Ruby in Practice

Ruby in Practice

JEREMY McANALLY
ASSAF ARKIN

with YEHUDA KATZ, DAVID BLACK,
GREGORY BROWN, PETER COOPER,
and LUKE MELIA

MANNING

Greenwich
(74° w. long.)

For online information and ordering of this and other Manning books, please visit
www.manning.com. The publisher offers discounts on this book when ordered in quantity.
For more information, please contact

> Special Sales Department
> Manning Publications Co.
> Sound View Court 3B   fax: (609) 877-8256
> Greenwich, CT 06830   email: orders@manning.com

 Manning Publications Co.
Sound View Court 3B
Greenwich, CT 06830

Development Editor: Nermina Miller
Copyeditor: Andy Carroll
Typesetter: Gordan Salinovic
Cover designer: Leslie Haimes

ISBN 9781933988474
Printed in the United States of America
1 2 3 4 5 6 7 8 9 10 – MAL – 14 13 12 11 10 09

For my wife, family, and God.
Thanks for not abandoning and/or smiting me,
depending on the case.

—J.M.

To my wife, Zoe.
You're the bestest!

—A.A.

brief contents

contents

preface

Between us, we speak a lot about Ruby at conferences and to user groups, and it's inevitable that at some point, whether after a talk (if we've given one) or when we're just hacking on something, someone will approach with a problem along the lines of, "I know Ruby, but I really don't know how to work with XML very well." "I know Ruby, but I can't really figure out how to get it to talk to our web service." "I know Ruby, but I'm having a problem getting it to integrate with our single-sign-on system." We welcome these questions and answer them gladly, because at least we know people are trying to use Ruby in the real world. But these questions also expose an information trend that this book aims to curb.

Many Rubyists have been worried for a while that because Ruby found a niche on the web with Ruby on Rails, this would become its *only* niche. Don't let us mince words here: Rails is a fantastic framework, but it certainly doesn't represent everything that Ruby can do. When we were given the chance to write this book, we were very excited about the opportunity to share our experience working with Ruby in environments outside (or at least on the edge of) the web. It's a wide area to cover, but it's one that a lot of people are working in and making progress in; at the same time, only limited information about it is generally available.

We've been using Ruby for a while now. It's been a long, wild road that we've driven down! Sometimes we've skidded off the side, sometimes we've dangerously strayed into other lanes, but we've driven forward—occasionally blazing new paths and at other times following the tracks of those before us. We've used Ruby in a lot of exotic places, and we couldn't have done it without the help of a lot of people.

Now it's our turn to pay it forward and to share what we have learned. This book has gone through many incarnations, authors, Rails versions, and revisions, but finally you hold in your hands the culmination of approximately 20 years of combined Ruby experience, 2 years of writing and revising (we Rubyists tend to be busy, slow people), and innumerable conversations. Enjoy.

acknowledgments

We would like to offer our deepest thanks to Manning Publications and their team: Michael Stephens, Nermina Miller, Megan Yockey, our copy editors, proofreaders, production team, and everyone else who had a hand in making this project happen. We know it's been a long road, and we deeply appreciate your bearing with us.

We'd also like to thank our contributors who collaborated with us on six chapters: Yehuda Katz, chapters 8 and 10; David Black, chapter 9; Gregory Brown, chapter 13; Peter Cooper, chapter 12; and Luke Melia, chapter 11. Their contributions have been invaluable.

The reviewers who took time out of their busy schedules to read the manuscript in its many iterations deserve special recognition. They are Pete McBreen, David Black, Greg Donald, Mike Stok, Phillip Hallstrom, Jason Rogers, Bill Fly, Doug Warren, Jeff Cunningham, Pete Pavlovich, Deepak Vohra, Patrick Dennis, Christopher Haupt, Robert McGovern, Scott Shaw, Mark Ryall, Sheldon Kotyk, Max Bolingbroke, Marco Ughetti, Tom Werner, Rick Evans, Chukwuemeka Nwankwo, and Bob Hutchinson.

We would thank our technical editor, Yossef Mendelssohn, except that he's probably too busy putting the hurt on some code or something. Also, for keeping us in check, Nick Sieger and Hamish Sanderson.

Jeremy would like to thank his wife (for not killing him, even though sometimes he's sure she wanted to during this whole process), his family (for not forgetting who he was, even though he rarely had time to visit), his coworkers (for not making fun of him for taking two years to write a book), and God (for the whole giving-him-life thing). He would also like to give a shout-out to his dogs, since they can't read.

Assaf would like to thank his wife for putting up with "Weekend plans? What weekend plans? I have some chapters to edit!" as well as his friends and coworkers for asking politely about the book but understanding that these things take time. Ruby, for bringing the fun back to programming. And the many people who wrote the libraries, tools, and blog posts that helped Ruby come this far. Without you, this book would not be possible.

about this book

Welcome to *Ruby in Practice*! This book is geared toward software developers who know Ruby or who are starting with Ruby and want to put their skills to use solving real software-development problems. We'll walk you through a series of common software scenarios, such as authenticating against LDAP or parsing XML, and show you how to approach and easily solve them using Ruby.

These solutions (and the chapters themselves) are discrete units that can be read in any order. If you're not interested in the web-related chapters, feel free to skip them. If you really want to learn all about reporting, skipping past the other chapters shouldn't affect your ability to understand that one. While we do suggest that you read them in order (because some chapters will make at least a little more sense after reading others), you don't have to. And, fear not: if a concept is discussed elsewhere in the book, it is noted so that you can find it easily enough.

Who should read this book

Ruby is gaining steam both on and off the web. This book is geared toward developers who want to explore using Ruby in environments that aren't necessarily "database-backed web applications." Experience in Ruby is assumed (and is fairly essential to get the maximum value from most of the discussions), but you don't need to be an expert to get started with this book. Even beginners will find their place, learning from examples that range from practical solutions to development challenges.

What this book doesn't include

This book isn't an introduction to the Ruby language. While it does discuss a number of language techniques, these discussions assume a working knowledge of Ruby. There is very little hand-holding when it comes to understanding the fundamentals of the code examples, so you would do well to either learn Ruby or at the least pick up a book to refer to when you come to something you don't understand.

This book also does not contain much introductory information on Rails. It is discussed in a few chapters (specifically in chapter 4), it's used as an example for various techniques, and it's often referred to in relation to web applications with Ruby, but this book will not teach you Ruby on Rails. Of course, it's not essential to know Rails to enjoy this book; you can read the whole book blissfully unaware of what `alias_method_chain` is. But if you are interested in learning it, we recommend you get one of the many books on the topic, since they cover it better than we could in the small space we devote to it.

How this book is organized

Ruby in Practice is composed of 13 chapters divided into 3 parts.

- Part 1—Ruby techniques
- Part 2—Integration and communication with Ruby
- Part 3—Ruby data and document techniques: Working with some form of data is the fundamental task of any application.

Part 1 (chapters 1-3) discusses techniques that will be useful when you start applying what you learn in the rest of the book. Techniques include metaprogramming and DSLs, testing and BDD, scripting and automating tasks.

Chapters 4-8 (part 2 of *Ruby in Practice*) are arranged in a problem/solution/discussion format, covering topics related to systems integration and communications. We discuss web services, messaging systems, e-mail and IM, and so on, and we show you how to put these technologies to use in your Ruby applications.

Part 3 (chapters 9-13) follows the same format, but focuses on data, presentation, and security. We discuss databases, parsing and generating XML, reporting, authentication, and so on. These chapters will equip you to work in a data-driven environment using Ruby as your primary tool.

The appendices cover topics related to the book, but they're not specific to any particular chapter. Appendix A is a quick treatise on getting a good Ruby environment set up on your system. Appendix B covers JRuby: how to install it, how to use Java with Ruby, and how to deploy Rails applications as WAR files. Appendix C discusses deploying Ruby web applications.

Code conventions

All source code in the book is in a `monospace` font, which sets it off from the surrounding text. For most listings, the code is annotated to point out key concepts, and numbered bullets are sometimes used in the text to provide additional information about the code. Sometimes very long lines will include line-continuation markers.

In the text, names of Ruby methods, classes, modules, and constants are also in a monospace font. Names of programs, such as ruby and java, are monospace when referring to the program executable or command-line usage; otherwise, they appear in regular type. Book and article titles, and technical terms on first mention, appear in italics.

Code downloads

The complete source code for the examples in this book is available for download from the publisher's web site at http://www.manning.com/RubyinPractice. This includes any code used in the book, with accompanying tests or spec files. A more frequently updated and forkable version of the code (meaning that you can clone your own version and make changes to be pushed back to our mainline version) is available at http://www.github.com/assaf/ruby-in-practice/.

Author online

The purchase of *Ruby in Practice* includes free access to a private forum run by Manning Publications where you can make comments about the book, ask technical questions, and receive help from the authors and other users. You can access and subscribe to the forum at http://www.manning.com/RubyinPractice. This page provides information on how to get on the forum once you're registered, what kind of help is available, and the rules of conduct in the forum.

Manning's commitment to our readers is to provide a venue where a meaningful dialogue between individual readers and between readers and the authors can take place. It isn't a commitment to any specific amount of participation on the part of the authors, whose contributions to the book's forum remain voluntary (and unpaid). We suggest you try asking the authors some challenging questions, lest their interest stray!

The Author Online forum and the archives of previous discussions will be accessible from the publisher's website as long as the book is in print.

About the cover illustration

The illustration on the cover of *Ruby in Practice* is taken from a collection of costumes of the Ottoman Empire published on January 1, 1802, by William Miller of Old Bond Street, London. The title page is missing from the collection and we have been unable to track it down to date. Each illustration bears the names of two artists who worked on it, both of whom would no doubt be surprised to find their art gracing the front cover of a computer programming book...two hundred years later.

The collection was purchased by a Manning editor at an antiquarian flea market in the "Garage" on West 26th Street in Manhattan. The seller was an American based in Ankara, Turkey, and the transaction took place just as he was packing up his stand for the day. The Manning editor did not have on his person the substantial amount of cash that was required for the purchase and a credit card and check were both politely turned down. With the seller flying back to Ankara that evening the situation was getting hopeless. What was the solution? It turned out to be nothing more than an old-fashioned verbal agreement sealed with a handshake. The seller simply proposed that the money be transferred to him by wire and the editor walked out with the bank information on a piece of paper and the portfolio of images under his arm. Needless to say, we transferred the funds the next day, and we remain grateful and impressed by this unknown person's trust in one of us. It recalls something that might have happened a long time ago.

The pictures from the Ottoman collection, like the other illustrations that appear on our covers, bring to life the richness and variety of dress customs of two centuries ago. They recall the sense of isolation and distance of that period—and of every other historic period except our own hyperkinetic present.

Dress codes have changed since then and the diversity by region, so rich at the time, has faded away. It is now often hard to tell the inhabitant of one continent from another. Perhaps, trying to view it optimistically, we have traded a cultural and visual diversity for a more varied personal life. Or a more varied and interesting intellectual and technical life.

We at Manning celebrate the inventiveness, the initiative, and, yes, the fun of the computer business with book covers based on the rich diversity of regional life of two centuries ago, brought back to life by the pictures from this collection.

Part 1

Ruby techniques

In these first three chapters, we'll look at techniques and tools we'll be using throughout the remainder of the book and that you'll be using throughout your Ruby career.

We'll cover advanced and essential language constructs, strategies (like test- and behavior-driven development), and Ruby tools to put these strategies to use in your applications. We'll round out this part with a thorough introduction to Rake, a useful Ruby tool for transforming database schemas, bootstrapping applications, running tests, and automating nearly any other task.

Ruby under
the microscope

1

This chapter covers

- Minimizing developer cycles
- Loading a lot of features in a little code

Often people, especially computer engineers, focus on the machines. They think, "By doing this, the machine will run faster. By doing this, the machine will run more effectively. By doing this, the machine will something something something." They are focusing on machines. But in fact we need to focus on humans, on how humans care about doing programming or operating the application of the machines. We are the masters. They are the slaves.

—Yukihiro Matsumoto, creator of Ruby

You've heard it all before, right? A new language or framework becomes the flavor du jour, and everyone starts talking about it. First there's a low rumble on websites, then someone gets ahold of it and does something cool, and out comes the marketing speak. I'm sure you can imagine Dave from marketing barking at you about another amazing technology: "You'll be more productive! Our synergistic approach to dynamic, domain-driven development will allow you to get to market quicker and get a better return on investment! Get a lower TCO and higher ROI over J2EE with our XP-driven Scrum model based on XML! Take apart your FOB and overhaul your BOB with our easy-to-use turnkey solution!" To some in the world of software development, it sounds like Ruby is all hype and buzz, but this book will show you that you can develop "real" software with Ruby.

Maybe you have heard the accolades and decided to read this book to find out if Ruby is right for you. Maybe you know Ruby already, and you chose this book to pick up practical techniques you can take back to the workplace. Whatever your reason for picking up our book, we're glad you did and we hope that we can help you learn more about using Ruby in the real world. But before we get down to the nuts and bolts, let's take a step back and gain some perspective.

1.1   Why Ruby now?

Here's a fact that surprises many people: Ruby came to the world the same year as Java—1995. Like many other open source technologies (such as Linux and MySQL) it took its time to mature and get noticed. So what happened in those 10 years that turned Ruby from a little-known language into a hot ticket item without the help of a big-vendor marketing machine? The adoption of Ruby on Rails, Ruby's premier web development framework, is the obvious answer, and it has without a doubt skyrocketed Ruby's popularity. It brought on hordes of developers who use Ruby exclusively with Rails, and even more developers who came for Rails, but stayed for Ruby.

Although Rails played a major role in getting Ruby into the mainstream, it still doesn't explain why it happened only recently, and not earlier. One thing that can help explain Ruby's meteoric rise is the recent rise in software complexity.

If you work for a big company, chances are you have to deal with complex problems. Sales across different channels, multiple products and markets, suppliers and distributors, employees and contractors, accounting and SOX compliance, market dynamics and regulations, and on and on. It's unavoidable: the problems of running any sizable business are complex. What about the solutions? You're probably thinking that there are no simple solutions to complex problems, and complexity is the nature of any real business. But do solutions have to be unnecessarily complex?

Given the complexity that naturally arises from these business problems, you don't want the technology you use to solve them to be unnecessarily complex. The more technology you throw at the problem—web servers and databases, online and batch processing, messaging protocols and data formats—the more complexity you add. The only way to alleviate this complexity conundrum is to look for simpler solutions to existing problems, efficiently using the developer cycles you have available.

1.1.1   Optimizing developer cycles

There has been a growing realization that software companies are targeting these business problems (one might call it the "enterprise" space) by offering overly complex solutions. We can't blame them. Complex solutions sell better. It's easier to obfuscate the solution and abstract the problem or to design a solution that solves every conceivable problem (even problems that the client doesn't have yet!) than to design a solid, simple solution that fits the problem domain. But as more developers realize that these "silver bullet" solutions create more problems than they solve, the momentum is shifting toward simpler, lightweight technologies.

OPEN SOURCE

Open source, with its organic development model, is able to adapt to this changing of tides better. For example, in the Java space, one can see a strong bias toward Spring and Hibernate as opposed to EJB. Many developers are defecting from a lot of spaces to Rails. Why? Those projects aren't afraid to reevaluate their approaches to accommodate current developer attitudes, because these sorts of projects are developed by the developers who use them every day in their own work.

We like to talk about large-scale systems, thousands of servers, petabytes of data, billions of requests. It's captivating, the same way we could talk about horsepower and 0 to 60 acceleration times. But in real life we often face constraints of a different scale. Can you do it with a smaller team? Can you get it done tomorrow? Can you add these new features before we go into beta? Most often businesses have to optimize not for CPU cycles, but developer cycles. It's easy to scale out by throwing more hardware at the problem, but, as many businesses have found out, throwing more people at the problem just makes the project late. That knowledge was captured years ago in Fred Brooks' *Mythical Man-Month*, but our bosses just decided to prove it empirically.

Minimizing developer cycles is probably the single most attractive feature of dynamic languages, and Ruby in particular. Simplifying software development has been the holy grail of the software industry. Say what you will about COBOL, it's much better than writing mainframe applications in assembly language. And believe it or not, productivity was a major selling point for Java, in the early days when it came to replace C/C++. It's the nature of software development that every once in a while we take a leap forward by changing the way we write code, to deal with the growing complexity that developed since the last major leap. And it's not the sole domain of the language and its syntax. One of the biggest criticisms against J2EE is the sheer size of its API, and the complexity involved in writing even the simplest of programs. EJB is the poster child of developer-unfriendly technology.

The true measure of a programming language's productivity is how little code you need in order to solve a given problem. Writing less code, while being able to do the same thing, will make you far more productive than writing a whole lot of code without doing much at all. This is the reverse of how many businesses view productivity: lines of code produced. If simple lines of code were the metric, Perl would win every time. Just as too much code can make your application unmaintainable, so can terse, short code that's "write only." Many of Ruby's language features contribute to creating short, sane, and maintainable code.

1.1.2   Language features

Ruby seems to hit the sweet spot and appeal to developers who value natural interfaces and choose to migrate away from languages that inherently promote complexity. But why? Why would developers move away from "proven" technologies to Ruby, which is, arguably, the "new kid," regardless of its positive aspects? Primarily because Ruby is a dynamic language that works well for applications and scripting, that supports the object-oriented and functional programming styles, that bakes arrays and hash literals into the syntax, and that has just enough metaprogramming features to make building domain-specific languages fun and easy. Had enough marketing? Of course, this laundry list of buzzwords is not as important as what happens when you combine all these features together. In combination, the buzzwords and abstract concepts become a powerful tool.

For example, consider Ruby on Rails. Rails is one incarnation in a long series of web application frameworks. Like so many web application frameworks before it, Rails deals with UI and remote APIs, business logic, and persistence. Unlike many web application frameworks before it, it does so effortlessly, without taxing the developer. In its three years of existence, it leapfrogged the more established frameworks to become the benchmark by which all other frameworks are judged.

All that power comes from Ruby. The simplicity of mapping relational databases to objects without the burden of XML configuration results from Ruby's combination of object-oriented and dynamic styles. The ease with which HTML and XML templates can be written and filters can be set up comes from functional programming. Magic features like dynamic finders and friendly URL routing are all forms of metaprogramming. The little configuration Rails needs is handled effortlessly using a set of domain-specific languages. It's not that Rails (or really Ruby) is doing anything new; the attractiveness comes from *how* it does things. Besides being a successful framework on its own, Rails showed the world how to use Ruby's combination of language features to create applications that, quite frankly, rock. Dynamic features like `method_missing` and closures go beyond conceptual curiosity and help you deliver.

So, why is Ruby popular now? This popularity can, for the most part, be traced to developers growing weary of complex, taxing development tools and to the emergence of Rails as a definite, tangible project that shows how Ruby can be used to create production quality software that's still developer friendly. Once you start working with Ruby, you'll probably realize this too. It takes about the same amount of effort to work with flat files, produce PDFs, make SOAP requests, and send messages using WebSphere MQ as it does to map objects to databases, send email, or parse an XML file. Wrap that into a nice, natural syntax, and you have a potent tool for software development.

Let's jump right into some Ruby code.

1.2   *Ruby by example*

We think the best way to illustrate Ruby's capabilities and features is by example, and what better way than by diving into some code? Let's take a fairly typical situation: you need to pull data from a database and create graphs with it. Perhaps you need to trace the sales performance of a range of products across all of your sales locations. Can we keep it simple?

First, we'll need to install three libraries: Active Record (an object-relational mapper for databases), Scruffy (a graphing solution for Ruby), and RMagick (ImageMagick bindings for Ruby, required by Scruffy). Let's do that using the Ruby-Gems utility:

```
gem install active_record
gem install rmagick
gem install scruffy
```

Assuming you have all the system prerequisites for these packages (for example, ImageMagick for RMagick to bind to), you should now have all you need.

TIP   RMagick can be a beast to set up. We suggest checking the project's documentation, the mailing list, and your favorite search engine if you have problems.

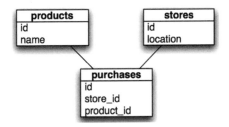

Now, let's set up our database. Figure 1.1 shows our schema diagram for the database.

You can use figure 1.1 as a model to create the tables (if you prefer to use some sort of GUI tool), or you can use the SQL in listing 1.1.

Figure 1.1 For our graph, we will build a simple domain model: products will have purchases, which belong to the stores where they happened.

Listing 1.1 SQL for graph example database

```
CREATE DATABASE `paper`;

CREATE TABLE `products` (
  `id` int NOT NULL auto_increment,
  `name` text,
  PRIMARY KEY (`id`)
);

CREATE TABLE `purchases` (
  `id` int NOT NULL auto_increment,
  `product_id` int default NULL,
  `store_id` int default NULL,
  PRIMARY KEY (`id`)
);

CREATE TABLE `stores` (
  `id` int NOT NULL auto_increment,
  `location` text,
  PRIMARY KEY (`id`)
);
```

Now, let's set up ActiveRecord to work with the database. ActiveRecord is typically used inside of a Rails application, and because we're not using it in that environment, it takes a few more lines of configuration. See our configuration and implementation code in listing 1.2.

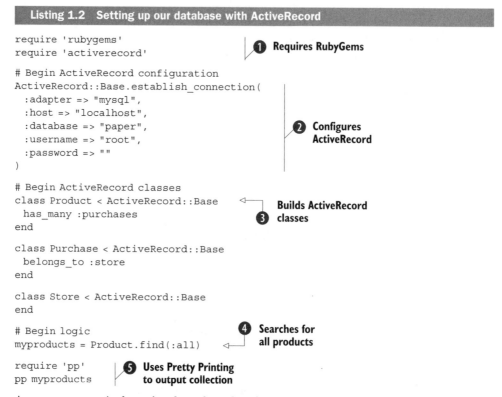

Listing 1.2   Setting up our database with ActiveRecord

```
require 'rubygems'
require 'activerecord'
```
❶ **Requires RubyGems**

```
# Begin ActiveRecord configuration
ActiveRecord::Base.establish_connection(
  :adapter => "mysql",
  :host => "localhost",
  :database => "paper",
  :username => "root",
  :password => ""
)
```
❷ **Configures ActiveRecord**

```
# Begin ActiveRecord classes
class Product < ActiveRecord::Base
  has_many :purchases
end
```
❸ **Builds ActiveRecord classes**

```
class Purchase < ActiveRecord::Base
  belongs_to :store
end

class Store < ActiveRecord::Base
end
```

```
# Begin logic
myproducts = Product.find(:all)
```
❹ **Searches for all products**

```
require 'pp'
pp myproducts
```
❺ **Uses Pretty Printing to output collection**

As you can see, it doesn't take a lot of code to get a full object-relationally mapped database connection. First, we import the RubyGems library ❶, so we can then import ActiveRecord. Next, we establish a database connection with ActiveRecord ❷. Normally this configuration data would live in a database configuration file in a Rails application (such as `database.yml`), but for this example we chose to run outside Rails, so we've used `establish_connection` directly. Next, we create ActiveRecord classes and associations to map our database ❸. Finally, we execute a query ❹ and output its results using Pretty Printing (pp) ❺.

   Just fill in some testing data (or download the script from the book's source code to generate some for you), and run the script. You should see something like the following output:

```
[#<Product:0x639e30 @attributes={"name"=>"Envelopes", "id"=>"1"}>,
 #<Product:0x639e08 @attributes={"name"=>"Paper", "id"=>"2"}>,
 #<Product:0x639c00 @attributes={"name"=>"Folders", "id"=>"3"}>,
 #<Product:0x639bb0 @attributes={"name"=>"Cardstock", "id"=>"4"}>]
```

Our database is set up and our query works, so let's move on to generating a graph from the data. First, remove those last two lines from listing 1.2 (they'll be superfluous by the time we're done). Now let's take the data we retrieved, process it, and build the graph using Scruffy. In listing 1.3, you'll see how to do that.

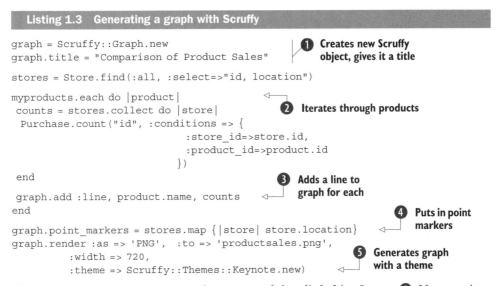

First, we create a `Scruffy::Graph` instance and do a little bit of setup ❶. Next, we iterate through the products we found earlier and calculate the sales counts for each store location ❷. Then we add a line on the graph showing the sales trends for that product across the stores ❸. Before we render the graph, we need to add the markers to indicate which sales location we're looking at ❹. Finally, we render the graph to a PNG file using one of Scruffy's built-in themes ❺.

If you open the graph and look at it, you can see that it is polished (ours looks like figure 1.2).

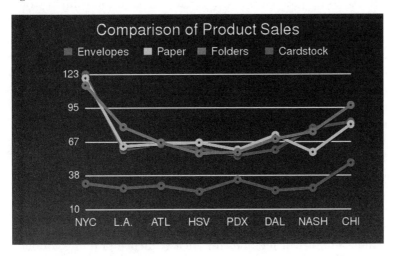

Figure 1.2   Our finished graph: in about 40 lines of code, we pulled data from the database, processed it, and graphed it in a rather attractive fashion.

Not bad for 40 lines of code, including whitespace, comments, and more verbose than required constructs. Sure, this example isn't representative of every situation—you can't develop a full CRM solution in Ruby with 40 lines of code—but it speaks volumes about the expressiveness of the language and the power of its toolkit.

In the next section and subsequent chapters, we'll look at a lot of the concepts that power this example, so you can start building applications and tools that take full advantage of Ruby's features.

1.3   Facets of Ruby

Now that we've discussed the "why" of Ruby, let's look at the "how." One of the goals of this book is to make you into a truly effective Ruby developer; we want you to be able to use Ruby to reframe problems and craft solutions. In this section, we'll discuss Ruby concepts and unique "Rubyisms" that will help you do this and that will power the examples and libraries you'll see throughout the rest of the book. We intend that you'll come away with a grasp of these advanced concepts and know how to craft code that is readable, expressive, and "good" (by whatever subjective method you use to measure that). If we're successful, you'll be able to use Ruby to do your job more effectively and develop more maintainable applications.

But what do we mean when we talk about reframing problems in Ruby? Every programming language has its own set of idioms and best practices. Once you're comfortable with the syntax and know your way around the libraries, you start to explore that which makes the language unique. You explore the character of the language, if you will: the way it promotes a certain style of programming and rewards you for following it. If you work with the language, it will work for you.

Object-oriented languages, for example, ask you to encapsulate behavior and data into objects, and they reward you for that in reuse. If you're coming from Java, you know the value of using JavaBeans and the standard collections library, of throwing and catching exceptions, and so on. Today we take those for granted, but in the early days of Java development, many developers would use Java as if it were C or Visual Basic. They wrote code that didn't follow Java idioms, which made it harder to maintain and use.

Like Java, Ruby has its own set of idioms. For example, in Ruby you often use *blocks* to keep your code simple and readable. You can write methods that extend classes with new functionality (metaprogramming). You enrich classes with common behavior by mixing in modules, fondly known as *mixins*. You can use *blocks* to abstract loops and even extend methods and reduce code duplication.

Let's say you were writing a script to interface with an old legacy server. It accepts TCP connections and operates on simple commands like LOGIN, GET, DELETE, and so on. Each time you start a session with the server, you need the same setup and tear-down, but you want to do different things during the socket's connection each time. You could write a number of methods for each sequence of events, duplicating the setup and teardown code in each one, or you could use a block. Listing 1.4 shows a simple implementation of this script.

Listing 1.4   Using blocks to reduce code duplication

```
def remote_session
  config = get_configuration_information
  sock = TCPSocket::new(config.host, config.port)
  yield sock       ❶
  sock.close
  log_results
end

# Send some data
def send_login
  remote_session {|sock| sock.send('LOGIN')           ❷
end

# A little more advanced
def login            ❸
  remote_session do |sock|
    sock.send('LOGIN')
    received = sock.recv(128)          ❹
    received == 'OK'
  end
end
```

First, we create a method to execute our setup and teardown, with a yield statement inside ❶. That yield statement tells Ruby to execute the block that is fed to the method as a parameter. Next, we create a simple method to send the LOGIN command to our server ❷. Note that a block is fed to this method as a parameter. The sock parameter is the socket from our setup method (remote_session) that is given to the block to use. We do the same for the login method ❸, but this time we send the login and do something with the returned data ❹. Notice the code duplication we've eliminated by putting all of our setup and teardown into a separate method; this is just one of the many facets of Ruby that make development with it that much cleaner and easier.

Ruby is a dynamic language, and as you get to explore that facet of Ruby, known as *duck typing*, you'll notice that you don't need to use interfaces and abstract classes as often. The way Ruby allows you to extend objects and use constructors relieves you from juggling factories. Iteration is often done with blocks and functions, whereas in nonfunctional languages you tend to use for loops and define anonymous classes.

Once you get the hang of all these ideas, you'll start reframing problems in terms of Ruby, rather than thinking out a solution in a language you're more familiar with, and writing it in the Ruby syntax. You will often find that reframing problems changes the way you think about code, and you'll discover new ways to become a better developer.

Imagine a method that queries the database for products based on different criteria. You could call the method with any number of arguments. But it's hard to understand exactly what criteria it's using if your code looks like this:

```
find_products nil, nil, nil, nil, 5, 50, 250
```

What does the 5 stand for? What about the 50? Some languages promote the idiom of method overloading, creating several methods with different signatures, depending on the expected call. But overloading doesn't always work if all the arguments are integers. In that case you'll want to follow a different idiom, creating an object, populating its fields, then passing it to the method. Those are all good idioms, but not the ones you'll likely use with Ruby.

Ruby has a convenient syntax for handling hashes, which you can use to simulate named arguments. Instead of method overloading and populating objects, you can write something like this:

```
find_products :category => 5, :price => 50..250
```

Duck typing even makes it possible to call the following line and let the method extract the identifier from the storage object:

```
find_products :category => storage, :price => 50..250
```

As you practice these idioms, you'll notice certain things change. For one, you'll have fewer methods in your objects, making your APIs easier to understand. In fact, you'll have fewer classes to deal with. In this example, we've eliminated an object to hold all the properties and a class to define it. With fewer classes and methods, it's easier to understand the overall design of your software and how all the pieces fit together.

This discussion has barely scratched the surface. This book is not a walkthrough of the Ruby language; we only wanted to give you a taste for the language's features. We could go on and on about all of the dynamic features of Ruby, but it would ultimately be redundant. We'll cover some of these concepts, features, and practices in this chapter, but throughout the book you'll see these and other Ruby idioms in practice, which is where real education happens: when you use your knowledge in practice. We hope that we can help you learn those mostly by example, with some explanations along the way. The more you invest in learning the language, the better a developer you'll be. There's always a learning curve, but fortunately there's not a lot to it with Ruby. You'll see the benefit of Ruby while you're learning and practicing the language, but you'll want to take that information and go deeper to get even better.

One of the killer apps for Ruby is the Ruby on Rails web application framework. Developers are attracted to the magic of Rails and the productivity gains therein, but, in reality, most of the magic is good Ruby programming applied to web applications. Think about this: what if you could make the same magic work for you in other domains, to make you a better developer for any problem you need to solve? What if you could take those same productivity gains and magic methods, and use them in *your* code? Let's look at some of the facets of this gem we call Ruby that can make this possible: duck typing, simplicity, efficiency, and functional programming.

1.3.1   *Duck typing*

Ruby uses dynamic typing rather than static typing, and Ruby's brand of dynamic typing has been dubbed *duck typing*. It's not so much that Ruby's typing behaves differently than most dynamically typed languages; it's merely that one thinks about objects based on behavior rather than type: if an object walks like a duck and quacks like a duck, then it must be a duck.

In a static typing system, an object's type is determined by its class definition at compile time. Static typing forces each object to declare its heritage, so you're always asking, "where are you coming from?" In dynamic languages, behavior is captured by the object, not the interface. Dynamic typing only cares about merits, so the question to ask each object is, "what can you do?"

You can do the same with reflection in Java or C#, but reflection hides your business logic in a haystack of type-bypassing code. With dynamic typing, you don't have to declare so many interfaces and abstract classes in anticipation of reuse, you don't have to write adapters and decorators as often, and you don't need to choose between readability and functionality. All these help you reuse code more often.

A byproduct of duck typing is that method calls do not check their recipient's type beforehand. Your code calls a method, and if it fails, it raises an exception. This concept sounds a little cloudy, so let's look at a piece of code to explain it. Let's say we have a method that calls `size` and returns it in a friendly message.

```
def print_size(item)
  puts "The item's size is #{item.size}."
end
```

Our method calls `size` on the object without regard for its class, so if you feed it an object that responds to the `size` method, it will work.

```
mystring = "This is a string."
print_size(mystring)          # => The item's size is 17.
myarray = [1,2,3,4,5]
print_size(myarray)           # => The item's size is 5.
myfile = File::Stat.new("readme.txt")
print_size(myfile)            # => The item's size is 432.
```

This is a perfect illustration of duck typing: all three objects walk and talk like ducks. We're expecting the object to do something, and we only have to ask: does it do that?

Duck typing is a trade-off. You no longer have a compiler that will catch type errors upfront, but you do have fewer opportunities for errors. In a statically typed language, you'll repeat the type declaration in multiple places: class definition, variable declaration, constructor, method arguments, and so on. If you need to refactor code, perhaps splitting a class into an interface and separate implementation, maybe adding a factory or writing a decorator, you end up making type changes in multiple places, and you'll want a type-checking compiler to help you minimize errors.

That's not a problem with Ruby. As you grow more familiar with Ruby, you'll notice that you don't have to declare types that often, or repeat them all over the place. You rarely need to separate interfaces and implementation classes, or conjure factories and decorators. When you have fewer types to deal with, type checking is less of an issue. What you get in return is being able to do more with less code, which means fewer places for bugs to hide. Give it a shot. We doubt you'll miss type checking.

If you do end up needing a way to assert that an object at least responds to a method, every object defines a method named `respond_to?` that will respond `true` or `false` depending on whether or not that object will respond to the method indicated:

```
3.respond_to?(:to_s)        # => true
3.respond_to?(:im_fake)      # => false
"string".respond_to?(:gsub) # => true
```

This isn't type checking, but it's a pretty good indicator of an object's identity if you need it. This is also useful if you want to branch depending on the parameter given to the method:

```
if param.respond_to?(:convert)
  param.convert
else
  MyClass.from_object(param)
end
```

This technique can help make your API simpler, and, depending on how the code is written, make your code shorter.

1.3.2 Simplicity

Ruby values simplicity. To be fair, all programming languages do, each striving for simplicity in its own way. But they don't all achieve it in the same way. A language cannot enforce simplicity any more than it can keep your code bug free, but it can certainly reward you for keeping things simple. Or, it can reward you for making things complex, often in the form of over-engineering.

As much as we hate to admit it, once we write a piece of software and release it to the world, the software becomes harder to change. Yet, it often needs to change to add new features, switch databases, support more protocols, or integrate with other systems. And so we plan for change.

Each language has its own patterns that deal with change. In a statically typed language like Java, you need to think about these requirements upfront: once the implementation has been fixed, it is hard to change. You tend to figure out the interfaces upfront, use factories liberally, allow for decorators, and so on. Because those changes are hard to make later on, you're better off doing them up front, just in case, even for cases that will never happen. In their own way, statically typed languages reward you for over-engineering.

In contrast, you'll find that it's much easier to make local changes with Ruby without affecting the rest of your code because it's a dynamic language. When change is easy to make, you don't have to plan as much for every eventuality. In dynamic languages, there's less need to design interfaces that are separate from the implementation, because it's possible to refactor the implementation without breaking code all around. You won't need to bury the business logic in layers of factories, decorators, listeners, and anonymous classes. That might seem hard to imagine if you have a strong background with statically typed languages, but as you get comfortable with Ruby, you'll notice it too. Ruby will reward you for keeping things simple, and saying no to code you don't need will reward you with quicker development and easier maintenance.

1.3.3 DRY efficiency

Ruby is a DRY language. DRY stands for: Don't Repeat Yourself. Syntactically, it's an efficient language: you can express the same thing with fewer lines of code. As we know, computers are fast enough that more lines of code do not slow them down, but what about you? When it comes to debugging and maintaining, the more code you have to deal with, the harder it is to see what it does and find the problems that need fixing. Ruby helps you keep your code short and concise.

Listing 1.5 shows this with a simple example. The first style is Ruby, but you'll notice that it looks similar to many other programming languages. The second style is the preferred way of doing it in Ruby: shorter and less repetitive (and if this is the last value in a method, the return is superfluous). There's not a lot to this example, but imagine that you could do this throughout your code, eliminating thousands of lines of unnecessary cruft.

Listing 1.5   A small example of DRY syntax

```
# The long way
record = Hash.new
record[:name]  = "Dave"
record[:email] = "admin@net.com"
record[:phone] = "555-1235"
return record

# The Ruby way
return { :name=>"Dave", :email=>"admin@net.com", :phone=>"555-1235" }
```

Though this example is a bit contrived, it illustrates part of a consistent effort to make Ruby's syntax efficient without being unreadable. Ruby's syntax has a lot of little features like this that end up giving you huge gains: blocks, iterators, open classes, and more. And many of these features are due to Ruby's ties to functional programming.

1.3.4   *Functional programming*

Ruby is an object-oriented language: it is objects all the way down. Like many other dynamic languages, functions are also first-class citizens. Couple that with outstanding support for closures, and it's easy to adopt a functional style of programming. But unlike more traditional functional programming languages, like LISP or Haskell, Ruby is easier to pick up, and it can let you enjoy both worlds of functional and procedural style.

Why is functional programming so important? For one, it helps you write shorter and more concise code, and some things are easier to express in functional style. For another, the functional style leads to code that doesn't depend on state and has fewer side effects. Code like that is much easier to mold and refactor, and it gives you more opportunities for reuse. It also makes it easier to build applications that scale.

The easiest way to build software that scales is using the "shared nothing" architecture. The less shared state you have to deal with, the easier it is to scale. Although Ruby comes with modern libraries that support threads, locks, mutexes, and other concurrency mechanisms, it helps that you don't have to use them often.

We're sure a lot of this discussion sounds like academia mixed with astronaut buzz talk. Functional programming hasn't yet hit the big time in the world of software development, but perhaps you're familiar with the Google MapReduce algorithm, which achieves unparalleled scalability by running tasks independently of each other. Its efficiency is achieved through two main algorithms or methods: map and reduce.

You can see Ruby's "map" in listing 1.6 as the obviously named `map` method; the "reduce" part in Ruby is most often done using the `inject` method.

Listing 1.6   Map is one way Ruby uses functional programming for parallelism

```
# Code that iterates in order to map one array to another
application_names = []
for application in applications
  application_names << application.visible_name
end

# Code that maps one array to another
applications.map { |application| application.visible_name }

# An even shorter way to express it in Rails and Ruby 1.9
applications.map &:visible_name
```

Code that has fewer dependencies is easier to run in parallel, taking advantage of modern multicode CPUs, or when deploying on a cluster of servers. There are other ways to do it, but functional programming makes it extremely easy.

Now let's look at one of the most attractive features of Ruby. In covering these facets of Ruby, we've been working our way toward one of the biggest features of the language: metaprogramming.

1.4   Metaprogramming

We talked in the beginning about reframing solutions in terms of Ruby. Software development bridges the gap between your ideas and applications you can use. The smaller that gap, the more quickly you can cross it. We're going to stop the analogies here, but the point is that you want to translate your ideas into code quickly and easily. The language you choose can increase or reduce this distance between ideas and your implementation (see figure 1.3).

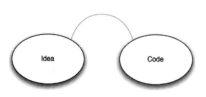

Figure 1.3   Some languages create a gulf between your ideas and working code.

But as you progress and become an expert with the tools of your trade (regardless of which language you use), this gap will slowly close. You'll be able to frame things in terms of a language's idioms, keeping the language's limitations, strengths, and so on, in the back of your mind. Your ideas are then much closer to real code (figure 1.4 illustrates this).

Most programming languages are content being what they are. Some languages are more generic, but they force you to deal with more details. Other languages help you deal with a specific domain problem but tend to be simple and inflexible, such as

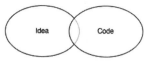

Figure 1.4   Ideas can more closely match the resulting code if your expertise and perspective create an overlap between the framing of an idea and the real code that will execute it.

SQL, RuleML, XML Schema, Ant, and CSS. Through *metaprogramming*, Ruby allows you to have a mixture of both. You can extend Ruby with mini-languages that can get you closer to the problem you're solving, and you can still use all the expressive power of Ruby (see figure 1.5).

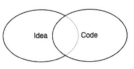

Figure 1.5 Ruby can be bent to your problem domain, making the overlap between your problem domain and real code significant.

This book isn't focused on teaching much Ruby "teachnique" in the sense of the core language, but there are a couple of powerful tools that will let you crank your developer volume all the way to 11 and give you the ability to solve problems with ease. We think it's worthwhile to spend a few minutes introducing you to these tools: metaprogramming and domain-specific languages.

1.4.1 Getting started with metaprogramming

The software industry always looks for that one silver bullet that can turn ideas into code without the "overhead" of software developers. We're not too worried about losing our jobs, but software that writes software is a wonderful tool, even if it only takes on part of the workload. Compilers that turn source code into machine code do that—they let us work with higher-level languages. Source code generators and IDE wizards give us a head start by writing boilerplate code and skeletons. And even further up the ladder, there's *metaprogramming*, writing code that writes code.

Methods that define methods

If you come from a background in Java or C#, you learned that objects and classes are different in one fundamental way. Objects are mutable, so you can change them by calling methods on them, but classes are immutable: their definitions are written down, and once compiled, cannot be changed. In Ruby, classes, like objects, are mutable. You can call a method on a class that will change the class definition.

Let's look at a simple example. Suppose we have a `Project` that has an `owner`, an attribute you can both get and set. Listing 1.7 shows two ways to express that. We can write a couple of methods, or we can call `attr_accessor`. By calling this method on the class, we allow it to change the class definition and essentially define a method for getting the value of the instance variable `@owner`, and a method for setting it.

Listing 1.7   Using `attr_accessor` to define accessor methods on your class

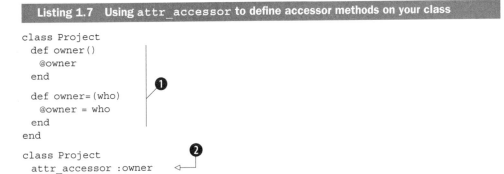

```
class Project
  def owner()
    @owner
  end

  def owner=(who)
    @owner = who
  end
end

class Project
  attr_accessor :owner
end
```

The class definitions in listing 1.7 both do the same thing: define an attribute owner that you can get and set. The first version is rather explicit ❶, but the second version uses a lot less code ❷. This seems a little contrived now, but imagine having 12 or 15 attributes in a class. Then you're going from 40 or 50 lines of code down to 1. That's a *huge* spread across an entire application. Even better, you describe the intent of what needs to happen (accessing an attribute) without having to be totally verbose about it.

But how does it work? Let's take a look at an implementation of `attr_accessor` in Ruby in listing 1.8. This is not *the* implementation from Ruby, but it has the same effect.

Listing 1.8   A reimplementation of `attr_accessor`

```
class Module
  def attr_accessor (*symbols)          ❶
    symbols.each do |symbol|
      class_eval %{
        def #{symbol}
          @#{symbol}
        end
                                         ❷
        def #{symbol}=(val)
          @#{symbol} = val
        end }
    end
  end
end
```

Using Ruby's open classes, we reopen the class definition of the Ruby core class `Module` ❶ and add a method, `attr_accessor`, to it. This method takes each provided symbol and executes a code block in the context of the class definition using `class_eval` ❷. You will become familiar with the `*_eval` family of methods in your metaprogramming. Check out table 1.1 for a summary of their usage.

Table 1.1   The `eval` family of methods

Method	Usage
`eval(str)`	Evaluates a string of code: `eval("puts 'I love eval!'")`

`instance_eval(str)`
`instance_eval { }`
	Evaluates a given string of code or a code block, changing the receiver of the call to `self`:
	
	`class Hider`
	`  def initialize`
	`    @hidden = "Hello, world!"`
	`  end`
	`end`
	
	`my_hidden = Hider.new`
	`my_hidden.instance_eval { puts @hidden }`
	`# => Hello, world!`

Table 1.1 The `eval` family of methods *(continued)*

Method	Usage

`class_eval(str)`
`class_eval { }`
	Evaluates a given string of code or a code block in the context of a class's definition:
	<pre>def printable_attribute(attr)
	  class_eval %{
	        def p_#{attr}
	          puts attr.to_s
	        end
	  }
	end
	
	class Printer
	  attr_accessor :name
	  printable_attribute :name
	end
	
	my_printer = Printer.new
	my_printer.name = "LaserPrint 5000"
	my_printer.p_name # => LaserPrint 5000</pre>

Now that we have added our method to the class definition, every instance of a `Module` or `Class` object has this method available to it.

Now let's look at a more complex example. We're further along in the development of our application, and we realize there will be a lot of projects to manage. We want to help users by giving them a way to tag projects, so they can then find projects through tags and through related projects. We need a separate table to hold the tags, and we need to add methods to retrieve projects by tags, to delete tag associations when a project is deleted, and so forth.

That's quite a lot of work: a lot of database work for inserting new tags, editing and deleting tags, not to mention searching. We decide to reinvent the wheel some other time, and instead we download a plugin called `ActsAsTaggable`. Listing 1.9 shows how we use it.

Listing 1.9 Using `ActsAsTaggable` to get a lot of features in one line of code

```
class Project < ActiveRecord::Base
  acts_as_taggable
end
```

Why is this a more complex example when it's no longer than the previous one? Because `acts_as_taggable` adds a lot of functionality to our `Project` model that would take us several days to do otherwise. Now our `Project` model has access to a set of tags in the database and has methods to search with baked right in (such as `find_tagged_with`). We can call `Project.find_tagged_with(:all => 'ruby')` and get an array of models that have the tag ruby. It required little code on our part: that is the power of metaprogramming.

Ruby is flexible enough that in addition to defining new methods, you can extend existing methods. Think of this as aspect-oriented programming baked into the language. It can also let you define complete classes, from the simple `Struct`, which declares a JavaBean-like class in one method call, to more complicated mechanisms, such as creating a collection of model classes from your database schema.

Now let's look at dynamic method definition.

Implementing methods dynamically

This style of metaprogramming happens at class definition, but metaprogramming can also be used to dynamically alter objects. With languages that have static (or early) binding, you can only call a method if that method is part of the class definition. With languages that have dynamic (or late) binding, you can call any method on an object. The object then checks its class definition to decide how to respond to the method call.

This means that in Ruby, if the method is not part of the class definition, the object calls `method_missing`. Typically, `method_missing` will throw an exception, but you can override it to do more interesting things. Let's try to create an XML document (an RSS feed for our projects) using `XML::Builder`. Take a look at listing 1.10.

Listing 1.10 Building an RSS feed for our projects

```
xml = XML::Builder.new
xml.rss "version"=>"2.0" do
  xml.channel do
    xml.title "Projects"
    xml.pubDate CGI.rfc1123_date(Time.now)
    xml.description "List of all our projects"
    for project in projects do
      xml.item do
        xml.title project.name
        xml.guid project_url(project), :permalink=>true
        xml.pubDate CGI.rfc1123_date(project.created_on)
        xml.description project.details
      end
    end
  end
end
```

If you're looking for the step where we use a DTD or XML Schema to generate source code, you won't find it. Builder uses `method_missing` to create elements based on the method name, attributes from the method arguments, and text nodes from the first argument, if it's a string. So a simplified version of that method might look like listing 1.11.

Listing 1.11 A simplified look at `XML::Builder`'s use of `method_missing`

```
def method_missing(sym, *args, &block)
  root_element = sym                        ❶

  args.each do |arg|                        ❷
```

```
  case arg
    when Hash
      build_elements(root_element)
    when String                          ❸
      add_element(root_element)
  end
 end
end
```

Using Ruby's open classes, Builder overrides the `method_missing` method. Builder takes the name of the missing method that is called ❶, and the value provided ❷, and makes elements out of them depending on the value's type ❸. You'll likely find coding like this sprinkled throughout your favorite and most-used libraries, including ActiveRecord.

Builder is one of those staple libraries you'll use quite often in your projects, and it's an interesting library to analyze if you're curious about metaprogramming. If you learn enough about it, metaprogramming can help you build mini-languages that you can use to reframe business logic in terms of the problem domains, rather than in terms of a language's syntax. We're talking about *domain-specific languages.*

1.4.2   *Domain-specific languages*

Functions, objects, libraries, and frameworks all help you work at a higher level of abstraction, closer to the problem. If you look at the software landscape, you'll see a lot of different specialty domains. You can imagine languages, each of which is designed to solve a specific set of problems by expressing solutions in a way that's easy and natural for that specific domain. Perhaps you hadn't heard of domain-specific languages (DSLs) before reading this book, but you certainly have used them. Do any of the following names sound familiar: SQL, regular expressions, HTML, Make, WSDL, .htaccess, UML, CSS, Ant, XSLT, Bash? These are all domain-specific languages.

Within the domain of relational databases, there needs to be a way to define new tables. There needs to be a way to query these tables and return the results, to create new records, to update and delete existing records. You could do those things by delving into low-level database APIs, creating the table structures directly, iterating over B-tree indexes to fetch records, performing joins in memory, and sorting the data yourself. In fact, many system developers used to do just that. Nowadays, we use SQL.

But DSLs have a limit: it's hard to create a programming language that has good support for variables, expressions, functions, objects, and all the tooling around it. So DSLs tend to be simple, static, and inflexible. HTML, for example, can express rich multimedia content, including text, images, audio, and video. But if you want to do anything dynamic, like pull-down menus, partial updates, or drag and drop, you need a more generic programming language. You'll want to use JavaScript. On the other hand, because JavaScript is a generic programming language, it will take a mountain of statements to create a page using the DOM API. But what if you could mix a generic programming language with a domain-specific language?

Let's look at XML Schema definitions, for example. The XML Schema language was originally designed to validate XML documents. With it, you can express what a valid XML document looks like, so you can check XML documents against these rules before deciding whether or not to process them. It's much easier to use than iterating over the DOM and checking whether the current element is allowed to follow the previous element, and whether it has all the right attributes.

But, like most DSLs, XML Schema has its limits. For example, you can check that a customer element has optional contact data, such as email, phone, or IM handle, but there's no easy way to require that at least one of these elements exists. There's no easy way to validate that all U.S. addresses have a state, or that the ZIP Code matches the address. But if we created a DSL using a powerful host language (like Ruby), we could come up with something that looks like listing 1.12.

Listing 1.12   A validation domain-specific language example

```
contact_information_verification do |the_persons|
  the_persons.name.is_required

  the_persons.address.is_required
  the_persons.address.must_be(10).characters_long

  the_persons.phone.must_be(10).characters_long

  the_persons.im_handle.must_not_be(in_existing_accounts)
end
```

This gives us a nice set of readable rules that can be updated by anyone (probably even your secretary), which will generate or execute the validations we need. DSLs can bring the same simplicity and abstraction to a lot of your specific problems.

NOTE   What we've created here is not *technically* a DSL in the purest sense, but an embedded DSL (EDSL)—a domain-specific language that's embedded inside a host language, in this case Ruby. Throughout this book, we'll show different Ruby libraries and tools that include their own mini-languages, all of which are EDSLs.

Think about code that expresses business rules or composes tasks, and you'll find many opportunities to simplify and reduce noise. DSLs don't just help your secretary or business manager keep your code up, they can also help you as a developer keep yourself sane. Using Ruby's metaprogramming capabilities, you can build these sorts of solid, literate tools and fluent interfaces.

1.4.3   *Refining your metaprogramming*

If you've never built a DSL, it can be slightly daunting to make sure your implementation stays flexible yet still clean. Even the masters have to take a step back to rethink things every once in a while. (For example, Rspec, a popular Ruby testing library, changed its DSL numerous times before settling on the current implementation.) But there are steps you can take to make sure that you're approaching the right problems the right way with metaprogramming, and to ensure that you aren't carrying around a hammer looking for a nail to hit.

The place to start is with the problem you solve over and over again. When you see a lot of repetition in your code, or when you find yourself getting bogged down by details, that's the right time to simplify things. Metaprogramming helps you simplify by creating an easier, more expressive way to write code. There's no point in writing a DSL that you will only use once, but it pays several times over if you use it repeatedly.

You could let your imagination run wild and use metaprogramming to solve problems you think you'll have someday, but you'll quickly realize that those are just mental exercises. Instead, look for patterns you have in your code right now, for practices and idioms you use often, and use metaprogramming to simplify those. This process is called *extraction*, and it's based on what you need and use, not what you could imagine doing some day. You'll notice that Rails, Rake, RSpec, and many of the other frameworks we cover in this book all came from extractions, from looking at existing solutions and finding better, easier ways to write those.

The best way to write a DSL is to practice *intentional programming*. Step away from the code and ask yourself, "if I were not limited by the language I use right now, if I could express the solution itself in some other language, what would my code look like?" Try to write that code as if that language already exists. You've just defined a DSL. Now you have to go and implement it, but the hardest part is behind you.

So how do you know you're successful? A good DSL has two interesting qualities. The first is that you'll want to use it. You know you're successful when, out of all the possible things you can do that day, just after coffee, you decide to write code using that DSL.

The second quality of a good DSL is that you can throw away the documentation and still use it, or you might say it follows the "the rule of least surprise." When the code comes naturally to you, it's easier to write and less painful to maintain. When we work with Rails, we never have to stop to ask, "how do we access the order_on field?" We know that in Rails it's accessed with the order_on method. We know that to find an employee record by their name, we use find_by_name. The rule of least surprise is one of those, "I'll know it when I see it" guidelines. Just ask your teammates what they expect to happen, and if you've followed the rule closely enough, they should be able to tell you.

Using method_missing and a few other fun metaprogramming tricks, you may work yourself into a position where you have a lot of methods that aren't explicitly defined. The Rails API is much larger than the API documentation indicates because there is so much runtime code generation that goes on. How do you make sure that your users and coworkers know what your code can do, that your code is testable, and, above all, that your intentions are clear (even six months from now)? You document, of course. And if you follow the rule of least surprise, you have little to worry about: other developers will intuitively know which methods to expect when it all makes sense.

But what about testing? Don't the dynamic features make it harder to test? Testing metaprogramming is no different from testing any other piece of code. There's nothing magical about it, no hidden traps. You can use any tool available for testing, and, in fact, in the next chapter we're going to talk about testing at length.

1.5   *Summary*

Ruby has gained a lot of popularity in recent times because it's a simpler, expressive alternative to other contemporary languages. This success is partially due to the emergence of Rails as a tangible tool that developers can use to develop production-quality software that's still developer friendly. Rails owes this friendliness to Ruby, which offers a lot of features, such as metaprogramming, that make Ruby more expressive and even fun.

As more and more developers pick up Ruby, they will want to use their current programming paradigms, like aspect-oriented programming or declarative programming, and development practices such as Scrum or test-driven development. Ruby has a number of libraries to help bring these old practices into your new environment (such as Ruleby or AspectR). In the next chapter, we'll concentrate on the most prevalent of these—test-driven development—and we'll look at testing Ruby code using the built-in testing library and some related third-party tools and libraries.

Testing Ruby

This chapter covers

- Testing principles
- Test-driven development
- Behavior-driven development
- Using stubs and mocks
- Testing your tests

How do you currently test your code? From what people tell us, it seems the most popular testing methodology is "works now, works later": they test their software by playing around with it, and if it works now, they assume it always will. If this is your approach, you've surely encountered many of the problems we did when we used that method: changes to one part of the system breaking another, unexpected edge cases (or non-edge cases!) causing the software to behave unexpectedly, and so on. Then comes the inevitable debugging. The whole business is a huge time and effort sink.

You can avoid this entire situation and gain more assurances along the way by using automated testing. Ruby makes it easy by including a unit-testing library with its standard distribution (and more tools are available via third-party libraries). But before we use that library, let's take a look at the basics of software testing.

2.1 Testing principles

Automated testing is a process in which code is written to test the behavior of other code. For example, if you wrote a shopping cart web application, you would write code that would call the various pieces of the application and verify its results (to ensure the `calculate_total` method gave you a correct total), test all the "moving parts" of your application (by calling a piece of code that uses the database to ensure your database code is behaving properly), and so on. These sorts of tests are called automated because, well, they are. You write the test code, you run it (typically inside a container specifically meant for testing), and it tests the code it's written to test. This means no more clicking around on your application for 10 minutes to ensure that one feature is functioning properly; no more writing that fake input file and hoping it treats other input files the same way; and no more wasting hours of time trying to nail down what part of your big system is causing that little error to pop up. (OK, so maybe not "no more," but at least a lot less!)

So what exactly do we mean by a *test*? A test at its core is a piece of code that ensures that another piece of code does what it's supposed to. In testing, you're seeking to set up a test state in your application and check for (the right) changes to that state after the tests run. You write tests that will verify the results of a method or other value-bearing code to ensure that, in most cases, the input is handled properly.

If you wanted to write tests for your method `get_results_as_string`, you would write a test to ensure it returned a string. You would also write a test that made sure it raised exceptions with the wrong input as a safeguard: you want it to complain when it's improperly used (you want to test what works, and what doesn't). You are testing the behavior of your code in an isolated environment to ensure it behaves as it should. This may sound abstract now, but we'll take a look at what these tests look like in Ruby later in this chapter.

2.1.1 Why bother with testing?

Many developers avoid testing because of all that extra code, and we'll certainly give it to you honestly: testing creates more code. But don't let that scare you. Although testing may cost you some keystrokes, you'll appreciate it later when it saves brain power and time. Testing keeps your other code in line; it lets you know if your code is still behaving the same way, rather than your having to think hard about whether or not it is, or, even worse, finding out it's not when you've deployed it and it crashes hard.

So, the first benefit of testing is obvious: you know that the code works. You could just run the code and see for yourself—there's no need to write automated test cases. But consider the huge time sink that would become: spending hours a day poking at your application, making sure each piece is working properly. Using automated tests gives you peace of mind and a productivity boost because if the tests pass (and if they're well-written tests) you can be assured your code is behaving properly.

As we all know, code has a sensitive personality: you fix things in one place, and it may get upset and break in another place. Testing helps you maintain the behavior of your application; if you add code or refactor it, how can you be sure that your application will behave the same way unless you test it? And what better way to test it than with consistent, automated tests? Let's say you refactor a class's methods and cut them down from 13 to 6. Can you be sure that the methods that are exposed to the rest of the application still behave the same? If you've written a solid test suite, it should be easy. Just run the tests, and if they all pass, it should presumably work in the same fashion as it did before.

Another benefit of automated tests is that they help with debugging. Some bugs are notoriously hard to find when you have to repeatedly run the code, each time going through manual steps like creating and deleting data to make the bug surface, fixing and testing it again to see if you got to the root of the problem. Test cases are more granular, and they tell you exactly what they're doing, so by running the test cases you can find bugs and fix them easily.

Testing and dynamic languages

Many critics of dynamic typing say that debugging dynamic languages is harder because the compiler doesn't help you with debugging through type checking, but testing can help you get over a dependence on this static compiler behavior. Because Ruby objects are defined by behavior rather than a static definition, you can use tests to verify their behavior more effectively than by relying on the compiler. Compilers don't test for nulls, string values, integers out of range, or partially constructed objects, and they are easily fooled by type casting. Testing gives you the same level of granularity with a much wider test spectrum, and as such, more information when trying to debug.

Now that we've covered the basic principles of testing, let's look at testing in Ruby. The "burden" of testing is much lighter in Ruby, thanks to its built-in testing libraries and third-party tools. In this section, we'll take a look at these tools and how they can help you effectively write tests and code faster and easier.

2.1.2 *Types of testing*

When people refer to testing, they are usually talking about *unit tests*. Unit tests test your code in small, discrete units: methods or classes or whatever small units of code you care to test. These tests are the core of all testing, because they test your code at its lowest level and verify its basic behaviors. Unit tests are the bread and butter of testing; typically these will be the first tests you write and will act as the foundation that other test types are built from. You wouldn't want to write tests for a database application and all of its queries without first writing a test to ensure it can connect and make a query, right?

Unit tests should be concentrated. They should test the smallest unit possible: a single method at a time, a single call signature at a time, a single class at a time, a single module at a time, and so on. In doing this, you create a set of tests that depends only on what's being tested, making their results more accurate. This way the `foo` method can't make the test for `bar` fail.

NOTE   Most developers initially have difficulty gaining this separation of concerns. Don't worry! There are plenty of techniques and libraries to help you out. Further on in this chapter, we discuss some of these strategies.

Higher up in the architecture we find *integration tests*. These tests involve larger pieces of code, and you can think of them as being something like compound unit tests. As the name suggests, they test the integration of your application's pieces. For example, Rails's integration tests allow you to test an entire application flow, from logging in, through filling a form, to getting a page with search results. Other integration tests could test a full application operation, like an e-commerce transaction or a sequence of actions like downloading, extracting, and using data. Their purpose is to make sure that all of the moving parts of your application, like your code, the database, any third-party code, and so on, are all moving in the right direction.

There are many other types of testing (functional tests, acceptance testing, regression testing, and so on), but these are beyond the scope of this book (and you may never need to write any of these sorts of tests if you have a testing/QA team). The remainder of this chapter will show you how to unit test your code using Ruby and its libraries, and we'll start by walking through a basic testing workflow.

2.1.3   *Testing workflow*

Developers typically don't test as much as they should. The excuses usually range from "It's too much code!" to "We don't have time for tests!" This temptation to skip testing is especially prevalent when tests are an afterthought to development. This tendency to ignore testing (along with a few more reasons we'll discuss a little later) is why we advocate a *test-first* approach to development. In a test-first approach, you write your tests before you write your code, using your tests as a way to describe the behavior of the code you will write. For example, if you were writing an application to process XML files, you would want to write tests that describe how the application would behave when fed a valid XML file, when fed an invalid XML file, when the process is complete, and so on, and then you would go back and write the code to make those tests valid.

The test-first methodology can follow one of two paths: *test-first development* or *test-driven development*. We've described test-first development above: write your tests, and then write your code to make the tests pass. Test-driven development (TDD) is the same idea, except that it adds an element of code refactoring to the mix. The basic process can be broken into five steps: add, fail, code, test, refactor (as shown in figure 2.1).

Figure 2.1   Test-driven development is a five-step process: add, fail, code, test, refactor.

In the first step, you add tests for any new code you want to write *before you write the code*. You write a test that tests for the right behavior of the method; if the method takes a string and returns its length, write a test that calls the method with "hello" and test for a return value of 5; if it should raise an exception when you pass it a nil, test for that. As tests are added, you create a specification of the behavior that your code should conform to.

Once the specification is laid out, you move on to the fail step. In this step you run the tests and ensure they fail. And for a reason. We use tests to deal with errors we make in the code, but we can make errors while writing test cases. We can set up an object with all the right values, but forget to call the method we're supposed to test, or call a method but forget to check its result, and such a test will always pass. Until you can make the test fail at least once, you have no certainty it's actually testing your code.

Next, you write code to make the tests pass: you implement the specification you've created with the tests. Write the method, module, or class, and if the tests pass, great! If the tests fail, go back and debug your code to make them pass. When they all pass, go back and refactor your tests and code so they're more effective (shorter but accomplish just as much or more).

But why bother with all this business?

2.2 *Test-driven development with Ruby*

The built-in Ruby testing library is similar to the libraries of other languages, such as Java and Python. The general architecture consists of test suites, built from methods, which make assertions about your code. These test suites are run by test runners, which invoke the tests and report the results. As shown in figure 2.2, a single runner may invoke a number of suites, which may hold a whole lot of tests (the ActiveRecord tests for mySQL have 1,035 tests with 3,940 assertions!).

So, let's get going on writing some tests. We'll start with a basic test: testing the length of a string. First, we'll need to create a test harness, which in Ruby is a class that inherits from `Test::Unit::TestCase`. Listing 2.1 shows our test case.

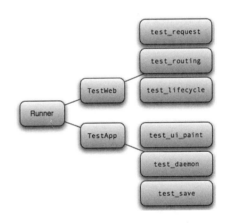

Figure 2.2   Test suites are composed of a collection of unit tests that are run one by one by a test runner.

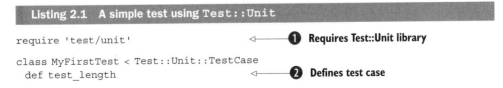

Listing 2.1   A simple test using `Test::Unit`

```
require 'test/unit'                              ❶ Requires Test::Unit library

class MyFirstTest < Test::Unit::TestCase
  def test_length                                ❷ Defines test case
```

```
    my_string = "Testing is fun!"
    assert_equal 15, my_string.length
  end
end
```

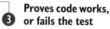

**Proves code works,
❸ or fails the test**

First, we need to `require` the `Test::Unit` library ❶ and create a class that inherits from `Test::Unit::TestCase`. We can then create methods that test the code ❷. Within these methods, we will make assertions ❸ about the code. Save this code to a file (for example, my_first_test.rb) and run it. You should see output that looks something like this:

```
Loaded suite my_first_test
Started
.
Finished in 0.00058 seconds.

1 tests, 1 assertions, 0 failures, 0 errors
```

You can see that we had one test (one method that contained tests), one assertion, and no failures. We had one `assert_equal` statement that evaluated to `true`, so we had no failures. The `assert_equal` method isn't the only assertion available; there are a number of assert methods, which are listed in table 2.1.

Table 2.1   Ruby's built-in testing library offers a large number of assertions baked right in.

Assertion	Description
`assert(boolean)`	Passes if `boolean` (that is, a boolean expression) is `true`.
`assert_equal(expected, actual)` `assert_not_equal(expected, actual)`	Passes if `expected == actual` or `expected != actual`.
`assert_nil(object)` `assert_not_nil(object)`	Passes if `object == nil` or `object != nil`.
`assert_match(pattern, string)` `assert_no_match(pattern, string)`	Passes if `string` matches or doesn't match `pattern` (such as a regular expression).
`assert_raise(exception...) {block}` `assert_nothing_raised(exception...) {block}`	Passes if the `block` raises or doesn't raise the provided `Exception`(s)
`assert_same(expected, actual)` `assert_not_same(expected, actual)`	Passes if `actual.equal?(expected)` or if `!actual.equal?(expected)`.
`assert_respond_to(object, method)`	Passes if `object` can respond to the given method.
`assert_throws(expected_sym) {block}` `assert_nothing_thrown {block}`	Passes if the `block` throws the provided symbol; `assert_nothing_thrown` passes if the provided `block` doesn't throw any symbols.
`assert_instance_of(class, object)`	Passes if `object.class == class`.

Table 2.1 Ruby's built-in testing library offers a large number of assertions baked right in. *(continued)*

Assertion	Description
`assert_operator(first, operator, second)`	Passes if the first object compared to the second object is `true` when using the provided `operator`.
`assert_kind_of(class, object)`	Passes if `object.kind_of?(class)`.
`assert_in_delta(expected, actual, delta)`	Passes if `actual - expected <= delta`.
`assert_send(send_array)`	Passes if method sent to object returns `true`.

Using these assertions, you can build sets of tests that check your code effectively, but, like your code, tests don't run in a vacuum. Often you need a little bit of setup before execution, or some teardown afterwards, such as reading in files or creating objects. Test::Unit provides a way to do that using the xUnit architecture. For example, if we wanted to test our string for length, emptiness, and hash value, it wouldn't make sense to instantiate the string in each method; instead we would use the setup method. Take a look at listing 2.2 to see what we mean.

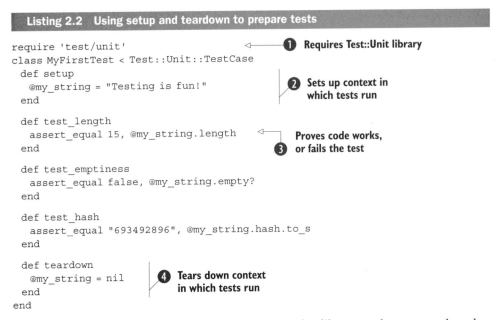

Listing 2.2 Using setup and teardown to prepare tests

```
require 'test/unit'                              ◁───────❶ Requires Test::Unit library
class MyFirstTest < Test::Unit::TestCase
  def setup
    @my_string = "Testing is fun!"              ❷ Sets up context in
  end                                              which tests run

  def test_length
    assert_equal 15, @my_string.length          ◁─────  Proves code works,
  end                                           ❸ or fails the test

  def test_emptiness
    assert_equal false, @my_string.empty?
  end

  def test_hash
    assert_equal "693492896", @my_string.hash.to_s
  end

  def teardown
    @my_string = nil                            ❹ Tears down context
  end                                              in which tests run
end
```

We start out the same way as last time: require the library and create a class that inherits from TestCase ❶. But this time, we do something a little different. We create a setup method that creates an instance variable to hold our string ❷. Now we refer to my_string as an instance variable throughout our tests (❸ and other places). Finally, we (superfluously) set my_string to nil in teardown ❹. The teardown method is special, like setup, and it's run after tests. Yes, this example is a little contrived (especially because we didn't do the whole testing cycle), but it's important to understand the concept before we take it into practice. Now that you have the concept, let's move on to an example that's a little more real world.

Let's say you're building an application to grab some XML reports from a remote server, pull some data out, then process the data you pull out. The reports, which are output from your payroll server, are catalogs of employees and hours worked; they are used by the application you're building to generate departmental expense reports. One of these reports might look something like this:

```xml
<payroll-report>
  <department name="Graphics">
   <employee name="Janice Partridge">
    <week id="1">40</week>
    <week id="2">38</week>
    <week id="3">30</week>
    <week id="4">40</week>
   </employee>
   <employee name="James Jones">
    <week id="1">33</week>
    <week id="2">23</week>
    <week id="3">30</week>
    <week id="4">25</week>
   </employee>
  </department>
  <department name="IT">
   <employee name="Andrea Lantz">
    <week id="1">40</week>
    <week id="2">41</week>
    <week id="3">45</week>
    <week id="4">39</week>
   </employee>
  </department>
</payroll-report>
```

Fairly simple, right? Departments have employees, which have weeks and hours. That's simple enough to implement, and we'll get to it soon, but first let's write the test cases. Take a look at listing 2.3.

Listing 2.3 Tests for our to-be-implemented XML reporter

```ruby
require 'test/unit'
require 'payroll_reporter'

class PayrollReporterTest < Test::Unit::TestCase          ❶ Creates a
  def setup                                                 PayrollReporter
    @my_reporter = PayrollReporter.new('test.xml')   ◁───   that tests can use
  end

  def test_department                          ◁────────┐
    assert_equal nil, @my_reporter.department(1234)       Tests
    assert_equal nil, @my_reporter.department("Development")   department
    expected = {"Andrea Lantz"=>                          data parsed
          {"week"=> [{"id"=>"1", "content"=>"40"},      ❷ from XML
          {"id"=>"2", "content"=>"41"},
```

```
                  {"id"=>"3", "content"=>"45"},
                  {"id"=>"4", "content"=>"39"}]}}
    assert_equal expected, @my_reporter.department("IT")
  end

  def test_employee
    assert_equal nil, @my_reporter.employee(234323)
    assert_equal nil, @my_reporter.employee("Mr. Mustache")
    expected = {"week"=> [
                  {"id"=>"1", "content"=>"40"},
                  {"id"=>"2", "content"=>"41"},
                  {"id"=>"3", "content"=>"45"},
                  {"id"=>"4", "content"=>"39"}]}
    assert_equal expected, @my_reporter.employee("Andrea Lantz")
  end

  def test_get_hours_for
    assert_equal nil, @my_reporter.get_hours_for("Miguel de Jesus")
    assert_equal 165, @my_reporter.get_hours_for("Andrea Lantz")
  end
end
```

3 Tests employee data parsed from XML

4 Tests that work hours were parsed and calculated correctly

First, we create an instance of the `PayrollReporter` class **1** in the setup method. The constructor takes a path to an XML file (we'll feed it a test file here). Next, we create a test for a method named `department`, which will retrieve the details (employees, for example) of a department **2**. We follow this with a test for a method named `employee`, which will do the same thing but for employees (it will retrieve a hash of their work hours) **3**. The last test we create is for a method named `get_hours_for`, which retrieves the total hours worked by an employee **4**. Then we run the tests and get a load of errors. If we create a stub file (a file that has all classes and methods defined but with no method bodies), we should see failures rather than errors.

We've added some tests and they are properly failing, so let's implement the code (which you can see in listing 2.4).

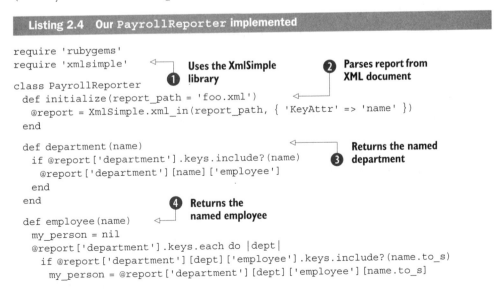

Listing 2.4 Our `PayrollReporter` implemented

```
require 'rubygems'
require 'xmlsimple'

class PayrollReporter
  def initialize(report_path = 'foo.xml')
    @report = XmlSimple.xml_in(report_path, { 'KeyAttr' => 'name' })
  end

  def department(name)
    if @report['department'].keys.include?(name)
      @report['department'][name]['employee']
    end
  end

  def employee(name)
    my_person = nil
    @report['department'].keys.each do |dept|
      if @report['department'][dept]['employee'].keys.include?(name.to_s)
        my_person = @report['department'][dept]['employee'][name.to_s]
```

1 Uses the XmlSimple library

2 Parses report from XML document

3 Returns the named department

4 Returns the named employee

```
      end
    end

  return my_person
  end
                                            Calculates work
  def get_hours_for(name)        ⟵————┘   ❺ hours for employee
    my_employee = employee(name)
    return nil if my_employee == nil

    total_hours = 0
    my_employee['week'].each do |week|
      total_hours += week['content'].to_i
    end

    total_hours
  end
end
```

We'll talk more about using and manipulating XML data later in this book, but for now we'll use a library named XmlSimple to do basic data extraction ❶. We implement each piece of the code individually. First the constructor, which takes a file path and opens it for parsing ❷. Then a department method to get the employees in a department ❸, and an employee method to get the work hours of an employee ❹. Last, a get_hours_for method to get the total work hours of an employee ❺. Now we need to run the tests to ensure they pass.

```
Loaded suite payroll_reporter_test
Started
...
Finished in 0.028279 seconds.

3 tests, 8 assertions, 0 failures, 0 errors
```

Excellent! Now that all of our tests pass, we can move on and refactor the current code and add new code (maybe a method to get an employee's work hours for a certain week or a whole department's work hours). As we add this code, we'll use the tests to ensure that the application's behavior is consistent. If the language of assertions and tests doesn't appeal to you, there is an alternative testing method.

2.3   *Behavior-driven development with RSpec*

Test cases help you ensure the code behaves as it should, but how do you know what it should behave like? We like to base our development on a written specification, which tells us what the code should do. The tests measure whether the code behaves according to the specification, and the code itself implements the expected behavior. A written specification makes it easier to work as a team, to work against in-development libraries and services, to communicate to stakeholders what the software does, and to track progress as the features are implemented.

In this section we'll talk about behavior-driven development, an approach that focuses on specifying, testing and implementing behavior (in that order), and we'll show you how to do that using RSpec.

2.3.1 *What is behavior-driven development?*

Specifications take many forms, from high-level architecture diagrams through storyboards and screen mocks, all the way down to capturing the behavior of each functional unit. The high-level specification is most likely to remain accurate because it doesn't capture a lot of details, and wholesale changes to the architecture and major components don't happen frequently. It's much harder to keep a functional specification synchronized with the code. If you have ever developed against a specification written as a Word document, you'll know what we're talking about. The specification starts out as the best ideas about the software to be written, and it's only during development that you find it contains wrong assumptions, which must be fixed in code. In a matter of days, the code starts to diverge from the document, and the document turns into a work of fiction.

Behavior-driven development (BDD) was conceived by Dan North to address this issue. To do BDD right, you start by writing a specification of the code, but instead of creating a static document, you create it in the same repository that holds the source code. The specification forms a template that describes the expected behavior, which you then fill up with test cases. As you make changes, you reflect those back into the specification and tests, changing them alongside the code. The process is illustrated in figure 2.3.

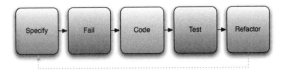

Figure 2.3   The behavior-driven development process starts with specification, adds tests, and builds an implementation that matches the specification and passes the tests.

If this sounds a bit conceptual, don't worry. In practice, it's easy to do. A specification document may initially look something like this:

```
describe "A new string" do
  it "should have a length of zero."
  it "should be empty."
end
```

This is Ruby code, and we'll explain what it does in just a moment. It's also a specification that's easy to read and understand. The behavior stands out, so we don't have to guess it from the code. When we run it through a tool, we get a report that looks the one shown in Figure 2.4. The report we generate has three colors: green for test cases that pass, identifying behaviors we implemented correctly; red for failing tests; and yellow for anything we specified but haven't implemented yet. It tells us where we stand so we can track progress on our project.

To go from the specification to working code, we'll start by adding test cases (see listing 2.6). From here on, we're following TDD practices: write a test that fails, then write the implementation to make the test pass.

We'll encounter the difference between BDD and TDD again when we decide to make a change to our specification. Perhaps we will realize we need to use a different

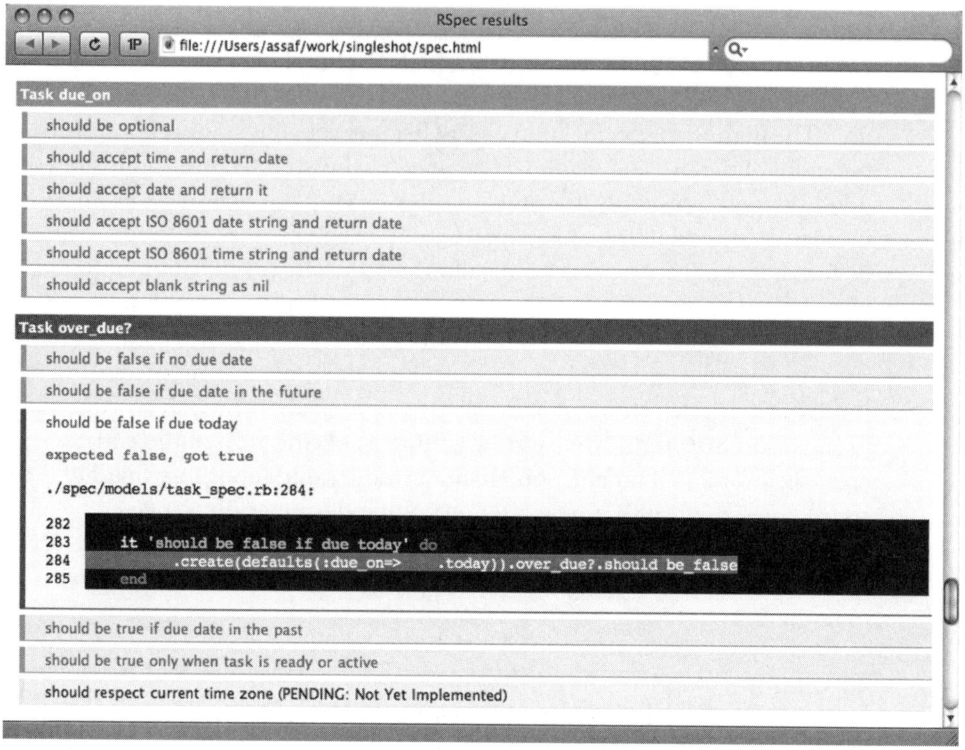

Figure 2.4   An HTML report showing successful, failing, and pending specifications

message format, present a task to the end user in a different way, or simplify a set of methods that are part of the public API. Whatever the reason, we're going to return to this file, change the specification to describe the new behavior, fill it up with a test case to check the new behavior, and work out the implementation to conform to both. BDD gives us a way to manage change, keeping the code and specification synchronized.

Now that we have covered the basics of BDD, let's look at a particular frame-work—one that's used extensively in the Ruby world and that also influenced BDD frameworks for languages as diverse as Java and FORTRAN. We're talking about RSpec.

2.3.2   *Testing with RSpec*

Let's build a suite of BDD tests using RSpec as we look at a simple spec for a class we'll create. We'll start by installing RSpec (`gem install rspec`), which provides us with the spec library we need to require in our code and the `spec` command-line tool we'll use to run these specification files. You can also use the command-line tool to generate reports like the one in figure 2.4 and to repeatedly run only failing tests. In chapter 3 we'll talk about Rake, and we'll show you how to set up your environment to automate these tasks.

Let's return to our previous string-testing example to get a grasp on BDD; listing 2.5 shows a basic spec for a new string object.

> ### The role of specification in agile development
>
> Agile development practices put emphasis on progress through small, incremental iterations, with a close feedback loop between developer and end users. Agile development is the antithesis of BDUF (Big Design Up Front) and the waterfall model. What agile practitioners discovered is that having one stage to cement the specification, followed by a marathon to implement it, led to disaster. No matter how good your intentions, it's impossible to predict everything up front. Business needs may change as you're building the software, technical difficulties require adjustments, and your customer may realize he needs something different when he sees the working code. To create software successfully, you need the ability to evolve its design as you're building it, working closely with end users to make sure it meets their expectations.
>
> To make agile practices work, you still need a specification. What you don't need is a specification that's cast in stone before the first day of development. It has to be a living, changing document that can adapt to evolving requirements. It's even better when it documents not what the software should have looked like, but what the delivered software actually does, and when it can be used to track progress. That makes BDD an important tool for agile development.

Listing 2.5 A context for an empty queue string

```
require 'rubygems'          ❶ Requires RSpec
require 'spec'

describe "A new string" do          Establishes a
  # Our specs will go here   ❷ new context
end
```

First, we require the needed libraries ❶, which make available the methods that we must have. Then we create a context ❷ for our string object: "A new string." This context will describe the expected behavior of a new string. We can list those behaviors without writing any code to test them yet, or we can go straight ahead and start adding code that will test these behaviors. Because this is a trivial example, we'll go ahead and add some real test cases, which you can see in listing 2.6.

Listing 2.6 A few specs for a string object

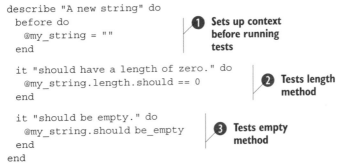

```
describe "A new string" do
  before do                  ❶ Sets up context
    @my_string = ""             before running
  end                           tests

  it "should have a length of zero." do
    @my_string.length.should == 0   ❷ Tests length
  end                                  method

  it "should be empty." do
    @my_string.should be_empty   ❸ Tests empty
  end                              method
end
```

The general setup of the contexts and specifications may look familiar to you, because they are somewhat similar to those in the TDD library. First, we specify a before block ❶, which will create an instance variable for us to use in our specifications (cleaning up after a test is done using an `after` block). Next, we create a specification that a new string should have a length of 0 ❷.

Note the use of the method `should`; the `should` and `should_not` methods are the primary verbs used in RSpec. These methods, combined with predicates (like `empty` ❸), allow you to specify various conditions. You use these predicates to describe how the object being tested should behave (`should throw_symbol`), exist (`should be_instance_of`), respond (`should respond_to`), and so on. Check out table 2.2 to see a list of the specification predicates that are available. You can find more details on the RSpec website (rspec.info).

Table 2.2   RSpec has numerous specifications you can use to verify the behavior of your application.

Specification	Description
`should be_predicate [args]` `should_not be_predicate [args]`	Uses the question mark form of the method provided as the predicate (e.g., `simple_object.should be_empty` calls `empty?` on the `simple_object`).
`should be_close(val, tolerance)` `should_not be_close(val, tolerance)`	Allows a value tolerance for floating-point specifications.
`should have_something [args]`	Calls `has_something?` on the receiver (e.g., `should_have_key` calls `has_key?`).
`should <operator> value` `should_not <operator> value`	Uses Ruby's operators to test (e.g., `should_be < 3` or `should_be =~ /hi/`).
`should include(item)` `should_not include(item)`	Specifies that a collection should or should not include `item`.
`should match(regex)` `should_not match(regex)`	Specifies that the receiver should or should not match the provided regular expression.
`should be_an_instance_of(class)` `should_not be_an_instance_of(class)`	Uses `instance_of?` to test the receiver's class.
`should be_a_kind_of(class)` `should_not be_a_kind_of(class)`	Uses `kind_of?` to test the receiver's class ancestry.
`should respond_to(symbol)` `should_not respond_to(symbol)`	Tests whether the receiver responds to the given symbol using `respond_to?`.
`should raise_error([ex], [mesg])` `should_not raise_error([ex], [mesg])`	When called on a `Proc`, specifies that a given exception should or should not be raised; if no exception is given, checks for any exception thrown. The parameter for `mesg` is a string or regular expression that is matched against the exception's message.

Table 2.2   RSpec has numerous specifications you can use to verify the behavior of your application. *(continued)*

Specification	Description
`should throw_symbol [:symbol]` `should_not throw_symbol [:symbol]`	When called on a `Proc`, tests whether a given symbol was thrown; if no symbol is given, tests for any symbol.
`should change(receiver, :method)` `should change { block }`	When called on a `Proc`, tests whether the value of `receiver.method` has changed after the `Proc` has executed; this method has a number of forms (check the latest documentation to see them all).

`should have(number).things`
`should_not have(number).things`
`should have_at_least(number).things`
`should have_at_most(number).things`
	Tests the receiver's count (`should_have`), lower limit (`should_have_at_least`), and upper limit (`should_have_at_most`) of the collection named for `things` (e.g., `my_array.should have(3).items`).

`should eql(arg)`
`should_not eql(arg)`
`should equal(arg)`
`should_not equal(arg)`
	Specifies that the receiver should or should not be equal to `arg` in object identity (`eql`) or merely value (`equal`).

`should satisfy { |arg| block }` `should_not satisfy { |arg| block }`	Tests whether the block evaluates to `true` when the receiver is passed as the only argument.

Getting back to our example, you can run the specs and make sure they pass (which they should!).

Now let's look at BDD with something a little more realistic. Let's say you want to test an `IntranetReader` object, which is a wrapper for your intranet's RSS feed. We'll create a spec for all the behaviors of the library. Remember, because we're using behavior-driven development, we want to start with a spec, and we need to specify behavior for whether or not the object has stories in it, whether it properly connected, whether the RSS is parsed correctly, and so on, rather than asserting values and conditions. Let's start with the most basic spec, which you can see in listing 2.7.

Listing 2.7   A basic spec for our `IntranetReader` class

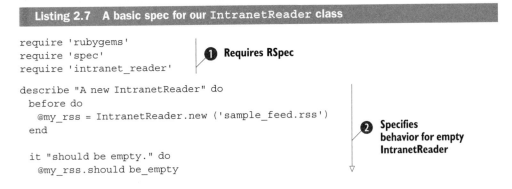

```
require 'rubygems'
require 'spec'                                    ❶ Requires RSpec
require 'intranet_reader'

describe "A new IntranetReader" do
  before do
    @my_rss = IntranetReader.new ('sample_feed.rss')
    end                                           ❷ Specifies
                                                     behavior for empty
                                                     IntranetReader
  it "should be empty." do
    @my_rss.should be_empty
```

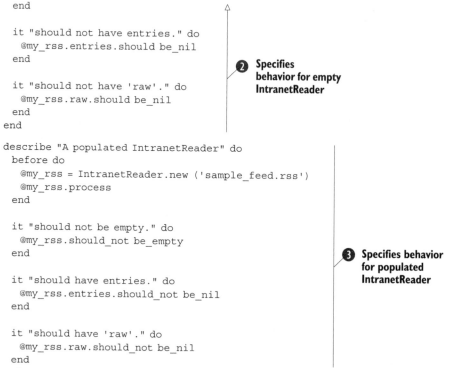

```
      end

      it "should not have entries." do
        @my_rss.entries.should be_nil
      end

      it "should not have 'raw'." do
        @my_rss.raw.should be_nil
      end
    end
    describe "A populated IntranetReader" do
      before do
        @my_rss = IntranetReader.new ('sample_feed.rss')
        @my_rss.process
      end

      it "should not be empty." do
        @my_rss.should_not be_empty
      end

      it "should have entries." do
        @my_rss.entries.should_not be_nil
      end

      it "should have 'raw'." do
        @my_rss.raw.should_not be_nil
      end
    end
```

❷ Specifies behavior for empty IntranetReader

❸ Specifies behavior for populated IntranetReader

This is similar to our specification in listing 2.6, except this time we've specified two contexts. First, we require our essential libraries ❶, and then we proceed to create a context for an empty IntranetReader ❷. Inside the context, we have specifications to check for the emptiness of the new object we've created. A second context holds specifications for a populated IntranetReader ❸. These specifications ensure that the object was populated properly.

If you run these specifications now (using the spec command like this: spec intranet_reader_spec.rb), you will get some errors (especially if you don't create an intranet_reader.rb file to require). It should look something like the following when they're failing "correctly." (The actual output includes stack traces of all failing tests, which we haven't included here.)

```
FFFFFF

...

Finished in 0.002936 seconds

4 specifications, 4 failures
```

Once you've reached this point, all you have to do is go back and implement code to make the tests pass, just like in test-driven development. Listing 2.8 shows our implementation using the SimpleRSS gem, but yours may look somewhat different.

Listing 2.8　**Our implementation of `IntranetReader`**

```ruby
require 'rubygems'
require 'simple-rss'
require 'open-uri'

class IntranetReader
  def initialize(url)
    @feed_url = url
  end

  def process
    @raw = open(@feed_url).read
    @rss = SimpleRSS.parse @raw
  end

  def entries
    @rss.items if @rss
  end

  def empty?
    @rss.nil? ? true : @rss.items.empty?
  end

  def raw
    @raw
  end
end
```

If you run the specifications and there are no failures, it's time to add and refactor tests, code, or both. Perhaps you'd like to implement a method to validate the RSS input before it's processed, or maybe you'd like to allow the user to search the RSS feed. Whatever you add, just remember: specify, code, test, refactor.

But what if your testing environment doesn't have access to the RSS feed? How do you mimic your production environment for testing? The next section will discuss a few strategies for dealing with this problem and a few techniques for setting up an environment for your tests.

2.4　A testing environment

As you read this chapter and start playing with tests, you may be wondering, "What if my test environment doesn't have access to certain parts of my application, like networked components or third-party services?" Fortunately for us, the pioneers of software testing devised a number of techniques to handle this sort of thing. In this section, we'll take a look at three of these techniques: fixtures, stubs, and mocks.

2.4.1　Setting up a baseline with fixture data

One of the earliest difficulties you'll encounter with testing is replicating the environment in which your code will run. Often the problem is not so much replicating the relationship among your code, but the external environment from the OS or network. Many developers use *fixtures* as a first crutch to get this sort of environment up and going. Fixture data (or fixtures) create a fixed, baseline environment for your tests to run in. For example, as with Ruby on Rails, you might use a YAML file to set up the database with an initial set of products so you can test your inventory management code against known data. Or, you might create a few data files that are prepopulated with data that would normally be generated by another application so you can test how your code reacts to existing data.

NOTE   In the Ruby development realm, you will probably most often hear the term "fixture" applied to Rails and its testing fixtures for databases. Don't be confused: the concept of a fixture existed before Rails was around and is useful outside of Rails.

There is no special technique necessary to use fixtures because you are simply constructing a baseline environment for testing. For example, let's say you were testing a component of your application that received the output from ps to check for the existence of a process. Listing 2.9 shows the original class and test.

Listing 2.9   A process checker class and test

```
require 'test/unit'

class ProcessChecker
  def initialize                          ❶ Gets output
    @ps_output = `ps -A`          ◁─┘       from ps
  end

  def rails_server?                       ❷ Checks for Rails
    @ps_output =~ /ruby script\/server/ ◁─┘  server script
  end

  # Other process-checking methods...
end

class TestProcessChecker < Test::Unit::TestCase
  def test_initialize                              Asserts output is in ❸
    my_checker = ProcessChecker.new                an instance variable

    assert my_checker.instance_variables.include?('@ps_output') ◁─┘
  end
end
```

As you can see, we have a `ProcessChecker` class that grabs the output from ps, stores it in an instance variable ❶, and checks that variable for various processes (in this case, we just check that the Rails server script is running) ❷. We then create a test that ensures that variable is actually set when the object is instantiated ❸. But now we're at a testing impasse. How do you test the results of the ps call? Will you have to start the Rails server script every time this test is run? What if the deployment environment doesn't even have Rails installed?

This is one situation where implementing a fixture makes sense. If you create standard data for the object to use instead of making a call to ps every time, you can ensure your tests will run the same everywhere (even on Windows!). Take a look at the revised version of the test in listing 2.10.

Listing 2.10 A revised test with fixture data

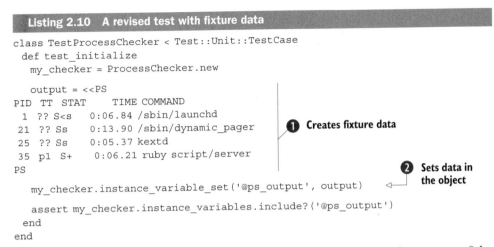

```
class TestProcessChecker < Test::Unit::TestCase
  def test_initialize
    my_checker = ProcessChecker.new

    output = <<PS
PID  TT  STAT      TIME COMMAND
  1  ??  S<s    0:06.84 /sbin/launchd
 21  ??  Ss     0:13.90 /sbin/dynamic_pager
 25  ??  Ss     0:05.37 kextd
 35  p1  S+     0:06.21 ruby script/server
PS

    my_checker.instance_variable_set('@ps_output', output)

    assert my_checker.instance_variables.include?('@ps_output')
  end
end
```

❶ Creates fixture data

❷ Sets data in the object

In this instance, we fill in some fixture data, which has static output from a run of the ps command **❶**. This data is then fed into the object via instance_variable_set **❷**. Now we can run this test on any platform (even though Windows will complain that it can't find ps) and it should behave the same way, because we now have a set of fixture data to work from.

NOTE   We are injecting the data in a way that makes our test case fragile **❷**. We recommend adding methods to your classes and modules that will assist in testing. We wanted to show what's possible when you don't have full control of the objects you're testing.

You could then go back to your tests to refactor or add to them, as in listing 2.11.

Listing 2.11 Our refactored and expanded tests

```
class TestProcessChecker < Test::Unit::TestCase
  def setup
    @my_checker = ProcessChecker.new

    output = <<PS
PID  TT  STAT      TIME COMMAND
  1  ??  S<s    0:06.84 /sbin/launchd
 21  ??  Ss     0:13.90 /sbin/dynamic_pager -F /private/var/vm/swapfile
 25  ??  Ss     0:05.37 kextd
 35  p1  S+     0:06.21 ruby script/server
PS

    @my_checker.instance_variable_set('@ps_output', output)
  end

  def test_initialized
    assert @my_checker.instance_variables.include?('@ps_output')
  end

  def test_rails_server
    assert @my_checker.rails_server?
  end
end
```

❶ Uses setup method to create an object to test

❷ Tests for the check method

Now that we've refactored to use the `setup` method ❶, it's trivial to add tests for the methods on the class ❷.

Fixtures make it easy to set a baseline environment for your tests, but they can't cover everything. For example, if you're using a database, fixtures often don't scale easily and become a hassle to maintain (you can find plenty of blog posts about the subject on Google). If you plan on running your software on multiple platforms, you may have to maintain a fixture for each platform in cases like the preceding example. There are alternative methods to get around these problems, and with a little work and abstraction we can take advantage of them. We can use fixtures to rake data, as discussed earlier, and we can use stubs and mocks to fake methods and components. Let's start with stubs.

2.4.2 *Faking components with stubs*

Stubs are "fake" objects or methods that mimic the behavior of "real" objects. A stubbed object creates a facade of a real object, seemingly behaving like the real object, but in actuality faking the real object's logic. This technique is useful for mimicking parts of your application that may not be available or that are performance intensive.

For example, let's say you have an application that orders products from one of your suppliers, but you don't want to order a room full of products while running your tests. In that case, you would create stubbed objects to fake the supplier service so your tests can still be run without buying anything. These objects would act like, expose the same API as, and return the same values as the real objects that interact with the remote service, except they wouldn't be interacting with the remote service. For a visual of the concept, see figure 2.5.

Let's look at this example in code. Let's say the supplier exposes a web service API to you and has included a natural Ruby wrapper for this service. The API exposes a `search` method for finding products, an `add_to_cart` method for adding products to your cart, and a `pur-chase` method for finishing your order. Your application receives the purchasing data in XML form, which is parsed and then given to the supplier object to execute the purchase. The supplier class has an `execute_purchase` method, which takes an array of product names and quantities from the XML purchasing data. Our test for a simple purchase is shown in listing 2.12.

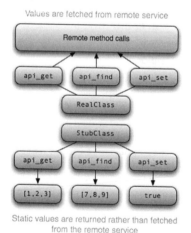

Figure 2.5   A stubbed class will seem to act like the real object but won't actually behave like it. In this case, the stub doesn't grab data from a remote service, but to the code consuming the API, it appears to.

Listing 2.12   Building tests for our supplier class

```
class TestSupplierInterface < Test::Unit::TestCase
  def test_execute_purchase
    data = [
      {:item_name => 'Red Rug', :quantity => 2},
      {:item_name => 'Set of Pens', :quantity => 17}
    ]

    my_supplier = MaterialSupplier.new
    assert my_supplier.execute_purchase(data)
  end
end
```

As you can see, we instantiate our class, call the `execute_purchase` method, and assert returns the truth value. If you run the tests, it should fail, so we're ready to implement the class. The class implementation for this particular supplier is shown in listing 2.13.

Listing 2.13   A class for handling purchasing from a supplier

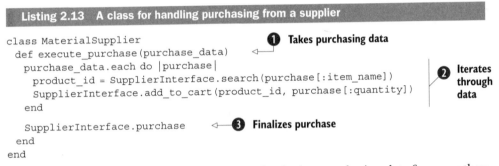

```
class MaterialSupplier                              ❶ Takes purchasing data
  def execute_purchase(purchase_data)
    purchase_data.each do |purchase|                                    ❷ Iterates
      product_id = SupplierInterface.search(purchase[:item_name])          through
      SupplierInterface.add_to_cart(product_id, purchase[:quantity])       data
    end

    SupplierInterface.purchase          ❸ Finalizes purchase
  end
end
```

As we mentioned, the `execute_purchase` method takes purchasing data from another part of your application ❶. The data is then iterated, the product name is searched for, its `id` is found, and it is added to the cart ❷. After the cart has been populated, we finalize the purchase ❸.

Now that we have a test and a class, how do we reliably test this? We can use the remote system to implement it, but we shouldn't depend on that all the time, especially if we want our tests to be consistent and reliable in every environment. Even if it is available, you probably don't want to (or shouldn't) send real requests to the remote server. So, we need to stub it.

To stub the `SupplierInterface` class, we need to create a class of the same name with input methods that return the right results (without making any requests to the remote service). Because we only use this class for testing, we'll include it in the same file as our test case (listing 2.12). Listing 2.14 shows the stubbed `SupplierInterface`.

Listing 2.14   A stubbed `SupplierInterface`

```
class SupplierInterface
  @@products = {                   ❶ Specifies
    1234 => 'Red Rug',               initial data
```

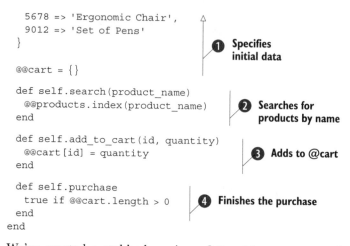

```
    5678 => 'Ergonomic Chair',
    9012 => 'Set of Pens'
  }                                    ❶ Specifies
                                          initial data
  @@cart = {}

  def self.search(product_name)
    @@products.index(product_name)     ❷ Searches for
  end                                     products by name

  def self.add_to_cart(id, quantity)
    @@cart[id] = quantity              ❸ Adds to @cart
  end

  def self.purchase
    true if @@cart.length > 0          ❹ Finishes the purchase
  end
end
```

We've created a stubbed version of SupplierInterface that works from data that we've statically created ❶. We use class-level hashes to implement searching (using the index method) ❷ and adding to a cart ❸. Because all we are testing at this point is whether we can add items to the cart and purchase them, we can just have the purchase method mimic the remote system and return true if the order is successful (if there are items in the cart) ❹. Now our tests should execute in the same manner, except using our local stubbed class instead of the remote service interface.

Stubbing is a useful technique for getting your tests up and running, but at the end of the day, stubs are still dumb objects. They pass back the value you ask for, but they don't verify that the right method calls are being made to them. This deficiency can make your tests weaker than they would be if you were to test those calls to the objects you're stubbing, because you could be missing out on a missed method call or a wrong parameter. Now let's take a look at another technique: mocks.

2.4.3 *Setting behavior expectations with mock objects*

Mock objects are similar to stubs, except they set expectations about your code's interactions with them. In our previous example, a mock object wouldn't have just stupidly taken the input for the search or add_to_cart methods—it would have verified that it received the right parameters or that the method was called in the first place. In doing this, it not only tests your code's actions on the returned values, it also tests your code's interactions with these objects: parameters passed, methods called, exceptions raised, and so on.

In this section, we'll look at a couple of ways to create mock objects. The first method we'll discuss is creating your own mock object patterns, no library required. We'll then take a look at using libraries such as Mocha to create mock objects.

Creating custom mocks

Before there were fancy mocking libraries, developers had to get their hands dirty and build their own mock objects. Unlike programming on punch cards, creating your own custom mock objects is still a valid practice. Sometimes there is a specific order or logic to how your application runs, and trying to shoehorn that into some mocking libraries' interfaces can sometimes be awkward. Building your own mock objects is simply easier.

Let's continue with our previous example. If we take our stubbed class and add expectations for each method, we can make it into a mock object. Listing 2.15 shows a revised version of the `SupplierInterface` stubbed class from listing 2.14.

Listing 2.15 Tests for shipping components

```
class SupplierInterface
  @@products = {
    1234 => 'Red Rug',
    5678 => 'Ergonomic Chair',
    9012 => 'Set of Pens'
  }

  @@cart = {}

  def self.search(product_name)                                    ❶ Expects
    $expectations[:search] = true if product_name.is_a?(String)  ←    a string
    @@products.index(product_name)                                    argument
  end

  def self.add_to_cart(id, quantity)
    $expectations[:add_to_cart] = true if id.is_a?(Integer) &&
      quantity.is_a?(Integer)          ←
    @@cart[id] = quantity                ❷ Expects two integers
  end

  def self.purchase
    $expectations[:purchase] = true      ←    Expects this method
    true if @@cart.length > 0            ❸    to be called
  end
end
```

Here we have created expectations about parameters (❶ and ❷) and an expectation that the `purchase` method will be called ❸, setting global variables appropriately. (This is not the best practice, but for the sake of brevity we'll keep it simple.) These expectations can then be evaluated in an updated test, as shown in listing 2.16.

Listing 2.16 An updated test to use our custom mock

```
class TestSupplierInterface < Test::Unit::TestCase
  def setup
    $expectations = {}
  end

  def test_execute_purchase
    data = [
      {:item_name => 'Red Rug', :quantity => 2},
      {:item_name => 'Set of Pens', :quantity => 17}
    ]

    my_supplier = MaterialSupplier.new
    assert my_supplier.execute_purchase(data)
```

```
[:search, :add_to_cart, :purchase].each do |meth|
    assert $expectations[meth],
      "#{meth} was not called or not called properly."
  end
 end
end
```

❶ Testing our expectations

As you can see, we have added a small piece of code ❶ to the end of the method that iterates over our known expectations (one for each method we expected to be called) to make sure they were set. If they weren't, the test fails. This technique makes our tests more robust, and, if used consistently, can make full test coverage a lot quicker than using simple stubs or nothing at all.

The only problem with custom mocks is they aren't formal, and, as a result, they are time-consuming to maintain. Fortunately there are a few libraries to formalize your mocks and speed up the development of your tests.

Creating mocks with Mocha

As mocking has become more popular, a number of libraries has been created that make the process much easier. In this section, we're going to discuss Mocha, one of the newer mocking libraries. Its mocking interface is much more intuitive and powerful than those of some other mocking libraries, so it's the one we'd recommend, were you to ask (and you are asking, because you are reading this book!).

TIP   If you find that Mocha doesn't work with your testing practices, or that it is "too magical," you may want to look into FlexMock, Jim Weirich's mocking library, or RSpec's mocking capabilities.

Mocha works via a mechanism it calls expectations (which is why we called our hash `$expectations` in the earlier examples). Mocha sets expectations on object behavior; so, for example, you might set an expectation that an object will have its `process` method called or that an object's `save` method will be called and it should return true. This is just like what we did before, except that Mocha makes the process much cleaner. Mocha expectations are defined by a single method, `expects`, and they can be attached to any object. When an expectation is attached to an object, a stub is automatically created and an expectation is set up. Listing 2.17 shows our example (from listing 2.16) refactored to use Mocha.

Listing 2.17   The previous mocking example, rewritten using Mocha

```
require 'rubygems'
require 'test/unit'
require 'mocha'                    ❶ Specifies an
                                     empty class
class SupplierInterface    ⏴
end

class TestSupplierInterface < Test::Unit::TestCase
  def test_execute_purchase
    data = [
      {:item_name => 'Red Rug', :quantity => 2},
      {:item_name => 'Set of Pens', :quantity => 17}
    ]
```

```
my_supplier = MaterialSupplier.new

SupplierInterface.expects(:search).with('Red Rug').returns(1234)
SupplierInterface.expects(:add_to_cart).with(1234, 2)

SupplierInterface.expects(:search).with('Set of Pens').
  returns(9012)
SupplierInterface.expects(:add_to_cart).with(9012, 17)

SupplierInterface.expects(:purchase).returns(true)

assert my_supplier.execute_purchase(data)
  end
end
```

② Sets up expectations for methods

❸ Expects purchase will complete

In this version of the code, we still verify behavior, but we don't have to spend the time to implement an entire class, and we get the benefit of being able to verify specific calls to a method. We first create a blank class, because all we're doing is attaching stubs to a dummy class ❶; in a real-world setting, this would be unnecessary, because there would be a real class to attach the stubs to. Next, we define expectations for each method and for calls to that method ❷. The final expectation is then set and the method tested ❸. When this test suite is executed, you should see something like the following:

```
Loaded suite purchasing
Started
.
Finished in 0.001637 seconds.

1 tests, 6 assertions, 0 failures, 0 errors
```

As you can see, assertions are created for each expectation that we set. These assertions verify the behavior of your code when calling the stubbed methods.

Ruby offers a number of utilities to take all sorts of measurements of your testing code. Now that we've taken a look at testing, specifying, stubbing, and mocking, we need to look at a few techniques that test your tests.

2.5 Testing your tests

No one is perfect. If testing helps to smoke out your imperfections, who's to say you won't create some in the process of writing test code? In other words, "Who's testing the testers?" In this section, we'll look two metrics for evaluating your testing code's coverage and quality.

2.5.1 Testing code coverage

As your applications grow in size, so will your test suites, and as your test suites grow in size, so will the chances that you'll miss testing a method or class here or there.

Typically, there isn't an issue with skipping a test here or there unless it's an important method that you forgot to test or a class that is used quite often. But Ruby offers a couple of tools that can help you ensure your code is covered with good quality tests 100%, and we'll look at them next.

TIP The ZenTest tool from Ryan Davis is another way to avoid skipping tests. If you run it over your code, it will generate stubs for code that you've written tests for or generate tests for code that doesn't have any. It's excellent if you're writing tests for the existing code or if you're doing TDD and want to exert less effort.

Testing coverage with rcov

The rcov utility from Mauricio Fernandez allows you to test the C0 coverage of your code (coverage of method and statements, but statements with conditions will not test fully). It can be installed using RubyGems (for example: `gem install rcov`) and executed using the `rcov` command. When executed with a test file as a parameter, it will crawl through the code and look at the test coverage for each class. Rcov collects this data and produces HTML/XHTML (or, optionally, text).

TIP Rcov can show your results in a simple text format if you feed it the `-T` option on the command line.

Rcov works by running over test suites and checking the line coverage of the code. You run it by invoking the `rcov` command followed by the list of files to test. As an example, we'll run rcov on a portion of Rails using the command `rcov test/*.rb -o coverage/` (the `-o` option allows you to specify an output directory). Figure 2.6 shows the generated HTML page.

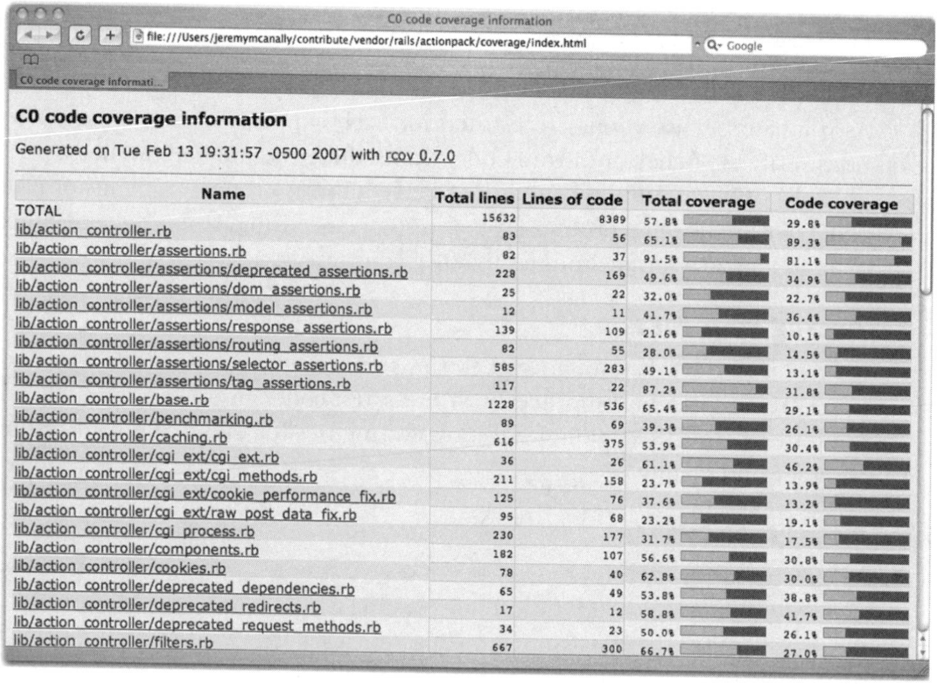

C0 code coverage information

Generated on Tue Feb 13 19:31:57 -0500 2007 with rcov 0.7.0

Name	Total lines	Lines of code	Total coverage	Code coverage
TOTAL	15632	8389	57.8%	29.8%
lib/action_controller.rb	83	56	65.1%	89.3%
lib/action_controller/assertions.rb	82	37	91.5%	81.1%
lib/action_controller/assertions/deprecated_assertions.rb	228	169	49.6%	34.9%
lib/action_controller/assertions/dom_assertions.rb	25	22	32.0%	22.7%
lib/action_controller/assertions/model_assertions.rb	12	11	41.7%	36.4%
lib/action_controller/assertions/response_assertions.rb	139	109	21.6%	10.1%
lib/action_controller/assertions/routing_assertions.rb	82	55	28.0%	14.5%
lib/action_controller/assertions/selector_assertions.rb	585	283	49.1%	13.1%
lib/action_controller/assertions/tag_assertions.rb	117	22	87.2%	31.8%
lib/action_controller/base.rb	1228	536	65.4%	29.1%
lib/action_controller/benchmarking.rb	89	69	39.3%	26.1%
lib/action_controller/caching.rb	616	375	53.9%	30.4%
lib/action_controller/cgi_ext/cgi_ext.rb	36	26	61.1%	46.2%
lib/action_controller/cgi_ext/cgi_methods.rb	211	158	23.7%	13.9%
lib/action_controller/cgi_ext/cookie_performance_fix.rb	125	76	37.6%	13.2%
lib/action_controller/cgi_ext/raw_post_data_fix.rb	95	68	23.2%	19.1%
lib/action_controller/cgi_process.rb	230	177	31.7%	17.5%
lib/action_controller/components.rb	182	107	56.6%	30.8%
lib/action_controller/cookies.rb	78	40	62.8%	30.0%
lib/action_controller/deprecated_dependencies.rb	65	49	53.8%	38.8%
lib/action_controller/deprecated_redirects.rb	17	12	58.8%	41.7%
lib/action_controller/deprecated_request_methods.rb	34	23	50.0%	26.1%
lib/action_controller/filters.rb	667	300	66.7%	27.0%

Figure 2.6 The rcov tool presents its results as HTML or text; the HTML view has nice graphs that illustrate code coverage and individual pages for each file tested.

As you can see, a percentage is given for each code file, along with a small bar graph. Running this on a smaller codebase will yield less spectacular results, but it's still a useful tool for making sure your code is completely covered.

Once you've mastered code coverage, it may beneficial to ensure your tests are of good quality and coverage; Heckle is a tool for testing just that.

2.5.2 Testing quality with Heckle

Heckle, from Ryan Davis, is a different kind of tool. Think of Heckle as your tests' worst nightmare. It tests the *quality* of your tests using a technique called fuzz testing. The problem with test cases is that merely passing doesn't guarantee you're putting the code to the test. Perhaps you're calling one method, but not testing for the changes it makes to the object. These kinds of errors happen on occasion, and you'll notice them when you change the test code slightly and the test still passes. Heckle takes your tests, messes with the test code, then runs them again to ensure that they fail when they should. If your tests don't notice crazy changes to your code, then either that code isn't covered or it isn't covered well.

TIP Heckle also supports RSpec. All you have to do is invoke RSpec with the `--heckle` option.

Think of Heckle as a way of testing your tests—checking them for coverage and quality. Let's say you have the class in listing 2.18.

Listing 2.18 A simple class to Heckle

```
class Customer
  def initialize(name = nil)
    @name = name
  end

  def tag
    tag = "Customer: "
    tag += @name.nil? ? "<unknown>" : @name
    tag
  end
end
```

This class will create a pretty simple object to represent customers and hold their names. Listing 2.19 shows a test for this class.

Listing 2.19 Our tests to Heckle

```
require 'test/unit'
require 'customer'

class TestCustomer < Test::Unit::TestCase
  def test_tag
    @customer = Customer.new('Mike Stevens')
    assert_equal 'Customer: Mike Stevens', @customer.tag
  end
end
```

For an example's sake, we have one test that tests the value returned by the tag method. If we were to run rcov on this, it would tell you that we have 100 percent coverage, but if we run Heckle, we'll see a different story:

```
Initial tests pass. Let's rumble.

*************************************************************************
***  Customer#tag loaded with 3 possible mutations
*************************************************************************

3 mutations remaining...
2 mutations remaining...
1 mutations remaining...

The following mutations didn't cause test failures:

def tag
  tag = "Customer: "
  tag = (tag + if @name.nil? then
    "\037B\e|H\020B\027\022W3_q\027\025G\f?bZHJ&p/P&\nP\016\036-#\031"
  else
    @name
  end)
  tag
end
```

One mutation that Heckle ran didn't cause a test failure when it should have. Note that it changed the value that is returned from tag from <unknown> to a long string of text. Because we didn't test for this, it didn't fail. So now we need to go back and add or refactor tests to catch the mutation. Listing 2.20 shows how we did it.

Listing 2.20   Our updated tests that can stand up to even a strong Heckling!

```
class TestCustomer < Test::Unit::TestCase
  def test_tag
    @customer = Customer.new('James Litton')
    assert_equal 'Customer: James Litton', @customer.tag
  end

  def test_tag_empty
    @customer = Customer.new
    assert_equal 'Customer: <unknown>', @customer.tag
  end
end
```

We added a test to test for an empty name attribute, and if we run Heckle again, we should see a different result:

```
Initial tests pass. Let's rumble.

*************************************************************************
***  Customer#tag loaded with 3 possible mutations
*************************************************************************

3 mutations remaining...
2 mutations remaining...
1 mutations remaining...
No mutants survived. Cool!
```

No mutants survived! Great! So we've fixed our tests to stand up even to fuzz testing. Now it's time to go back and create more tests, more code, and heckle again and again. Even though Ruby makes this cycle easier, it can get annoying to make a change, run the tests, make a change, run the tests, and so on ad nauseum.

2.6 *Summary*

Ruby's testing facilities almost make it too hard not to test! In this chapter, you've been exposed to TDD and how to do it with Ruby. You should be able to build test suites for new and old code and expand those tests over time. You were also shown how to do BDD using the RSpec library, starting with the specification and working your way through to implementation.

We also discussed how to mimic a production environment while testing, using techniques like fixtures and fake objects. You learned how to build stubs and mocks (both from scratch and using Mocha) in order to mimic code functionality. In the last stretch, we looked at a couple of secondary tools that can help you out when writing tests. The rcov tool will ensure your code is covered, and the Heckle tool will help you ensure your code is covered well.

In the next chapter, we'll start looking at using Ruby with other technologies. The rest of this book is about practical techniques, many of them using other technologies, but before we dig into that content, we need to take a look at the basics of integration and automation with Ruby.

Scripting with Ruby

This chapter covers

- Reading and writing CSV data
- Generating daily reports
- Producing a comparison report
- Generating customized printable reports

One of the greatest assets of Ruby is its ability to scale small. As a software developer, you have learned about the difficulties of scaling large: applications with millions of lines of code, handling terabytes of data and serving billions of hits a day, taking advantage of multicore architectures and server farms. The rest of this book is about working with big services: messaging, web services, databases, and so on. Scaling up and scaling out are tough challenges that excite the imagination, but they're not all that software can do for you. We thought it would be prudent to take a chapter and show you how Ruby can help you out doing everyday "stuff."

In our daily lives, there are a lot of small problems waiting to be solved. Some solutions take a minute to develop and may fit in a single line, yet are just as important as much larger, attention-grabbing problems. Consider a commit hook that runs the test suite before allowing a commit, attaches the commit message to an open ticket, and sends a notification to the development team. It's not rocket science, nor an opportunity for the next billion-dollar company, but it makes life easier. Simple solutions like that automate repetitive tasks, double-check what we're doing, and smooth our workflow so we can get more done without spending the night at the office.

3.1 *Scripting with Ruby*

If you talk to developers proficient with scripting languages—command-line languages like bash, or programming languages like Ruby, Perl, and Python—you'll learn that their environment is full of little scripts. Each script on its own does very little, but in combination they cut down on unnecessary workload and help us concentrate on the truly creative tasks.

In practice, scripts come in all shapes and forms. You can write a trivial Greasemonkey script to change the color scheme of a website or remove intrusive ads and annoying sidebar widgets. A lot of build systems use fairly complex scripts to build complex applications targeting multiple platforms. System administrators rely on an arsenal of scripts that run in the background, on a schedule or from the command line, doing everything from deploying to monitoring to controlling and alerting.

In this chapter, we'll show you some simple, even throw-away, scripts. Not because we have limited space, but because we think writing such scripts is a good habit to pick up. There's always room in your life for little scripts that do dumb work so you don't have to.

To illustrate, we're going to pick a fun project for our very first solution. We're going to inflict our recent travel photos on all our friends. Instead of inviting them over to watch a slide show (we know they'd have an "emergency" at home that night), we'll serve those photos one by one using Twitter.

Problem

You need to take a collection of high-resolution images, and scale them down to show fully in the browser, looking like Polaroid pictures. Next, you'll make them available on the web for everyone to see (using our Amazon S3 account), and announce each image to the world using your Twitter account.

Solution

We're going to write two different scripts:

- The first will scale down and add a Polaroid effect to our images, upload them to our Amazon S3 account, and write list of URLs (one for each image) so we can check the images before unleashing them on the world.
- The second will pick one image and post a link for that image to our Twitter account. We're going to schedule this script to run once an hour, Twittering a different image each time it runs.

We're going to need two Ruby gems for that, so let's start by installing them:

```
$ gem install aws-s3
$ gem install twitter
```

We'll start with the first script, shown in listing 3.1.

Listing 3.1   Turn our photos into smaller, Polaroid-like images, and upload to Amazon S3

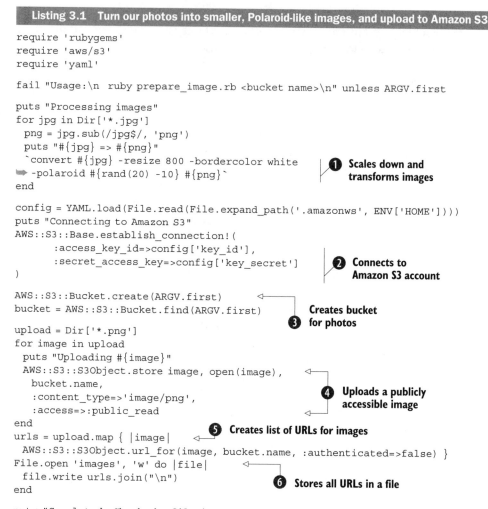

```
require 'rubygems'
require 'aws/s3'
require 'yaml'

fail "Usage:\n  ruby prepare_image.rb <bucket name>\n" unless ARGV.first

puts "Processing images"
for jpg in Dir['*.jpg']
  png = jpg.sub(/jpg$/, 'png')
  puts "#{jpg} => #{png}"
  `convert #{jpg} -resize 800 -bordercolor white
   -polaroid #{rand(20) -10} #{png}`
end

config = YAML.load(File.read(File.expand_path('.amazonws', ENV['HOME'])))
puts "Connecting to Amazon S3"
AWS::S3::Base.establish_connection!(
      :access_key_id=>config['key_id'],
      :secret_access_key=>config['key_secret']
)

AWS::S3::Bucket.create(ARGV.first)
bucket = AWS::S3::Bucket.find(ARGV.first)

upload = Dir['*.png']
for image in upload
  puts "Uploading #{image}"
  AWS::S3::S3Object.store image, open(image),
    bucket.name,
    :content_type=>'image/png',
    :access=>:public_read
end
urls = upload.map { |image|
  AWS::S3::S3Object.url_for(image, bucket.name, :authenticated=>false) }
File.open 'images', 'w' do |file|
  file.write urls.join("\n")
end

puts "Completed. Check the file images for list of URLs."
```

- **1** Scales down and transforms images
- **2** Connects to Amazon S3 account
- **3** Creates bucket for photos
- **4** Uploads a publicly accessible image
- **5** Creates list of URLs for images
- **6** Stores all URLs in a file

First, we need images that are just big enough to show fully in a web browser. Our photos are high resolution, so we need to scale them down to 800 pixels wide. We also want to make them look like Polaroid pictures, with a white border, and tilt them randomly between -10 and 10 degrees. We're going to use the `convert` program to do that transformation **1**.

We connect to our Amazon S3 account **2**, and since Amazon S3 stores files in buckets, we start by making sure we have a bucket ready **3**. Next, we upload these images one by one (for simplicity, the originals are JPEG and the Polaroids are PNG), and tell Amazon to make them publicly readable **4**. We get the URL for each of these images **5** and store them in a file called images **6**.

To use the script, we first need to supply our Amazon Web Services account credentials. We'll put those in a separate file, so we can reuse them with different scripts, and so we can share this script without sharing our account information. You'll need a file called .amazonws in your home directory that looks like this:

```
key_id: <your AWS access key id>
key_secret: <your AWS secret access key>
```

This is the command to run the script and tell it which bucket to use:

```
$ ruby upload_images.rb ruby_in_practice
```

Now let's turn to the second script, shown in listing 3.2.

Listing 3.2   Twitter a link to an image

```
require 'rubygems'                                          Reads all image  ❶
require 'twitter'                                           URLs from file
require 'yaml'

fail "Usage:\n  ruby twitter_image.rb <message>\n" unless ARGV.first
file_name = File.join(File.dirname(__FILE__), 'images')
images = File.readlines(file_name)
fail "No images to twitter, images file is empty" if images.empty?
message = "#{ARGV.first} #{images.first}"

config = YAML.load(File.read(File.expand_path('.twitter', ENV['HOME'])))
twitter = Twitter::Base.new(
                  config['email'],         ❸ Connects      Creates message
                  config['password']          to Twitter   for first image  ❷
                  )                           account
puts "Posting #{message} to twitter"
twitter.post(message)                      ◄──❹ Posts message

File.open file_name, 'w' do |file|          ❺ Writes remaining
  file.write images[1..-1].join("\n")          URLs to file
end
```

We start by reading all the URLs from the images file ❶, but we're only going to Twitter the first image, so we'll create a message for only one image ❷. Next, we connect to our Twitter account ❸ and post that message ❹. Finally, we'll write the remaining URLs back to the file ❺, so we can process the next URL when the script runs again.

As before, we're going to use a configuration file that lives in the home directory. The .twitter file looks like this:

```
email: <email>
password: <password>
```

We're not going to run this script from the command line. Instead, we'll schedule it to run once an hour using cron:

```
$ echo "0 * * * * $(pwd)/twitter_image.rb \"Check out this photo \"" > jobs
$ crontab jobs
```

Discussion

There are several libraries we could use to resize images and apply interesting transformations. The first that comes to mind is RMagick. RMagick is a Ruby wrapper around the excellent ImageMagick processing library. It has everything we need to create fun images for our project, yet we decided not to use it. The trick to scaling down is always looking for the simplest, shortest solution to the problem.

A true script ninja will get the job done with the minimum amount of effort. Not that RMagick is all that complicated, but we decided to do something else instead. We typed `convert --help` on the command line, scanned the help page for the three settings we wanted to use, tested them (again, from the command line) against a couple of images, and pasted the command into our Ruby script. The `convert` program is a command-line interface to ImageMagick, and for our case it was simpler and faster to use than opening up the RMagick API documentation.

We didn't build any sophisticated error handling into either script. The first one we're going to run from the command line, and if it fails, we'll just run it again. The second script runs as a background job, and because we don't want to miss posting any image, we made sure it only discards an image's URL after posting a message about that image. If it fails, it will pick up where it left off the next time it runs.

Eventually, it will run out of images to post and start failing. We're going to notice that no new images appear on our Twitter stream, check that the images file is empty, and remove the cron job. If we wanted to be smarter, we could also build an auto-remove feature into the script itself.

You probably noticed that we took other shortcuts as well. We placed the original photos, the PNG Polaroids, the list of URLs, and the two scripts all in the same directory. We mixed code with data, original content with temporary files. That's not modular or organized as you'd expect a large-scale application to be. Then again, this is not a large-scale application that will keep on running into the next millennium. It's the simplest script we could write in the least amount of time; we're going to use it once and discard it.

If this is your first foray into scripting, we do hope you'll think this example is inelegant, maybe downright ugly. Like we said, scripts come in all shapes and forms. Some scripts manage critical systems and others are integral parts of larger applications—you'll want to use your best development skills to write those. There's a place for writing scripts that are well thought out, easy to maintain, thoroughly documented, tested, and tested some more.

But we also wanted to introduce you to a different world of scripting. One that's more focused on getting mundane tasks out of the way by automating them. There are times when investing less is the best course of action, and simple is the best way to start.

We also showed you how easy it is to glue things together with Ruby. We kept things simple by using an image-transformation program instead of diving headfirst into an API, and by keeping our authentication credentials in a text file. Instead of using a database server, we stored state in a text file, and we used cron to schedule our tasks instead of using a scheduling component. Of course, we benefited from the simplicity of AWS-S3 and the Twitter gem.

In the next section, we're going to take another look at scripting, this time scripting Windows applications using OLE Automation and Mac OS X applications using OSA.

3.2 Automating with OLE and OSA

Scripting languages are easier to program with than low-level programming languages. If you've ever written an Excel macro, created a workflow using Word and Outlook, or programmed with AppleScript, you know what we're talking about. Application scripting—desktop and server applications alike—is done through APIs designed specifically for the task at hand, and is simplified to work from any programming language. In this section, we're going to take a look at automating applications on the Windows platform using OLE Automation, and Mac OS X applications using Open Scripting Architecture (OSA).

OLE Automation provides scripting support for Windows applications. Microsoft Office is a set of desktop applications that use OLE Automation, typically in combination with the Visual Basic for Applications (VBA) scripting language. OLE is just as easy to use from Ruby programs running on the Windows platform, as we'll demonstrate by using Ruby and Microsoft Outlook.

OSA provides scripting support for applications running on Mac OS X. It was designed specifically for AppleScript, so some experience with AppleScript is helpful, but it is easy enough to use from the more powerful Ruby language. We'll use the same example to automate Apple's iCal calendar application.

Let's start with OLE Automation and Microsoft Outlook.

3.2.1 Automating Outlook with Ruby

The example we'll use is a fairly trivial one, but one that would be easier to develop in Ruby than either VBA or AppleScript.

During development we often have to take shortcuts to get something done. Maybe we're trying to get a demo running, or giving other developers a piece of code so they can start working again. We mark those things we haven't finished with comments that say TODO or FIXME. And as much as we hate to admit it, we don't always go back and fix that code—mostly we forget about it. So we're going to create a simple script that will read these comments from the source code and adds tasks in Outlook or To Do items in iCal to remind us about them.

Problem

Given a directory containing Ruby source files, find all the TODO and FIXME comments buried in the source code, and create a task item for each one in Outlook.

Solution

You can see the entire script in listing 3.3.

Listing 3.3 Turn TODO and FIXME comments into Outlook tasks

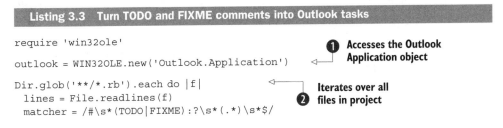

```
require 'win32ole'

outlook = WIN32OLE.new('Outlook.Application')          ❶ Accesses the Outlook
                                                          Application object
Dir.glob('**/*.rb').each do |f|                        ❷ Iterates over all
  lines = File.readlines(f)                               files in project
  matcher = /#\s*(TODO|FIXME):?\s*(.*)\s*$/
```

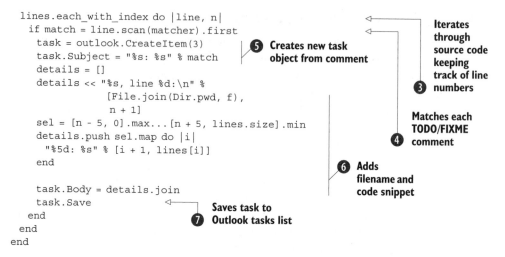

```
lines.each_with_index do |line, n|
  if match = line.scan(matcher).first
    task = outlook.CreateItem(3)
    task.Subject = "%s: %s" % match
    details = []
    details << "%s, line %d:\n" %
              [File.join(Dir.pwd, f),
               n + 1]
    sel = [n - 5, 0].max...[n + 5, lines.size].min
    details.push sel.map do |i|
      "%5d: %s" % [i + 1, lines[i]]
    end

    task.Body = details.join
    task.Save
  end
end
end
```

⑤ Creates new task object from comment

Iterates through source code keeping track of line numbers ③

Matches each TODO/FIXME comment ④

⑥ Adds filename and code snippet

⑦ Saves task to Outlook tasks list

We start by obtaining the Outlook Application object using the Ruby-OLE bridge ❶. We'll need that object later on, to create Outlook tasks. Next, we use the `Dir.glob` method to iterate through all the Ruby files in the current directory and each subdirectory and read each file ❷. We need the line number of each comment, so we use `each_with_index` to iterate through each line while keeping track of the line number ❸.

Using a regular expression, we match each line containing a TODO or FIXME comment ❹. Some people put a colon after the TODO/FIXME, and some don't, so our regular expression handles both cases. For each comment, we create an Outlook task using the comment text as the task subject ❺. Next, we add the filename, line number, and a code snippet to the task body ❻, before saving the task in Outlook ❼.

Try running this script on your project's directory and watch as all TODO and FIXME comments show up in your Outlook tasks list.

Discussion

The Ruby-OLE (win32ole) bridge is part of the Ruby standard library when running Ruby on the Windows platform, so there's no need to install anything else. You only need to require win32ole in your code.

The translation between OLE and Ruby objects is straightforward, but it uses OLE naming conventions. If you read the documentation for Outlook OLE objects, you'll notice that we're using the same methods (`CreateItem`, `Save`) and properties (`Subject`, `Body`) documented there.

In this example, and the next one, we use the glob pattern `**/*.rb` to match any Ruby file in the current directory and any of its subdirectories. You can easily extend this to match other file types; for example, to search for Ruby and eRuby files, you can write `**/*.{rb,erb}`. To keep the example simple, we wrote it to look only for Ruby comments based on the hash sign, so you'll want to change that if you're searching for other types of comments.

If you're familiar with C's versatile `printf` function, you'll be happy to know Ruby includes both `printf` and `sprintf` in the core library (`scanf` is also available in the standard library, so you need to require it explicitly). The percent operator (`%`) is a shortcut

> **Slash and backslash**
>
> You'll notice throughout this book that our examples use *forward slashes* as directory separators (/, also known as *slashes*). Most Windows applications use *backward slashes* by convention (\, also known as *backslashes*), although the Windows APIs work equally well with both slashes and backslashes. The DOS command line is one application that doesn't; it only accepts backslashes in command-line arguments, leading many developers to believe that Windows doesn't support slashes at all.
>
> Since slashes are supported on Windows, and are used as path separators on *nix operating systems and in URLs, we recommend using slashes as a matter of practice. The Ruby standard library uses slashes as the default separator, and some methods, like `Dir.glob`, only work with slashes. You can find out if your platform supports an alternative path separator by looking at the value of `File::ALT_SEPARATOR`, but using `File::SEPARATOR` or just /, will make your code run on different operating systems and support more third-party libraries.

for `sprintf`; when the left-side expression is a string, that string is used to format the arguments provided by the right-side expression. So, for example, the expression

```
"%s: %s" % match
```

is shorthand for

```
sprintf("%s: %s", match[0], match[1])
```

The task subject is short and concise. We basically copy the comment text over, but it's not all that useful if we can't tell which line of what file it comes from, so we use the task body to convey that information, adding the filename and line number.

If we have to deal with a lot of TODO/FIXME tasks—and we often do—we'd want some way to prioritize which task to do first, so the more information we get, the better. You'll notice we added a snippet of the source code surrounding the comment to the body of each task:

```
sel = [num - 5, 0].max .. [num + 5, lines.size].min
details.push sel.map { |i| "%5d: %s" % [i + 1, lines[i]] }
task.Body = details.join("\n")
task.Save
```

We used the current line number to create a range of lines, up to five lines before and five lines after. So if the comment appears on line 7, our selection would be the range `2..13`. All we have to do then is transform each integer in that range into the text of that line, and join the lines together.

We're going to use most of this code in the next section, only changing it to deal with iCal instead of Outlook.

3.2.2 *Automating iCal with Ruby*

Now let's turn our attention to Mac OS X and write the same example to automate iCal.

Problem

Given a directory containing Ruby source files, find all the TODO and FIXME comments buried in the source code, and create a To Do entry for each one in iCal.

Solution

For this solution, we decided to access iCal's scripting objects using the Appscript library. We explain why in the discussion, so for now, let's get Appscript installed. The gem name is actually rb-appscript:

```
$ sudo gem install rb-appscript
```

You can see the entire script in listing 3.4. You'll notice it's similar to the Outlook script in listing 3.3. The main difference is using a method call to create the To Do item and set all the relevant properties.

Listing 3.4   Turn TODO and FIXME comments into iCal To Dos

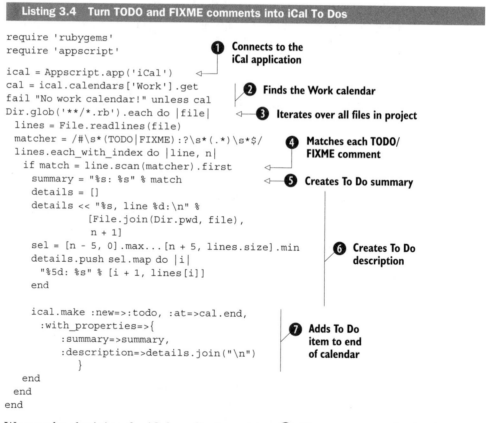

```
require 'rubygems'
require 'appscript'
                                    ❶ Connects to the
                                       iCal application
ical = Appscript.app('iCal')
cal = ical.calendars['Work'].get        ❷ Finds the Work calendar
fail "No work calendar!" unless cal
Dir.glob('**/*.rb').each do |file|      ❸ Iterates over all files in project
  lines = File.readlines(file)
  matcher = /#\s*(TODO|FIXME):?\s*(.*)\s*$/  ❹ Matches each TODO/
  lines.each_with_index do |line, n|           FIXME comment
    if match = line.scan(matcher).first
      summary = "%s: %s" % match          ❺ Creates To Do summary
      details = []
      details << "%s, line %d:\n" %
              [File.join(Dir.pwd, file),
               n + 1]
      sel = [n - 5, 0].max...[n + 5, lines.size].min  ❻ Creates To Do
      details.push sel.map do |i|                          description
        "%5d: %s" % [i + 1, lines[i]]
      end

      ical.make :new=>:todo, :at=>cal.end,
        :with_properties=>{
          :summary=>summary,              ❼ Adds To Do
          :description=>details.join("\n")   item to end
            }                                of calendar
    end
  end
end
```

We start by obtaining the iCal application object ❶. There are several calendars, and we want to add To Dos to the Work calendar, so we look it up ❷.

We use the `Dir.glob` method to iterate through all the Ruby files in the current directory and each subdirectory and read each file ❸, matching lines that contain a TODO or FIXME comment ❹. For each comment, we create a summary from the comment text ❺. We collect the filename, line number, and a code snippet to provide more details ❻. Then it's just a matter of creating a new `todo` item at the end of the calendar with these two properties ❼.

Discussion

To understand this example in full, you need to understand a bit about how Apple-Script works, so let's start with a simple AppleScript example in listing 3.5.

Listing 3.5   AppleScript example for adding a To Do item to iCal

```
tell application "iCal" to
  make new todo at end of calendar "Work"
    with properties {summary:"FIXME now"}
```

AppleScript was designed to simplify scripting by using an English-like syntax. Some of that syntax comes directly from the API, so understanding the syntax helps in understanding how to use the relevant APIs.

The example in listing 3.5 loosely translates into a method call (`make`) with one anonymous argument (`todo`) and two named arguments (`at end` and `with proper-ties`). The value of the first named argument is an object reference; it doesn't point to an actual object but denotes a location—the end of a list. Since we're adding a To Do item, iCal will use that reference to plant the new item at the end of the To Do list. The second named argument is similar to a Ruby hash. These arguments are then used to call the `make` method on the iCal application.

The Ruby equivalent, using the Appscript library, would look like listing 3.6.

Listing 3.6   Ruby example for adding a To Do item to iCal using Appscript

```
ical = Appscript.app('iCal')          ◁— Finds iCal application
ical.make :new=>:todo, :at=>ical.calendars['Work'].end,    | Creates new To Do
  :with_properties=>{ :summary=>'FIXME now' }              | item in Work calendar
```

There are two libraries you can use to automate Mac OS X applications. Appscript (from appscript.sourceforge.net) is based on the AppleScript model and so supports all the flexibility and capabilities of scripting OSA (Open Scripting Architecture) applications. The other one is RubyOSA (from rubyosa.rubyforge.org), which makes OSA feel more Ruby-ish. If you want to get a feeling for RubyOSA, check out listing 3.7.

Listing 3.7   Ruby example for adding a To Do item to iCal using RubyOSA

```
`open -a iCal`                              ◁─────┐   Starts iCal running
ical = OSA.app('iCal')      ◁— Finds iCal application  | before we can call its API
cal = ical.calendars.find { |cal| cal.name == 'Work' }
position = if cal.todos.empty?                        | Finds last item
     cal.todos.last                                   | in To Do list
    else
      cal.todos.last.after
    end

ical.make OSA::ICal::Todo, :at=>position,       | Adds new To Do
  :with_properties=>{ :summary=>'FIXME now' }   | item to calendar
```

Unfortunately, some things get lost in translation, and a few automation tasks we worked on could not be done in RubyOSA. If you want to master a single library, we recommend picking up Appscript.

Another way of adding To Do items to your calendar is by using the Cocoa API to create them in the calendar store. You can do a lot more things using the Cocoa APIs than is possible with the OSA APIs; in fact, you can build an entire native application using the Ruby/Cocoa bridge. For our example, this would be overkill, and we don't have room in this book to cover Ruby/Cocoa in full. But to whet your appetite, we'll look at a simple example. Listing 3.8 uses the Cocoa API to talk to Growl. Add it to the end of listing 3.5, and the script will show a Growl notification when it completes.

Listing 3.8 Growl notification using Cocoa API

```
require 'osx/cocoa'
dnc = OSX::NSDistributedNotificationCenter.defaultCenter
dnc.postNotificationName_object_userInfo_deliverImmediately(
  :GrowlApplicationRegistrationNotification, nil,
  { :ApplicationName=>'TODO/FIXME', :AllNotifications=>['Completed'] },
  true)
dnc.postNotificationName_object_userInfo_deliverImmediately(
  :GrowlNotification, nil,
  { :ApplicationName=>'TODO/FIXME', :NotificationName=>'Completed',
   :NotificationTitle=>'TODO/FIXME comments added to iCal' }, true)
```

Next, we're going to look at a different kind of automation, using Rake to automate multiple tasks and their dependencies.

3.3   *Using Rake*

Rake is a build tool similar in principle to Make. Briefly, it allows you to define tasks, establish dependencies between tasks, and execute those tasks (and their dependencies) from the command line. In chapter 8, we'll look at Ruby Gems and show you how to use Rake to build and package your gems.

Since Rake tasks are written in Ruby, Rake is flexible enough that you can use it to automate different types of tasks. Rails and Merb are two web application frameworks that use Rake for development tasks; Vlad the Deployer, which we also cover in chapter 8, uses Rake for deployment tasks. In fact, Rake has become such an indispensable tool that it's now included in most distributions of Ruby 1.8 (such as One-Click Installer, for Mac OS X) and it's available as part of Ruby 1.9. You can read more about Rake at rubyrake.org.

In this section, we're going to cover the basics of Rake, and we'll do that through two examples that build on each other, to create a template Rakefile that you can easily apply to your own applications.

If you don't already have Rake installed, start by installing it:

```
$ gem install rake
```

Now let's get started.

3.3.1 Using tasks

Rake is all about tasks, so we'll start by looking at the very basics of working with tasks: how to use Rakefile to define tasks, how to invoke tasks from the command line, and how to use tasks as prerequisites of other tasks. Rake's dependency mechanism takes care of executing all the necessary tasks, and only those. If you don't get it on the first read, don't despair; use Rake a few times in your own projects, and you'll quickly pick it up.

Problem

You're starting a new project, and you plan to use RDoc to generate documentation and RSpec for behavior-driven development. These commands require specific command-line options, which are not the same for every project and can be run in different ways. How can you make it less painful by automating these tasks?

Solution

Rake will look for a file called Rakefile (or rakefile). It's a regular Ruby file, but it has a specific name and is loaded by Rake so Rakefile can make use of methods like task and file that are part of the Rake API. We'll create it in the root directory of our project and add all the necessary tasks to use RDoc and RSpec effectively. Listing 3.9 shows what our Rakefile looks like.

Listing 3.9 Rakefile for creating RDoc documentation and running RSpec tests

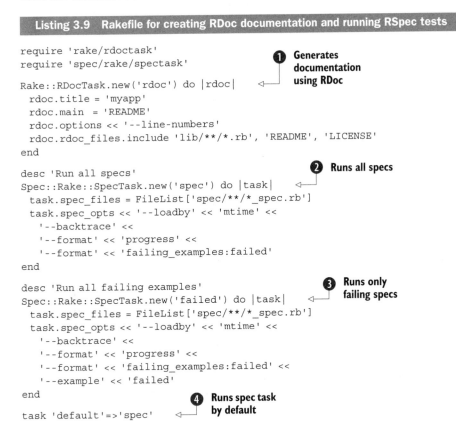

```
require 'rake/rdoctask'
require 'spec/rake/spectask'                        ❶ Generates
                                                       documentation
Rake::RDocTask.new('rdoc') do |rdoc|                   using RDoc
  rdoc.title = 'myapp'
  rdoc.main = 'README'
  rdoc.options << '--line-numbers'
  rdoc.rdoc_files.include 'lib/**/*.rb', 'README', 'LICENSE'
end

desc 'Run all specs'                                 ❷ Runs all specs
Spec::Rake::SpecTask.new('spec') do |task|
  task.spec_files = FileList['spec/**/*_spec.rb']
  task.spec_opts << '--loadby' << 'mtime' <<
    '--backtrace' <<
    '--format' << 'progress' <<
    '--format' << 'failing_examples:failed'
end

desc 'Run all failing examples'                      ❸ Runs only
Spec::Rake::SpecTask.new('failed') do |task|            failing specs
  task.spec_files = FileList['spec/**/*_spec.rb']
  task.spec_opts << '--loadby' << 'mtime' <<
    '--backtrace' <<
    '--format' << 'progress' <<
    '--format' << 'failing_examples:failed' <<
    '--example' << 'failed'
end                                                  ❹ Runs spec task
                                                        by default
task 'default'=>'spec'
```

```
desc 'Clean temporary directories and files'
task 'clobber' do      <┐
  rm_rf 'tmp'                    ❺  Cleans up at end
  rm_f 'failed'
end
```

We start out by using `Rake::RDocTask` to configure the documentation tasks ❶. There are three—rdoc, rerdoc, and `clobber_rdoc`—all created together using the same configuration. Next, we define two tasks for running specs (we'll explain more about them in the discussion that follows). The first task (`spec`) runs all our specs ❷, while the second task (`failed`) runs only those examples that failed in the previous run ❸. We're strong believers in behavior-driven development, so we run `spec` as part of the default task ❹. Last, we use the `clobber` task to clean up ❺ all the temporary files and directories created by the other tasks.

Discussion

Let's start by finding out which tasks we just defined:

```
$ rake --tasks
rake clobber       # Clean temporary directories and files
rake clobber_rdoc  # Remove rdoc products
rake failing       # Run all failing examples
rake rdoc          # Build the rdoc HTML Files
rake rerdoc        # Force a rebuild of the RDOC files
rake spec          # Run all specs
```

RDoc is a tool for generating API documentation from comments found in Ruby source files. You can run it from the command line using the `rdoc` command. It's a simple command to use, but when working with multiple projects, it's easy to forget which options to use with what project. Do we include the license file on this project? Which file is the main documentation page? What else should we include besides the lib directory?

That's the first thing we're going to automate. Instead of having to remember which command-line options to use, we'll create one task to take care of all that. We'll use `Rake::RDocTask` for that, so to generate documentation for the current project, all we need to do is run `rake rdoc`.

We do the same for RSpec (we covered RSpec in chapter 2). We use `Spec::Rake::SpecTask` to define a task that runs all the specification files it finds in the spec directory, and we set it up to use our preferred options. In fact, we have two tasks for RSpec. The first, called `spec`, runs all the specs and uses two formatters. One formatter, `progress`, shows a progress bar so we get an indication of its location. You can also pick other options, such as `--format specdoc` to have all the specifications listed to the console, `--colour` to add a touch of color, `--format html:specs.html` to generate an HTML report.

Specifications are collections of examples, and examples are much like tests in that they either fail or pass. The second formatter, `failing_examples`, logs all the failed examples into the failed file. If there are any failures after running `rake spec`, they're all collected in that file. Now we can go and fix the code, but instead of running all the specifications over again (which is time-consuming!) we're going to run the few examples that failed in the previous run, using `rake failed`. We fix anything that's still broken and keep repeating until there are no more failing examples left to run.

If you run the `rake` command without giving it a task name, Rake will attempt to run the `default` task. And by default, there is no default task, so we created one. We like the practice of testing the code as often as possible, so we made the default task run the `spec` task. We did that by adding it as a prerequisite.

Rake allows you to invoke a given task any number of times, but it will only attempt to execute the task once—the first time it's invoked. That makes tasks different from, say, Ruby methods. You can reference the `rdoc` task from as many places in the Rakefile as you want, and all of these can trigger it, but it will only execute once. This is fine, because we only need to generate the documentation once. This feature is particularly useful for complex Rakefiles, where the same task may be referenced from multiple places. For example, we might want to generate the documentation on its own, so we can access it during development, but also as part of a task that creates a zip package of our project, and as part of another task that generates the documentation and uploads it to a website. We may also have a fourth task that goes through the whole release process, directly depending on the package and site update tasks; effectively depending on the `rdoc` task twice (once in the documentation task and once in the release task). Since Rake will invoke the `rdoc` task once, on first use, we can use these transitive dependencies liberally.

Some tasks never execute. Tasks have prerequisites and actions, so when Rake invokes a task, it starts by first invoking all the task's prerequisites, which must come before any of the task's own actions. It then asks the task whether or not it should execute, and if the task responds positively, Rake goes and executes all the actions in sequence.

When would a task not execute? Let's see what happens when we run the `rdoc` task twice in a row. We're going to use the `--trace` flag, so Rake will report every task invoked and executed. You can see the result of running `rake rdoc --trace` twice in listing 3.10.

> **Listing 3.10 Listing 3.10 Running `rake rdoc` twice with `--trace`**

```
$ rake rdoc --trace
(in /Users/assaf/Ruby In Practice/CH3/3.3)
** Invoke rdoc (first_time)
** Invoke html/index.html (first_time)
** Invoke README (first_time, not_needed)
** Invoke LICENSE (first_time, not_needed)
** Invoke Rakefile (first_time, not_needed)
** Execute html/index.html

                README:
                LICENSE:
Generating HTML...

Files:   2
```

```
Classes: 0
Modules: 0
Methods: 0
Elapsed: 0.148s
** Execute rdoc
$ rake rdoc --trace
(in /Users/assaf/Ruby In Practice/CH3/3.3)
** Invoke rdoc (first_time)
** Invoke html/index.html (first_time, not_needed)
** Invoke README (first_time, not_needed)
** Invoke LICENSE (first_time, not_needed)
** Invoke Rakefile (first_time, not_needed)
** Execute rdoc
```

Both times, Rake starts by invoking the task rdoc. It then invokes all its prerequisites (in this case, html/index.html), and finally executes the task, which by itself doesn't do anything interesting. All the work is actually done by the html/index.html task. You can see from listing 3.10 that this task executes on the first run, but not on the second one.

Rake invokes the html/index.html task by first invoking all its prerequisites (README, LICENSE, and rakefile). It then asks the task if it needs executing. In the first run, there is no html/index.html file in the current directory, so the task executes, generating all the documentation into the html directory, and with it the html/index.html file. In the second run, the file already exists, so the task has nothing to do. Rake calls the needed? method on the task, and the method returns false, so Rake doesn't execute any of its actions.

That works out quite nicely. If the documentation already exists, the task doesn't do anything, and the whole process completes quickly by skipping unnecessary tasks.

Rake allows you to define file tasks (using Rake::FileTask or simply with the file method). You use file tasks to create or update files, and the task name is the same as the file it represents. A file task will execute in two cases: if the file does not already exist, or if any of its prerequisites are newer than the file itself.

The html/index.html task is a file task. We know it will execute if the file does not already exist, and it will also execute if any of the prerequisites are newer than the file. So if we updated the README file, it would detect that the file is newer and generate the documentation all over again. What if we change the title option by updating the Rakefile? The Rakefile is also a prerequisite, and being newer than html/index.html will force it to regenerate the documentation. So there you have it. A very simple mechanism for tracking transitive dependencies that makes sure tasks execute, but only when they're needed.

The tasks we have covered so far, documenting and running the specs, all generate files in our working directory. All these files are generated by tasks, so we don't have to keep them around. If you like to keep your desk clean and tidy, you'll want to do the same with your working directory. We're going to use the clobber task for that.

You can see, at the end of listing 3.9, that we defined the clobber task to remove the failed file and the tmp directory, both of which are generated by the spec/failed task. We don't have to worry about the html directory, because `Rake::RDocTask` took care of that. It defined one task called `clobber_rdoc` specifically to remove the html directory, and you can use that task to clean up after the rdoc task. Separately, it defined the `clobber` task to invoke the `clobber_rdoc` task.

Yes, you can define the same task multiple times. In fact, when you call methods like `task` or `file`, Rake first looks to see if a task exists, and if not, creates it. Then it tasks any prerequisites or actions, and adds those to the existing task. So one thing we can do is write different tasks that create temporary files in the working directory, and next to each of these tasks, enhance the `clobber` task to clean up only those files and directories. Rake also allows us to create composite tasks, like `Rake::RDocTask`, without regard for the order in which tasks are defined.

You might be asking how we know `clobber` uses `clobber_rdoc`? We used the `--prereqs` option to list all the tasks and their dependencies, as shown in listing 3.11.

Listing 3.11 Listing all the tasks and their prerequisites

```
$ rake --prereqs
(in /Users/assaf/Ruby In Practice/CH3/3.3.1)
rake clobber
    clobber_rdoc
rake clobber_rdoc
rake default
    spec
rake failed
rake html
rake html/index.html
    README
    LICENSE
    Rakefile
rake rdoc
    html/index.html
rake rerdoc
    clobber_rdoc
    rdoc
rake spec
```

Check out the `rerdoc` task, which always recreates the documentation: it first cleans up the documentation directory, then runs the `rdoc` task.

We're almost done with our introduction to Rake. Before we move on, we want to add one more useful tip. Notice how we cleaned up an entire directory by calling `rm_rf`? This method is defined by `FileUtils`, a standard library that's part of Ruby and provides a lot of convenience methods for copying, removing, linking, and otherwise working with files. Usually you would have to `require 'fileutils'`, but Rake makes these methods directly accessible in your Rakefile.

3.3.2 *File tasks*

In this section, we're going to expand on file tasks and show you how to use three features of Rake that will help you automate tasks that deal with and process files. We're going to use the file task to create first a file and later a directory from a list of prereq-uisites. We'll use `FileList` to manage lists of files and show you how it's easier to use and more powerful than a simple array. And we'll use rules to tell Rake how to convert a file of one type into another.

Problem

To get your code ready for release, you need to perform two additional tasks. You kept your code modular by writing several JavaScript files, but for performance reasons you want to serve a single JavaScript file to your users. You want to automate a task that will merge these JavaScript files into a single file. You also wrote your documentation using Textile, a lovely markup language, but you're going to serve HTML pages to your users. You want to automate a task that will convert your Textile files into HTML.

Solution

We started building our Rakefile in the previous section (see listing 3.9), and in this section we're going to add tasks to it. You can see those additional tasks in listing 3.12.

> **Listing 3.12   Tasks to merge JavaScript files and create HTML from Textile documents**

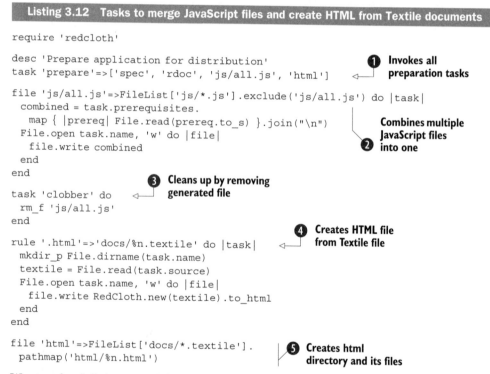

```
require 'redcloth'

desc 'Prepare application for distribution'                    ❶ Invokes all
task 'prepare'=>['spec', 'rdoc', 'js/all.js', 'html']            preparation tasks

file 'js/all.js'=>FileList['js/*.js'].exclude('js/all.js') do |task|
  combined = task.prerequisites.
    map { |prereq| File.read(prereq.to_s) }.join("\n")         Combines multiple
  File.open task.name, 'w' do |file|                           JavaScript files
    file.write combined                                        ❷ into one
  end
end
                          ❸ Cleans up by removing
task 'clobber' do            generated file
  rm_f 'js/all.js'
end
                                        ❹ Creates HTML file
rule '.html'=>'docs/%n.textile' do |task|    from Textile file
  mkdir_p File.dirname(task.name)
  textile = File.read(task.source)
  File.open task.name, 'w' do |file|
    file.write RedCloth.new(textile).to_html
  end
end

file 'html'=>FileList['docs/*.textile'].        ❺ Creates html
  pathmap('html/%n.html')                          directory and its files
```

We start by defining one task, `prepare`, that will invoke all the tasks we want to auto-mate ❶. Some of these were defined before (see listing 3.9), and the other two we define now. We start with a task to create the `js/all.js` file by merging all the JavaScript files found in the `js` directory ❷. We also enhance the `clobber` task to clean up by discarding `js/all.js` ❸. Next, we teach Rake how to convert any Textile file it finds in the `docs` directory into an HTML file, using the RedCloth library ❹.

This is just a rule, it doesn't process any specific file, but it sets the stage for the next task that will find all the Textile files in the docs directory and use them to generate HTML files in the html directory ❺.

To run this Rakefile, first install the RedCloth gem (gem install redcloth) and invoke the prepare task:

```
$ rake prepare
```

Discussion

Let's start with the file task that creates the combined js/all.js. A naïve implementation would just iterate over a list of files, read the contents of each one, merge them, and create a file from the result. We could write it like this:

```
file 'js/all.js' do |task|
  combined = ['js/utils.js', 'js/effects.js'].
    map { |prereq| File.read(prereq.to_s) }.join("\n")
  File.open task.name, 'w' do |file|
    file.write combined
  end
end
```

As we learned in section 3.3.1, this task will create the scripts/all.js file when it executes, but it will not execute if the file already exists. We can make it execute each time, but what we're really interested in is making it execute whenever one of the source files (utils.js or effects.js) changes. We do that by specifying these two files as prerequisites, so that our task executes whenever one of the prerequisites is more recent than the file created by the task.

We want to keep our Rakefile DRY, so in addition to specifying the prerequisites once, we're going to use the prerequisite list from within the task definition. Our revised task looks like this:

```
file 'scripts/all.js'=>['js/utils.js', 'js/effects.js'] do |task|
  combined = task.prerequisites.
    map { |prereq| File.read(prereq.to_s) }.join("\n")
  File.open task.name, 'w' do |file|
    file.write combined
  end
end
```

Now all we have to do is add new prerequisites to the task definition whenever we add new files in the js directory. Simple, and so easy to forget, so let's instead ask the task to pick up all the files in the js directory and process them.

Rake has a powerful tool for dealing with lists of files called, not surprisingly, FileList. It's very similar to Ruby's Array, and it implements all the same methods, so you can use a file list just like an array. We can list each file individually, but FileList can also use file patterns (aka glob patterns). Instead of listing each individual file, we'll use FileList['js/*.js'] to pick up all the JavaScript files in the js directory.

Can you spot the bug? Once we create the js/all.js file, the glob pattern will pick it up as well, and our task will merge all the files including js/all.js itself, doubling its size. It will keep doubling each time we run the task. Oops! Fortunately, we can also tell FileList to exclude files that match a certain pattern, so we'll change our definition to use FileList['js/*.js'].exclude('js/all.js'). You can see the final version in listing 3.12.

We'll explore another way to use FileList in a moment, but first, let's talk about rules. We decided to write our documentation using Textile (http://www.textism.com/tools/textile/), a very simple markup language. Textile documents are very easy to write with a text editor, and they easily convert into HTML. A Textile document would look something like listing 3.13.

Listing 3.13   Example Textile document that we'll convert to HTML

```
h1. Welcome

Myapp is *the best* something something.

New features in Myapp 2.0:
* Super fast
* Never breaks
* Saves kittens

Hear what other people have to say:

bq. Myapp has totally changed my life!
-- Anonymous

Developed for: "Ruby in Practice":http://www.manning.com/mcanally/
```

To turn Textile documents into HTML, we're going to use RedCloth (for documentation, see http://redcloth.org). We can tell Rake how to convert any Textile file into any HTML file by writing a rule. Let's say we use rule '.html'=>'.textile'. We don't have a task to create the welcome.html file, but we're still going to ask Rake to invoke that task. Rake will look for a matching rule that can pair the target file (the file we want to create) with an existing source file, and if it finds a match, it will use the rule to create a new file task.

Because our rule applies to any file with the .html extension, it will match against the target file. The rule also tells Rake how to convert the target filename into a source filename, which, in this example, involves a simple substitution of filename extension. Since the source file exists, Rake will create a new file task with the name welcome.html, the source welcome.textile, and the action specified by the rule.

The example we gave in listing 3.12 is a bit more complicated. It uses a pathmap to convert one filename to another: docs/%n.textile replaces the filename extension with .textile and prefixes it with the docs directory. That way, we can use our rule to convert the docs/welcome.textile file into html/welcome.html.

But first, we need to know all the HTML files we want to create. Remember that at this point, we only have Textile files to work with, so we'll use FileList to list all the Textile files in the docs directory, and pathmap to convert that to a list of the HTML files we want to create:

```
file 'html'=>FileList['docs/*.textile'].pathmap('html/%n.html')
```

This one line is responsible for generating the html directory and all its files, only when necessary, while still updating the generated files when we modify the corresponding Textile documents. It's this combination of simplicity and power that makes Rake what it is.

3.4 Summary

In this chapter, we took a look at Ruby from a slightly different perspective: from that of a scripting language. We showed how to use Ruby to automate everyday tasks and drive other applications and services. In our first solution, we looked at simply using Ruby to interact with Twitter. Then we turned to platform-specific scripting with OSA and OLE and showed you how to drive applications using each of these technologies. Finally, we showed you how to use Rake to automate everyday tasks cleanly.

This foray into "scaling small" was fun, wasn't it? In the next part of the book, we'll turn our attention to working with "bigger" technologies: databases, web applications, and so on. The next two chapters will take a look at working with the Web and Ruby, specifically advancing your Rails knowledge and then applying that to creating Web services.

Part 2

Integration and communication

More and more applications need to perform some type of communication with the outside world, and even more applications are required to integrate with existing legacy technologies. In chapters 4 through 8, we'll look at how you can expose your application's functionality to the outside world and how to hook into existing interfaces and services. We'll end this segment by looking at Ruby deployment options, including gems and automated deployment with Capistrano.

Ruby on Rails techniques

> **This chapter covers**
> - Using third-party libraries with helpers
> - Keeping code DRY using metaprogramming
> - Sharing code using plugins and gems
> - Benchmarking and profiling Rails applications

"Another Ruby book that teaches Rails?" No, we're not going that far! This chapter is not an introduction or tutorial on Rails; rather, it is a discussion of techniques related to Ruby on Rails. There's a middle-documentation problem that's arisen in the Rails community, and this chapter is meant to fill a few of the gaps that many other books and documentation sources leave open. We'll cover extending the Rails framework, through library code, plugins, and more, and we'll finish by talking about profiling your Rails code. Let's start by looking at Rails' helper mechanism.

4.1 Extending Rails

A lot of Rails developers see the magic going on in Rails and wonder how to capture that same simplicity in their own helpers or other Ruby scripts. As we've found out, using metaprogramming (remember that from chapter 1?) along with a few of Rails' built-in mechanisms will give you maximum syntactic sugar while also making it easy to develop.

There are three essential types of extensions to Rails: helpers, libraries, and plug-ins. Helpers are view-specific extensions that expose new functionality to views or expose deeper functionality from controllers or models to views. Libraries are just that: they are part of your overall application, but separate from its models, views, and controllers. Plugins are essentially libraries that are in a redistributable format.

4.1.1   *Using helpers to expose Ruby libraries*

Surprisingly, many new Rails developers misunderstand the relationship between Ruby and Rails. Rails is written in Ruby, and as such can take advantage of any library that Ruby can. Some libraries are written specifically for, or with support for, Rails applications. Most libraries are general-purpose—they're still fully functional inside Rails, but we wish they would be as easy to use as the rest of Rails: using convention over configuration, keeping code simple and DRY, and so forth. In this section, we'll take one such general-purpose library and make it more Rails-friendly using helpers.

Problem

You have an existing Ruby library that you would like to expose to a Rails application in a natural way.

Solution

There are three main types of libraries or components we can create for Rails: a helper that lives in app/helpers, a library that lives in lib/, and plugins. In this instance, let's say we want to build a source-code browser and employ syntax highlighting. We'll create a helper to expose the Ultraviolet syntax highlighting library to a Rails application.

Ultraviolet's syntax is pretty nice, but we don't want to put something like the following in our views or controllers if we can help it:

```
result = Uv.parse(code, "xhtml", "ruby", false, "amy")
```

The first parameter is the code we want to parse, followed by the format to output, followed by the syntax file to use (Ultraviolet lets you use TextMate syntax and theme files), followed by `true` or `false` to indicate whether we need line numbers, followed, finally, by the name of the theme we want to use. Putting all that through an application will not only junk up the code, it will also cause a lot of duplication. (Most likely, three of these arguments are always the same in a given application, and repeating them all through the codebase makes it hard to change the code when you decide to switch themes, or maybe to turn line numbers off throughout your application.) We need to figure out a way to make it friendlier.

To get started, we'll first install Ultraviolet using RubyGems with a command something like the following:

```
gem install ultraviolet
```

Now we need to consider what a call to Ultraviolet would ideally look like when we call it from a view. We want to simplify as much as possible; perhaps it would be best to require only the code and make the other parameters optional. Of course, we'll want

Using Gems With Rails 2.1 or later

Rails 2.1 adds support for using Ruby gems as plugins and libraries. If you upgraded to Rails 2.1 or later, or you are starting a new project, we recommend using this feature to manage your gems. Your config/environment.rb file will look like this:

```
Rails::Initializer.run do |config|
  config.gem 'ultraviolet', :lib=>'uv'
  ...
end
```

Most times, Rails can infer which file to require by default. For some gems, we have to specify the library's main file explicitly, as we do here. If you're using configuration to load gems, you don't need to use `require` in your source code.

Now you can ask Rails to install the application's gem dependencies by running Rake:

```
rake gems:install
```

This task installs system-wide gems that all your applications can use when running on the current machine. When deploying, it's easier to deploy the application along with all its dependencies. You can do that by unpacking the gem dependencies into the application's `vendor/gems` directory, using this command:

```
rake gems:unpack
```

it to be semantically correct, so the `Uv.parse` call has to go in lieu of a better-named method, like `highlighted_code` or simply `code`. Perhaps it should look something like the following:

```
code("puts 'hello!' if code.ruby?")
```

So how do we do it? First, we need to either create a helper by creating a new file (we recommend something like uv_helper.rb or edit application_helper.rb in the app/helpers directory). Inside we need to define a `code` method (shown in `Application-Helper` here):

```
require 'uv'

module UvHelper
  def code(code)
  end

end
```

Next we need to look at putting the call to Ultraviolet in place. We could take the code as the sole argument and hard-code the other values, but it would be pretty nice to be able to specify a different theme or syntax if we ever needed to (and it's trivial to add).

Let's create a method that requires just the code argument, but accepts all the remaining optional arguments:

```
def code(code, format='xhtml', syntax='ruby',
      line_numbers=false, theme='amy')
  Uv.parse(code, format, syntax, line_numbers, theme)
end
```

As you can see, we give default values to the parameters that won't change often, so when it's called in a view, the only required argument will be the code we want to highlight.

Now we need to create a controller, an action, and a view and place the following code inside the view.

```
<html>
  <head><title>Syntax highlighting!</title></head>
  <body>
    <%= code('@items.each {|item| puts item }') %>
  </body>
</html>
```

If you view the action in a browser, you should see that the code is monospaced, but it doesn't have any color! That's because we didn't tell Ultraviolet to copy its CSS and other related files to the right place, or tell our view to include that CSS file.

To do that, we'll add a method to copy the CSS files from Ultraviolet to our application's `public/stylesheet` directory:

```
def copy_files
  Uv.copy_files 'xhtml', "#{RAILS_ROOT}/public/stylesheets"
  File.rename "#{RAILS_ROOT}/public/stylesheets/css/",
        "#{RAILS_ROOT}/public/stylesheets/syntax/"
end
```

Here, we first tell Ultraviolet to copy the files to our stylesheets directory, and we then rename the directory it creates to something more sensible.

Now we need to go back and add a few lines to our `code` method. It should look something like the following:

```
def code(code, format='xhtml', syntax='ruby',
      line_numbers=false, theme='amy')
  unless File.exist?("#{RAILS_ROOT}/public/stylesheets/syntax")
    copy_files
  end

  Uv.parse(code, format, syntax, line_numbers, theme)
end
```

Now the helper checks for the existence of the theme CSS files, and if they aren't there it copies them. This may not be necessary if you don't plan on sharing this helper at all, but if you do, this copy should happen only once, so the performance hit is negligible.

TIP   If you develop this code into a full plugin, you can use the plugin's install.rb file to copy over the CSS files during installation.

Now we need to create a method to include the stylesheet in our view. We could use stylesheet_link_tag directly, but then we'd have to worry about which theme we were using. In the interest of abstraction and making our lives easier, we'll create a custom method:

```
def theme_stylesheet(theme='amy')
  stylesheet_link_tag "syntax/#{theme}"
end
```

Now, if we add that to the <head> of our view, the code in the view should be properly highlighted, and look something like what you see in figure 4.1.

The final version of our syntax highlighting helper is shown in listing 4.1.

Listing 4.1   The whole Ultraviolet helper

```
require 'uv'

module UvHelper
  def code(code, format='xhtml', syntax='ruby',
           line_numbers=false, theme='amy')
    unless File.exist?("#{RAILS_ROOT}/public/stylesheets/syntax")
      copy_files
    end

    Uv.parse(code, format, syntax, line_numbers, theme)
  end

private

  def copy_files
    Uv.copy_files 'xhtml', "#{RAILS_ROOT}/public/stylesheets"
    File.rename "#{RAILS_ROOT}/public/stylesheets/css/",
                "#{RAILS_ROOT}/public/stylesheets/syntax/"
  end

  def theme_stylesheet(theme='amy')
    stylesheet_link_tag "syntax/#{theme}"
  end
end
```

Our helper should be complete and ready to use in our application. No syntax is safe from our highlighting now!

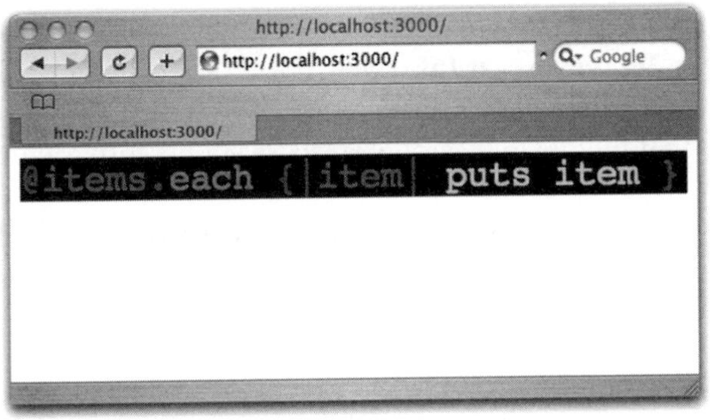

Figure 4.1   The output from our syntax highlighting library

Discussion

Helpers are a great way to expose third-party functionality to your application or to abstract your own logic to avoid duplication or a lot of unnecessary code. In this instance, we could potentially be saving ourselves a lot of keystrokes while also preserving the flexibility of the original API from Ultraviolet. We built in the most common use case for our needs, and left the rest to be explicitly specified. This "operation by common convention" is how Rails manages to stay so simple and useful: the most common usage is dead simple. Think about how easy it is to map a database to a class or to create really nice AJAX effects.

Of course, this isn't the only Ruby library you could expose to Rails, nor are helpers only useful for exposing Ruby libraries to Rails. There are a great number of Ruby gems that would be (or are) very helpful to a Rails application when exposed properly: RedCloth, which parses Textile into HTML; any of the loads of time-handling libraries such as Chronic; and the list goes on. Helpers are also useful for abstracting away parts of your views that are common: setting a special page title on each page, building your navigation menu, common layouts and widgets, and so on.

But helpers are only really useful to your views; what about the rest of your application? This is where other options, such as library code that lives in lib/ and plugins come in. These mechanisms can help deal with duplication in a number of other places in your application.

4.1.2   *Metaprogramming away duplication*

A big part of the Rails design philosophy is DRY—Don't Repeat Yourself—but it's very easy to repeat yourself in a Rails application: putting the same validation in a number of models, repeating that bit of markup on nearly every page, using that same idiom over and over in your controllers. It takes a keen eye to see when to extract pieces of code into reusable elements, but once you see what needs to be extracted, you need to know what to do with it.

Problem

You have a lot of code that is very similar in structure and function that you would like to consolidate as much as possible.

Solution

When you are building more complex models, validations and other related calls can become quite large. One of Jeremy's recent projects sported some models whose validations, plugin calls, and callbacks added up to over 30 lines at times. One way to shorten a lot of the code that builds up in models is to enact metaprogramming and abstract it away.

For example, let's say you were working on a project that had a lot of URL fields: links for feeds, links for web pages, links for product pages. Your models just have a lot of fields that are URLs, and you need to validate the fields, so you write something like this:

```
validates_presence_of :url
validates_length_of :url, :minimum => 12
validates_format_of :url, :with => /^((http|https) :
```

```
((([A-Za-z0-9$_.+!*(),;\/?:@&~=-])|%[A-Fa-f0-9]{2}){2,}(#([a-zA-Z0-9]
[a-zA-Z0-9$_.+!*(),;\/?:@&~=%-]*))?([A-Za-z0-9$_+!*();\/?:~-]))/,
  :message => "isn't a valid URL."
```

As you can see, there are only a few simple validations for the field. This doesn't seem major, until you take a step back and realize that you're doing these validations 25 to 30 times in your application on differently named attributes, sometimes two or three times per model. If you decide to add to one of them or remove one of them, that's a lot of unnecessary work.

The better way is to metaprogram a little library to help you clean them up. Listing 4.2 shows one such library. Place the code in a file (ours is named validates_url.rb) in the lib/ folder.

Listing 4.2 A URL validation library

```
module ValidatesUrl                        ❶ Validates the
                                             record's attribute
  def validates_url(attribute = :url)    ←┘
    validates_presence_of attribute
    validates_length_of attribute, :minimum => 12
    validates_format_of attribute, :with => /^((http|https):
((([A-Za-z0-9$_.+!*(),;\/?:@&~=-])|%[A-Fa-f0-9]{2}){2,}(#([a-zA-Z0-9]
[a-zA-Z0-9$_.+!*(),;\/?:@&~=%-]*))?([A-Za-z0-9$_+!*();\/?:~-]))/,
      :message => "isn't a valid URL."
end

end

                                           ❷ Adds validates_url method
ActiveRecord::Base.send(:extend, ValidatesUrl)  ←┘  to ActiveRecord::Base
```

Basically, what we've done in listing 4.2 is to wrap the validations in a method, so we can simplify our code and call validates_url on each attribute ❶ we want to validate. And since most often we'll want to validate an attribute called url, we made that the default attribute name.

Finally, we extend ActiveRecord::Base with our method so it's available to all of our models ❷. We extended the class, adding a new method we can call on the class itself. Specifying validation rules in Rails is done by calling methods on the class during its definition.

Extending classes is one of the metaprogramming techniques that makes Rails so easy and powerful to use. This is different from adding methods to a class, methods we can then call on objects of that class: we can do that as well, but we would use include instead of extend.

So, the validates_url method is now available to our models. Of course, we'll remove the older validations so they don't look like the model in listing 4.3.

Listing 4.3 Our model, pre-metaprogramming

```
class Blog < ActiveRecord::Base
  validates_presence_of :url
  validates_length_of :url, :minimum => 12
  validates_format_of :url, :with => /^((http|https):
```

```
➥  ((([A-Za-z0-9$_.+!*(),;\/?:@&~=-])|%[A-Fa-f0-9]{2}){2,}(#([a-zA-Z0-9]
➥  [a-zA-Z0-9$_.+!*(),;\/?:@&~=%-]*))?([A-Za-z0-9$_+!*();\/?:~-]))/,
      :message => "isn't a valid URL."
    validates_presence_of :feed_url
    validates_length_of :feed_url, :minimum => 12
    validates_format_of :feed_url, :with => /^((http|https):
➥  ((([A-Za-z0-9$_.+!*(),;\/?:@&~=-])|%[A-Fa-f0-9]{2}){2,}(#([a-zA-Z0-9]
➥  [a-zA-Z0-9$_.+!*(),;\/?:@&~=%-]*))?([A-Za-z0-9$_+!*();\/?:~-]))/,
      :message => "isn't a valid URL."
  end
```

Instead, they're cleaner and read much better, as you can see in listing 4.4.

Listing 4.4   Our metaprogrammed model

```
class Post < ActiveRecord::Base
  validates_url
  validates_url :feed_url
end
```

Using this sort of metaprogramming can shear off tons of code cruft that's floating around in your applications.

Discussion

Metaprogramming in Ruby is a powerful concept, and it's metaprogramming that gives Rails its real power. Methods like `acts_as_list`, ActiveRecord's attribute mapping, and nearly every model-related plugin, depend on metaprogramming to function. In this example, we've only shown one side of metaprogramming. There are many more techniques we can use, some of which we'll show later in this book.

Now let's look at taking this sort of code and making it reusable.

4.1.3   *Turning your code into reusable components*

After a while, you will build a considerable toolkit of helpers and libraries, but what if you want to share those with your friends, family, fleeting acquaintances, and business colleagues? The easiest way to do that is to extract the code into a plugin.

Problem

You'd like to share your recently metaprogrammed code with others as a plugin.

Solution

In this section, we'll extract the URL validation library into a plugin that we can distribute.

First, generate a plugin using `script/generate`.

```
$ script/generate plugin validates_url

  create vendor/plugins/validates_url/lib
  create vendor/plugins/validates_url/tasks
  create vendor/plugins/validates_url/test
  create vendor/plugins/validates_url/README
  create vendor/plugins/validates_url/Rakefile
  create vendor/plugins/validates_url/init.rb
  .
```

```
create vendor/plugins/validates_url/test/validates_url_test.rb
```

It should have generated a number of files for you, including a Rake file, a code file, and a few installation necessities. Next, copy the code from your library in lib/ to the validates_url.rb file in the plugin's directory.

Now that the code is basically in the right place, we need to move some of the pieces around. Pull the call to extend out from the bottom of the main code file and place it in init.rb. The code in your init.rb file is executed in order to initialize the plugin and execute any code hooks (such as extending a class) that your plugin needs to work. Then fill out the README with some basic information, and you've just written your first Rails plugin!

Using gems to distribute Rails plugins

You can also use gems to distribute Rails plugins (Rails 2.1 or later). We'll discuss gem packaging and distribution in chapter 8, but let's look at the difference between gems and non-gem plugins.

You can install gems system-wide and use them across all your applications, or unpack gems into the application directory and distribute them alongside the application. You'll find unpacking easier to use when deploying Rails applications. Gems unpack into the vendor/gems directory, and if you want to develop the gem alongside your application, you can start by creating it in a directory under vendor/gems.

By convention, you use the lib directory to hold the Ruby files that make up your gem. Any Rails-specific initialization goes in the rails/init.rb file.

Configuring your Rails application to use a system-wide gem is done in the config/environment.rb file. Rails uses that information to list (rake gems), install (rake gems:install), and unpack (rake gems:unpack) gems.

Each environment has a separate configuration file, and you can use these files to specify gems that are only used in a specific environment, such as gems used for development or testing but not in production.

Discussion

As you can probably tell, Rails plugins are basically libraries and helpers that have explicit places for code hooks, an install/uninstall script, and a README. Their simplicity, though, makes them very easy to write while still being useful. This example covers the core of writing a plugin, but there are a few little pieces that it doesn't cover.

First, plugins are given install and uninstall scripts, which should be used for any sort of setup/teardown that your plugin needs to do. For example, if we were to port our Ultraviolet helper to a plugin, we would probably want to call copy_files in the install task and delete the copied files in the uninstall task rather than doing it on the first request. This would not only knock down the small performance hit that you take from doing it on the first request, but you can also deal with any errors that might arise before your application is running rather than after. Many plugins use the install hook to show further instructions for installation, like the `restful_authentication` plugin that shows you the README file with further installation and generation instructions.

Plugins also have their own sets of Rake tasks, which can be used to do repeated tasks related to the plugin. For example, if you had a plugin that worked with Amazon's S3, and you wanted to clear off your testing bucket, you might have a `rake:bucket:clear` task. These tasks sit right alongside Rails' tasks in the `rake -T` listing, so they're easily accessible to developers using your plugin.

Now let's turn our attention to Rails performance.

4.2   Rails performance

One of the sticking points for some developers, when it comes to Rails, is the performance. Of course, performance is a rather relative term when you have so many moving parts in a framework: database performance, rendering performance, dispatch performance, and so on. Any or all of these can play a part in your performance problems, but you can't fix the problem until you know what it is. In this section, we'll look at how to profile a Rails application and find your problem spots.

The simplest way to do it is to take a look in your log files. When you see something like the following, you can pretty much guarantee it's a problem area:

```
Processing HomeController#home (for 127.0.0.1 at 2007-08-31 10:15:30) [GET]
  Session ID: 39ba59dc6b7a6eb672cf3a0e89bdc75d
  Parameters: {"action"=>"home", "controller"=>"home"}
Rendering home/home
Completed in 26.39205 (1 reqs/sec) | Rendering: 0.09310 (1%) | 200 OK
[http://localhost/home/home]
```

If you don't see anything that apparent, or if there are a lot of code branches in that method, you'll have to dig a little deeper into the workings of your code. Rails provides a benchmarking helper just for this purpose, which is a really handy tool for simple analysis of pain points in your code.

4.2.1   Benchmarking a Rails application

Benchmarking is a really easy way of getting a lot of data about the performance of your Rails applications. Rails offers two ways of getting benchmark data. The first is to use `script/performance/benchmarker`, which takes a line of code on the command line, benchmarks it, and report back.

Let's say you thought your `Order` model's `cancel!` method was getting out of hand. You could do something like this to find out:

```
$ script/performance/benchmarker 'Order.find(:first).cancel!'
```

As a result, the script will give you a simple report of the measurements it took.

```
user  system  total    real
#1  0.000000  0.000000  0.000000 ( 0.017904)
```

Of course, if you actually had problematic code, it would return much larger numbers. This is great for testing things outside the context of your application, but Rails also offers a simple helper for benchmarking inside your application.

Problem

You need to benchmark your Rails inside your application.

Solution

Rails offers a single method named benchmark that allows us to benchmark blocks of code throughout an application. Let's say we have a model method that looks like this:

```
def create_council_members(members)
  members.each do |member|
    new_member = Member.create(member[:attributes])

    new_member.association = Club.find_by_associate(member[:friend])
    new_member.unverified! if new_member.association.unverified?
  end
end
```

We're having trouble telling which part of the code is causing the problem, but we know it's in this method because of the log files. If we were to wrap that segment of code into a benchmark block, we could get a better idea of what's going on:

```
def create_council_members(members)
  members.each do |member|
    Member.benchmark("Creating a member") do
      new_member = Member.create(member[:attributes])
    end

    Club.benchmark("Associating a member") do
      new_member.association = Club.find_by_associate(member[:friend])
      new_member.unverified! if new_member.association.unverified?
    end
  end
end
```

If we make a few requests and look inside the log file, we will see something like the following snippet:

```
Creating a member (0.34019)
Associating a member (0.90927)
[...]
Creating a member (0.29010)
Associating a member (0.90902)
[...]
Creating a member (0.35069)
Associating a member (1.0937)
```

The time measurements are in parentheses and are usually quite telling. In this case, associating a member takes a lot longer!

Discussion

Benchmarking models is great, but if you find yourself seeing high render times in your logs, you can benchmark blocks of code in views in a similar manner. Views also have a benchmark method, as you can see in the following code.

```
<% benchmark "Content tree menu" do %>
  <%= build_content_tree %>
<% end %>
```

This helper is great if you're rendering a menu or complex trees of content and can't seem to nail down the performance problem. If you find you need more data than either of these provides, perhaps you need to look into profiling.

4.2.2   *Profiling a Rails application*

Profiling offers runtime analysis of your Rails applications, breaking down each method call and showing its share of the execution time. Profiling is a very useful way to get in-depth information on your Ruby code in general, but it's usually a little less friendly than the way Rails provides.

Problem

You are having performance issues with a Rails application and would like to find your application's trouble spots.

Solution

Rails offers a script that lives in performance/ named `profiler`, which will use the Ruby profiler to profile your Rails application. You invoke it in basically the same manner as you invoke the benchmarker.

For example, let's say you wanted to profile the confirmation of reservations in your hotel-booking application. The following line would invoke the profiler with your `confirm!` method:

```
$ script/performance/profiler 'Reservation.confirm!'
```

Rails then produces a report to the console that includes *a lot* of information, some of which is actually useful:

```
Loading Rails...

Using the standard Ruby profiler.
  %    cumulative   self              self     total
 time    seconds   seconds   calls  ms/call  ms/call  name
12.20     0.10      0.10      188     0.53     0.64    Array#select
  .
  .
  .
 5.12     0.82      0.04       1      1.00     0.98    Reservation#done!
  .
  .
  .
 0.00     0.82      0.00      17      0.00     0.00    Proc#new
 0.00     0.82      0.00       1      0.00   820.00    #toplevel
```

We'll say it again: the profiler produces *a lot* of data. Some of it is interesting (who knew `Array#select` was the worst offender?), some of it is useless (of course #toplevel doesn't have a performance hit!), and some of it is useful (the `done!` method appears to be what's killing the performance in this case). The important thing to analyze here is not only the percentages and times, but the calls (in the fourth column). We would worry about `Array#select` if the 12 percent it takes up weren't spread across 188 calls; on the other hand, the `done!` method on our model eats up 5 percent in *one* call. That's where a performance problem lies.

Discussion

If you'd like to get more information and fancier reporting on your Rails application, a library called ruby-prof can help you out. It's written in C, it's much faster, and it integrates directly with the Rails profiler script (which will automatically use ruby-prof if it's available). For example, if you want to generate an HTML report for a graph profile, you can do this:

```
$ script/performance/profiler 'Reservation.confirm!' graph_html
```

The ruby-prof library is available as a Ruby gem and you can check out its RDoc at http://ruby-prof.rubyforge.org/.

4.3   Summary

In this chapter, we looked at a number of techniques that Rails developers should be employing. First, we looked at adding your own extensions to Rails and building reusable components from your own code. We then looked at gauging the performance of your Rails application, and suggested a few practical tools and tips to get you started. In the next chapter, we'll take a deeper look at Ruby and web services, including an in-depth look at REST and REST clients.

Web services
5

This chapter covers

- Using HTTP from Ruby
- Building REST services with Rails
- Using REST services with ActiveResource
- Using SOAP with SOAP4R

Throughout this book, we show you ways of integrating Ruby with different applications and services. Some scenarios depend on a particular protocol or architecture, such as using Lightweight Directory Access Protocol (LDAP), sharing data through a relational database, or moving messages around with WebSphere MQ (WMQ). In this chapter, we'll explore the web architecture and look at how we can use web services across language, platform, and application boundaries.

To this end, we'll focus on Service Oriented Architecture (SOA) with Ruby. SOA is not a particular product, technology, or protocol—it's an architecture for building services with the intent to reuse them in different contexts and combine them into larger applications. In this chapter, we're going to choose common protocols and message formats and discuss three common styles for building web services: plain HTTP, REST, and SOAP.

First, we'll cover the foundation and show you how to use HTTP and URLs. Then we'll venture into the world of RESTful web services and show you how to handle

90

resources, representations, and the uniform interface. Finally, we'll talk about SOAP and using SOAP4R as a means for integrating with services developed around the SOAP stack, and in particular J2EE and .Net applications.

5.1 Using HTTP

The basic building blocks of the web are the HTTP protocol and the use of URLs for addressing, and the content is mostly HTML and various media types like images, music, and video. In this chapter, we're going to focus on the programmatic web, which is all about machines talking to machines and application-to-application integration. As a result, we'll pay much more attention to structured data formats like XML, JSON, and even CSV.

5.1.1 HTTP GET

We're going to start with the simplest scenario and show you how to retrieve data from a remote web service and then how to parse the resulting document into structured data that you can process with Ruby. For this example we picked CSV. Although most people equate web services with XML, there's a surprising abundance of structured data out there that is not XML. In this section, we'll take the opportunity to show you how easy it is to use non-XML data, delivered over the web.

Problem

You're building a market intelligence application that needs to retrieve historical stock prices about various public companies. That information is publicly available on the web, but you need to retrieve it and parse it into data you can use.

Solution

For this example, we're going to use Google Finance to get historical stock prices for Google itself. Google Finance has a URL you can use without registering or authenticating. It provides historical data in the form of a CSV document.

Ruby provides two libraries for working with HTTP. For full HTTP support, we'll turn to Net::HTTP, which we cover in the next section, but for the common use case of reading data from a web service, we'll use the more convenient open-uri.

So, to start, we're going to construct a URL and use the open method to create a connection and read the data:

```
url = "http://finance.google.com/finance/historical?q=NASDAQ:#{symbol}&
➡ output=csv"
data = open(url).read
```

Not all data on the web is HTML or XML, and in this example we retrieve a CSV document. We're going to use FasterCSV to parse the document (you will learn more about FasterCSV in chapter 13). Let's parse the document into a set of rows, and convert each row into a hash:

```
csv = FasterCSV.parse data, :headers=>true, :converters=>:numeric
csv.map { |r| r.to_hash }
```

Now we're going to roll all of this into a single method called historical_ stock_prices, so we can use it to read historical stock prices in our applications.

We're also going to follow another Ruby idiom that allows us to either require the file as a library or run it from the command line as a script. Listing 5.1 shows the entire program.

Listing 5.1   Get historical stock prices from Google Finance

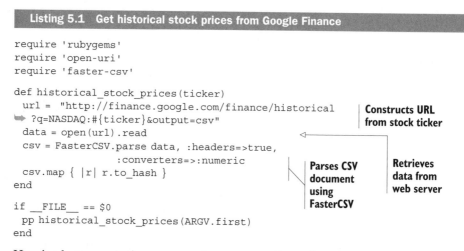

```
require 'rubygems'
require 'open-uri'
require 'faster-csv'

def historical_stock_prices(ticker)
  url = "http://finance.google.com/finance/historical
    ?q=NASDAQ:#{ticker}&output=csv"
  data = open(url).read
  csv = FasterCSV.parse data, :headers=>true,
                  :converters=>:numeric
  csv.map { |r| r.to_hash }
end

if __FILE__ == $0
  pp historical_stock_prices(ARGV.first)
end
```

Constructs URL from stock ticker

Retrieves data from web server

Parses CSV document using FasterCSV

Here's what we get when we run the program from the command line, showing one line from the actual result:

```
$ ruby historical.rb GOOG
=> {"High"=>522.07, "Open"=>521.28, "Close"=>514.48, "Date"=>"10-Sep-07",
"Volume"=>3225800, "Low"=>510.88}
```

Discussion

Using the open-uri library is the easiest way to GET content from an HTTP server. It's designed to be simple to use and to handle the most common cases.

Our example was simple enough that we could treat the URL as a string. In more complex use cases, you will want to use URI objects instead. URI is a library that can parse a URI into its components, like host, path, and query string. You can also use it to construct URIs from their component parts and manipulate them. It includes classes for supporting HTTP and FTP URLs, email (mailto:), and LDAP URIs, and is easily extended.

The open-uri library adds a read method to HTTP and FTP URIs, so let's see how we would use it:

```
uri = URI("http://finance.google.com/finance/historical?output=csv")
uri.query << "&q=NASDAQ:#{CGI.escape(ticker)}"
data = uri.read
```

Note that we're using CGI.escape to properly escape a value before including it in the query string. It's not necessary for our example, since all the stock-ticker symbols we want to deal with are ASCII characters, but it's generally a good idea to deal with special characters like = and & appearing in query string parameters.

The read method returns the content of the HTTP response as a String. Most times that's all we care for, and we like the convenience of it. Occasionally, however, we'll want more information from HTTP headers; for example, to determine the content type of the response, or to handle redirects.

In Ruby, each object implements a single class, but you can also add methods to an object instance, in addition to those provided by its class. There are several ways of doing this.

First, open-uri uses the `extend` method to add metadata methods to the `String` object it returns. We can use that to access various HTTP headers, like this:

```
puts "The actual URL after redirection: #{data.base_uri}"
puts "Content type: #{data.content_type}"
puts "Last modified: #{data.last_modified}"
puts "The document: #{data}"
```

If you access the web from behind a proxy server, you can tell open-uri to use that proxy server using the `:proxy` option. You can set the `HTTP_PROXY` environment variable and open-uri will pick it up by default. So let's use that to run our example from behind a proxy server:

```
$ export HTTP_PROXY="http://myproxy:8080"
$ ruby historical.rb GOOG
```

In the next example, we'll use open-uri to access a local server, bypassing the proxy, and using HTTP Basic Authentication:

```
open(url, :proxy=>nil, :http_basic_authentication=>["john", "secret"])
```

For downloading larger documents, open-uri will also allow you to use a progress bar. Check the open-uri documentation for more details.

Now that we have covered retrieving data from a web server, let's see how we can send data to a web server by making an HTTP POST request.

5.1.2   HTTP POST

The previous section was a simple scenario using GET to access publicly available information. In this section, we'll turn it up a notch and use HTTP POST to submit data, add authentication for access control, and handle status codes and errors.

Problem

In your network, you have an existing service that can receive and process orders. You need a way to turn orders into XML documents and send them over to the order-processing service.

Solution

Let's start with the data. To make this solution easy to use, we're going to support two types of arguments. The XML document can be passed directly, in the form of a string, or the data can be passed as a `Hash`, with the method converting it into an XML document.

For this simple example, we're going to use the XmlSimple library, so let's install it first:

```
gem install xml-simple
```

We will use XmlSimple to convert a hash into an XML document:

```
if Hash === data
  data = XmlSimple.xml_out(data, 'noattr'=>true, 'contentkey'=>'sku',
    'xmldeclaration'=>true, 'rootname'=>'order')
end
```

The XML document we're going to create will look like this:

```
<?xml version='1.0' standalone='yes'?>
<order>
  <item>
    <quantity>1</quantity>
    <sku>123</sku>
  </item>
  <item>
    <quantity>2</quantity>
    <sku>456</sku>
  </item>
</order>
```

Now that we have the data, it's time to create an HTTP connection. We'll start by parsing the URL string into a `URI` object, and set up Net::HTTP to use either the HTTP or HTTPS protocol:

```
uri = URI.parse(url)
http = Net::HTTP.new(uri.host, uri.port)
http.use_ssl = true if uri.scheme == 'https'
```

Next, we're going to set the HTTP headers. We don't want the server to accept partial documents, which could happen if the connection drops, so we're going to tell it exactly how long the document is. And for extra measure, we're going to use an MD5 hash to make sure the document is not corrupted:

```
headers = { 'Content-Type'=>'application/xml',
  'Content-Length'=>data.size.to_s,
  'Content-MD5'=>Digest::MD5.hexdigest(data) }
```

In this example, we make a single request, so we'll let Net::HTTP deal with opening and closing the connection:

```
post = Net::HTTP::Post.new(uri.path, headers)
post.basic_auth uri.user, uri.password if uri.user
response = http.request post, data
```

We send the request, and we don't expect any data in the result, but we do want to know if our request was successful, so the last thing we'll do is look at the status code returned by the server. A successful response is anything with a 2xx status code. Some services return 200 (OK), but others may return 201 (Created), 202 (Accepted), or 204 (No Content). In this case, we expect 201 (Created) with the location of the new resource, but we'll also respond favorably to any other 2xx status code. All other responses are treated as error conditions:

```
case response
  when Net::HTTPCreated; response['Location']
```

```
  when Net::HTTPSuccess; nil
  else response.error!
end
```

Listing 5.2 shows all these pieces merged into a single file.

Listing 5.2 Using HTTP POST and XmlSimple to send a document to the web server

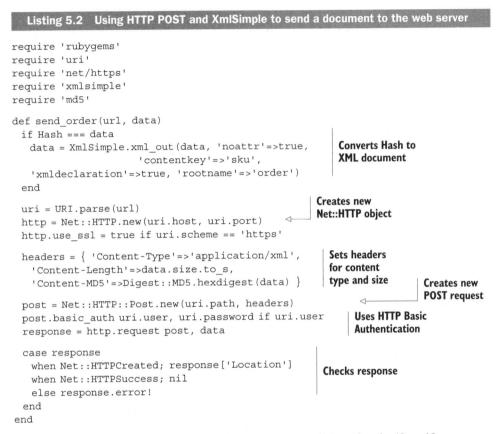

```
require 'rubygems'
require 'uri'
require 'net/https'
require 'xmlsimple'
require 'md5'

def send_order(url, data)
  if Hash === data
    data = XmlSimple.xml_out(data, 'noattr'=>true,     Converts Hash to
                     'contentkey'=>'sku',              XML document
    'xmldeclaration'=>true, 'rootname'=>'order')
  end

  uri = URI.parse(url)                                Creates new
  http = Net::HTTP.new(uri.host, uri.port)  ←         Net::HTTP object
  http.use_ssl = true if uri.scheme == 'https'

  headers = { 'Content-Type'=>'application/xml',      Sets headers
    'Content-Length'=>data.size.to_s,                 for content
    'Content-MD5'=>Digest::MD5.hexdigest(data) }      type and size     Creates new
                                                                        POST request
  post = Net::HTTP::Post.new(uri.path, headers)  ←
  post.basic_auth uri.user, uri.password if uri.user  Uses HTTP Basic
  response = http.request post, data                  Authentication

  case response
    when Net::HTTPCreated; response['Location']
    when Net::HTTPSuccess; nil                         Checks response
    else response.error!
  end
end
```

Now let's see how we can send a new order with three lines of code (four if you count the print statement):

```
order = { 'item'=>[ { 'sku'=>'123', 'quantity'=>1 },
               { 'sku'=>'456', 'quantity'=>2 } ] }
url = send_order('https://order.server/create', order)
puts "Our new order at: #{url}" if url
```

Discussion

Ruby has several libraries for dealing with XML, and which one you choose depends on the use case. When you need maximum flexibility and the ability to handle elements, attributes, and text nodes, you can use REXML to work with the XML document tree. For performance-intensive applications, you can use libxml, a native XML library. If you have data that you need to convert into an XML document, you can use Builder instead (we'll look at using it later in this chapter). Some XML documents map nicely into a hash, in which case XmlSimple is true to its name. For this particular example, we chose XmlSimple because it fits nicely with what we wanted to do, but throughout this book we will use different XML libraries, always choosing the one that's best for the task at hand.

Some developers prefer to write or use APIs where authentication information is passed as a separate argument on each method call, or stored once in an object. We prefer to pass authentication information in the URL itself. You'll notice that the previous example takes the username and password from the URL and applies it to the POST request, using HTTP Basic Authentication. Since HTTP Basic Authentication passes the username and password as clear text, we'll use that in combination with HTTPS to encrypt the request from snooping eyes. A URL with authentication information in it will look like https://john:secret@example.com/create.

HTTP is a connectionless protocol; it handles each request individually. The server doesn't care whether we send each request in a separate connection or send multiple requests in a single connection. HTTP 1.1 provides keep-alive connections that we can use to open a connection once and send multiple requests—the benefit is that we don't have to create a TCP connection for each request, and it gives us better latency. We can do this:

```
http.start do |conn|
  response = conn.request post, data
end
```

Our example makes a single request. We could have opened the connection, made that one request, and closed it. In fact, we did just that when we called the request method on the Net::HTTP object; it was just masked behind a single method call. If your code is making several requests to the same server, consider explicitly opening a connection and using the connection object to make those requests.

As you've seen, the Net::HTTP library covers all the features of the HTTP protocol, from one-line requests all the way to persistent connections, from GET requests to documents and forms, with support for HTTPS and HTTP Basic Authentication. It supports all the common HTTP verbs like GET and POST, the less common ones like HEAD and OPTIONS, and even the WebDAV headers. It supports all the HTTP headers, and response codes help you distinguish between successful response codes, redirects, and errors.

Keep in mind, though, that Net::HTTP is a low-level library. Unlike open-uri, it will not set the proxy server for you; you'll need to do that yourself when creating connections. Most often, we use Net::HTTP for one-off tasks, or to write more convenient libraries. In section 5.2.3, we'll talk about one such library called ActiveResource that provides RESTful access to remote resources, built from Net::HTTP.

Before we do that, let's look at the other side of HTTP—the server side. We showed you how a client can retrieve data from and send data to a web server. Next we'll show you how to implement a simple web server that client applications can retrieve data from.

5.1.3 *Serving HTTP requests*

Now that we know how to access a web service, let's build a simple service. In the previous chapter, we talked about Rails, and as you'll see later in this chapter, Rails is a great framework for building web services. Yet, not all web services need a full-fledged framework, and sometimes working close to the protocol (HTTP) is better, so in this section we'll show you a simple service built straight into the HTTP server.

Problem

You have an analytics console that you could use to monitor traffic across all servers in the network. It works by pulling log files from each server and batch processing them. To make it work with your server, you need to set up a simple service that provides all the log files for a given day.

Solution

Ruby comes with a built-in web server called WEBrick, a simple and lightweight server that is an adequate choice for development and prototyping. For production, though, we recommend using Mongrel or Thin. Both are faster and more stable than WEBrick, and you can use them as standalone servers, or to deploy a cluster of load-balanced application servers behind Apache or Nginx.

In this example, we'll use Mongrel as a standalone server, and we'll start by installing it:

```
gem install mongrel
```

Next, we'll define the `LogService`, which needs to implement a single method called `process`, which handles the HTTP request and sets the response:

```
class LogService < Mongrel::HttpHandler
  def process(request, response)
    ...
  end
end
```

A request that ends with `/YYYY-MM-DD` retrieves all the log files for that particular day. A request that ends with `/last` retrieves the last set of log files, which happens to be yesterday's date:

```
case request.params['PATH_INFO']
when /^\/(\d{4}-\d{2}-\d{2})$/
  package $1, response
when '/last'
  package (Date.today - 1).to_s, response
else
  response.start 404 do |head, out|
    head['Content-Type'] = 'text/html'
    script = request.params['SCRIPT_NAME']
    out.write "<h1>Request URL should be #{script}/last "\
          " or#{script}/[yyyy]-[mm]-[dd]</h1>"
  end
end
```

If we get a request we cannot process, we return the 404 (Not Found) status code, but we also include a short HTML snippet explaining the correct URL format. We do that to help our users, since getting the request URL wrong is a common mistake.

The `package` method will handle all valid requests, so let's look at it next. We're going to use the RubyZip library:

```
gem install rubyzip
```

Strictly speaking, we want to create an empty zip file, add all the log files into it, use default compression, and return that file to the client. We're going to decide on the zip filename first, and we'll make sure to use a distinct filename for each day:

```
zip_filename = "logs-#{date}.zip"
```

We're not going to create a file with that name. Imagine two requests coming at the same time, attempting to write into the same zip file at once. Not good. So instead, we'll create a temporary file:

```
tmp_file = Tempfile.open(zip_filename)
```

Next, we'll use RubyZip to add the log files:

```
Zip::ZipOutputStream.open(tmp_file.path) do |zip|
  Dir.glob("#{@path}/*-#{date}.log").each do |filename|
    zip.put_next_entry File.basename(filename)
    zip << File.read(filename)
  end
end
```

The `glob` method is named after the glob pattern, which we can use to match any number of files. An asterisk (*) matches any filename or partial filename, a question mark (?) matches any single character, and a double asterisk (**) matches directories recursively. You can find a few more options in the `Dir.glob` documentation. Here we'll find all filenames that contain the date and end with the extension *log*, such as errors-2007-10-05.log.

Once we have created the zip file, we'll return it to the client:

```
response.start 200 do |head, out|
  head['Content-Type'] = 'application/zip'
  head['Content-Length'] = File.size(tmp_file.path)
  head['Content-Disposition'] = %{attachment; filename="#{zip_filename}"}
  while buffer = tmp_file.read(4096)
    out.write buffer
  end
end
```

It's a simple matter of returning the status code 200 (OK) and copying the file over to the Mongrel response, which we do one block at a time to keep the service from eating up all available memory.

We're just about done. We have a Mongrel `HttpHandler` that responds to GET requests by returning a zip file with all the log files for a given date, and we can use that as a building block for a larger application that includes several services by simply registering the handler on a given URL. We're not going to show you a larger application here. Instead we'll make it possible to run this service from the command line:

```
service = LogService.new(path)
puts "Starting Mongrel on port #{port}, serving log files from '#{path}'"
mongrel = Mongrel::HttpServer.new('0.0.0.0', port)
mongrel.register '/logs', service
mongrel.run.join
```

We set up the server to listen on IP 0.0.0.0, which means any network card including localhost. You can also specify a specific IP address or host name, or only allow requests from the same machine by listening to localhost (127.0.0.1).

Let's run the server:

```
ruby log_service.rb ~/logs
Starting Mongrel on port 3000, serving log files from '/home/assaf/logs'
```

To retrieve all the latest log files, simply open your browser and head over to http://localhost:3000/logs/last.

Now let's merge all that code into a single file, shown in Listing 5.3.

Listing 5.3 A service for packaging log files and serving them as a zip file

```
require 'rubygems'
require 'mongrel'
require 'zip/zip'

class LogService < Mongrel::HttpHandler

  def initialize(path)
    @path = path
  end

  def process(request, response)                        ◁─┐ Accepts only
  unless request.params['REQUEST_METHOD'] == 'GET'      ◁─┘ GET requests
      return response.status = 405
    end
    case request.params['PATH_INFO']
    when /^\/(\d{4}-\d{2}-\d{2})$/                       Determines
      package $1, response                              resource from
    when '/last'                                        request path
      package (Date.today - 1).to_s, response
    else
      response.start 404 do |head, out|                 ◁─── Returns 404 if
        head['Content-Type'] = 'text/html'                   resource not found
        script = request.params['SCRIPT_NAME']
        out.write "<h1>Request URL should be #{script}/last"\
                " or #{script}/[yyyy]-[mm]-[dd]</h1>"
      end
    end
  end

private

  def package(date, response)
    zip_filename = "logs-#{date}.zip"
```

```
    tmp_file = Tempfile.open(zip_filename)     ◁─── Creates a temporary file
    begin
      Zip::ZipOutputStream.open(tmp_file.path) do |zip|
        Dir.glob("#{@path}/*-#{date}.log").each do |file|
          zip.put_next_entry File.basename(file)          Uses RubyZip to
          zip << File.read(file)                          compress files
        end
      end
      response.start 200 do |head, out|          ◁───┐ Returns successful
        head['Content-Type'] = 'application/zip'       │ (200) response
        head['Content-Length'] = File.size(tmp_file.path)
        head['Content-Disposition'] = %{attachment;
          filename="#{zip_filename}"}
        while buffer = tmp_file.read(4096)
          out.write buffer                     Streams file
        end                                    to the client
      end
    ensure                       Discards
      tmp_file.close!    ◁────┘   temporary file
    end
  end
end

if __FILE__ == $0
  unless path = ARGV[0]
    puts "Usage:"
    puts " ruby log_service.rb <log_dir> [<port>]"     Handles
    exit                                               command-line
  end                                                  arguments
  port = ARGV[1] || 3000
  service = LogService.new(path)
  puts "Starting Mongrel on port #{port}, serving log files from '#{path}'"
  mongrel = Mongrel::HttpServer.new('0.0.0.0', port)
  mongrel.register '/logs', service          Starts a new
  mongrel.run.join                           Mongrel server
end
```

Discussion

This example shows you how to set up a simple web service without going the route of a web framework. We do advocate using web frameworks when they help you get better results with less work, and in the next section we'll delve into RESTful services using Rails. Sometimes, though, a web framework just gets in the way, and we wanted to make you feel comfortable using the simplest solution for each situation.

Another thing web frameworks do is hide, or abstract away, the HTTP protocol. In our experience, you'll do better if you learn how to use HTTP with all its richness, whether you're writing the code yourself, learning how to use a web framework, or evaluating a library for use in your application. Our service only supports GET requests, so we used the status code 405 (Method Not Allowed) to deny all other HTTP methods. That status code tells the client exactly why his request was rejected.

Along with the response, we sent three headers. The first, Content-Type, tells the client the file type, and a web browser can use this information to open the file with the right application. The second, `Content-Length`, tells the client how long the response is, which is particularly useful for large responses, and for showing a progress bar of the download. The HTTP protocol allows the server to close the connection once it's done sending the request, but if the connection drops (and sometimes it does), the client doesn't know whether or not it received the full response. The `Content-Length` header gets around that problem. We also used the `Content-Disposition` header to suggest a filename. Without this header, a request to /logs/last would attempt to download and save a file called "last." With this header, the browser will offer to save the file under a name like logs-2007-10-05.zip.

The last thing we did was send the request progressively, in blocks of 4,096 bytes. That allows the client to start reading in, and if necessary, to start saving the response, without waiting for the server to be done reading the file. It also saves the server from loading the entire file, which could well be gigabytes of data, into memory. Paying attention to these details will improve the performance and scalability of your applications, and the responsiveness of your web servers.

Now that we have covered the basics of HTTP, we're going to go one step further and explore the REST style. We'll show you how to create resources, handle multiple representations, and use the uniform interface to build RESTful web services.

5.2 REST with Rails

So far, we've shown you how to build services and clients that use the HTTP protocol. We'll take this a step further now and show you how to build RESTful services using Rails.

The Representational State Transfer (REST) architectural style is modeled after the web. Basically, it codifies the principles and methods behind web servers that lead to the creation of the largest distributed system ever built. For some people, "distributed" is about the plumbing—sending messages to remote servers. However, we're also thinking of the way large-scale systems emerge from smaller services built independently by different groups of people—systems that are distributed in design and in implementation.

When we follow the REST style, we follow those same web principles: modeling our services in terms of resources, making sure they are addressable as URLs, connecting them by linking from one resource to another, handling representations based on content type, performing stateless operations, and so forth. In the following sections, we'll show an example using Rails. You'll also quickly realize why we picked Rails for this task.

5.2.1 RESTful resources

Besides being the largest collection of useless information, personal opinions, and short video clips, the web is also a large-scale system built from resources. Each page is a resource identified by its URL. We use links to navigate from one resource to another, and forms to operate on those resources. Applying these same principles, we can build web services that are simple for both people and applications to use, and we can wire them together to create larger applications.

Problem

You're designing a task manager that your employees will use to manage their day-to-day assignments. You're also planning several applications and workflows that will create and act upon these tasks. How can you design your task manager as a web service that both people and applications can use?

Solution

Obviously one part of the solution is supporting programmable web formats like XML and JSON, which we'll handle in the next section. Before we get to deal with that, we need to understand how to structure our resources so we can consume them from web browsers and client applications.

When we develop a web service, our aim is to build the service once and support any number of clients that want to connect to it. The more client applications that can reuse our service, the more we get out of the initial effort that goes into building that service. We're always on the lookout for those principles and practices that would make our service loosely coupled and ripe for reuse. In this section, we're going to do just that by applying REST principles to a task manager.

We'll start by identifying the most important resources we need to provide. We have one resource representing the collection of tasks, which we'll make apparent by using the URL path /tasks. And since we also plan to operate on individual tasks, we'll give each task its individual resources, and we'll do so hierarchically by placing each task in a resource of the form /tasks/{id}.

We'll handle all of these through the `TasksController`, so the first thing we'll do is define the resource so Rails can map incoming requests to the right controller. We do that in the config/routes.rb file:

```
ActionController::Routing::Routes.draw do |map|

  # Tasks resources handled by TasksController
  map.resources :tasks
end
```

Retrieving the list of all tasks in the collection is done by the `index` action:

```
class TasksController < ApplicationController
  # GET on /tasks
  # View: tasks/index.html.erb
  def index
    @tasks = Task.for_user(@user_id)
  end

  ...
end
```

For individual tasks, we're going to use the `show` action when the client asks to retrieve that one task:

```
# GET on /tasks/{id}
# View: tasks/show.html.erb
def show
  @task = Task.find(params[:id])
end
```

What else would we want to do with a task? We'll want to change (update) it, and we'll need to offer a way to delete it. We can do all three on the same resource. We can use HTTP GET to retrieve the task, PUT to update the task, and DELETE to discard it. So let's add two more actions that operate on a member task:

```
# PUT on /tasks/{id}
def update
  @task = Task.find(params[:id])
  @task.update_attributes! params[:task]
  respond_to do |format|
    format.html { redirect_to:action=>'edit', :id=>task.id }
    format.xml { render :xml=>task }
  end
end

# DELETE on /tasks/{id}
def destroy
  Task.find (params[:id]).destroy

  head :no_content
end
```

We got a bit ahead of ourselves. Before we can do all these things with a task, we need some way to create it. Since we have a resource representing the collection of tasks, and each task is represented by its own resource, we're going to use HTTP POST to create a new task in the collection:

```
# POST on /tasks
def create
  task = Task.create!(params[:task])
  respond_to do |format|
    format.html { redirect_to:action=>'show', :id=>task.id}
    format.xml { render :xml=>@task, :status=>:created,
      :location=>url_for(:action=>'show', :id=>task.id) }
  end
end
```

We can now start to write applications that create, read, update, and delete tasks. The beauty is that we've done it entirely using one resource to represent the collection and one resource to represent each member, and we've used the HTTP methods POST (create), GET (read), PUT (update), and DELETE (delete). When it comes time to develop another service, say for managing users or orders, we can follow the same conventions, and we can take what we learned from one service and apply it to all other services.

We're not done, though. We want to expose this service to both people and applications. Our employees are going to use a web browser; they're not going to send a POST or PUT request, but do that using forms. So we need two forms: one for creating a task, and one for updating an existing task. We can place those inside the task list and individual task view respectively. For larger forms—and our tasks will require several fields, taking up most of the page—we want to offer separate pages linked from existing view pages, so we're going to offer two additional resources.

From the tasks list, we're going to link to a separate resource representing a form for creating new tasks, and following our hierarchical design, we'll assign it the URL path /tasks/new. Likewise, we'll associate each individual task with a URL for viewing and editing it:

```
# GET on /tasks/new
# View: tasks/new.html.erb
def new
  @task = Task.new
end

# GET on /tasks/{id}/edit
# View: tasks/edit.html.erb
def edit
  @task = Task.find(params[:id])
end
```

Now it's becoming clearer why we choose to lay out the resources hierarchically. If you like tinkering with the browser's address bar, try this: open the edit form for a given task, say /tasks/123/edit, and change the URL to go up one level to the task view at /tasks/123, and up another level to the tasks list at /tasks. Besides being a nice browser trick, this setup helps developers understand how all the resources relate to each other. This is one case where picking intuitive URLs is worth a thousand words of documentation.

So let's pause and review what we have so far:

- GET request to /tasks returns the list of all tasks.
- POST request to /tasks creates a new task and redirects back to the tasks list.
- GET request to /tasks/new returns a form that we can use to create a new task; it will POST to /tasks.
- GET request on /tasks/{id} returns a single task.
- PUT request on /tasks/{id} updates that task.
- DELETE request on /tasks/{id} deletes that task.
- GET request on /tasks/{id}/edit returns a form that we can use to update an existing task; it will PUT these changes to /tasks/{id}.

We didn't get here by accident. We intentionally chose these resources so that we need to keep track of only one reference (URL) to the tasks list and one reference to each individual task. Helping us was the fact that we can use all four HTTP methods, which already define the semantics of operations we can do against these resources. Notice that while adding more actions to our controllers, we made no change to our routing configuration. These conventions are a matter of practical sense, and Rails follows them as well, so our one-line definition of the resource captures all that logic, and all we had to do was fill in the actions.

Next, we're going to add a couple of actions that are specific to our task manager and extend our resource definition to cover those.

The first resource we're going to add is for viewing the collection of completed tasks. We can follow the same rules to add resources for viewing pending tasks, tasks scheduled to complete today, high-priority tasks, and so forth. We're going to place it at the URL path /tasks/completed.

The second resource we're going to add will make it easier to change task priority. Right now, making a change to the task requires updating the task resource. We want to develop a simple AJAX control that shows five colored numbers and sets the task priority when the user clicks on one of those numbers. We'll make it easy by providing a resource to represent the task priority, so we can write an onClick event handler that updates the resource priority directly. We'll associate the priority resource with the URL path /tasks/{id}/priority.

Let's add these two resources together and create the routes shown in listing 5.4.

Listing 5.4   Defining our task manager resources in config/routes.rb

```
ActionController::Routing::Routes.draw do |map|

  # Tasks resources handled by TasksController
  map.resources :tasks,
    :collection => { :completed=>:get },
    :member => { :priority=>:put }
end
```

Next, let's add the controller actions to TaskController:

```
# GET on /tasks/completed
# View: tasks/completed.html.erb
def completed
  @tasks = Task.completed_for_user(@user_id)
end

# PUT on /tasks/{id}/priority
def priority
  @task = Task.find(params[:id])
  @task.update_attributes! :priority=>request.body.to_i
  head :ok
end
```

Will it work? We certainly hope so, but we won't know until we check. Rails resource definitions are easy to work with, but we still occasionally make mistakes and create something different from what we intended. So let's investigate our route definitions using the routes task:

```
$ rake routes
```

The output should look something like listing 5.5.

Listing 5.5   Routes for our RESTful tasks list

```
completed_tasks GET   /tasks/completed       {:action=>"completed"}
          tasks GET   /tasks                 {:action=>"index"}
                POST  /tasks                 {:action=>"create"}
       new_task GET   /tasks/new             {:action=>"new"}
completion_task PUT   /tasks/:id/completion {:action=>"completion"}
      edit_task GET   /tasks/:id/edit        {:action=>"edit"}
           task GET   /tasks/:id             {:action=>"show"}
```

```
PUT    /tasks/:id          {:action=>"update"}
DELETE /tasks/:id          {:action=>"destroy"}
```

The actual output is more verbose; we trimmed it to fit the page by removing the controller name (no surprise, it's always "tasks") and the formatting routes, which we'll cover in the next section. You can see how each HTTP method (in the second column) and URL template (third column) map to the correct controller action (rightmost column). A quick peek tells us all we need to know.

The leftmost column deserves a bit more explanation. Rails creates several friendly looking routing methods that we can use instead of the catch-all `url_for`. For example, since our tasks list needs a link to the URL for the task-creation form, we can write this:

```
<%= link_to "Create new task",
    url_for(:controller=>'tasks', :action=>'new') %>
```

Or, using the named-route method, we can shorten it to this:

```
<%= link_to "Create new task", new_task_url %>
```

Likewise, we could have the task list link to each task's individual page:

```
<%= link_to task.title, task_url(task) %>
```

Or we can include a link for the task-editing form:

```
<%= link_to "Edit this task", edit_task_url(task) %>
```

We're done, so let's have a look at what our controller looks like with all the actions brought together in one file. As we write it up, we're going to make a couple of minor tweaks. First, we'll use named routes instead of `url_for`. Second, we'll add a filter to load the task into the controller, for the benefit of actions operating on individual tasks. Listing 5.6 shows the resulting controller.

Listing 5.6   Routes for our RESTful tasks list

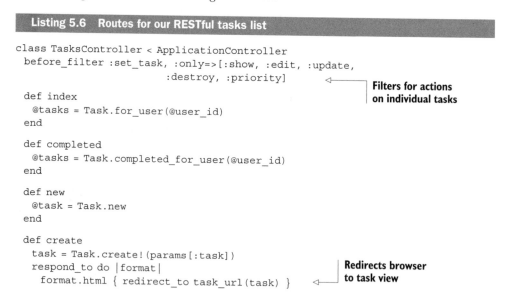

```
class TasksController < ApplicationController
  before_filter :set_task, :only=>[:show, :edit, :update,
                            :destroy, :priority]          ◁──── Filters for actions
                                                                on individual tasks
  def index
    @tasks = Task.for_user(@user_id)
  end

  def completed
    @tasks = Task.completed_for_user(@user_id)
  end

  def new
    @task = Task.new
  end

  def create
    task = Task.create!(params[:task])
    respond_to do |format|
      format.html { redirect_to task_url(task) }          ◁──── Redirects browser
                                                                to task view
```

```
      format.xml { render :xml=>task, :status=>:created,
            :location=>task_url(task) }
  end
end

def show
end

def edit
end

def update
  @task.update_attributes! params[:task]
  respond_to do |format|
    format.html { redirect_to edit_task_url(@task) }
    format.xml { render :xml=>@task }
  end
end

def priority
  @task.update_attributes! :priority=>request.body.to_i
  head :ok
end

def destroy
  @task.destroy
head :no_content
  end

private

  def set_task
    @task = Task.find(params[:id])
  end
end
```

**Returns XML document
for new task**

**Associates
controller with
task from URL**

Discussion

We showed you how to build a simple RESTful web service using Rails. However, there
are a few more things worth noting about this example and how we used Rails to apply
the principles of REST.

One of the core principles of REST is the uniform interface. HTTP provides several
methods you can use on each resource; the four we're showing here are POST (create), GET (read), PUT (update), and DELETE (delete). They have clear semantics, and
everyone understands them the same way. Clients know what GET does and how it differs from DELETE, servers operate differently on POST and PUT, caches know they can
cache the response to a GET but must invalidate it on DELETE, and so forth. You can
also use that consistency to build more reliable applications; for example, PUT and
DELETE are idempotent methods, so if you fail while making a request, you can simply
repeat it. The uniform interface saves us from having to reinvent and document these
semantics for each and every application, and it helps that we can always do the same
thing the same way.

Unfortunately, while we get this variety for the programmable web, web browsers
have not yet caught up, and some cannot properly handle PUT and DELETE. A common

workaround is to use POST to simulate PUT and DELETE by sending the real HTTP method in the _method parameter. Rails understands this convention, and so do many AJAX libraries like Prototype.js and jQuery, so you can safely use these with Rails to keep your resources RESTful.

You will notice, in our example, that when updating an existing resource (the task), we respond to the PUT request with the default status code 200 (OK) and an XML representation of the updated resource. On the other hand, when creating a resource, we respond to the POST request with the status code 201 (Created), an XML representation of the new resource, and the Location header. The latter tells the client application that we just created a resource and where to find that resource, to retrieve and update it later on. In both responses, we return a document that may be different from the one we received, perhaps with added fields like id, version, and updated_at. Either way, we're using the full semantics of the HTTP protocol to distinguish between creating a resource and updating an existing one.

People work differently from applications, however, and when responding to a web browser, we need to consider the user experience. The way browsers work, if we simply responded to a POST request with a render, and the user then refreshed the page, the browser would make another POST request—the double-submit problem. We don't want that to happen, so we redirect instead. We also don't need to send back a representation of the resource, or its location; instead, we take the user back to the tasks lists.

You may be wondering, what happens if someone makes a request to /tasks/456, but there is no such task? Clearly this should return a 404 (Not Found) response, yet we show no such thing in our example. One way in which Rails simplifies deployment is by taking care of all these details and applying default behavior, so you don't have to worry about it unless you want to change the way it behaves. So we let Rails figure it out.

When we call Task.find and it can't find a task with that identifier, it throws an ActiveRecord::RecordNotFound exception. Rails catches this exception and maps it to the 404 (Not Found) status code. The default behavior is to send back a static page that you can find (and customize to your application) in public/404.html.

Likewise, if we tried to create or update a task by sending a field it doesn't understand, such as an XML document with the element <address> (our tasks don't have an address field), Rails will throw an ActiveRecord::RecordInvalid or Active-Record::RecordNotSaved exception. It will then catch this exception and map it to a 422 (Unprocessable Entity) status code.

Rails similarly deals with unsupported content types by returning 406 (Not Acceptable), which we'll put into action in the next section. You can add your own logic for catching and dealing with these exceptions, and you can introduce your own exception and handling logic. Have a look at ActionController::Rescue, particularly the rescue_from method.

One common mistake web developers make is storing a copy of an object in the session, like this:

```
Task.find_by_user(session[:user])
```

What's wrong with this code? Updating the user's record in the database, or even deleting it, will not update the session, and the session will keep using stale data. It is much better to store the record identifier, which doesn't change, and access the record as necessary. The common alternative looks like this:

```
Task.find_by_user_id(session[:user_id])
```

This code works better, as long as you're using sessions. When developing applications that use a web service, it's much easier to work with HTTP Basic Authentication, as we've shown in the previous sections. It's easier to use than going through a custom login form and then carrying the session cookie around.

Fortunately, it's a trivial matter to write controllers that support both means of authentication. Simply add a filter that can use HTTP Basic Authentication or the session to identify the user, and store their identifier in the `@user_id` instance variable. We recommend doing that in `ApplicationController`, which is why we're not showing this filter in our example.

We talked about the ease of mapping resources for CRUD (create, read, update, delete) operations. Resource mapping is another area where we encourage you to explore more. You can take hierarchical resources one step further and create nested resources, such as /books/598/chapters/5. You can use the `to_param` method to create more friendly URLs, such as /books/598-ruby-in-practice/chapters/5-web-services. Also, have a look at some of the form helper methods that will generate the right form from an ActiveRecord object, using the most suitable resource URL. This combination will not only make it easier to develop web applications, but also help you do the right thing from the start.

When building RESTful web services, another thing we have to deal with are multiple content types. We briefly touched upon this, using HTML for end users and XML for applications, and in the next section we'll explore it further, adding support for JSON and Atom.

5.2.2   *Serving XML, JSON, and Atom*

Every resource has a representation. In fact, a given resource can have more than one representation. Users accessing our task manager will want to see an HTML page listing all their tasks, or they may choose to use a feed reader to subscribe to their task list, and feed readers expect an Atom or RSS document. If we're writing an application, we would want to see the tasks list as an XML document or JSON object, or perhaps to pull it into a calendar application in the form of an iCal list of to-dos and events.

In this section, we're going to explore resources by looking at multiple representations, starting with HTML and adding XML, JSON, and Atom representations for our tasks list.

Problem

As you're building your task manager, you realize you need to support a number of clients, specifically feed readers and programmable clients, by adding XML, JSON, and Atom representations to the tasks list.

Solution

One reason we recommend Rails for building web services is the ease of adding different representations for the same underlying resource. So let's start with a simple action that displays the current task list in one of several formats:

```
def index
  @tasks = Task.for_user(@user_id)
end
```

Since most Rails examples look like this and only support HTML, we won't fault you for thinking this example shows just an HTML output, but in fact it supports as many formats as we have views. When you leave it up to Rails to render the response, it tries to find a suitable view based on the action name and expected format. If we wrote a view called index.html.erb, Rails would use it to render HTML responses. If we added a view called index.xml.builder, Rails would use this one to render XML responses. For Atom, we would use index.atom.builder, and for iCal, index.ics.erb.

Notice the pattern here? The first part tells Rails which action this view represents, the second part tells it which format it applies to, and the last part tells it which templating engine to use. Rails comes with three templating engines: ERB (eRuby), Builder, and RJS. This is a new feature introduced in Rails 2.0. Earlier versions were less flexible, and always matched a combination of format and templating engine, so for HTML it would default to ERB by looking up the view index.rhtml, and for XML it would default to Builder by looking up the view index.rxml. Rails 2.0 gives you more flexibility in mixing and matching formats and templating engines, and also makes it easier to add new template handlers (for example, for using Liquid templates or HAML).

In a moment, we're going to show you Builder, when we use it to create an Atom feed for our tasks list. For XML and JSON, we're not going to go through the trouble of creating and maintaining a custom view. Instead we'll let ActiveRecord do a trivial transformation of our records into an XML document or a JSON object:

```
def index
  @tasks = Task.for_user(@user_id)
  case request.format
  when Mime::XML
    response.content_type = Mime::XML
    render :text=>@tasks.to_xml
  when Mime::JSON
    response.content_type = Mime::JSON
    render :text=>@tasks.to_json
  when Mime::HTML, Mime::ATOM
    # Let Rails find the view and render it.
  else
    # Unsupported content format: 406
    head :not_acceptable
  end
end
```

The preceding code shows the long way of doing things. You can see the short way to respond with different content types in listing 5.7.

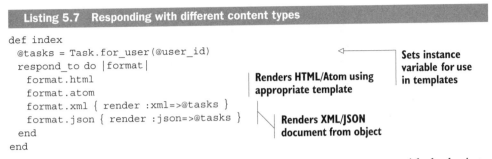

Listing 5.7 Responding with different content types

```
def index
  @tasks = Task.for_user(@user_id)         ◁──────┐  Sets instance
  respond_to do |format|                           │  variable for use
    format.html                                     │  in templates
    format.atom              Renders HTML/Atom using
    format.xml { render :xml=>@tasks }   appropriate template
    format.json { render :json=>@tasks }
  end                                    Renders XML/JSON
end                                      document from object
```

We're using the respond_to method to match each format we support with the logic to render it. It's similar to the case statement in the previous code example, but simpler to specify and more declarative. We're also letting the render method do all the hard work by asking it to convert the array into an XML document or JSON object and to set the Content-Type header appropriately. It's shorter to write and easier to maintain.

Now it's time to handle the Atom view, for which we'll create a view file called index.atom.builder, as shown in listing 5.8.

Listing 5.8 An Atom feed for our tasks list

```
atom_feed do |feed|
  feed.title "My tasks list"           Sets feed title and
  feed.updated @tasks.first.created_at  updates timestamp

  @tasks.each do |task|
    feed.entry task do |entry|          Produces one
      entry.title task.title            feed entry for
      entry.content task.description, :type => 'html'   each task
    end
  end
end
```

The call to atom_feed creates an XML document with the right wrapping for a feed, including the XML document type declaration, feed element with ID, and alternate link back to our site. It also creates an AtomFeedBuilder object and yields to the block. From the block, we're going to create the feed title, specify the last update, and add all the feed entries.

We now have a tasks resource that responds to GET and returns the task list in different content types: HTML for web browsers, Atom for feed readers, and either XML or JSON for client applications.

Discussion

The HTTP protocol allows clients to request data in a particular format using content negotiation. When the client sends a request to the server, it uses the Accept header to indicate all the content types it supports in order of preference. The server can pick the most suitable content type and use it when responding to the client. If the server doesn't support any of the listed content types, it simply responds with 406 (Not Acceptable). Another status code, 415 (Unsupported Media Type), tells the client that the server does not support the content type of a POST or PUT request.

That's the basic idea behind content negotiation. In some cases, it's clearly the right thing to do. We can use one resource URL and send it to all our clients, and each client can see a different representation of the same resource. A web browser will see an HTML page, a feed reader will see an Atom feed, and other applications may see XML or CSV.

Another approach uses different resource URLs for each representation. Some people prefer this approach, since it allows you to manage different representations. For example, if you want to download a CSV document using a web browser, you need a URL that will always send back a CSV document.

There is no one best way to construct these URLs, but there are two common conventions. One adds a query parameter that indicates the expected content type. For example, you can decide to use the `format` query parameter, and use a URL like /tasks?format=xml. Another convention is to use an extension suffix on the URL path, such as /tasks.xml. We recommend using the extension suffix for the simple reason that saving the document with a web browser will retain the suffix, and a file called tasks.xml will always open in the right application.

How does Rails handle this? When we use the built-in mechanism to decide on the content type, as we did in listing 5.7, Rails picks up the expected format from the `format` query parameter, or from the URL path suffix, or from the `Accept` header, in order of preference. Which way you request different content types is up to you—a Rails application can support all three.

You'll notice that in listing 5.6, when we wrote an action to create a new task, we did this:

```
Task.create!(params[:task])
```

Multiple representations work both ways. If we can create a response and send back an XML document, we had better be able to process a request by accepting the same XML document. When Rails processes an XML request, it converts the XML document into a `Hash`, using the document element's name for the parameter name. The preceding example expects the document to contain the element <task> and passes the `Hash` to ActiveRecord.

It works the same way for HTML forms, if you follow the simple naming guidelines set by Rails. In our forms, we will have fields like `task[title]` and `task[priority]`. Rails uses this naming convention to figure out how the fields relate to each other, and turns them into a `Hash` parameter, so we can use the same line of code to process an XML document or the submission of an HTML form.

It helps that we're using Rails' form helper methods:

```
<% form_for @task do |f| %>
  <%= f.text_field :title %>
  <%= f.text_field :priority %>
<% end %>
```

The `form_for` creates the <form> element, figures out the action URL, and takes care to map the field names from `title` to `task[title]`. Give it a new record and it will point the form to the URL for creating a new resource (`tasks_url`, `POST` method); give it an existing record and it will point the form to the URL for updating an existing resource (`task_url(@task)`, `PUT` method). That is why we used `Task.new` to render the form in the new action: we can use a single template to both create and update a record. Rails comes with built-in support for HTML forms, XML, JSON, and YAML, and if that's not enough, you can always add custom parameter parsers. Have a look at `ActionController::Base.param_parsers` for more information.

In listing 5.8 we showed you how to use AtomFeedBuilder, a templating mechanism for generating Atom feeds. AtomFeedBuilder itself extends the more generic XML templating mechanism provided by `Builder::XmlMarkup`. Let's take a moment to look at Builder and what you can do with it.

Builder is a simple templating mechanism for creating XML documents from Ruby code. Because it always produces well-formed documents, some developers even use it to generate XHTML pages. It's available as a gem you can use in any application that needs to generate XML, and it's also included as part of Rails. Builder is very simple to understand and intuitive to use, and it's a good example of what can be done with a little bit of metaprogramming.

When you call a method on a `Builder` object, it takes the method name and uses it to create an XML element with the same name. This is done through `method_missing`, and there is no need to specify any of these methods in advance. AtomFeedBuilder only specifies a few methods that do a lot more than just generate an XML element, so it defines `entry` but doesn't bother to define `title` or `content`.

As you can imagine from this example, passing a string argument to a `Builder` object will use that value for the element content, a hash argument specifies the element's attributes, and blocks are used to nest one element within another.

Besides these, there are some special methods you can call, such as `tag!` to create an element with a given name (for example, to handle special characters or namespaces), `text!`, `cdata!`, `comment!` (each of which do exactly what you think they would), and `instruct!` to create the XML declaration at the top of the document.

We mentioned before that you can use different URLs for the various response representations. When we defined the tasks resource, Rails created several named route methods like `tasks_url` and `task_url`. What we didn't show before is that, in addition, Rails created named route methods that accept a format and return a URL that specifies that output format in the form of a path suffix. These method names start with `formatted_` and accept an additional argument that specifies the output format, and they will show up when you run the `rake routes` task. Let's add a link that users can use to subscribe to the Atom feed, using a named route:

```
<%= link_to "Subscribe", formatted_tasks_url(:atom) %>
```

In this section, we showed you how to build a RESTful web service. But what if you want to access that service from another application? In the next section, we'll talk about ActiveResource, Rail's way of accessing remote resources using an ActiveRecord-like API.

Method_missing and BlankSlate

Builder uses `method_missing` in an interesting way. Ruby's objects use method passing—when you call a method on an object, Ruby first tries to match it against a known method definition, and if it doesn't find any method, passes it on to the object's `method_missing`. The default implementation throws `NoMethodError`. Builder, on the other hand, uses `method_missing` to catch method calls and convert them into XML elements, so we don't need to declare an XML Schema or build any skeleton objects to get this simple creation of XML documents from Ruby code.

Existing object methods may clash with XML element names; for example, names like *id* and *type* are commonly used as element names. To solve that, Builder uses `BlankSlate`, a class that has most of its standard methods removed. (In Ruby 1.9 you can achieve the same using `BasicObject`.)

5.2.3   *Using ActiveResource*

We started this chapter by showing you how easy it is to use open-uri and Net::HTTP. Well, easy is a relative term. Building a client library to access our task manager service will still require a fair amount of boilerplate code—more than we care to write, test, and maintain. We also showed you some principles and conventions for designing RESTful web services. In this section, we'll take it a step further and show you how we can use them to develop a client library for the task manager using ActiveResource.

Problem

Now that the task manager service is up and running, you need to develop your work-flow application. As part of that application, you'll need to create and manage tasks. You want to reuse our task manager service, and you want to get it done before the day is over.

Solution

We'll build a client application that uses ActiveResource to access the task manager service. We'll start by writing a class to represent the resources for handling a task list and individual tasks:

```
class Task < ActiveResource::Base
  self.site = 'https://john:secret@taskmanager.example.com/'
end
```

Remember from section 5.1.2, we're using the URL to specify the username and password for accessing the service, and these map to HTTP Basic Authentication, using HTTPS when we need to access it over public networks.

We've not yet implemented a single method in our new `Task` class, but let's first see what we can do with it. Let's start by creating a new task:

```
task = Task.create(:title=>'Read about ActiveResource', :priority=>1)
puts 'Created task #{task.id}'
=> 'Created task 1'
```

Doesn't this code look very familiar? We're using ActiveResource here to operate against remote resources, but the patterns are the same as in the previous section, where we used ActiveRecord to access the database.

Let's see what happens behind the scenes of the `create` method:

```
task = Task.new
task.title = 'Read about ActiveResource'
task.priority = 1
task.save
```

It starts by creating a new object in memory and setting its attributes, and it saves the object by making a POST request to the resource /tasks, with an XML document containing the task definition. Our simple implementation, you may recall from section 5.2.1, receives the XML document, parses the attributes, and uses them to create a record in the database. It then tells the client what the new task resource is, which is all our ActiveResource needs to know.

Let's follow up by updating the task:

```
task.title << ' and try this example'
task.save
```

This time, since the task already exists, we make a PUT request to the resource and updated it. So we can create and update resources. We can also read and delete them:

```
task = Task.find(1)
task.delete
tasks = Task.find(:all)
Task.delete(tasks.first.id)
```

All of this is just a matter of conventions. ActiveResource follows the same conventions we used when we built the task manager service, so we got all this functionality just by specifying a URL.

How do we know our Task class sends requests to the right URL? We assumed it uses XML by default, but is there a way to find out for sure? Let's try the equivalent of the `rake routes` task:

```
puts Task.collection_path
=> /tasks.xml
puts Task.element_path(1)
=> /tasks/1.xml
```

We built our task manager around all the common patterns, but we also added two resources specific to our task manager. We had one resource for listing all the completed tasks, and we'll want to use that from our client as well. Let's list those tasks:

```
Task.find(:all, :from=>:completed)
```

As you can guess, this is just a request against the /tasks/completed.xml path. We also had a resource for quickly updating the task priority, which we designed to support our AJAX controls. Let's try to use that as well:

```
task.put(:priority, nil, 5)
```

This time, the request goes to /tasks/{id}/priority, substituting the task identifier in the URL template. The put method takes two additional arguments, the first being a hash that is passed along as query string parameters, and the second being the body of the message. Remember from section 5.2.1, we're passing a priority number in the body of the message.

As you might expect, there are other custom methods you can use, like get, post, and delete. We're going to hide the details of put from the application by wrapping it in a method; in fact, we'll add a couple more to create an ActiveResource class that represents our task manager service. The result is shown in listing 5.9.

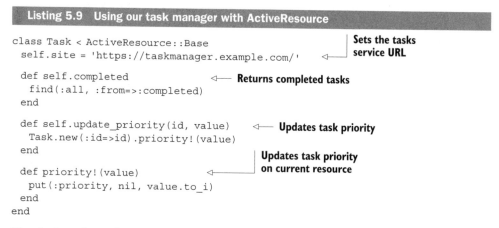

Listing 5.9   Using our task manager with ActiveResource

```
class Task < ActiveResource::Base                              Sets the tasks
  self.site = 'https://taskmanager.example.com/'    ◁───┐  service URL

  def self.completed           ◁─── Returns completed tasks
    find(:all, :from=>:completed)
  end

  def self.update_priority(id, value)    ◁─── Updates task priority
    Task.new(:id=>id).priority!(value)
  end
                                         Updates task priority
  def priority!(value)          ◁───────┘ on current resource
    put(:priority, nil, value.to_i)
  end
end
```

Now let's try it out by running this snippet using script/console:

```
Task.site.user_info = 'john:secret'

puts 'Completed tasks'
Task.completed.map { |task| task.id }.to_sentence
=> "1, 2 and 3"

puts 'Changing priority for task 123'
Task.update_priority(123, 5)
Task.find(123).priority
=> 5
```

Discussion

As you've seen from our examples, Rails makes it extremely easy to build web services that follow the REST principles and work equally well with web browsers and the programmable web. In fact, a lot of that simplicity comes directly from following these principles. We didn't have to tell our client how to create, read, update, or delete the resource—those all followed from using the proper HTTP methods. All we had to do is point our client at the right place. Likewise, we didn't have to build two different task manager applications for people and for applications. We managed both at the same time by using different content types.

If you follow Rails conventions, you get the basic CRUD operations for free. In practice, that's often not enough, and you'll find that you need more specific resources and you'll need to layer additional actions into your controllers. We showed you how easy it is to add these custom methods on both the server and the client sides. There are, of course, other things you'll need to do. A fully functional task manager would need to handle deadlines and exceptions, send notifications, and even spawn workflows that would involve even more tasks and interact with other services. Those are all possible to do within the constraints of REST; unfortunately, it's more than we can show in the limited span of one chapter.

In the last three solutions, we have talked extensively about Rails, but we want you to take their general principles home with you even if you use other web frameworks or programming languages. The first principle was the recommended practice of building RESTful web services and the benefits that come from following the REST architectural style. The other was the benefit of picking up on conventions, which can help you design better, develop faster, and end up with code that's easier to understand and maintain. If nothing else, there will be less to document. Conventions are not just for Rails; when you're building your own applications, think how conventions could help you work less and get more done.

The SOAP messaging protocol is another way to harness the HTTP protocol and build services that cross languages, platforms, and applications. In the following sections, we'll turn our attention to SOAP using the built-in SOAP4R library.

5.3   SOAP services

When it comes to talking with J2EE, .Net, and legacy applications, the first option that comes to mind is SOAP. And yes, Ruby does come with a SOAP stack called, not surprisingly, SOAP4R.

SOAP4R supports SOAP 1.1 with attachments, and service definitions specified using WSDL 1.1. Security options include HTTP Basic Authentication, SSL/TLS, and a separate library that covers WS-Security (WSS4R). SOAP4R participates in interoperability testing, and if you're working at the level of WS-I Basic Profile compliance, you can expect it to work with the various Java SOAP stacks (Axis, Glue, CXF), .Net, and others.

In the next two sections, we'll cover the basics of using SOAP4R as we implement a simple task manager service and a client application to invoke it.

5.3.1   Implementing the service

The appeal of the SOAP protocol is in crossing language and platform boundaries, so there's no need to build the service in Ruby in order to use it from Ruby. We can easily imagine the task manager being a service implemented in Java and the client application in Ruby, or the other way around. Regardless, we want to make this chapter self-contained, so we're going to show you how to implement the service in Ruby, and also how to invoke it using Ruby.

We're picking up on the same task manager service we developed in the previous sections of this chapter, but this time using SOAP instead of REST.

Problem

You need to develop a task manager service that you can use from a variety of client applications using the SOAP messaging protocol.

Solution

We recommend contract-first service development. In our experience, it leads to more robust services that are easier to reuse and maintain. In contract-first, we start by specifying the functionality offered by the service, typically in the form of human-readable documentation and a WSDL service definition. Once that's done, we use the service definition to start building the service implementation and any applications that need to invoke the service. In fact, once we have a service definition, we can branch off to develop both pieces in parallel.

We also prefer document style with literal encoding, fondly known as *doc/lit*, which makes it easier to evolve the service definition over time, so we're going to use that for our service definition. Since WSDL is verbose and we only have so much space in this book, we'll keep our example to the bare minimum. We'll build our service to support a single operation, for creating a new task, and only care about two parameters, the task title and priority.

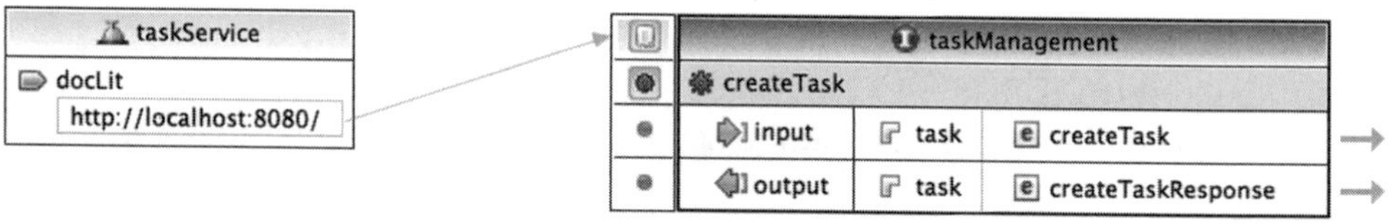

Figure 5.1 Simple task manager service

Figure 5.1 shows a simple outline of the service definition, visualized using Eclipse Web Service Toolkit. It was generated from the WSDL document given in listing 5.10.

Listing 5.10 WSDL describing our task manager service

```
<?xml version="1.0" encoding="utf-8"?>
<definitions name='taskService'
 targetNamespace='http://example.com/taskManager'
 xmlns='http://schemas.xmlsoap.org/wsdl/'
 xmlns:tns='http://example.com/taskManager'
 xmlns:xsd='http://www.w3.org/2001/XMLSchema'
 xmlns:soap='http://schemas.xmlsoap.org/wsdl/soap/'>
<types>
  <xsd:schema elementFormDefault='unqualified'
     targetNamespace='http://example.com/taskManager'>
    <xsd:element name='createTask'>
      <xsd:complexType>
        <xsd:sequence>
          <xsd:element name='title' type='xsd:string'/>
          <xsd:element name='priority' type='xsd:int' minOccurs='0'/>
        </xsd:sequence>
      </xsd:complexType>
    </xsd:element>
    <xsd:element name='createTaskResponse'>
      <xsd:complexType>
        <xsd:sequence>
```

```
        <xsd:element name='id' type='xsd:string'/>
      </xsd:sequence>
    </xsd:complexType>
  </xsd:element>
  </xsd:schema>
</types>

<message name='createTask'>
 <part name='task' element='tns:createTask'/>
</message>
<message name='createTaskResponse'>
 <part name='task' element='tns:createTaskResponse'/>
</message>

<portType name='taskManagement'>
 <operation name='createTask'>
   <input message='tns:createTask'/>
   <output message='tns:createTaskResponse'/>
 </operation>
</portType>

<binding name='taskManagementDocLit' type='tns:taskManagement'>
 <soap:binding transport='http://schemas.xmlsoap.org/soap/http'
     style='document' />
 <operation name='createTask'>
  <soap:operation style='document' />
  <input>
    <soap:body use='literal'/>
  </input>
  <output>
    <soap:body use='literal'/>
  </output>
 </operation>
</binding>

<service name='taskService'>
 <port name='docLit' binding='tns:taskManagementDocLit'>
   <soap:address location='http://localhost:8080/'/>
 </port>
</service>
</definitions>
```

Like any full-featured stack, SOAP4R allows us to work directly with SOAP messages using the low-level SOAP object model, and to do our own routing between incoming messages and application components. Even for our simple example, doing that would be tedious, so instead we'll use the WSDL service definition to create a service skeleton and extend it with the application logic.

We'll start by creating a working directory for the server side, and run the wsdl2ruby.rb command-line tool to create the service skeleton files:

```
$ mkdir server
$ cd server
$ wsdl2ruby.rb --wsdl ../taskService.wsdl --type server --module TaskManager
```

Now let's have a look at the generated files.

The first file, taskService.rb defines a class called `TaskManagement`. The name comes from the `portType`, and you will notice that SOAP4R capitalizes the first letter, since Ruby class names are CamelCase. It defines a single operation for creating a new task. When you look at the source code, you will notice that it specifies the input and output messages with all their message parts (one each, in this case), the declared faults (of which we have none), and the document encoding in use. All that information comes from the WSDL document and is used to configure SOAP4R.

The second file, taskServiceMappingRegistry.rb defines mapping between the XML elements used in the messages and the Ruby classes holding that data. As SOAP messages come in, they get converted into Ruby objects that our application can easily handle. In this case, the `createTask` element is parsed to instantiate a `CreateTask` object. Likewise, the `CreateTaskResponse` object we return from the method will convert into a `createTaskResponse` element to be sent back in the response message.

Notice that this file contains two mapping registries, one called EncodedRegistry (SOAP encoding) and one called LiteralRegistry (literal encoding). Since we specified doc/lit, only the second mapping is defined and used.

The third file, taskServiceServant.rb contains the actual service skeleton. SOAP4R refers to it as "servant," which simply means the logic behind the service interface. The file defines a single method in the `TaskManagement` class that returns a fault. It's this skeleton file that we're going to fill up with application logic to implement the task manager service.

We're going to keep this example very simple. We'll specify a couple of classes, `CreateTask` and `CreateTaskResponse`, to hold the request and response messages, and implement the `createTask` method to create a new task record in the database and return the task identifier. You can see the full service implementation in listing 5.11.

Listing 5.11   Our task manager servant

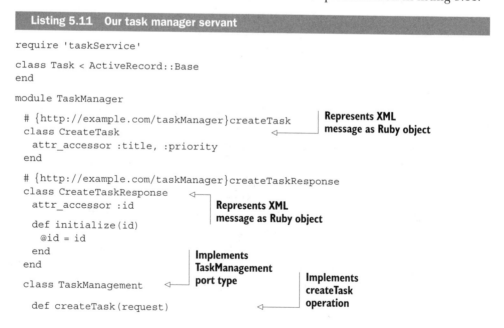

```
require 'taskService'

class Task < ActiveRecord::Base
end

module TaskManager

  # {http://example.com/taskManager}createTask
  class CreateTask                                    ◁——— Represents XML message as Ruby object
    attr_accessor :title, :priority
  end

  # {http://example.com/taskManager}createTaskResponse
  class CreateTaskResponse       ◁——┐
    attr_accessor :id                  Represents XML message as Ruby object

    def initialize(id)
      @id = id
    end
  end
                                     Implements TaskManagement port type
  class TaskManagement   ◁——┘
                                                  Implements createTask operation
    def createTask(request)   ◁——┘
```

```
    task = Task.create :title=>request.title, :priority=>request.priority
    return CreateTaskResponse.new(task.id)
  end

 end

end
```

The common practice is building a number of services (or servants) and configuring a web server to host them all, exposing each one on a different endpoint URL. For this example, though, we only have one service, so we'll use the quick prototype standalone server provided by taskService.rb. In addition to the service definition, this file defines a standalone server application called `TaskManagementApp`. The only thing we need to do is start it (see listing 5.12).

Listing 5.12 A simple task manager SOAP service

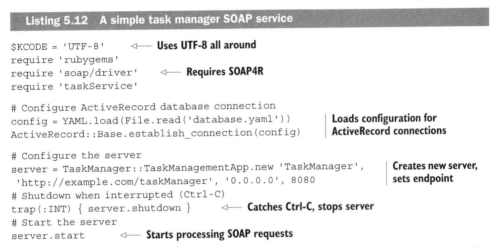

```
$KCODE = 'UTF-8'                 <-- Uses UTF-8 all around
require 'rubygems'
require 'soap/driver'            <-- Requires SOAP4R
require 'taskService'

# Configure ActiveRecord database connection
config = YAML.load(File.read('database.yaml'))          | Loads configuration for
ActiveRecord::Base.establish_connection(config)         | ActiveRecord connections

# Configure the server
server = TaskManager::TaskManagementApp.new 'TaskManager',     | Creates new server,
 'http://example.com/taskManager', '0.0.0.0', 8080             | sets endpoint
# Shutdown when interrupted (Ctrl-C)
trap(:INT) { server.shutdown }        <-- Catches Ctrl-C, stops server
# Start the server
server.start          <-- Starts processing SOAP requests
```

We're almost ready to run. We're using ActiveRecord to access the database, so we also need to specify the database connection configuration. We'll do that in a separate file called database.yaml, which for our database setup looks like this:

```
adapter: mysql
host:  localhost
username: dev
password: dev
database: task
```

Using ActiveRecord outside of Rails

ActiveRecord is a key piece of the Rails puzzle and provides the model part of the Model-View-Controller (MVC) design pattern, mapping Ruby objects to database tables. It's also an outstanding object-relational mapping framework on its own, and you can, as many developers do, use it outside of Rails. All it takes is installing the ActiveRecord gem, requiring it from your application, and using `establish_connection` to configure the database connection.

Now let's start the server:

```
$ ruby server.rb
```

We'll write a client application that uses this service in the next section, so keep the service running and you can test the client application against it.

Discussion

We showed you how easy it is to get started developing SOAP services with Ruby. Before we move to the next section, there are a few more things you'll need to know when building real live services.

SOAP4R comes in two flavors. It's part of the Ruby standard library available in your Ruby installation, and it is also available as a packaged gem that you can install from the public gem repository at http://RubyForge.org.

Like any standard library, SOAP4R gets updated with major releases of the Ruby runtime, and as we're writing this book, Ruby 1.8.6 is the predominant runtime shipping with SOAP4R 1.5.5. The gem version is updated more frequently and is currently at version 1.5.8 and pushing toward 1.6. We recommend you stay up with the latest enhancements and bug fixes by installing and using the SOAP4R gem in your environment.

If your service is sending and receiving text in languages other than English, you should consider using UTF-8 encoding. In our experience, it is far easier to use UTF-8 encoding all around than to switch encoding for each document or message. The Ruby global variable $KCODE specifies the default encoding used by the runtime, and SOAP4R picks up on it as the default encoding, so make sure to set $KCODE to UTF8 before requiring SOAP4R.

Our example was simple enough that we wrote the XML Schema type definitions inline, but for larger services you'll want to create separate type libraries and reuse these definitions across multiple services. This is fairly easy to do by aggregating them into XML Schema documents and importing those documents into various WSDLs. You will also want to use another SOAP4R tool called xsd2ruby.rb to read these XML Schema documents and create XML/Ruby mapping files, which you can then reuse in your code.

We did rapid prototyping by letting SOAP4R create a simple standalone server that uses WEBrick, the default web server that ships with Ruby. That's good enough for development and testing, but for production you should consider using Mongrel instead. The easiest way is to install the mongrel-soap4r gem, which lets you configure Mongrel for hosting SOAP4R services.

We cannot complete this section without mentioning ActionWebService. It's a lightweight framework on top of SOAP4R designed specifically for use inside Rails applications. It's particularly useful if you want to expose SOAP services as part of a Rails application, and it lets you implement the service operations inside your controllers. You can also use it to invoke SOAP services from within a Rails application.

ActionWebService is also a good fit if you prefer code-first service development and want to define your services from working code. It has a simple, declarative API that feels very similar to the annotations used in J2EE and .Net. We like the

ActionWebService API, but we prefer contract-first design, especially when using SOAP across different languages and platforms, which is why we wrote this example using WSDL and SOAP4R.

Now let's turn our attention to service invocation and write a SOAP client to invoke the task manager service.

5.3.2   Invoking the service

The promise of services is reuse, which emphasizes the client side of the application. In this section, we'll show you how to write a client application to use the task manager service, and not surprisingly, it will be easier and quicker to write than the service itself.

Problem

You want to develop a client application that can use the task manager service described in the WSDL document.

Solution

In the previous section, we showed you how to use SOAP4R and a WSDL file to implement a simple task manager service. In this section, we'll use the same WSDL document to create two clients for that service.

SOAP4R refers to client stubs as "drivers," and for legacy reasons the base class for all drivers is called `SOAP::RPC::Driver`. But don't get confused—that same driver will also support doc/lit services like the one we're using here.

Since we already have a WSDL service definition, we'll use `WSDLDriverFactory` to create a new driver for the task manager service:

```
wsdl = File.expand_path('taskService.wsdl')
SOAP::WSDLDriverFactory.new(wsdl).create_rpc_driver
```

The driver reads the WSDL service definition and adds all the operations available to the service, along with the endpoint URL and protocol bindings, so we can immediately begin using it. Messages are mapped from their internal SOAP representation to Ruby hashes:

```
response = driver.createTask(:title=>'Learn SOAP4R', :priority=>1)
puts "Created task #{response['id']}"
```

That's all there is to it. We can start adding more operations to our WSDL, create more complex message definitions, all the while using the same basic patterns. You can see the entire client application in listing 5.13.

Listing 5.13   Task manager client using WSDLDriver

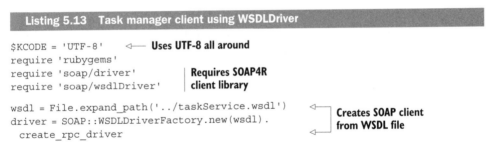

```
$KCODE = 'UTF-8'      ⟵── Uses UTF-8 all around
require 'rubygems'
require 'soap/driver'          Requires SOAP4R
require 'soap/wsdlDriver'      client library

wsdl = File.expand_path('../taskService.wsdl')   ⟵┐  Creates SOAP client
driver = SOAP::WSDLDriverFactory.new(wsdl).        │  from WSDL file
  create_rpc_driver                              ⟵┘
```

```
response = driver.createTask(:title=>'Learn SOAP4R',
                            :priority=>1)
puts "Created task #{response['id']}"
```
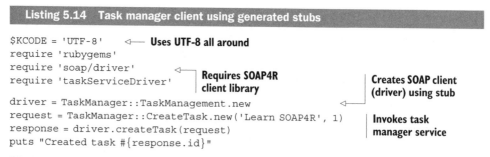
Invokes task
manager service

SOAP::RPC::Driver can also map SOAP messages to and from Ruby objects, and when working with larger and more complex operations we prefer that, so the next step is to generate these mappings. Instead of doing it ourselves, we'll turn again to the wsdl2ruby.rb command-line tool:

```
$ mkdir client
$ cd client
$ wsdl2ruby.rb --wsdl ../taskService.wsdl --type client --module TaskManager
```

Let's have a look at the generated files.

The first file, taskService.rb, defines Ruby classes to represent each element we use in our messages, so in the source code are ready definitions for CreateTask and CreateTaskResponse.

The second file, taskServiceMappingRegistry.rb, specifies the mapping between XML elements and these Ruby classes. We covered that mapping in the previous section, when we showed how it is used by the service.

The third file, taskServiceDriver.rb, defines TaskManagement, again using the portType name for the class name, with the single operation we defined in the WSDL. It also includes a basic driver implementation that loads all the mappings and remembers the default endpoint URL. As before, all that information comes from the WSDL and is used here to configure SOAP4R, and once we generate this stub, we no longer need to reference the WSDL file.

Listing 5.14 shows how we would use the TaskManagement driver with the typed message parts in place of the WSDL driver and hashes.

Listing 5.14 Task manager client using generated stubs

```
$KCODE = 'UTF-8'    ◁── Uses UTF-8 all around
require 'rubygems'
require 'soap/driver'
require 'taskServiceDriver'      Requires SOAP4R
                                 client library
driver = TaskManager::TaskManagement.new                 Creates SOAP client
                                                         (driver) using stub
request = TaskManager::CreateTask.new('Learn SOAP4R', 1)
response = driver.createTask(request)                    Invokes task
puts "Created task #{response.id}"                        manager service
```

Discussion

There are several strategies for working with SOAP services. If you're building an infrastructure piece, you may need to work with the bare metal, using the SOAP object model (classes like SOAPBody and SOAPString) to create and parse messages directly, making dynamic invocations using a generic invoke method. If you're building business applications, you'll want to work at a higher level of abstraction by using WSDL. WSDL documents help you define the service contract, from which you can quickly build client stubs and server skeletons that handle all the details of XML and messaging.

We advocate contract-first design and keeping your services compliant with WS-I Basic Profile as the way to build services that interoperate across J2EE, .Net, Ruby, and many other platforms and languages.

Deploying Ruby services on Java/C WS stacks

At the time of this writing, a few alternatives are emerging for building and deploying SOAP services using Ruby. Unfortunately, these are so new that we did not get a chance to cover them in this book.

One interesting possibility is to use JRuby and scripting support in Java 1.6 to deploy Ruby services on any number of Java-based WS stacks. One example we've seen is based on Axis2, another uses the Tuscany project (an SCA container that allows you to mix services written in different languages). If you prefer using Ruby MRI, have a look at C-based WS stacks that offer Ruby bindings, such as the Ruby bindings for Axis/C, provided by WS02, the lead developer of Axis.

5.4   *Summary*

In this chapter, we've shown you what you need to know to get started building web services with Ruby. We covered the basics of the web architecture using open-uri and Net::HTTP, how to build RESTful web services using Rails, and how to exchange messages using the SOAP protocol.

There are a few more libraries worth mentioning. This is Ruby, after all, and a lot of developers new to Ruby are surprised to find out how many libraries already exist for handling common tasks.

Want to talk to eBay's web services? eBay4R is the easiest way to get started. How about Amazon's on-demand services? Ruby has libraries for using Amazon S3, EC2, SQS, and SimpleDB. SAP NetWeaver? Have a look at sapnwrfc, optimized for NetWeaver web services. SalesForce? You can use the low-level RForce, or if you're much more comfortable with ActiveRecord, have a look at ActiveSalesForce.

We'll show you another example when we talk about asynchronous messaging in chapter 7 and integrate our internal business application with a web service, using WMQ and ActiveSalesForce. But first, we'll talk about automating communication, starting with e-mail and IM in the next chapter.

Automating communication

With the proliferation of communication technologies like the telephone, the internet, and cell phones, people are more connected than ever before, and recent software advances have allowed us to automate these communications: electronic call center menus, widespread email, instant messaging (IM) bots, and so on. This sort of communications automation software can make your life much easier when it comes to handling interactions with coworkers, employees, and customers. For example, you might want to send out an email to 500 customers when their product has shipped. As invisible and minor as this software seems, it is a very big piece of the infrastructure of modern businesses.

In this chapter, we'll look at techniques for creating this sort of software, looking at code examples extracted from real systems doing this sort of work every day.

We'll start by looking at email, discussing how to send, receive, and process it. Then we'll take a look at some instant communication mediums, such as AOL Instant Messenger (AIM) and Jabber.

6.1   *Automating email*

Email is one of the most popular technologies on the web today, but, thanks to spammers, the concept of "automated email dispersion" has bad connotations, even though this sort of mechanism is probably one of the most common internet applications. It's often used in consumer applications. Purchased a product from an online shop? Chances are you've received an automatically generated email message. Signed up for a new service lately? You've probably received an activation notice via email.

But these are all business-to-consumer use cases. What about automating email for things like your continuous integration server or process-monitoring software? You can use email as a powerful way to alert or update people about the state of a system. You could also use automated email reception for tasks like creating new tickets in your development ticketing system or setting up autoresponders for email addresses (for example, a user sends an email to autoresponse@yourdomain.com, and then emails are automatically responded to with the message in the body for that address). Email's ubiquity makes it a powerful tool for communication in your Ruby applications, and in this section we'll show you how to harness email to do your (Ruby-powered) bidding. We'll cover the basics, like sending and receiving, and then look at processing email with Ruby.

Let's first take a look at your options for sending email messages with Ruby.

6.1.1   *Automating sending email*

Ruby has a few options for sending email messages. First, there's a built-in library, Net::SMTP, which is very flexible but also very difficult to use compared with others. There are also other high-level solutions such as TMail or Action Mailer (built on top of TMail), which work just fine, but we've found that a gem named MailFactory works the best. MailFactory gives you nice facilities for creating email messages while requiring very little in the way of dependencies.

> ### Testing SMTP
> If you don't have an SMTP server like Sendmail handy, then Mailtrap is for you. Written by Matt Mowers, Mailtrap is a "fake" SMTP server that will write (or "trap") the messages to a text file rather than sending them. You can grab Mailtrap via Ruby-Gems (`gem install mailtrap`) or download it and find out more at rubyforge.org/projects/rubymatt/.

Problem

You need to automate sending email from your Ruby application to alert your system administrators when Apache crashes.

Solution

Ruby's built-in SMTP library is fairly low-level, at least in the sense that it makes you feed it a properly formatted SMTP message rather than building it for you. MailFactory is a library (available via RubyGems) that helps you generate a properly formatted message, which you can then send via the built-in SMTP library.

Creating a message with MailFactory is as simple as creating a `MailFactory` object, setting the proper attributes, and then getting the object's string value, a properly formatted SMTP message. Listing 6.1 shows a short example.

Listing 6.1 Constructing a basic `MailFactory` object, attribute by attribute

```
mail = MailFactory.new              ⟵── Creates new MailFactory
mail.text = "This is the message!"
mail.subject = "Re: Ruby in Practice"
mail.from = "Jeremy <jeremy@rubyinpractice.com>"    Sets message
mail.replyto = "Assaf <assaf@rubyinpractice.com>"   attributes
mail.to = "You <you@yourdomain.com>"

mail.to_s                                    ⟵┐   Converts to formatted
# => [Your properly formatted SMTP message]   ┘   SMTP message
```

As you can see, setting up a `MailFactory` object is fairly straightforward: instantiate, populate, and output the message to a string.

Now, all you need to do is feed the message to Net::SMTP to send it. To send an email to your system administration team every time your Apache web server process crashes, you just need to build a MailFactory object, giving it a string of recipients, and then send it via Net::SMTP. Listing 6.2 shows our implementation.

Listing 6.2 Sending email to administrators

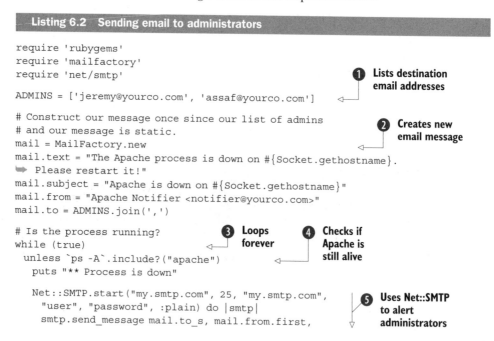

```
require 'rubygems'
require 'mailfactory'
require 'net/smtp'                                    ❶ Lists destination
                                                         email addresses
ADMINS = ['jeremy@yourco.com', 'assaf@yourco.com']  ⟵┘

# Construct our message once since our list of admins   ❷ Creates new
# and our message is static.                               email message
mail = MailFactory.new                               ⟵┘
mail.text = "The Apache process is down on #{Socket.gethostname}.
➥ Please restart it!"
mail.subject = "Apache is down on #{Socket.gethostname}"
mail.from = "Apache Notifier <notifier@yourco.com>"
mail.to = ADMINS.join(',')

# Is the process running?          ❸ Loops      ❹ Checks if
while (true)                     ⟵┘  forever       Apache is
  unless `ps -A`.include?("apache")  ⟵┘            still alive
    puts "** Process is down"

    Net::SMTP.start("my.smtp.com", 25, "my.smtp.com",    ❺ Uses Net::SMTP
      "user", "password", :plain) do |smtp|                 to alert
      smtp.send_message mail.to_s, mail.from.first,         administrators
```

```
                  mail.to          ⑤  Uses Net::SMTP to
      end                              alert administrators
    end

    sleep 5
  end
```

First, we build an array of administrator email addresses **❶**. Then we use this and other information to build the `MailFactory` object **❷**. Next, we constantly loop like a daemon **❸** (we could also take this out and run the script in a `cron` job or something like that), grabbing the output of `ps` **❹** and checking it for the term "apache." If it's not found, we send a mail to the administrators using Net::SMTP **❺**. The `start` method takes parameters for the SMTP server address and port, the "from" domain, your username and password, and the authentication scheme (could be `:plain`, `:login`, or `:cram_md5`). An SMTP object is then yielded to the block, which we can call methods on to send email messages (e.g., `send_message`).

Discussion

We like to use MailFactory to build the SMTP message like this, but it's not required. If you're comfortable building properly formatted messages or are grabbing the messages from another source, MailFactory isn't required. There are also alternatives to MailFactory, like TMail, which both generates and parses email messages. You don't even have to use the built-in library for sending messages; if you're really masochistic, you could just use a `TCPSocket` and talk SMTP directly!

> **SMS messages**
>
> A lot of cell phone carriers let you send SMS messages via email. This is a cheap and efficient way to reach people instantly when one of the options discussed later isn't available.

One thing to note about our example is that it likely won't work on Windows. The `ps` utility is a *nix-specific utility, which means that if you're on Linux, Solaris, or Mac OS X, you should be fine, but if you're on Windows, you're out of luck. If you really want to implement something like this on Windows, you can take a few other routes. One is to use one of the many WMI facilities available, either through the `win32` library or one of the other WMI-specific packages. You could also seek out a `ps` alternative on Windows, many of which are available if you just do a web search for them.

If these approaches strike you as too low-level, then Action Mailer might be for you. Action Mailer is Ruby on Rails' email library, and it offers a lot of niceties that other approaches don't. This isn't a book all about Rails, so we won't go into Action Mailer here, but if you're interested, you can check out a book dedicated to Rails or the Action Mailer documentation at am.rubyonrails.org.

Now that you're familiar with sending email with Ruby, let's take a look at receiving it.

6.1.2   *Receiving email*

Ruby has built-in libraries for both POP3 and IMAP reception of messages, but unfortunately they're not API-compatible with one another. In this section, we're only interested in processing incoming emails quickly. We don't intend to keep them around, so we don't need the more advanced IMAP.

We're going to concentrate on the POP3 library (Net::POP3), but if you're interested, the example is available for the IMAP library in the downloadable source code for this book.

Problem

You need to perform actions at a distance, like being able to restart the MySQL server when away from the office. You don't always have SSH access, but you can always email from a cell phone.

Solution

Ruby's POP3 library, Net::POP3, is fairly simple to operate. To grab the messages from your inbox, you simply use the `start` method on the `Net::POP3` class and manipulate the object given to its block. Check out the example in listing 6.3.

Listing 6.3   Fetching email using POP3

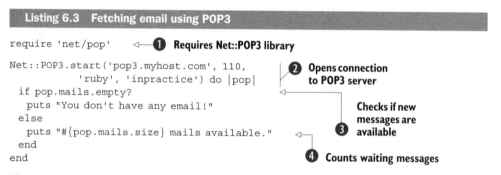

```
require 'net/pop'        ←─❶  Requires Net::POP3 library

Net::POP3.start('pop3.myhost.com', 110,          Opens connection
           'ruby', 'inpractice') do |pop|    ❷  to POP3 server
  if pop.mails.empty?
    puts "You don't have any email!"              Checks if new
  else                                            messages are
    puts "#{pop.mails.size} mails available."  ❸  available
  end
end                                          ❹  Counts waiting messages
```

Net::POP3, like Net::SMTP and all other Net modules, is part of the Ruby standard library, which ships with every Ruby implementation. Unlike core library modules (like String, Array, and File) you have to require standard library modules in order to use them ❶. Once you've gotten the library properly in place, you can take a few approaches to getting your mail. You could instantiate an object and work with it, but we think our approach here (using the class method and a block) is cleaner and more concise ❷. The parameters for the `start` method are the connection's credentials: host, port, login, and password. Next, we interact with the object yielded to the block to see how many messages are present in the current fetch. If there are no email messages, we output a message indicating as much ❸, but otherwise we output how many messages were found ❹.

For this problem, we need to set up a system that will restart a MySQL server when a message is sent to a specific email address with the subject "Restart MySQL." To build a system like that, we need to grab the emails from the address's inbox, iterate through them, and check each message for "Restart MySQL" in the subject. You can see our implementation in listing 6.4.

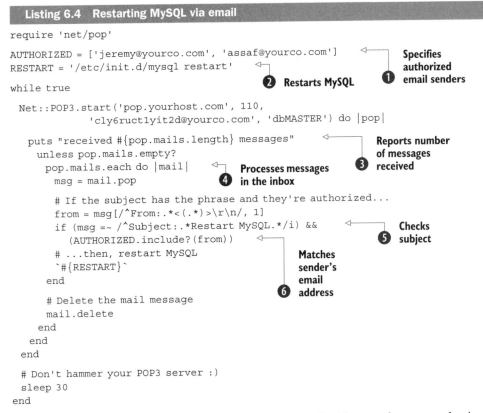

Listing 6.4   Restarting MySQL via email

```
require 'net/pop'

AUTHORIZED = ['jeremy@yourco.com', 'assaf@yourco.com']          ◁       Specifies
RESTART = '/etc/init.d/mysql restart'       ◁                            authorized
                                        ❷ Restarts MySQL        ❶      email senders
while true

  Net::POP3.start('pop.yourhost.com', 110,
            'cly6ruct1yit2d@yourco.com', 'dbMASTER') do |pop|

    puts "received #{pop.mails.length} messages"          ◁       Reports number
      unless pop.mails.empty?                                     of messages
        pop.mails.each do |mail|       ◁                  ❸      received
          msg = mail.pop           ❹ Processes messages
                                        in the inbox
          # If the subject has the phrase and they're authorized...
          from = msg[/^From:.*<(.*)>\r\n/, 1]
          if (msg =~ /^Subject:.*Restart MySQL.*/i) &&    ◁       Checks
             (AUTHORIZED.include?(from))       ◁           ❺      subject
            # ...then, restart MySQL                Matches
            `#{RESTART}`                            sender's
          end                                       email
                                             ❻      address
          # Delete the mail message
          mail.delete
        end
      end
  end

  # Don't hammer your POP3 server :)
  sleep 30
end
```

First, we set up a couple of constants: one for the email addresses that are authorized to restart MySQL ❶, and one for the command we'll use to restart MySQL ❷. Next, we output a message telling how many messages we've received ❸. We then iterate through the messages ❹, checking for the proper subject ❺ and From address ❻. If the sender is authorized and the subject contains "Restart MySQL," we run RESTART and MySQL is restarted. Having read the message, we discard it and sleep for 30 seconds before checking to see if another message is waiting for us.

Discussion

The production system that this solution is based on had a few more things that administrators could do via email, such as managing indexes and creating databases. It also allowed administrators to send multiple commands per email. But we decided to strip this solution down to give you a base to work from that you can expand or completely change to suit your whim. You could change this to manage other long-running processes, execute one-off jobs, or even send other emails out.

You're probably wondering about security. We wanted to make it possible to send an email from any device, specifically from cell phones. Even the simplest of cell phones lets you send short emails, usually by sending a text message (SMS) to that address instead of a phone number. You can try it out yourself if you have any email addresses in your phone book.

Unfortunately, cell phones won't allow you to digitally sign emails, so we can't rely on public/private key authentication. We can't rely on the sender's address either, because those are too easy to guess and forge. Instead, we used a unique inbox address that can survive a brute force attack and gave it only to our administrators. We kept this example short, but in a real application we'd expect better access control by giving each administrator his own private inbox address and an easy way to change it, should he lose his phone.

In spite of that, it's always a good idea to double-check the sender's address. We'll want our task to send back an email response, letting the administrator know it completed successfully. And sometimes these responses come bouncing back, so we'll need a simple way to detect administrator requests and ignore bouncing messages, or we'll end up with a loop that keeps restarting the server over and over.

POP3 is usually good enough for most instances, but on some networks APOP (Authenticated POP) is required. If your host uses APOP authentication, you can give the `start` command a fifth Boolean parameter to indicate that Net::POP3 should use APOP. If we wanted to enable APOP on our previous example, the call to the `start` method would look something like this:

```
Net::POP3.start('pop.yourhost.com', 110,
                'cly6ruct1yit2d@yourco.com', 'dbMASTER', true)
```

In this example, we extracted information from the raw POP message using regular expressions. This works for simple cases, like what we've done here, but as your needs get more complicated, the viability of this approach breaks down. In the next section, we'll take a look at a much more robust solution to email processing: the TMail library.

6.1.3 *Processing email*

Now that you know how to send and receive email, you can start thinking about how to leverage these techniques to solve bigger problems. In this section, we'll combine these two techniques and take a look at one subsystem in a production ticketing system.

Problem

You have a ticketing system built with Rails. It's running great, but creating tickets is a bit laborious, so you want to allow users to open tickets via email. You need to process and respond to ticket-creation email messages in your Ruby application.

Solution

The smartest flow for the new ticket-creation system seems to be to receive an email, process its contents, put the relevant data in an instance of your model, and delete the mail. Then, pull the model on the front end with a web interface. So, we'll assume you have a `Ticket` model like the following:

```
class Ticket < ActiveRecord::Base
  has_many :responses
end
```

Listing 6.5 shows our implementation of the mail-handling script. We'll analyze it piece by piece.

Listing 6.5   Creating tickets via email

```ruby
require 'net/pop'
require 'tmail'
require 'net/smtp'

while true
  Net::POP3.start('mail.yourhost.com', 110,          ❶ Connects to POP3 server
    'tickets@yourco.com', 't1xeTz') do |pop|
    unless pop.mails.empty?

      # Iterate each mail                        ❷ Processes each
      pop.mails.each do |mail|                      new email
        # Parse the email we received                    ❸ Parses email
        ticket_mail = TMail::Mail.parse(mail.pop)            header and body

        # Create a new Ticket instance
        new_ticket = Ticket.new
        new_ticket.owner = ticket_mail.from
        new_ticket.subject = ticket_mail.subject       ❹ Creates database
        new_ticket.text = ticket_mail.body                record from email
        new_ticket.save

        # Create and send the new email
        new_mail = TMail::Mail.new        ❺ Sends response email
        new_mail.to = ticket_mail.from
        new_mail.from = 'Jeremy <jeremy@jeremymcanally.com>'
        new_mail.subject = "Ticket Created! :: #{ticket_mail.subject}"
        new_mail.date = Time.now
        new_mail.mime_version = '1.0'
        new_mail.set_content_type 'text', 'plain'
        new_mail.body = "A new ticket has been created for
➥ you.\n===========\n\n#{ticket_mail.body}\n\nThanks!"

        Net::SMTP.start('my.smtp.com', 25, 'my.smtp.com',
                    'user', 'password', :plain) do |smtp|
          smtp.send_message new_mail.encoded, new_mail.from,
                        new_mail.to
        end

        # Delete the received mail message
        mail.delete
      end

    end
  end

  sleep 30
end
```

In this implementation, we first receive our email messages using Net::POP3 ❶. Then we iterate through the messages ❷ and use TMail's message-parsing abilities to get a usable object with attributes ❸. We then create a new instance of our ActiveRecord model, Ticket ❹, and populate it with the data from the email. Finally, we use TMail to build a new email object (notice the API similarities to MailFactory) ❺, and send that email using Net::SMTP.

Discussion

TMail is available as a standalone gem (`gem install tmail`), but you'll also find it as part of the standard Rails distribution, included in the Action Mailer module. Action Mailer itself is a wrapper around TMail and Net::SMTP that uses the Rails framework for configuration and template-based email generation. You can learn more about Action Mailer from the Rails documentation. In this particular example, the email message was simple enough that we didn't need to generate it from a template, and we chose to use TMail directly.

NOTE   *Astrotrain*   Jeremy's coworkers at entp have written a great tool named Astrotrain, which turns emails into HTTP posts or Jabber messages for further processing. You can send an email to my_token_1234@ yourhost.com and get a post to something like http://yourhost.com/ update/?token=my_ token&hash=1234. You can find out more and get the source at http://hithub.com/entp/astrotrain/tree/master.

Now that you have a solid grasp of automating email, let's take a look at another problem domain in communication automation: instant messaging.

6.2   *Automating instant communication*

Sometimes, email just isn't quick enough. Thanks to technologies like online chat and instant messaging, we can now be connected directly with one another, chatting instantly. And the ubiquity of technologies like AIM, Jabber, and others finally make them a viable solution for business communication. Automating these sorts of communications opens up interesting possibilities: customer service bots, instant notification from your continuous integration system, and so on.

This section will concentrate on using two of the most popular options for instant communication: AIM and Jabber.

6.2.1   *Sending messages with AIM*

Once released independently of the America Online dial-up client, the IM component of the AOL system quickly became one of the most popular systems for private messaging. It might not have the same tech appeal as Jabber or GTalk, but it's an instant messaging workhorse that commands half the market share and is used for both personal and business accounts. Contacting users or employees through AIM is a good way to make sure your communication is heard as quickly as possible.

Problem

You need to send server information via instant messages using AIM.

Solution

The Net::TOC library (`gem install net-toc`) provides a very flexible API for interacting with the AIM service. The first approach you can take to using it is a simple, procedural connect/send/disconnect approach. Listing 6.6 shows an example of sending an IM.

Listing 6.6   Sending an IM with Net::TOC

```
require 'rubygems'
require 'net/toc'
```

```
client = Net::TOC.new('yourbot', 'p@$$w0rd')
client.connect
```
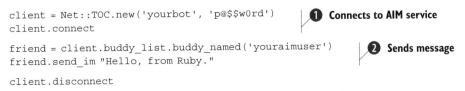 **①** **Connects to AIM service**

```
friend = client.buddy_list.buddy_named('youraimuser')
friend.send_im "Hello, from Ruby."
```
② **Sends message**

```
client.disconnect
```

First, we create an object and connect to the AIM service **①**. Then we find a user (in this case, "youraimuser"), send a simple message **②**, and disconnect from AIM. This approach works well when you're simply sending messages, but it gets awkward when you want to deal with incoming messages.

Fortunately, Net::TOC has a nice callback mechanism that allows you to respond to events pretty easily. These events range from an IM being received to a user becoming available. See table 6.1 for a full listing.

Table 6.1 A full listing of the Net::TOC callbacks

Callback	Description
`on_error { |err| }`	Called when an error occurs. Use this to provide your own error-handling logic.
`on_im { |message, buddy, auto_response| }`	Called when an IM is received; parameters include IM message and sender. Use this to receive and respond to messages.
`friend.on_status(status) { }`	Called when the given friend's status changes; the `status` parameter should be one of the following: `:available`, `:online`, `:idle`, `:away`. Use this to track when friends go online or offline and to see changes in their status message.

These callbacks make interactions with users much cleaner than if you tried to shoehorn them into the sequential method. Let's say you wanted to get information from a server simply by sending an IM to an AIM bot. Listing 6.7 shows an implementation using Net::TOC's callbacks.

Listing 6.7 Sending the results of uptime over AIM

```
require 'rubygems'
require 'net/toc'

def get_server_information
  <<-TXT
uptime
------
#{`uptime`}

disk information
----------------
#{`df -k`}\n
  TXT
end

client = Net::TOC.new("youruser", "pa$zWu2d")

client.on_im do | message, buddy |
  friend = client.buddy_list.
```
① **Returns information about server**

② **Callback responds to new IMs**

```
➡ buddy_named(buddy.screen_name)
   friend.send_im(get_server_information)          ❷ Callback responds
 end                                                   to new IMs

client.connect
client.wait      ⟵—❸  Starts waiting for new IMs
```

To get the server information, we create a `get_server_information` method ❶.
Next, we use the `on_im` callback to respond to any IMs we receive ❷. The callbacks
basically function as a declarative way to define behavior when something happens,
and, as you can see here, the block we provide will be called when an IM is received.
When this happens, the buddy is found (to get a `Net::TOC::Buddy` object) and an IM
is sent via the `send_im` method. Finally, once the callback is set up, we connect and
wait for IMs to come in to fire the callback ❸.

Discussion

Little bots and automations like this are becoming more and more popular. Developers are beginning to realize the potential uses for them: information lookups, customer management, workflows, and so on. Many IRC channels for open source
packages (including Ruby on Rails) now have IRC bots that will give you access to a
project's API by simply sending a message like "api ActionController#render." Developers looking for a solution to handle peer and management approval in code reviews
or to alert their coworkers of Subversion activity could use an AIM bot like this one.

If you're interested in embedding AIM chat features in a Rails application, your
options are slim and aren't very slick, but it is possible. We're not aware of any Rails
plugins that currently handle AIM communications dependably. The best way we've
found to handle this is to build an external daemon that you integrate with your Rails
application. For example, you could use the daemons gem to generate a daemon
script, give it full access to the Rails environment by including environment.rb, and
then run it along with your Rails application. This will allow your daemon to have
access to your application's models, making integration a snap.

If you find that the people you need to communicate with don't like AIM, you can
use libpurpl, the library that powers Pidgin, a multiprotocol chat client. There is a
Ruby gem named ruburple that hooks into libpurpl, but many people seem to experience sporadic success with building it. If you're able to build it, it's a great way to
access a number of chat protocols easily. If that doesn't work for you, you can also use
XMPP and Jabber to access other chat protocols. We'll talk about Jabber next.

6.2.2 *Automating Jabber*

Jabber is an open source IM platform. The great thing about Jabber is that you can have
your own private Jabber server, which you can keep private or link with other Jabber servers. So, you can have your own private IM network or be part of the public Jabbersphere.
In addition, XMPP (the Extensible Messaging and Presence Protocol that Jabber runs
on) offers a nice set of security features (via SASL and TLS). XMPP servers can also bridge
to other transports like AIM and Yahoo! IM. You can learn more about setting up and
maintaining your own Jabber server from the Jabber website at http://www.jabber.org/.

Problem

You want your administrators to be able to manage MySQL via Jabber messages sent from your Ruby application.

Solution

Ruby has a number of Jabber libraries, but the most advanced and best maintained is xmpp4r. In this section, we'll look at using a library built on top of xmpp4r named Jabber::Simple, which simplifies the development of Jabber clients in Ruby. You'll need to install both gems (xmpp4r and xmpp4r-simple) to use these examples.

Jabber and Rails

If you're interested in using Jabber with Rails, take a look at Action Messenger, which is a framework like Action Mailer but for IM rather than email. The Action Messenger home page is http://trypticon.org/software/actionmessenger/.

The process for interacting with Jabber is very similar to the process for interacting with AIM, but the API exposed in Jabber::Simple is slightly, well, simpler. Take a look at listing 6.8 for an example.

Listing 6.8   Building a simple `Jabber::Simple` object

```
require 'rubygems'                                         Connects to    Adds recipient
require 'xmpp4r-simple'                                    XMPP server    to roster

im = Jabber::Simple.new('you@jabberserver.com', 'p@s$')  ◁              Sends IM to
im.roster.add('them@jabberserver.com')                     ◁              recipient
im.deliver('them@jabberserver.com', "Hello from Ruby!")  ◁
```

First, we create a new `Jabber::Simple` object. When creating this object, you must provide your login credentials, and the account will be logged in. The new object is essentially an XMPP session with a nice API on top of it. The `roster` attribute provides an API to the logged-in account's contact list, which allows you to add and remove people. Finally, we use the `deliver` method to send a message to the person we added to this account's contact list.

Contact list authorization

When you add someone to an account's contact list, the person being added will have to authorize the addition of her account to your contact list. You can use the `subscript_requests` method to authorize requests for adding your bot. See the Jabber::Simple documentation for more information.

Jabber::Simple doesn't implement anything akin to the callbacks in Net::TOC, but the mechanism for receiving messages is fairly straightforward. As an example, let's say you wanted to expand on our earlier MySQL control service (from listing 6.4) to allow your administrators to stop, start, or restart the server over IM. Listing 6.9 shows one implementation of this script.

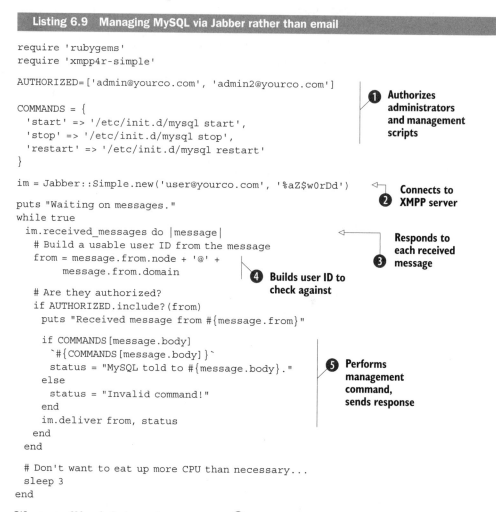

Listing 6.9   Managing MySQL via Jabber rather than email

```ruby
require 'rubygems'
require 'xmpp4r-simple'

AUTHORIZED=['admin@yourco.com', 'admin2@yourco.com']        ❶ Authorizes
                                                              administrators
COMMANDS = {                                                  and management
  'start' => '/etc/init.d/mysql start',                       scripts
  'stop' => '/etc/init.d/mysql stop',
  'restart' => '/etc/init.d/mysql restart'
}

im = Jabber::Simple.new('user@yourco.com', '%aZ$w0rDd')     ❷ Connects to
                                                               XMPP server
puts "Waiting on messages."
while true
  im.received_messages do |message|                         ❸ Responds to
    # Build a usable user ID from the message                  each received
    from = message.from.node + '@' +                           message
        message.from.domain
                                                            ❹ Builds user ID to
    # Are they authorized?                                     check against
    if AUTHORIZED.include?(from)
      puts "Received message from #{message.from}"

      if COMMANDS[message.body]
        `#{COMMANDS[message.body]}`
        status = "MySQL told to #{message.body}."           ❺ Performs
      else                                                     management
        status = "Invalid command!"                            command,
      end                                                       sends response
      im.deliver from, status
    end
  end

  # Don't want to eat up more CPU than necessary...
  sleep 3
end
```

We start off by defining a few constants ❶: AUTHORIZED is an Array of Jabber users that we permit to issue commands, and COMMANDS is a Hash of command sequences we'll use to control the MySQL server. Next, we create our Jabber::Simple object ❷ and call the received_messages method ❸. This method gives us an iterator that will yield each message received since the last received_messages call.

Now we need to figure out who sent us the message. The message.from attribute is actually a Jabber::JID object that gives us access to some of the internal Jabber data. Earlier in the chapter, we used email to administer MySQL, and we had to worry about spoofing the sender's address. XMPP uses server-to-server authentication to eliminate address spoofing, so we can trust the sender's identity. Since we need to know only the username and domain, we extract that and build a usable string ❹.

Next, we check to see if the user who sent us the message (now in `from`) is authorized to be doing so, and if so, we try to issue the command ❺. If they sent a bad command (i.e., not "start," "stop," or "restart"), we tell them so. Otherwise, we go to the next message or begin listening for new messages again.

Discussion

The Jabber::Simple library is nice, but if you like to get down to the bare metal, you could use xmpp4r directly. It offers a higher level API (not quite as high as Jabber::Simple, but tolerable), but it also gives you access to much of the underlying mechanics. This access could be useful if you're building custom extensions to XMPP or you want to do some sort of filtering on the traffic.

6.3 *Summary*

We've taken a look at a few approaches to communication automation in this chapter. Email automation has been in use for years in certain arenas, but we are seeing it expand out into more business applications (some of which were discussed here) and into the consumer world (with things like Highrise from 37signals and Twitter). AIM bots have been around for years (Jeremy can remember writing one in 1997!), but they're no longer exclusively in the territory of 13-year-olds and spammers—they've moved into the business-tool arena. Voice over IP (VOIP) seems to be moving in that same direction, with technologies like Asterisk and tools like Adhearsion.

All this is to say that we are beginning to see people use existing methods of communication in new and different ways. Fortunately, the Ruby community is constantly building new tools to work with these technologies, and many of them, like Adhearsion, are pioneers in their field. Another area where Ruby has pioneered is databases, where ActiveRecord and some of the new ORM libraries are pushing the boundaries of DSL usage in database programming.

Now that we have covered the use of email and instant messaging for automation, we'll turn our attention to technologies designed specifically for exchanging messages between applications, and we'll talk about asynchronous messaging using the open source ActiveMQ, big-iron WMQ, and Ruby's own reliable-msg.

Asynchronous messaging 7

> **This chapter covers**
> - Using ActiveMQ and Stomp
> - Using reliable-msg
> - Using WebSphere MQ

Asynchronous messaging is one of the most effective ways of building a loosely coupled system while maintaining a sense of coherence in the system. Coupling the publish/subscribe architecture with a reliable delivery broker gives you a solid architecture for integration with heterogeneous (or homogeneous) systems. In this chapter, we'll look at a few options for asynchronous messaging in Ruby, including how to integrate these solutions with Rails. We'll start with two open source messaging servers, ActiveMQ and Ruby-native reliable-msg, before moving on to WMQ, the granddaddy of message-oriented middleware.

7.1 Open source messaging servers

When building an application that requires asynchronous messaging, open source messaging servers are a compelling option. In this section, we'll take a look at two such options. The first, ActiveMQ (available from http://activemq.apache.org) is a Java-based messaging middleware developed by the Apache Software Foundation.

It's a popular mid-size solution attractive not only for its price tag (free!) but also for packing the right combination of features and performance while requiring minimal setup and administration. The second, reliable-msg, is a pure-Ruby implementation suitable for small-scale deployments.

You can connect to ActiveMQ in a variety of ways, including REST and XMPP, both of which we covered in previous chapters, or through the JMS API, an option that's available when deploying on JRuby (see appendix B). In this chapter, we're going to use Stomp, the Streaming Text Orientated Messaging Protocol. It's an open protocol that supports a variety of messaging brokers and programming languages, and, in combination with StompConnect, any messaging broker that supports the Java Message Service (JMS) API.

7.1.1 Using ActiveMQ

In this section, we'll look at using ActiveMQ with the stomp gem, a library that gives you the ability to interface with services over the Stomp protocol. Stomp offers a lightweight format for compatible clients to interact with message brokers. This means that although we're talking to ActiveMQ in this section, you could just as easily use the stomp gem with any Stomp-compatible message broker (a list of which is on the Stomp website at http://stomp.codehaus.org).

You first need to get your ActiveMQ instance installed and configured (see the ActiveMQ and Stomp websites for information on how to do that). You'll want to use RubyGems to install the stomp library:

```
$ gem install stomp
```

Problem

Your Ruby application needs to integrate with a monitoring service that uses a message broker to get information from the services it's monitoring.

Solution

The service we're integrating with processes error messages from the /queue/errors queue. It receives XML messages in a simple format:

```
<?xml version="1.0" encoding="UTF-8"?>
<error>
  <type>StandardError</type>
  <message>Something is broken.</message>
  <backtrace>
   NameError: uninitialized constant X
     from (irb):1
  </backtrace>
</error>
```

We're going to generate this XML document using Builder, which is the same library we used in chapter 5 to generate Atom feeds from a Rails application. Builder is available as a separate gem (gem install builder). You can see the method generating this XML document in listing 7.1.

Listing 7.1   A method that takes a Ruby error object and generates XML from it

```
def generate_xml(error_object)
  payload = ""

  builder = Builder::XmlMarkup.new(:target => payload)       ❶ Generates
  builder.instruct!                                            the payload

  builder.error do |error|                                   ❷ Writes
    error.type error_object.class.to_s                          document
    error.message error_object.message                          element
    error.backtrace error_object.backtrace.join("\n")
  end

  payload
end
```

Our generate_xml method takes an error_object as a parameter, from which we'll grab information to generate the XML. First, we start a new Builder document by creating an instance of Builder::XmlMarkup and telling it to generate the XML declaration ❶. Then we build our document using methods on the builder object ❷.

Now, what's the best architecture for our error reporter? Since we'll be catching exceptions and reporting them to the error-reporting service, it seems like a good idea to avoid creating an instance every time. We'll probably want to build a class and use class methods to handle the functionality. Listing 7.2 shows our implementation of this class.

Listing 7.2   Implementing our error reporter

```
require 'rubygems'
require 'stomp'
require 'builder'

class ErrorReporter
  def self.report!(error_object, queue='/queue/errors')      ❶ Pushes message
    reporter = Stomp::Client.new                                to queue
    reporter.send queue, generate_xml(error_object)
  end                                                        ❷ Uses Stomp client
                                                               to queue message
  private
  def self.generate_xml(error_object)
    payload = ""

    builder = Builder::XmlMarkup.new(:target => payload)
    builder.instruct!

    builder.error do |error|
      error.type error_object.class.to_s
      error.message error_object.message
      error.backtrace error_object.backtrace.join("\n")
    end

    payload
  end
end
```

Here you can see that we define a method called report! ❶, which takes an error_object as a parameter, along with the name of the queue you want to push the messages to (defaulting to /queue/errors). Next, we create our Stomp::Client object ❷ and tell it to send a message to the queue identified in the parameters with a payload containing XML from the generate_xml method we created earlier (listing 7.1).

Now, we just have to implement this in some code:

```
def error_method
  FakeConstant.non_existent_method!
rescue StandardError => error_obj
  ErrorReport.report! error_obj
end
```

When running that code, an error will be raised and reported via our ErrorReporter. If you check the queues in your message broker's web interface, you should see a message that has XML for the error object. That works great, but let's build a message consumer so we can test it more easily.

To consume messages with a Stomp::Client object, you use the subscribe method, which allows you to define behavior for responding to messages being pushed to a queue. The behavior is defined by providing a block to the subscribe method; you can see a primitive example of this in listing 7.3.

Listing 7.3 Processing all messages from the queue

```
client = Stomp::Client.new          ⟵── Uses Stomp client to consume messages
client.subscribe('/queue/testing") do |message|    Subscribes to queue,
  puts message.body                                  consumes each message
end

# Join the listener thread
client.join
```

Running the code in listing 7.3, then pushing messages into the /queue/testing queue will cause the payload of those messages to be printed to the console. The resulting message object is actually a Stomp::Message object, which also contains a little bit more information about the frame if you need it (specifically, the frame headers and command). We also join the thread; otherwise, the script would exit and the listener thread would be killed off.

So, to make a consumer for our error reporter, we'll need to pop the messages off the queue and process the XML inside of our subscribe call. We'll use REXML to parse the XML document and work with the elements tree. Our implementation is in listing 7.4.

Listing 7.4 Our testing consumer for the error reporter

```
require 'rubygems'
require 'rexml/document'
require 'stomp'

client = Stomp::Client.new
```

```
client.subscribe('/queue/errors') do |message|          ❶ Parses the XML
  xml = REXML::Document.new(message.body)    ◄──┐          message body
                                               │
  puts "Error: #{xml.elements['error/type'].text}"  │
  puts xml.elements['error/message'].text      │    ❷ Prints text value of
  puts xml.elements['error/backtrace'].text     │       various elements
  puts                                         │
end
```

```
client.join
```

We create a `Stomp::Client` object and invoke `subscribe`. When a message is received, we push the message body over to REXML ❶ and pull attributes out to print them to the console ❷. If you run this script and throw a few errors to the error reporter, your console should look something like the following:

```
Error: NameError
uninitialized constant NonExistentConstant
my_script.rb:3:in `test_call'
my_script.rb:12

Error: NameError
uninitialized constant IDontExist
application.rb:9:in `invoke!'
application.rb:20
```

Discussion

In these examples, we've only shown you a few features of the stomp gem. To keep the examples short, we left many features out, but the library is actually quite full-featured.

For example, it supports authentication in the message broker, so if we wanted to log in as a user on the broker listening on the `localhost` at port `13333`, we'd simply do something like the following when creating the `Stomp::Client` object:

```
client = Stomp::Client.new('username', 'pass', 'localhost', 13333)
```

The library also supports reliable messaging using client-side acknowledgement. For example, let's say you wanted to make sure that your authorization messages were being received. Your code, at its base level, might look something like the following:

```
message = nil
client = Stomp::Client.new
client.send '/queue/rb', "Hi, Ruby!"

client.subscribe('/queue/rb', :ack => 'client') { |msg| message = msg }

client.acknowledge message
```

To learn more about these and other features (like transactional sending), you can check out the Stomp home page or generate the RDocs for stomp on your local machine.

If Java and ActiveMQ aren't available to you, or you don't want to go through the effort of setting them up, there is also a pure Ruby Stomp server. It's available as a gem named stompserver, which you can install by executing the following:

```
$ gem install stompserver
```

> **Stomp documentation**
>
> The stomp gem doesn't actually generate its documentation when it installs itself, so you'll need to navigate to its directory and run `rdoc` to generate it yourself. RDocs aside, we found that the test suite was one of the best locations for information on how to use the library. The same goes for RubyWMQ and other libraries we cover in this book. Chalk it up to a developer community devoted to test-driven development.

While it's not production quality, it's great for testing your application locally without creating a lot of overhead on your system. Although it is useful, stompserver isn't the best pure-Ruby asynchronous messaging solution available. In the next section, we'll take a look at the best pure-Ruby option we've found: Ruby Reliable Messaging.

7.1.2 *Using reliable-msg*

If your preference is to stay in Ruby rather than using a tool from another language, or if your requirements don't allow for extraneous software installation, perhaps a pure Ruby solution is in order. Assaf wrote a pure Ruby reliable-messaging library named Ruby Reliable Messaging. In this section, we'll take a look at using this library to fulfill your asynchronous messaging needs in a small setting where no heavy lifting is required.

To get started, you'll want to install the Ruby Reliable Messaging gem, which is named reliable-msg:

```
$ gem install reliable-msg
```

Next, you'll want to start the Reliable Messaging library's message broker, which is a daemon that exposes brokering over DRb:

```
$ queues manager start
```

> **DRb**
>
> DRb (Distributed Ruby) is a standard library that you can use to write distributed applications. Using DRb, client applications can call Ruby objects that exist on a remote server using a fast binary protocol over TCP/IP. Similar in nature to RMI and DCOM, DRb was designed to make RPC calls between objects running on different machines and for interprocess communication. Because it was only designed to support Ruby clients and servers, its main benefits are speed and simplicity.

Problem

You want to utilize asynchronous messaging, but you need to stay in the Ruby language.

Solution

The Reliable Messaging library functions primarily through the `ReliableMsg::Queue` class and its `put` and `get` methods. These obviously named methods will put messages into the queue and get them out. Listing 7.5 shows an example.

Listing 7.5 Demonstrating the Reliable Messaging library's core functionality

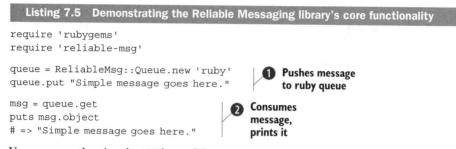

```
require 'rubygems'
require 'reliable-msg'

queue = ReliableMsg::Queue.new 'ruby'           ❶ Pushes message
queue.put "Simple message goes here."              to ruby queue

msg = queue.get                                  ❷ Consumes
puts msg.object                                     message,
# => "Simple message goes here."                    prints it
```

You can see the simple API here. We create a `ReliableMsg::Queue` object and use the
put method to place an object in the queue ❶. Next, we use the `get` method to pop
the first object (the string we just created) off the queue ❷. Then we use the `object`
method to get the object from the message and output it to the console (in this case,
we just had a string). This simple API makes it very easy to focus more on the business
logic around your messaging rather than the messaging itself.

While reliable-msg isn't meant for heavy-traffic messaging, it does offer one unique
advantage over the other solutions that aren't Ruby from top to bottom: native object
handling. When you place a message in the queue, the reliable-msg library does this:

```
message = Marshal::dump(message)
```

What does that mean for you? It means that you can put any type of object into the
queue and have it serialized natively in Ruby. No more XML serialization, no tiptoeing
around serialization limitations, and no more worrying about serialization problems.
Of course, this means that you can only integrate with Ruby clients, but this section is
all about pure Ruby messaging.

Let's say you want to use a queue to pass work-order information from your Rails
application to your Ruby application on a different host that processes and dispatches
work orders. Your `WorkOrderMessage` class might look something like listing 7.6.

Listing 7.6 Passing data from a Rails application to a Ruby application

```
class WorkOrderMessage
  attr_accessor :requester, :requested_work, :date_due

  def initialize(params)
    raise "Invalid arguments provided." unless params.is_a?(Hash)

    @requester = params[:requester]
    @requested_work = params[:requested_work]
    @date_due = params[:date_due]
  end

  def unique_id
    "#{@requester.slice(0,5).strip.upcase}-" +
    "#{@date_due.strftime('%m%d%y')}-#{@requested_work.hash}"
  end

  def report!
    puts "Order #{unique_id} received."
    puts "from #{@requester}, due #{@date_due.strftime('%D')}"
```

```
    puts "Work requested:"
    puts @requested_work
    puts
  end
end
```

In the class, we have `attr_accessors` for various attributes, a couple of methods to format the information in a variety of ways, and a constructor that takes a `Hash` as its single parameter so we can pass from a request action to a create action and to the constructor directly.

In our Rails application, we then would have a `create` action like the one in listing 7.7.

Listing 7.7   Creating a work order in the database and passing a message

```
def create
  @work_order = WorkOrder.new(params[:work_order])      ←——  ❶ Stores work order
  @work_order.save!                                              in database

  mq = ReliableMsg::Queue.new('orders_queue')
  message = WorkOrderMessage.new(params[:work_order])          ❷ Queues message to
  mq.put message                                                  process work order

  flash[:notice] = "Work order submitted."
  redirect_to(work_orders_path)
rescue ActiveRecord::RecordInvalid
  render :action => 'new'
end
```

First, we create an `ActiveRecord` object (`WorkOrder`) and save it to the database ❶. If that's successful, we proceed to create our `WorkOrderMessage` object and place it in the queue ❷. The rest of the method will place a confirmation message in the `flash` and redirect the user to the index of the `work_orders` controller.

Blocking your Rails application

The only downside to this approach is that it blocks your Rails application when placing the message in the queue, which means that if you're moving around big objects or have a slow or busy queue, your users will have to wait until it's done (or worse, the request may time out). See the following discussion section for a few tips on how to avoid this.

Now we need to create a message consumer for our Ruby application. Again, we'll use the `get` method to grab the message from the queue and process it. See listing 7.8 for our implementation of a simple consumer.

Listing 7.8   Consuming messages from the queue

```
require 'rubygems'
require 'reliable-msg'                                        ❶ Opens connection
                                                                to orders queue
queue = ReliableMsg::Queue.new 'orders_queue'         ←——
```

```
while true                          ◄── ❷ Loops forever
  while true
    break unless queue.get do |msg|
      msg.report!

                                        ❸ Processes each
      # If you had a Processor class...   message from queue
      Processor.process! msg
      true
    end
  end
  sleep 10 # No messages?  Hold on!
end
```

First we create our `Queue` object ❶, and then we start looping so that the consumer is always available ❷. When we get a message ❸, we call its `report!` method to give us a report of what its work order contains, then we tell our `Processor` class (assuming we have one) to process it.

Discussion

We said that the method we showed for Rails integration may cause problems if you have high traffic or big message objects. There are two popular options for Rails integrated messaging: AP4R and ActiveMessaging.

AP4R builds on reliable-msg and offers a number of Rails-specific features that will make your life much easier when trying to handle messaging. If you're interested in the minimal setup and configuration of reliable-msg and want to use it in combination with Rails applications, we recommend checking out AP4R.

ActiveMessaging is another alternative for integrating messaging providers into Rails applications. Its strength is in supporting WMQ, Stomp, JMS, Amazon Simple Queue Service, and reliable-msg, letting you switch between providers as your project needs change. It requires more setup than AP4R, but it has the clear advantage of supporting more messaging services.

If these libraries strike you as too much to set up or too much code to add to your applications, you could also use something like Spawn or BackgrounDRb to handle the sending (and optionally consuming) of messages. These options are simpler and possibly cleaner, but they aren't as integrated or powerful.

In our examples, we didn't cover some of the more advanced features of reliable-msg. For example, you can specify the delivery method. By default, it's "best effort" (`:best_effort`), which means it will try to deliver the message once, and if it fails, the message will be discarded. Let's say you wanted a little more resilience. You decide to change the delivery behavior to repeat delivery six times, and if it fails, to place the message in the `dead-letter` queue:

```
queue.put message, :delivery => :repeated
```

You can also set the `:delivery` argument to be `:once`, which will try to deliver the message once, and if it fails, the message will be placed in the `dead-letter` queue. These parameters can also be set on `Queue` objects so that the behavior becomes the default for any `message` object passed to it:

```
queue = Queue.new("my_queue", :delivery => :repeated)
```

This will cause any message put in that queue to be delivered using the `repeated` method rather than the default. The reliable-msg library also has a very flexible consumption API and a number of options for persistence. You can read more about these in RDocs, which are generated when you install the gem.

Viewing gem documentation

If you want to view the documentation for gems on your system, run `gem server` from your favorite command line. This script will start a web server on port 8808; you can navigate to it and browse a list of the gems you have installed and their accompanying documentation.

7.2 *WebSphere MQ*

What happens when you combine powerful message-oriented middleware with a powerful programming language? In the next two sections, we're going to look at Ruby-WMQ, a library for using WMQ from Ruby.

The best thing about RubyWMQ is how it's implemented. It's essentially a thin wrapper around the WMQ client API, which means you get access to all the WMQ options and flags, and full control over message descriptors and headers. The `get` and `put` methods work exactly like you expect them to, as do browsing and retrieving related messages, managing queues, and running WMQ commands. If you know WMQ, there's little new to learn here, and you'll be up and running in a few minutes.

RubyWMQ also brings with it all the useful Ruby idioms, like using hashed arguments, blocks, and the `each` method. As you'll see in the following example, it's easy to get productive with RubyWMQ and to write code that's simple, readable, and reliable. So let's get started.

7.2.1 *Queuing messages*

We're going to use WMQ for integration, and we'll start by using Ruby as the message producer. For the rest of the chapter, we'll be looking at an environment with several applications that invite people to register and create new accounts. To capture and handle all that information, we're going to use WMQ as a message bus across all these applications. All our applications will use a common format (using XML) and a queue to collect all these messages. Now let's put it to use.

Problem

Your web application allows users to register and create new accounts. Whenever a user creates an account, you need to capture some of that account information, create an XML message, and push that message into the `ACCOUNTS.CREATED` queue.

Solution

Since we covered Rails in previous chapters, we're going to use it again in this chapter. We're doing that so we can focus on RubyWMQ rather than the details of building a web application. However, what you will learn here is not specific to Rails or web applications.

Installing gems with C extensions

RubyWMQ is Ruby code mixed with a native C library. There are other gems that mix Ruby code with C extensions, some of which we cover in this book: MySQL, Mongrel, Hpricot, and RMagick.

On Windows, these C libraries are installed as DLLs, but on other operating systems they download as source code and need to be compiled and linked on your machine. If you're curious what C extensions look like, check out one of these gems' ext/ directories. Typically gems that use C extensions include an extconf.rb file, which uses the mkmf library to generate the Makefile. The rest is handled by make and gcc.

To run the examples in this section, you will need to have a development environment that includes these build tools. Some installations include them by default, but if yours doesn't, you will have to install them separately. If, for example, you're using Ubuntu, you will need to run this command: `apt-get install build-essential ruby1.8-dev`. We talk more about installation and setting up your environment in appendix A.

Let's first have a look at our existing `AccountsController`. It has several actions, but we're only interested in the `create` action that responds to POST requests and creates new accounts. Listing 7.9 shows what this action looks like.

Listing 7.9 `AccountsController` create action for creating a new account

```ruby
def create
  @account = Account.new(params['account'])
  if @account.save
    # Created, send user back to main page.
    redirect_to root_url
  else
    # Error, show the registration form with error message
    render :action=>'new'
  end
end
```

After we create the new account record, and before we respond to the browser, we're going to send a new message using RubyWMQ. Let's keep that code separate and add a new method called `wmq_account_created`.

To start with, this method will need to create an XML document with the new account information. The actual account record contains more information than we want to share, such as the user's password and the record's primary key, so we'll be selective with the few attributes we want to share:

```ruby
attributes = account.attributes.slice('first_name', 'last_name',
                'company', 'email' }
```

There's another attribute we want to share: the name of the application that created this account. Since we're very Web savvy, we always refer to applications by their domain name, so we'll use the domain name to set the value of this attribute:

```ruby
attributes.update(:application=>request.host)
```

Now, let's turn these attributes into an XML document with the root element "account":

```
xml = attributes.to_xml(:root=>'account')
```

A typical message will look like this:

```
<?xml version="1.0" encoding="UTF-8"?>
<account>
  <first-name>John</first-name>
  <last-name>Smith</last-name>
  <company>ACME Messaging</company>
  <email>john@example.com</email>
  <application>wmq-rails.example.com</application>
</account>
```

Next, we're going to connect to the queue manager. We want to keep the connection configuration in a separate file, so we don't have to dig through source code whenever we need to change it.

In fact, we want to keep several connection configurations that we can use in different environments. Typically, we'll use one queue manager that we run locally for development, another one for testing, and the real deal in production. We'll even configure those differently; for example, we'll use nonpersistent queues for development and testing. If you worked with Rails before, you know that it uses a YAML file to specify the database connection configuration—one for each environment. We'll use a similar structure to configure RubyWMQ. Listing 7.10 shows a sample wmq.yml configuration file.

Listing 7.10   A config/wmq.yml configuration file

```
development:                            | Uses local queue manager
  q_mgr_name: DEV.QM                    | for development

test:
  q_mgr_name: TEST.QM

production:
  q_mgr_name:  VENUS.QM
  connection_name: venus.example.com(1414)    | Uses central queue
  channel_name:    SYSTEM.DEF.SVRCONN          | manager for production
  transport_type:  WMQ::MQXPT_TCP
```

Loading YAML files is a trivial matter (see chapter 11 for a longer discussion about YAML and configuration). We need to pick the right configuration based on our current environment:

```
config_file = File.expand_path('config/wmq.yml', RAILS_ROOT)
config = YAML.load(File.read(config_file))[RAILS_ENV].symbolize_keys
WMQ::QueueManager.connect(config) do |qmgr|
  ...
end
```

Now that we have an XML document and an open connection, it's a simple matter of putting the message in the right queue:

```
qmgr.put :q_name=>'ACCOUNTS.CREATED', :data=>xml
```

One thing we found helpful during development is keeping a trace of all the messages created by the application. It helps when we need to troubleshoot and look for lost messages. So let's expand this single line to create a WMQ::Message object. The message identifier is set when we put the message in the queue, so we can log it afterwards:

```
message = WMQ::Message.new
message.data = xml
qmgr.put :q_name=>'ACCOUNTS.CREATED', :message=>message
logger.info "WMQ.put: message #{message.descriptor[:msg_id]} in
    ACCOUNTS.CREATED"
```

Now let's assemble all these pieces into working code. Since we might use RubyWMQ elsewhere in our application, we'll handle the configuration in a single place that is shared by all controllers. Listing 7.11 shows the ApplicationController and the method we added to load the right configuration.

Listing 7.11   The app/controllers/application.rb file modified to read WMQ configuration

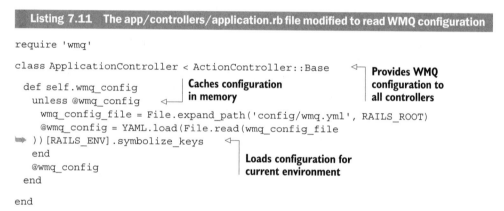

```
require 'wmq'

class ApplicationController < ActionController::Base          ◁  Provides WMQ
  def self.wmq_config                    Caches configuration     configuration to
    unless @wmq_config   ◁──┘            in memory                all controllers
      wmq_config_file = File.expand_path('config/wmq.yml', RAILS_ROOT)
      @wmq_config = YAML.load(File.read(wmq_config_file
➡  ))[RAILS_ENV].symbolize_keys   ◁──┐
    end                               Loads configuration for
    @wmq_config                       current environment
  end
end
```

Listing 7.12 shows AccountsController with an action that creates new messages and the wmq_account_created method. Controllers expose all their public methods as actions, and since this method is not an action, we'll make it private.

Listing 7.12   AccountsController queues new accounts in ACCOUNTS.CREATED

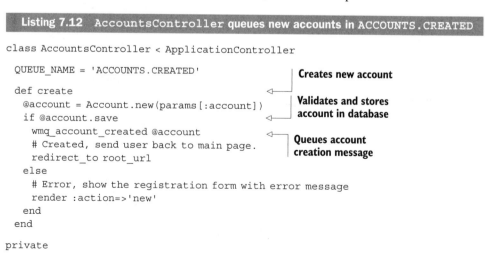

```
class AccountsController < ApplicationController

  QUEUE_NAME = 'ACCOUNTS.CREATED'                      Creates new account

  def create                                ◁──┘
    @account = Account.new(params[:account])           Validates and stores
    if @account.save                        ◁──┘       account in database
      wmq_account_created @account          ◁──┐
      # Created, send user back to main page.         Queues account
      redirect_to root_url                            creation message
    else
      # Error, show the registration form with error message
      render :action=>'new'
    end
  end

private
```

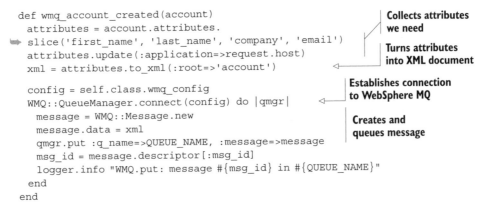

```
def wmq_account_created(account)
  attributes = account.attributes.
  slice('first_name', 'last_name', 'company', 'email')
  attributes.update(:application=>request.host)
  xml = attributes.to_xml(:root=>'account')

  config = self.class.wmq_config
  WMQ::QueueManager.connect(config) do |qmgr|
    message = WMQ::Message.new
    message.data = xml
    qmgr.put :q_name=>QUEUE_NAME, :message=>message
    msg_id = message.descriptor[:msg_id]
    logger.info "WMQ.put: message #{msg_id} in #{QUEUE_NAME}"
  end
end

end
```

Collects attributes
we need

Turns attributes
into XML document

Establishes connection
to WebSphere MQ

Creates and
queues message

And we're done. We just changed an existing controller to create XML messages and deliver them to other applications using WMQ.

Discussion

Writing the code was easy, but we sometimes make mistakes, and we can't tell for sure this will work in production. Not without a test case. So let's write a test case to make sure we're sending the right information on the right queue. We test the controller in listing 7.13.

Listing 7.13   Test case for putting message in ACCOUNTS.CREATED

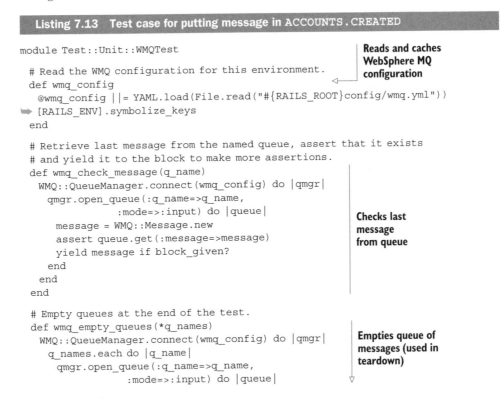

```
module Test::Unit::WMQTest

  # Read the WMQ configuration for this environment.
  def wmq_config
    @wmq_config ||= YAML.load(File.read("#{RAILS_ROOT}config/wmq.yml"))
      [RAILS_ENV].symbolize_keys
  end

  # Retrieve last message from the named queue, assert that it exists
  # and yield it to the block to make more assertions.
  def wmq_check_message(q_name)
    WMQ::QueueManager.connect(wmq_config) do |qmgr|
      qmgr.open_queue(:q_name=>q_name,
                      :mode=>:input) do |queue|
        message = WMQ::Message.new
        assert queue.get(:message=>message)
        yield message if block_given?
      end
    end
  end

  # Empty queues at the end of the test.
  def wmq_empty_queues(*q_names)
    WMQ::QueueManager.connect(wmq_config) do |qmgr|
      q_names.each do |q_name|
        qmgr.open_queue(:q_name=>q_name,
                        :mode=>:input) do |queue|
```

Reads and caches
WebSphere MQ
configuration

Checks last
message
from queue

Empties queue of
messages (used in
teardown)

```
      queue.each { |message| }              ↑  Empties queue of
    end                                        messages (used in
  end                                          teardown)
 end
end

end

class AccountsControllerTest < Test::Unit::TestCase
  include Test::Unit::WMQTest

  def setup
    @q_name = 'ACCOUNTS.CREATED'
    @attributes = { 'first_name'=>'John', 'last_name'=>'Smith',
              'company'=>'ACME', 'email'=>'john@acme.com' }
  end
                                                         Places new
                                                         message in
  def test_wmq_account_created      ⟵ Tests account creation    queue
    post :create, :account=>@attributes              ⟵
    wmq_check_message @q_name do |message|           Checks message
      from_xml = Hash.from_xml(message.data)         existence and contents
      app = @account.merge('application'=>'test.host')
      assert_equal app, from_xml['account']
    end
  end

  def teardown              Empties queue
    wmq_empty_queues @q_name   before next text
  end                      ⟵

end
```

The second half of listing 7.13 is our test case, and it's a very simple one. We POST to the create action with new account information, which pushes a new message to the queue. We then ask RubyWMQ to retrieve the new message, assert that the message exists, then yield to the block. In the block, we specify another assertion, checking the message content against the expected values.

We may want to use RubyWMQ in more places, so we abstracted the common features into a separate module, Test::Unit::WMQTest, that we can mix into other test cases. We have one method to return the queue manager configuration (wmq_config), another to check a message on any given queue (wmq_check_message), and a third that we use during teardown to empty the queue before running the next test (wmq_empty_queues).

If test cases fail, we could end up with messages filling the queue, which would lead to the wrong result the next time we run the test, so we discard all the messages from the test queue during teardown. That explains why we need a separate queue manager for running tests.

Running WMQ commands

You can also use RubyWMQ to run commands and perform administrative tasks. For example, if you're sharing this code with other developers, they will need the ACCOUNTS.CREATED queue in their development or test queue manager. You can set it up with a simple script or a Rake task:

Running WMQ commands (*continued*)

```
namespace :wmq do
  desc 'Creates WebSphere MQ queues on development and test environments'
  task :setup=>:environment do
    wmq_configs = YAML.load(File.read(File.expand_path(
      'config/wmq.yml', RAILS_ROOT)))
    ['development', 'test'].each do |environment|
      config = wmq_configs[environment].symbolize_keys
      puts "Connecting to #{wmq_config[:q_mgr_name]}"
      WMQ::QueueManager.connect(wmq_config) do |qmgr|
        puts "Creating ACCOUNTS.CREATED queue"
        qmgr.mqsc('define qlocal(ACCOUNTS.CREATED) defpsist(no)')
      end
    end
  end
end
```

So, now that we know the basics of producing messages, let's look at another form of integration: consuming and processing messages.

7.2.2 *Processing messages*

In this section, we're going to use WMQ for integration by receiving and processing messages. If you recall from the previous section, we have several applications that push account-creation messages to a single queue. In this section, we're going to turn these messages into sale leads in a customer-relationship management (CRM) database.

Problem

You have several applications through which users can create new accounts, and each of these applications pushes a message to the ACCOUNTS.CREATED queue. We want to batch process these messages and use them to create sale leads in our CRM database.

Solution

We're looking at batch processing messages here, so we're going to develop a stand-alone program that we can schedule to run at night.

We'll start by reading the connection configuration, using the same YAML configuration file we specified in listing 7.10. This time around, we're not running inside Rails. Instead, we'll pass the environment name using the WMQ_ENV environment variable:

```
ENV = ENV['WMQ_ENV']
wmq_config = YAML.load(File.read('config/wmq.yml'))[WMQ_ENV].symbolize_keys
```

Next, we'll open a connection to the queue manager and open the queue for reading:

```
WMQ::QueueManager.connect(wmq_config) do |qmgr|
  qmgr.open_queue(:q_name=>'ACCOUNTS.CREATED', :mode=>:input) do |queue|
    ...
  end
end
```

We need to pick up and process each message from the queue. There are a couple of ways of doing that. We can call get to retrieve each message and repeat until there are no more messages to receive (when get returns false). We showed you how to use the get method when we covered test cases in the previous section. We're much more fond of using Ruby idioms, however, so let's do that instead:

```
queue.each(:sync=>true) do |message|
  ...
end
```

The each method iterates over every message in the queue and passes it to the block. It also makes our code more reliable. The :sync=>true option tells WMQ to use synch-points. If the block throws an exception and doesn't catch it, the message goes back to the queue so we can process it again. WMQ marks the failed delivery attempt and will decide how long to wait before redelivery and how many failures to tolerate before filing the message in the dead-letter queue. Meanwhile, even if it failed on one message, the loop will continue processing the remaining messages. As simple as it is, this code is fault tolerant and can deal with failures like losing the database connection or someone tripping over the power cord.

This loop terminates once it's done processing all the messages in the queue, which is exactly what we wanted it to do. Remember, we're running this program on a night schedule to batch process all messages queued during the day. Of course, we could also run this program continuously and have it pick up messages as they become available, blocking to wait for new messages. All we need to do is add option :wait=>-1.

We're going to use REXML to parse the XML document in the message:

```
xml = REXML::Document.new(message.data)
```

There are certain elements whose contents we're interested in, such as the person's name and email address. We want to map those into a Hash and pass that to the Lead.create method. However, the names don't exactly match: Lead uses one convention for naming database columns, and the XML message has a different naming convention for its elements. Then there's the application name (the application XML element) that we want to store as the lead source (the lead_source column in the database). What we need here is a transformation. Let's define that:

```
transform = { :first_name=>'first-name',
              :last_name=>'last-name',
              :company=>'company',
              :email=>'email',
              :lead_source=>'application' }
```

The convention we're using here is to name the target on the left and its source on the right, for example, extracting the value of lead_source from application. This makes it easy to iterate over the transformation and map each value from its XML source to its Hash target. We'll use the XML Path Language (XPath) expressions to extract each value:

```
attributes = transform.inject({}) { |hash, (target, source)|
  nodes = xml.get_text("/account/#{source}")
  hash.update(target=>nodes.to_s)
}
```

```
# And create the sale lead record in the database...
Lead.create!(attributes)
```

Where did `Lead` come from? We're using ActiveRecord in this example, so `Lead` maps to the database table `leads`, and since ActiveRecord knows how to extract the class definition from the database schema, all we need to do is specify the class:

```
class Lead < ActiveRecord::Base
end
```

So now let's wrap this example into a single file we can run from the command line. Listing 7.14 shows essentially the same code we developed so far, with the addition of error logging.

When you look at listing 7.14, you may notice this chapter's key lesson. There are a handful of lines dedicated to setting up the environment and to turning an XML document into an ActiveRecord. Yet, what we set out to show you in this chapter—how to easily build programs that can reliably retrieve and process messages—is captured in two lines of code: each and the following end. It really is that simple.

Listing 7.14 Processing messages from WMQ to create new leads

```
require 'rubygems'
require 'wmq'
require 'active_record'

WMQ_ENV = ENV['WMQ_ENV']

# Set up logging and configure the database connection.
LOGGER = Logger.new(STDOUT)                                    Sets up ActiveRecord
ActiveRecord::Base.logger = LOGGER                             logging and database
database = YAML.load(File.read('config/database.yml'))         connection
  [WMQ_ENV].symbolize_keys
ActiveRecord::Base.establish_connection database

# Define the Lead class.
class Lead < ActiveRecord::Base        Uses ActiveRecord to
end                                     access leads table

# Read the WMQ configuration and open a connection.
wmq_config = YAML.load(File.read('config/wmq.yml'))            Connects to queue manager
  [WMQ_ENV].symbolize_keys                                     per configuration
WMQ::QueueManager.connect(wmq_config) do |qmgr|
  qmgr.open_queue(:q_name=>'ACCOUNTS.CREATED', :mode=>:input) do |queue|
    queue.each(:sync=>true) do |message|
      begin                                                    Processes each
        # Parse the document, transform from XML to attributes. message with
        xml = REXML::Document.new(message.data)                synchpoint
        transform = { :first_name=>'first-name',
                  :last_name=>'last-name',
                  :company=>'company',
                  :email=>'email',
                  :lead_source=>'application' }
        attributes = transform.                        Transforms XML
          inject({}) { |hash, (target, source)|        document into a Hash
```

```
        nodes = xml.get_text("/account/#{source}")
        hash.update(target=>nodes.to_s)
      }
      # Create a new lead.
      lead = Lead.create!(attributes)
      LOGGER.debug "Created new lead #{lead.id}"
    rescue Exception=>ex
      LOGGER.error ex.message
      LOGGER.error ex.backtrace
      # Raise exception, WMQ keeps message in queue.
      raise
    end
  end
 end
end
```

Transforms XML document into a Hash

Creates new lead record in database

Logs errors but lets WMQ deal with message

Discussion

That's really all there is to our solution. We wrote a simple program that can batch process messages and create new records in the database. It's simple, yet reliable, and isn't fazed when the database goes down or it encounters an invalid message.

Integrating with WebSphere MQ and SalesForce

Which database are we going to use? Tough call. How about SalesForce? Wouldn't it be interesting if we could turn this example into one that uses Ruby to integrate all our internal applications with SalesForce's SaaS CRM solution?

We can change out our solution to create a new sale lead in SalesForce with these three simple steps.

Step 1: install the ActiveSalesForce gem:

```
$ gem install activesalesforce
```

Step 2: load the ActiveSalesForce connection adapter by adding this line as the last require at the top of the file:

```
require 'activesalesforce'
```

Step 3: change the database.yml configuration file to use ActiveSalesForce as the connection adapter. Let's do that for the development environment:

```
development:
  adapter: activesalesforce
  url: https://test.salesforce.com
  username: <your username>
  password: <your password>
```

And we're done! Now when you run this program, it will process a day's worth of messages and turn them into sales leads that will show up in your SalesForce account.

7.3 *Summary*

Integrating with systems that are totally foreign to your development environment can be trying, but solutions like asynchronous messaging make it much easier. Fortunately Ruby has a number of mature libraries that work with a variety of messaging vendors. In this chapter, we looked at using RubyWMQ to work with WMQ. This solution works well for large-scale deployments, where WMQ is a requirement.

We also looked at ActiveMQ (open source high-throughput message-oriented middleware), using the Stomp protocol. What you learned here will also apply to other messaging services that support the Stomp protocol, and that includes many of the JMS providers out there. Last, we looked at a lightweight alternative that requires minimum setup and configuration—the Ruby Reliable Messaging library.

Now that we have talked about developing web applications and using Web services and asynchronous messaging, let's look at some options for deploying Ruby applications.

Deployment 8

This chapter covers

- Using gems to distribute libraries and applications
- Using Capistrano to deploy and manage servers
- Using Vlad to deploy and manage servers
- Monitoring servers with God.rb

Much has been written on the topic of deploying applications written in Ruby on Rails. However, not all Ruby applications are web applications, and not all web applications use Rails. This chapter will focus on the deployment concerns that arise when deciding how to create Ruby applications and how to release those applications into a live environment once done.

For veteran Rails developers, a lot of this will be familiar: we will discuss using Capistrano to deploy applications, packaging up reusable components in Ruby gems, and using God to monitor a deployed application. However, we will go beyond the common uses of these tools and explain how to customize them for a variety of server-based applications, beyond Rails.

Keep in mind that the process of deploying live applications can be complex. The topic could easily fill an entire book of this size. This chapter will focus on tools written in Ruby that can help you deploy applications and libraries. If you're interested specifically in web applications, you can find setup and configuration instructions in appendix C.

8.1 Creating deployable packages with RubyGems

When deciding how to structure new Ruby programs, it's worth taking some time to decide how you will deploy them. While some of the programs you create will be yours and yours alone, you may also find yourself creating code for hundreds or even thousands of developers. This may be because you are writing open source software, or because others will use your code in a large enterprise situation, or even because you are writing commercial code to be used by those who purchase it.

In this section, we will look at how to create skeletons for your code that will make it easy to release and deploy to other developers. Because Ruby's gem system is designed to be robust and decentralized, this section will focus on building Ruby gems and creating your own secure gem repositories.

Using the latest version of RubyGems

RubyGems is an extension of Ruby and not part of the official Ruby 1.8 distribution, although some distributions do contain it. The One-Click Ruby Installer (for Windows and Mac OS X) includes RubyGems, as do Mac OS X 10.5 (Leopard) and JRuby. RubyGems will become part of Ruby 1.9 and above.

If you do not have RubyGems installed, we recommend downloading RubyGems 1.2 or later from the RubyForge website and installing it by unpacking the archive file and running the setup.rb file found there. For example:

```
$ wget http://rubyforge.org/frs/download.php/38646/rubygems-1.2.0.tgz
$ tar xzf rubygems-1.2.0.tgz
$ cd rubygems-1.2.0
$ sudo ruby setup.rb
```

If you already have RubyGems installed, we recommend upgrading to 1.2 (which may require upgrading to Ruby 1.8.6). You can check which version of RubyGems you have by running the command `gem --version`. To upgrade to the latest version, use this command:

```
$ gem update --system
```

You can find more information about installing Ruby and setting up RubyGems in appendix A.

8.1.1 Using RubyGems in your organization

Suppose we run the IT department of a medium-sized programming firm. Pretty much everyone's writing Ruby code, but project groups are having difficulties sharing code. For instance, one team spent all month writing some code to send alerts out via AIM, and another team was several days into implementing the same code before they realized it had already been done. To avoid such problems, we want to provide a centralized repository of Ruby libraries produced by different teams in our organization.

Problem

You want to use the RubyGems system to allow your teams to integrate their packages into their existing libraries of Ruby code. You want them to be able to use their existing tools and to have downloaded gems integrate seamlessly into their existing repositories. Finally, you want to be able to support dependencies and requirements, as well as provide support for automatically installing C extensions.

Solution

We can use Ruby tools to generate gem skeletons and fill in information about dependencies and C extensions. We can then host these gems on a server and give the developers a URL that they can use with the gem command-line utility to pull gems from the company repository instead of from the default RubyForge repository.

Let's tackle these problems one at a time. First, let's take a look at generating empty gems that you can fill with the appropriate information. We're going to use the newgem utility to build the skeleton. It allows you to build a full skeleton, including a website to upload to RubyForge and automates other gem-related tasks. However, we're going to use the --simple switch to tell newgem to generate only enough code to get us up and running. Here's the command:

```
newgem ruby_in_practice --simple
```

Inside the directory created by this command, you should see a pretty simple structure containing a series of files at the root level (LICENSE, README, Rakefile, and TODO). There's a directory for your library (lib) and one for your tests (spec). There will also be a folder called script that includes generator scripts for Rubigen (which we will not be discussing here).

The main work we'll be doing here is inside of the Rakefile file, which holds the configuration for the gem we'll be building. You'll want to replace the sample information at the top, which will automatically be used further down in the gem specification. By default, the created gem will include all of the files in your lib and spec directories; you can change that by modifying the s.files declaration to include other files (where "s" refers to the variable that holds Gem::Specification). You can add dependencies by using s.add_dependency inside the gem specification. For instance, if you wanted to require hpricot 0.5 or higher, you would add this line:

```
s.add_dependency "hpricot", ">= 0.5"
```

You can include dependencies that are private to your organization or common gems that are on the main RubyForge server.

Your gem specification should look like the one in listing 8.1.

Listing 8.1   Gem specification

```
GEM = "ruby_in_practice"
VERSION = "0.1.0"
AUTHOR = "Sample McSample"
EMAIL = "sample@example.com"
HOMEPAGE = "http://sample.example.com"
SUMMARY = "A sample gem for Ruby in Practice"
```

```
spec = Gem::Specification.new do |s|
  s.name = GEM
  s.version = VERSION
  s.platform = Gem::Platform::RUBY
  s.has_rdoc = true
  s.extra_rdoc_files = ["README", "LICENSE", 'TODO']
  s.summary = SUMMARY
  s.description = s.summary
  s.author = AUTHOR
  s.email = EMAIL
  s.homepage = HOMEPAGE

  s.add_dependency "hpricot", ">= 0.5"

  s.require_path = 'lib'
  s.autorequire = GEM
  s.files = %w(LICENSE README Rakefile TODO) + Dir.glob("{lib,specs}/**/*")
end
```

When, later on, we install and use the gem in our application, RubyGems will add the gem's lib directory to the LOAD_PATH, so we can easily require these files from our application. To prevent naming conflicts, by convention we use a file that has the same name as the gem. You will notice that newgem generated the file lib/ruby_in_practice.rb. That will be the starting point for loading up the code that makes up our gem.

If your gem requires more than one file (and most do), we recommend placing additional files in a subdirectory that follows the same naming convention. In our case, that would be the lib/ruby_in_practice directory. Listing 8.2 shows an example of a lib/ruby_in_practice.rb file that requires additional files from the gem when it loads.

Listing 8.2   Requiring Ruby files from a gem

```
require 'ruby_in_practice/parser'
require 'ruby_in_practice/lexer'
require 'ruby_in_practice/interactive'
```

Requiring ruby_in_practice from an external file will automatically push the items under s.require_path (in this case lib) into the load path, so requires like those in listing 8.2 will work perfectly.

Discussion

The gem tool provides a variety of commands for installing, building, searching, serving, and performing many other gem-management tasks. You can learn more by running gem help commands.

Making a gem release is usually a more involved process. We like to run the full set of test case on our gem before packaging it for distribution. There are also other release tasks you may want to automate, like creating a changelog, tagging the release in source control, uploading the gem to a gem server, and so forth. Instead of running these tasks manually for each release (and sometimes getting them wrong), it's easier to automate the entire process using Rake. If you look into your gem repository, you will notice that most gems are built with the help of Rake.

As you get more involved with gem development, you'll want to explore different tools that will streamline different parts of the process. Newgem, which we just covered, takes the pain out of creating a new skeleton library and Rakefile for your gems. Another such tool is the rubyforge gem, which automates the process of making a new gem release via the RubyForge website.

Most gems consist entirely of Ruby code, but some contain portions of C code. C code is useful for talking to third-party and system APIs (e.g., a graphics or sound library), and for optimizing sections of critical code. Including C extensions is pretty simple too, assuming you have a working extconf.rb file already. Create a new directory called ext inside the gem skeleton, and place your extconf.rb file and any required C files into it. Then, add the following line to the gem specification:

```
s.extensions = "ext/extconf.rb"
```

This tells the gem installer to run extconf.rb and then to `make` and `make install` the generated Makefile. This will produce the same effect as manually installing the extension.

Here, too, there are a variety of tools you can use. Ruby can easily call out to C code, but if you're wrapping a library with a large C/C++ API, you'll find it easier to use tools like SWIG (http://www.swig.org) to generate the wrapper code for you.

Now that we've looked at how to package a gem, let's distribute it to other developers in the company by setting up a central gem repository.

8.1.2   Setting up a RubyGems repository

If you have an organization that needs to share Ruby code written by different departments, or if there's another reason you're distributing code to be used by others, you're going to want to start by setting up your own repository.

Problem

You need to deploy various software packages to a remote server where it will run, but managing dependencies has become quite complex. Additionally, it's difficult to manage the process of getting your files to the server and keeping track of which versions are running. Having already set up a server in the previous section, you want to incorporate your newly organized dependency system into your deployments.

Solution

To solve this problem, we'll package up and version the code into gems, and deploy the gems onto the server that will be running the code. Using the binary features of RubyGems, we can create a binary with the package that will run the code and that we can execute and monitor on the remote server. Because we will be using gems, we'll be able to specify both RubyForge dependencies and dependencies on our own gem repository.

We've already looked at the basics of packaging up code into gems. In order to use `rake package` and `rake install` to test our gem locally, we need to develop our code inside a gem structure. This means we need to make a few changes to the gem specification from listing 8.1 to add support for a binary that will run our code. We'll add a bin directory under ruby_in_practice, and add a file called ruby_in_practice under it. The binary will typically look something like the one in listing 8.3.

```
#!/bin/env ruby
require 'ruby_in_practice'
RubyInPractice.start
```

This binary assumes that you have a module somewhere in your codebase called `RubyInPractice` with a class method called `start`. This is a convenient way to structure your code—it keeps your binary very simple, and it's unlikely to need to change between versions. Keep in mind that in Ruby, `Dir.pwd` is the directory that the binary was run from, while `File.dirname(__FILE__)` is the directory that the code is in. This allows you to flexibly decide where to store support files like logs and PID files.

In order to make sure that our binary will get deployed along with our code, we'll need to make some changes to the gem specification we put together for listing 8.1. Let's take a look at just the gem specification part of the Rakefile in listing 8.4.

```
spec = Gem::Specification.new do |s|
  s.name = GEM
  s.version = VERSION
  s.platform = Gem::Platform::RUBY
  s.has_rdoc = true
  s.extra_rdoc_files = ["README", "LICENSE", 'TODO']
  s.summary = SUMMARY
  s.description = s.summary
  s.author = AUTHOR
  s.email = EMAIL
  s.homepage = HOMEPAGE                        Specifies binaries
                                               directory
  s.bindir = "bin"
  s.executables = "ruby_in_practice"           Specifies executables
                                               to install
  s.add_dependency "hpricot", ">= 0.5"

  s.require_path = 'lib'                                Adds bin to file list
  s.autorequire = GEM                                  for gem package
  s.files = %w(LICENSE README Rakefile TODO) +
    Dir.glob("{lib,specs,bin}/**/*")
end
```

Now, all we need to do is package up the gem, drop it on our server, and run `gem install` on the server. If we have a company-wide gem server, we could drop it on that server and deploy from there. We can specify dependencies and C extensions just as before, and our app will gracefully refuse to run if a dependency is not met. Say goodbye to dependency hell!

The `gem server` command will open up a server on port 8808, making the local repository available to users via the `--source` parameter to the normal `gem` command. Listing 8.5 shows some examples.

Listing 8.5   Using a custom repository with the `gem` command

```
gem install rails --source=http://example.com:8808
gem list --source=http://example.com:8808
gem query -nrails --source=http://example.com:8808
```
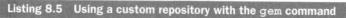

Our users will be able to install a gem ❶, list all available gems ❷, query the gem list for those matching a particular pattern ❸, and use many other commands available via the `gem` command. In essence, our server has become an alternative to the canonical RubyGems server. For more information on the available commands, run the `gem help` command from your command line.

Discussion

When you create your repository using `gem server`, you also have a number of options that will allow you to customize how you expose your repository to the world. Those options are detailed in table 8.1.

Table 8.1   The available options to the `gem server` command

Option	Effect
`--daemon`	Runs the server in daemon (background) mode.
`--p[ort]=PORT`	Runs the server on the designated port; if you use port 80, your users will be able to access the gem server without supplying a port to `gem -source`.
`--d[ir]=LOCATION`	Specifies the location of the gem repository.

As indicated in table 8.1, you can specify a location for the gem server that you expose. Say, for instance, that the server you are using for gems also has its own set of gems that you do not wish to expose (to make for more readable `gem list` output, for instance). You could install the gems you wish to expose in a custom location via `gem install -i`, and then use the `location` parameter to `gem server` to expose just those gems.

Assuming you are in the directory that will contain just the gems you want to expose, listing 8.6 shows how to do this.

Listing 8.6   Using a custom location for gem server

```
gem install rails -i ./gems
gem server -d ./gems --daemon
```

Listing 8.6 demonstrates how to install the gems into a new directory ❶ and then call `gem server` with the necessary settings ❷. You don't need to call the directory gems, but it's conventional and good practice to do so.

Ruby gems are the standard mechanism for deploying libraries, command-line tools, plugins, and even full libraries like Rails. Deploying web applications involves a different process. Besides pushing Ruby code, you'll want to manage the web server, update the database schema, and perform other management tasks. In the next section, we'll talk about Capistrano and Vlad the Deployer, two tools designed specifically for deploying and managing web applications.

8.2 *Deploying web applications*

So now you know how to deploy libraries and simple command-line applications. Web applications tend to be more complex. Besides the application and libraries, you have to take care of the web server itself, manage the database, process log files, mount network drives, and so forth. You might be deploying to a cluster of machines and configuring and managing multiple servers. These tasks call for a different kind of deployment and management tool.

In this section, we're going to discuss two such tools: Capistrano and Vlad the Deployer. Capistrano was developed originally for deploying Rails applications, but it can be used for many other remote deployment and management tasks. We'll look at a couple of examples of that. Vlad provides all the same features but is based entirely on Rake.

8.2.1 *Simplifying deployment with Capistrano*

Suppose we maintain a daemon written in Ruby that needs to be deployed to four production servers. We also need to test it on a staging server before pushing to production. We use subversion and release the daemons to the server from trunk when the release is ready. Our daemon is started and stopped via a shell command (`daemon_ctl start` and `daemon_ctl stop`). The `start` and `stop` commands handle cleaning up any zombie PID files.

Problem

You want to make sure that all four releases of your daemon make it to production, and that if any of them fail, they silently roll back. You have a production environment with four servers, and a staging environment with a single server. Both environments have identical requirements.

Solution

For this task, we're going to use Capistrano. Before setting this up, however, we'll need to gather information. Capistrano requires the username for the remote servers and subversion repository, the URL for the repository, and the directory the code will be checked out to.

Once we've gathered all this information, we need to add a file called "Capfile" to the root of our source tree. Deployment with Capistrano uses recipes, which are similar to Rake tasks. You'll find recipes on the web for managing Apache web servers, deploying Rails applications, using source control, starting and stopping background processes, migrating database schemas, and much more. These are placed in the Capfile and are loaded by the `cap` command-line tool. The Capfile we'll need for this problem is pretty straightforward. Listing 8.7 shows a sample of what we'll need.

Listing 8.7 Capfile for deploying a simple daemon

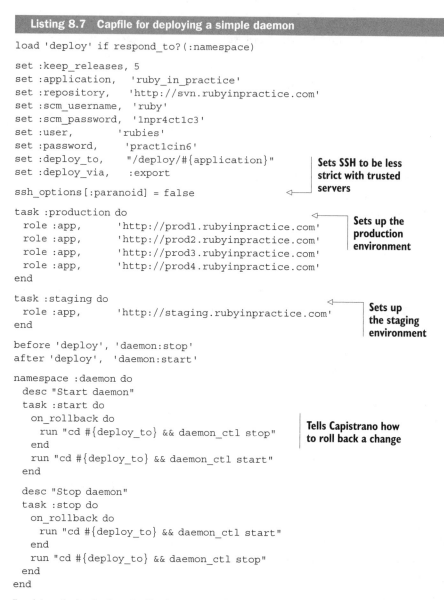

```
load 'deploy' if respond_to?(:namespace)

set :keep_releases, 5
set :application,   'ruby_in_practice'
set :repository,    'http://svn.rubyinpractice.com'
set :scm_username,  'ruby'
set :scm_password,  '1npr4ct1c3'
set :user,          'rubies'
set :password,      'pract1cin6'
set :deploy_to,     "/deploy/#{application}"          Sets SSH to be less
set :deploy_via,    :export                           strict with trusted
                                                      servers
ssh_options[:paranoid] = false        ◄──────┘

task :production do                           ◄─────  Sets up the
  role :app,     'http://prod1.rubyinpractice.com'    production
  role :app,     'http://prod2.rubyinpractice.com'    environment
  role :app,     'http://prod3.rubyinpractice.com'
  role :app,     'http://prod4.rubyinpractice.com'
end

task :staging do                              ◄─────  Sets up
  role :app,     'http://staging.rubyinpractice.com'  the staging
end                                                   environment

before 'deploy', 'daemon:stop'
after 'deploy', 'daemon:start'

namespace :daemon do
  desc "Start daemon"
  task :start do
    on_rollback do                                    Tells Capistrano how
      run "cd #{deploy_to} && daemon_ctl stop"        to roll back a change
    end
    run "cd #{deploy_to} && daemon_ctl start"
  end

  desc "Stop daemon"
  task :stop do
    on_rollback do
      run "cd #{deploy_to} && daemon_ctl start"
    end
    run "cd #{deploy_to} && daemon_ctl stop"
  end
end
```

In this relatively simple Capistrano recipe, we set up our environment, set up different environments for production and staging, and create two new tasks to start and stop the daemon. In order to be sure that the daemon will be turned off while we deploy and turned back on after we deploy, we used `before` and `after` filters to trigger the daemon at the appropriate times.

The most interesting parts of the Capistrano recipe are the `on_rollback` callbacks. Capistrano will automatically execute the rollback functions if any of the deployments fail, allowing you to specify that if the deployments fail, your daemons will turn back on.

Reusing recipes

Don't have time to reinvent the wheel? A quick search on Google will reveal Capistrano recipes that you can copy and paste into your Capfile and get started by building on other people's experience.

A great source for recipes is Deprec, available from http://deprec.rubyforge.org. Deprec is a collection of canned Capistrano recipes for setting up a production Rails server from scratch. And we do mean from scratch. It will copy SSH public keys over, install the entire Ruby on Rails stack, set up a working web server (Apache or Nginx), and get you up and running with minimum fuss.

Discussion

As you can see, it's pretty simple to use the default Capistrano deployment recipe to deploy non-Rails applications. That's because Capistrano's default code mainly handles checking code out of your source control system and deploying it to a remote location. You can use the `run` command to call out to shell commands on your remote servers, and they will be fired on all remote servers.

If necessary, you can use the `sudo` command to run the commands with superuser privileges. This allows you a fair bit of flexibility, effectively allowing you to do anything through Capistrano that you'd be able to do by manually logging in to your remote servers. Capistrano uses SSH to log into the remote server as the current user; if you maintain separate accounts, you can tell Capistrano to log in as a different user by passing `USER=name` as a command-line argument.

An important caveat of using `run` and `sudo` is that each command is run separately, and history is not preserved. That's why we used `run "cd #{deploy_to} && daemon_ctl stop"` in listing 8.7 instead of two separate run calls. That is typically not a problem, but it sometimes requires the creation of fairly convoluted code. In this respect, at least, a passing knowledge of the intricacies of bash can be quite helpful.

It is quite common to use Capistrano to deploy against and manage multiple environments. Our example was based on two environments, one for staging and one for production, and we used Capistrano tasks to configure each of these environments. For example, to deploy to the staging server, you would run this command:

```
$ cap staging deploy
```

To deploy to all the production servers, you'd run this command:

```
$ cap production deploy
```

Remember that `staging` and `production` are ordinary tasks. You can choose whatever name suits you. Just remember to run these tasks ahead of any task that requires the configuration, by placing it first on the command line.

Next, let's take a look at using Capistrano to intercept the incoming SSH stream in order to tail all of our remote logs at once.

8.2.2 *Tailing remote logs with Capistrano*

Now that we have our daemon purring away on four remote servers, we might want to look at the remote logs. Typically, you will want to see the logs from all four servers at once, with some sort of line-header indicating what server it's from. Since Capistrano uses Net::SSH, we can intercept the incoming stream, examine it, modify it, and then output it.

Problem

You want to connect to all of your remote servers, tail the logs, and have the results outputted to your local monitor.

Solution

We're going to use Net::SSH's incoming stream to get what we need. Capistrano's run and sudo commands both take an optional block with three arguments. The first argument is the channel, which is a Net::SSH::Connection::Channel object. You can get the full information about the object in the Net::SSH RDoc, but we will mainly use this object to extract information about which connection is being used. The next argument is the stream, which will be :err if the SSH connection returns an error. Finally, the last argument is the data being returned from the remote server.

This all comes together in listing 8.8, where we add support for tailing remote logs to our Capistrano recipe.

Listing 8.8   Tailing a remote log

```
desc "Tail log file to console"
task :tail do
  run "tail -f #{deploy_to}/log/daemon.log" do |channel, stream, data|
    server = channel[:server]
    puts if @last_host != server          ◁———  Specifies remote server name

    data.each { |line| puts "#{server}: #{line}" }    ◁———┐ Prints data
    break if stream == :err    ◁———┐                        │ to screen

    @last_host = server         Breaks if server
  end                           returns an error
end
```

As you can see, the recipe is pretty simple: we run a command on the remote server and then process it. We use an instance variable called @last_host to track the previous returned message, so we can put a blank line between messages from different servers.

Discussion

There's not much to say about this recipe because it's so straightforward. You'll probably want to take a look at the Net::SSH documentation, just to satisfy yourself about the internals (and especially if you want to go further with remote tailing), but the basics are pretty, well, basic. It's possible to get more adventurous and make each host use a different color for output. That's left as an exercise for the reader, but you might want to check out the ansi-colors gem, which allows you to do things like "string".red.on_white.

Interactive tasks using HighLine

When Capistrano needs to prompt you for input, it uses a terminal I/O library called HighLine. HighLine has a lot of interesting features for writing interactive tasks that require user intervention. You can use it to create colored output, to ask questions, to present a menu of choices, and to hide passwords entered on the console. You can find more about highline at http://highline.rubyforge.org.

We won't discuss HighLine at length here, but we'll show you a couple of examples:

```
task "time" do
  Capistrano::CLI.ui.say("The time is <%= color(Time.now, BOLD) %>")
end

task "nuke_everything" do
  if Capistrano::CLI.ui.ask("Nuke everything!?") == 'yes'
    nuke!
  else
    puts "Better safe then sorry."
  end
end
```

Another tool for remote deployment and management is Vlad the Deployer.

8.2.3 Deploying with Vlad the Deployer

As promised, let's dive into using Vlad the Deployer to handle deployment tasks. Capistrano and Vlad fulfill the same role but differ in the way you define and configure tasks. Vlad is based on Rake, which we covered in chapter 3, and if you're already using Rake extensively you may find it more familiar.

As we write this, Vlad the Deployer is still not quite up to snuff (it wouldn't be trivial to tail logs with Vlad as we did with Capistrano, for example), but for simple deployment, it's certainly a sight to behold.

Problem

As in section 8.2.1, you have a daemon that needs to be deployed to four servers via subversion. The deployment should roll back if any of them fail.

Solution

Vlad the Deployer is a Ruby package written by the Ruby Hit Squad. It aims to resolve several perceived core deficiencies with Capistrano. Specifically, it is dramatically smaller than Capistrano, weighing in at only 500 lines of code. It uses Rake as its core, so you can leverage your existing Rake knowledge in your deployment process. If you like using Rake for various development and management tasks, you'll appreciate being able to intermix deployment into your existing arsenal (you could force running all tests before deploying).

The starting point for Vlad is your existing Rakefile. To make use of Vlad, you must first require and load it:

```
require 'vlad'
Vlad.load
```

The load method supports a variety of configuration options for loading different recipes. For example, listing 8.9 shows a sample Rakefile that loads Vlad along with the Subversion and Mongrel recipes (these two are provided by Vlad).

Listing 8.9   Rakefile loading Vlad with Subversion and Mongrel recipes

```
require 'vlad'
Vlad.load :scm=>:subversion, :app=>:mongrel
```

The load method also loads the config/deploy.rb file, where you collect all the deployment configurations and tasks used by Vlad. Listing 8.10 shows a config/deploy.rb file that performs the same deployment tasks we used Capistrano for earlier.

Listing 8.10   config/deploy.rb for Vlad the Deployer

```
set :domain,        'rubyinpratice.com'
set :deploy_to,     '/deploy/ruby_in_practice'
set :repository,    'http://svn.rubyinpractice.com'

role :app,          "prod1.#{domain}"
role :app,          "prod2.#{domain}"
role :app,          "prod3.#{domain}"
role :app,          "prod4.#{domain}"

namespace 'daemon' do
  desc "Start daemon"
  remote_task 'start' do
    run "cd #{deploy_to} && daemon_ctl start"
  end

  desc "Stop daemon"
  remote_task 'stop' do
    run "cd #{deploy_to} && daemon_ctl stop"
  end
end

namespace 'vlad' do
  task 'update' => 'daemon:stop'

  task 'start' do
    task('daemon:start').invoke
  end

  task 'deploy' => ['update', 'migrate', 'start']
end
```

Discussion

Since Vlad uses Rake, you can use Rake's prerequisites and task actions to chain together tasks and add new behaviors to existing tasks.

In listing 8.10 we defined two remote tasks, daemon:start and daemon:stop. We enhanced Vlad's update task to run daemon:stop as a prerequisite, stopping the daemon before running the actual update. In contrast, we enhanced Vlad's start task to include a new action that will run the daemon:start task.

To trigger a Vlad deploy, run rake vlad:update vlad:migrate vlad:start. Alternatively, you can write a simple vlad:deploy task that runs all these tasks in sequence, as we did in listing 8.10.

To deploy new code, automatically stopping and starting the daemon as necessary, run this command:

```
$ rake vlad:deploy
```

Now that we've covered two ways to get your code onto the server, let's tackle keeping your code running once it's on the remote server. We'll look at a little Ruby utility called God that should handle most, if not all, of your monitoring needs.

8.3 Monitoring with God.rb

Once you have your daemon running on the remote server, you'll want to keep an eye on it. If it starts consuming too many system resources, you'll want to restart it; if it goes down, you'll want to be notified.

The tool we're going to discuss in this section is called God. God's influence is monit, a well-known Unix system-management tool. Whereas monit uses its own syntax and miniconfiguration language, God allows you to write notification rules directly in Ruby, for more flexibility and control. It also solves some of the most annoying issues that were present in monit, especially when handing daemons and PIDs. In short, God is everything that monit is as well as everything people wanted monit to be. You can find God at http://god.rubyforge.org.

8.3.1 A typical God setup

In section 8.2 we deployed a daemon process to our production servers. We'll continue with the same scenario, and use God to monitor the daemons running on our production servers.

Problem

You want to watch your daemon and make sure it stays up. Additionally, you want a way to gracefully start and stop the daemon, and to make sure it's not gobbling up all your system resources.

Solution

In listing 8.11, we'll use God.rb to set up our monitoring environment, which will include monitoring, graceful startup and shutdown, and resource-usage monitoring.

Listing 8.11 Watching daemon processes with God.rb

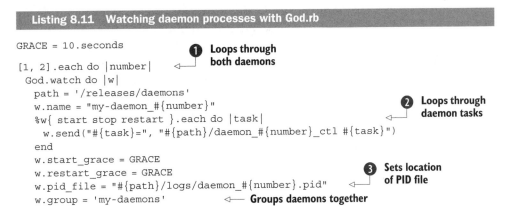

```
  w.interval = 30.seconds                          ❹  Cleans zombie
  w.behavior(:clean_pid_file)     ◄─┘                 PIDs

  w.start_if do |start|                            ◄──❺  Starts condition
    start.condition(:process_running) do |c|
      c.interval = 5.seconds
      c.running = false
    end
  end
                                                   ❻  Restarts
  w.restart_if do |restart|           ◄─┘             conditions
    restart.condition(:memory_usage) do |c|
      c.above = 50.megabytes
      c.times = [2, 3]
    end

    restart.condition(:cpu_usage) do |c|
      c.above = 30.percent
      c.times = 5
    end
  end
                                       ❼  Sets lifecycle
  w.lifecycle do |on|            ◄─┘      conditions
    on.condition(:flapping) do |c|
      c.to_state = [:start, :restart]
      c.times = 5
      c.within = 5.minutes
      c.transition = :unmonitored
      c.retry_in = 10.minutes
      c.retry_times = 5
      c.retry_within = 2.hours
    end
  end

  end
end
```

In order to avoid having to type the entire configuration file twice, we loop over the daemon numbers ❶. If we add additional daemons, we'll probably want to add more daemons to this list. Also note that this God configuration file is appropriate for our staging environment, where we have both daemons on the same server. We can use the exact same script on the production environments by removing the daemon numbers that will not be run on the server in question.

We also loop over the start, stop, and restart tasks, so we can easily change the command that is used to manage the daemons later ❷ without having to change it in three places. We specify the location of the PID file that will be created by the daemon ❸, which, in this particular case, will be inside the log directory in our release directory.

Because we rely on PID files, we must consider the possibility that our code will be killed without the opportunity for the PID to be correctly cleaned. This is called a "zombie PID," and it can wreak havoc with our daemon start script. That's why God provides the :clean_pid_file behavior, which will wipe out existing PIDs before it attempts to start up your code ❹.

We use one rule to monitor each daemon process every 5 seconds and start it if it's not already started or if it crashed ❺. Two additional rules will restart the process if it runs amok, which we define as eating up 50MB of memory two out of three times, or if it uses over 30 percent of CPU five consecutive times ❻. These are checked at the default 30-second interval.

Finally, we can set some events to occur across state changes (called lifecycle conditions). In this case, we want to handle the situation where God keeps trying to start the process, but it keeps failing (the `flapping` condition) ❼. We try more frequently early on, but then taper off as time goes on, and eventually give up. Specifically, if the daemon gets started or restarted five times in five minutes, we stop monitoring for ten minutes (in case the problem was intermittent and goes away if you leave it alone for a bit). If the flapping occurs more than five times over two hours, we give up.

Discussion

The configuration file in listing 8.11, while designed to handle the special case we developed in sections 8.2.1 and 8.2.2, is still very similar to the configuration file that the creator of God.rb uses to monitor his mongrels at http://en.gravatar.com, and which he makes available on the God.rb site (http://god.rubyforge.org). Chances are your configuration file will look similar as well. After all, there's not much difference between monitoring one server or another.

As you noticed, God's condition syntax is pretty easy to use. For every event (`start`, `stop`, `restart`), you can specify conditions that should trigger the event. In our example, we chose to trigger the `start` event if the daemon is not running, and check its status every 5 seconds. We also protect against runaway conditions like memory leaks and infinite loops by restarting the daemon. In our example, we trigger a restart if memory usage goes beyond 50MB in two out of the last three times we checked it. We trigger a restart if CPU usage goes above 30 percent five times in a row.

Obviously these limits will be different, depending on the application you're monitoring and the environment it's running, as would the reaction time. When God checks the process status, memory consumption may be high because the garbage collector didn't get the chance to claim unused memory yet. Likewise, CPU usage could reach 100 percent when running a critical section of code. By telling God to ignore these momentary spikes, we reduce the chance of false positives.

In our example, we set the `start` condition to check every 5 seconds, restarting a crashed daemon as soon as possible. For the `restart` tasks, we use a 30-second interval: if our daemon enters an infinite loop, God will notice that within the first 30 seconds, but will take an additional two minutes before making a decision and reacting. Unfortunately, picking up the right setup is a trade-off between response time and accuracy, and it's more art than science.

Monitoring our servers for failure and overcapacity creates a self-healing environment. Sometimes, an attempt to recover from a spike in load will create even more burden on the server, leading to a domino effect of ever-increasing restarts, or *flapping*. For that reason, we also monitor and react to lifecycle changes; for example, backing off from restarting a process when it looks like our attempt at recovery leads to cascading failure.

Likewise, monitoring for lifecycle changes can alert system administrators to bugs in the code, areas that need optimization, or the need for a hardware upgrade. We'll look at that next.

8.3.2 Notifications

Now that we have an infrastructure for keeping our daemons up and running, we'll probably want to be notified if they go down. In particular, when the flapping condition gives up after two hours of failures, we probably want the entire team to be notified. On the other hand, more minor issues can be sent to the team lead only.

Problem

You want to set up God.rb to notify the entire team after a flapping failure, but only the team lead if the process is restarted due to excess CPU or RAM usage.

Solution

Listing 8.12 shows how we can set up God to send emails.

Listing 8.12 Telling God.rb how to notify our team members

```
God::Contacts::Email.message_settings = {
  :from => 'daemon_master@example.com'
}

God::Contacts::Email.server_settings = {
  :address => 'daemons.example.com',
  :port => 25,
  :domain => 'example.com',
  :authentication => :plain,
  :user_name => 'daemon_master',
  :password => 't3hm4n'
}

{ 'lead' => 'lead@example.com',
  'joe'  => 'joesmith@example.com',
  'john' => 'theman@example.com',
  'mark' => 'marky@example.com' }.each do |name, email|
  God.contact(:email) do |c|
    c.name  = name
    c.email = email
    c.group = 'developers'
  end
end
```

To simplify setting up large numbers of email addresses, we've looped through a `Hash` and set the emails all at once. If you have a very large number of emails to set up, you might do something similar but with an external YAML file.

Now that we have our emails and groups set up, listing 8.13 shows how we can attach our notifications to the conditions specified in listing 8.11.

Listing 8.13 Monitoring with notifications

```
require 'emails.god'

GRACE = 10.seconds

[1, 2].each do |number|
  God.watch do |w|
    path = '/releases/daemons'
    w.name = "my-daemon_#{number}"
    %w{ start stop restart }.each do |task|
      w.send("#{task}=", "#{path}/daemon_#{number}_ctl #{task}")
    end
    w.start_grace = GRACE
    w.restart_grace = GRACE
    w.pid_file = "#{path}/logs/daemon_#{number}.pid"
    w.group = 'my-daemons'
    w.interval = 30.seconds

    w.behavior(:clean_pid_file)

    w.start_if do |start|
      start.condition(:process_running) do |c|
        c.interval = 5.seconds
        c.running = false
        c.notify = 'lead'
      end
    end

    w.restart_if do |restart|
      restart.condition(:memory_usage) do |c|
        c.above = 50.megabytes
        c.times = [2, 3]
        c.notify = 'lead'
      end

      restart.condition(:cpu_usage) do |c|
        c.above = 30.percent
        c.times = 5
        c.notify = 'lead'
      end
    end

    w.lifecycle do |on|
      on.condition(:flapping) do |c|
        c.to_state = [:start, :restart]
        c.times = 5
        c.within = 5.minutes
        c.transition = :unmonitored
        c.retry_in = 10.minutes
        c.retry_times = 5
        c.retry_within = 2.hours
        c.notify = 'developers'
      end
    end

  end
end
```

❶ Notifies lead developer about restart

❷ Notifies all developers about flapping

For simplicity, we broke the configuration file into two parts. The first specifies the email addresses to use (listing 8.12). The second (listing 8.13) uses the same monitoring configuration that we explored in section 8.3.1, with the addition of notifications. We added notification to the lead developer whenever the daemon is restarted after a crash or is forced to restart due to memory or CPU consumption ❶. Flapping conditions are typically a sign our code is going out of control, so we notify the entire developers group ❷.

Discussion

Now that we have a configuration file, it's time to use it. We'll start by testing it out, and for that we'll run God in the console:

```
$ sudo god -c config.god -D
```

You'll see messages from God as it's loading the configuration file and monitoring the processes. That will help you troubleshoot any problems with your configuration file. To stop God, press Ctrl-C.

Once you know the configuration file works, it's time to deploy God as a background process. You can do that using init scripts, `launchd`, or whatever works best in your environment. Here is an example of a cron task that runs God on every boot:

```
@reboot god -c /etc/god/config.god
```

You can then check whether God is running:

```
$ sudo god status
my-daemons:
  my-daemon_1: up
  my-daemon_2: up
```

Other commands allow you to start and stop tasks, load new configurations, and terminate god. Run `god --help` for more information.

8.4 *Summary*

Deploying Ruby applications is a complex topic. Most people use a mix of Ruby, Unix, and hand-rolled tools in their full deployment solution. What most people don't know, is how mature the existing Ruby tools are. In fact, because Ruby is a flexible and powerful language for running command-line scripts, you should also consider using these tools for tasks not specific to Ruby, such as deploying PHP applications or monitoring various servers and processes in your environment.

For automated deployment to a remote server, you can use either Capistrano or Vlad the Deployer to automate even fairly complex, transactional remote tasks. To share code within your organization, the RubyGems infrastructure has become extremely stable with version 1.0, allowing you to create, within your organization, a repository akin to the one people use for their day-to-day packaging systems.

For monitoring, you can say goodbye to the arcane monit tool and say hello to the pure-Ruby God.rb. God.rb even handles emailing and fairly complex monitoring rules, so you'll never need to manually SSH into your server to find out why your app is down again.

The landscape is only getting better with time. Capistrano, Vlad, and God.rb get better with every release, and as Ruby improves, so will these tools. Compared with old-school Unix utilities that are stuck in the '90s and require some fairly advanced system programming knowledge to hack on, the choice is clear. Ruby deployment tools have arrived.

We just covered web applications and deployment, and through some of the examples showed you how to build Ruby applications that use relational databases. In the next chapter, we're going to delve deeper into databases and show you more options for handling data storage from Ruby applications.

Part 3

Data and
document techniques

Working with some form of data is the fundamental task of any application, whether it's a database, a text file, XML, or JSON.

In chapters 9 through 13, we'll show you some Ruby tools for working with data in the most common formats and environments, from databases to structured data. Then we'll show you how to take that data and index, search, and report on it.

9
Database
facilities and techniques

This chapter covers

- Using plain text data storage
- Automating contacts in an address book
- Using Ruby's API for gdbm
- Using relational databases

So far we've taken a look at a number of technologies and how to use them with Ruby. This chapter will introduce key database tools available with, and for, Ruby. We'll take a broad view of what it means for something to be a database. Our working definition will be that a database is a storage unit external to your program where data can be stored. This definition includes highly evolved structures like relational databases, but also includes, potentially, plain-text files.

We'll also stipulate that the stored data has to have some intelligence about itself. A file containing a stream of words—though it may be loaded into a program as a string or an array—will not count as a database, because the file itself does not preserve any information about the structure of the data.

A flat file in YAML format, however, will count as a database, under our definition. As you'll see, it's possible and not even terribly difficult to wrap a YAML file in a workable API and reap the benefits of addressing your data structurally while also having access to it in text form. Text files are not the whole story, of course. Ruby ships with several flavors of the Berkeley database (DBM) system. We'll also look at tools available for creating and manipulating relational databases in Ruby.

Throughout the chapter, we'll work with a specific example: the implementation of an API for storing personal contacts—an address book. We're not so much concerned here with implementing the whole address book as with implementing the programming interface to the database facilities. Examples will include a certain amount of address-book implementation, but primarily we'll be looking at how to set up a database in which contact information can be stored, and how to talk to such a database in Ruby. We'll implement the API twice, once for YAML storage and once for gdbm. We'll then use the MySQL and database interface libraries (DBI) to move data from one database format to another.

We're going to start with YAML, a data-serialization tool that can, with a little assistance from Ruby, form the kernel of a simple data-persistence library.

9.1   *Using plain-text files for data persistence*

Using YAML as a data-persistence tool is an example of the more general case of using plain-text files for this purpose. You'll find other ways to do this in Ruby, such as the CSV (comma-separated values) facility in the standard library. XML files fall into this category, too.

None of these are full-fledged database systems. What they have in common with such systems is that they include information about the data, together with the data. CSV files don't contain *much* information about the data, but they do preserve ordering and, often, something like column or header information. XML preserves relationships in and among nested data structures. YAML does something similar with the avowed goal of being somewhat easier to read than XML, and more suitable for storing arbitrary Ruby data structures.

In looking at plain-text data-storage techniques, then, we'll focus on YAML as the one that offers the richest combination of complexity on the data end and editability on the text end.

NOTE   This example covers YAML persistence, but we also cover YAML elsewhere in more depth. See chapter 10 for in-depth coverage of using YAML as a persistence mechanism.

YAML is a data-serialization format: Ruby objects go in, and a string representation comes out. The strings generated by YAML conform to the YAML specification. YAML, itself, is not specific to Ruby; Ruby has an API for it, but so do numerous other languages. Here's a Ruby example in an irb session:

```
>> hash = { :one => 1, :two => 2, :colors => ["red","green","blue"] }
=> {:colors=>["red", "green", "blue"], :one=>1, :two=>2}
>> require 'yaml'          ❶
=> true
>> puts hash.to_yaml       ❷
```

```
---
:colors:
- red
- green
- blue
:one: 1
:two: 2
```

YAML is part of the Ruby standard library. You just have to load it ❶, and then your objects can be serialized to YAML using the to_yaml method ❷.

Objects serialized to YAML can be read back into memory. Picking up from the last example:

```
>> y_hash = hash.to_yaml
=> "--- \n:colors: \n- red\n- green\n- blue\n:one: 1\n:two: 2\n"
>> new_hash = YAML.load(y_hash)
=> {:colors=>["red", "green", "blue"], :one=>1, :two=>2}
>> new_hash == hash
=> true
```

The YAML.load method can take either a string or an I/O read handle as its argument, and it deserializes the string or stream from YAML format into actual Ruby objects.

While objects are in serialized string form, you can edit them directly. In other words, YAML gives you a way to save data and also edit it in plain-text, human-readable form. Part of the incentive behind the creation of YAML was to provide a plain-text format for representing nested data structures that wasn't quite as visually busy as XML.

Problem

You need a way to automate the storage and retrieval of professional and personal contacts (an address book), but you want it to be in plain text so that you can edit the entries in a text editor as well as alter them programmatically.

Solution

We'll write code that uses YAML, together with simple file I/O operations, to provide a programmatic interface to a plain text file containing contact entries.

First things first: let's start with a test suite. Aside from the merits of writing tests in general, this will allow us to create examples of how the code should be used before we've even written it. There's no better way to describe how you want an API to work than to write some tests that put it to use.

We'll create two classes: Contact and ContactList. The initializer for Contact will take the contact's name as the sole argument and will yield the new Contact instance back to the block, where it can be used to set more values. Listing 9.1 shows the class declaration and setup method for the test suite—you can place this code in a file called contacts_y_test.rb (the "y" indicates that this is for the YAML implementation). Our API for the contact code has already started to take shape.

Listing 9.1   Class declaration and setup method for testing the contact code

```
require "test/unit"
require "contacts_y"        ❶
class TestContacts < Test::Unit::TestCase
```

```
def setup
  @filename = "contacts"
  @list = ContactList.new(@filename)          ❷

  @contact = Contact.new("Joe Smith")         ❸
  joe.email = "joe@somewhere.abc"             ❹
  joe.home[:street1] = "123 Main Street"      ❺
  joe.home[:city] = "Somewhere"
  joe.work[:phone] = "(000) 123-4567"
  joe.extras[:instrument] = "Cello"

  @list << @contact          ❻
  end
end
```

In addition to test/unit, we load what will eventually be our implementation file: contacts_y.rb ❶. After the loading preliminaries, we instantiate a contact list along with a filename ❷, and a contact with a name ❸. In addition to the name, the contact has an email address ❹, and several apparently deeper hash-like data structures: home, work, and extras ❺. *The* ContactList object itself appears, not surprisingly, to have an array-like interface, judging by the appearance of the append operator (<<) ❻.

Now it's time to write some tests for business logic. The setup method inserts one Contact object into the list. What about retrieving an object? Listing 9.2 shows a method that does exactly that.

Listing 9.2   Testing the removal of a Contact object from a ContactList object

```
def test_retrieve_contact_from_list      ❶
  contact = @list["Joe Smith"]
  assert_equal("Joe Smith", contact.name)
end

def test_delete_contact_from_list        ❷
  assert(!@list.empty?)
  @list.delete(@contact.name)
  assert(@list.empty?)
end
end
```

Listing 9.2 includes a method that retrieves a contact ❶ and one that removes a contact from the list ❷. These two methods go in the test file after the setup method. We'll also close out the class so that we can write the implementation and get the test to pass.

Let's start with the ContactList class. We'll give each ContactList instance an array, in which it will store the actual Contact objects. The business of the ContactList class will consist mostly of deciding what, and when, to pass along to this array: inserting contacts, removing contacts, and, of course, persisting contacts to a YAML file and reading contacts from a file.

The initial implementation of ContactList is shown in listing 9.3. We're not using YAML yet, but we'll need it, so it's being loaded. (We're also not yet using the contacts accessor methods, but we'll use it a little later so it's best to put it in now.) Most of the action is in the `@contacts` array, which is expected to contain `Contact` objects. The code in listing 9.3 can be saved to contacts_y.rb.

Listing 9.3 Initial implementation of the `ContactList` class

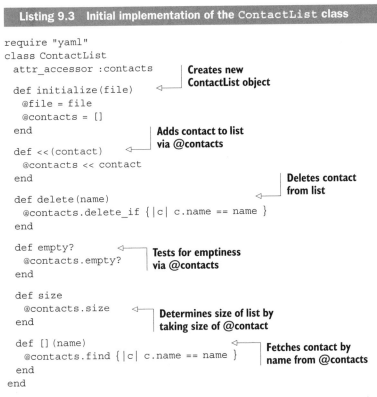

```
require "yaml"
class ContactList
  attr_accessor :contacts

  def initialize(file)            ◁──── Creates new
    @file = file                         ContactList object
    @contacts = []
  end
                                  ┌── Adds contact to list
  def <<(contact)          ◁──────┘   via @contacts
    @contacts << contact
  end
                                        ┌── Deletes contact
  def delete(name)                 ◁────┘   from list
    @contacts.delete_if {|c| c.name == name }
  end

  def empty?           ◁────┐ Tests for emptiness
    @contacts.empty?        │ via @contacts
  end

  def size
    @contacts.size     ◁────┐ Determines size of list by
  end                       │ taking size of @contact

  def [](name)                    ◁────┐ Fetches contact by
    @contacts.find {|c| c.name == name }│ name from @contacts
  end
end
```

The `@contacts` array fields requests for array-like operations. Some of these operations work the way they do out of the box for any Ruby array (such as `empty?`, `size`, and `<<`). Others require special implementation to make sure they do the right thing for a list of `Contact` objects. Note that `delete` and `[]` use a name lookup to figure out which contact you want to operate on.

Next comes the implementation of the `Contact` class, which will be responsible for storing the contact information itself. We want to be able to store separate contact info for home and work. Each of these sets of data will be stored as a hash and accessed as an attribute of the `Contact` object. The name and email properties will be separate, stored as individual attributes rather than parts of any of the hashes, as shown in listing 9.4.

Listing 9.4 The `Contact` class we use to store contact records

```
class Contact
  attr_reader :name, :email, :home, :work, :extras
  attr_writer :name, :email
  def initialize(name)
    @name = name
```

```
    @home = {}
    @work = {}
    @extras = {}
  end
end
```

Now, we can run the tests:

```
$ ruby contacts_y_test.rb
Loaded suite contacts_y_test
Started
..
Finished in 0.000594 seconds.

2 tests, 3 assertions, 0 failures, 0 errors
```

Success: no failures, no errors.

Now let's get to the YAML side of things. We want a `ContactList` object to know how to save itself, in YAML format, to a file, and we want the `ContactList` *class* to know how to load a YAML file into a new `ContactList` instance. Listing 9.5 shows a test for these functions; you can paste this test into the existing test class.

Listing 9.5   Saving and loading a `ContactList` object

```
def test_save_and_load_list
  @list.save
  relist = ContactList.load(@filename)
  assert_equal(1,relist.size)
  contact = relist["Joe Smith"]
  assert_equal("Joe Smith", contact.name)
end
```

To get these new assertions to succeed, we have to add `save` and `load` methods to the `ContactList` class, as shown in listing 9.6.

Listing 9.6   Second set of methods for the `ContactList` class

```
def save
  File.open(@file, "w") do |fh|
    fh.puts(@contacts.to_yaml)          ❶
  end
end

def self.load(file)          ❷
  list = new(file)
  list.contacts = YAML.load(File.read(file))          ❸
  list
end
```

These two methods can be pasted into the class definition for `ContactList`. Note that `load` is a class method, so it's defined directly on the `ContactList` class object (represented in context by `self` ❷).

It's in the `load` and `save` methods that you can see the use of YAML, and it's very simple. When you want to save the list, you convert its `@contacts` array to YAML and print the resulting string to the file ❶. When you want to read the list in, you use the `load` class method of YAML, passing it a string consisting of the contents of the file ❸. (You can also pass an open `File` object to `YAML.load`.)

The new tests pass. And so, with rather little fanfare, we have data persistence. Running the tests will create a file called "contacts", containing the YAML representation of the Joe Smith contact. This brings us to the other side of the YAML coin: the ability to edit the YAML file itself. You do have to be a bit careful, because the YAML specification has rules you have to follow. But as long as you follow the YAML rules, you can make as many changes as you want to the file between reads.

Listing 9.7 shows the contacts file resulting from running the tests for the contact classes.

Listing 9.7   The contacts output file, in YAML format

```
---
- !ruby/object:Contact
  email: joe@somewhere.abc
  extras:
    :instrument: Cello
  home:
    :city: Somewhere
    :street1: 123 Main Street
  name: Joe Smith
  work:
    :phone: (000) 123-4567
```

You don't want to touch the first two lines, which are YAML's business. But you can change the values of the strings, or add more data, and all your changes will be happily absorbed into the in-memory `Contact` objects next time you use the `Contact` class.

Discussion

YAML provides easy serialization of objects to strings, and it's not much harder to save those strings to a file. Whether or not you decide it's technically correct to call this a database, it certainly has database-like properties. You don't *have* to edit your YAML files by hand; you can treat them as a black box. But it's nice to know that they're easy to edit.

Still, plain-text files are far from the only game in town. We'll look next at Ruby's API for gdbm, the GNU version of the Berkeley DB database system.

9.2   *Using the (g)dbm API*

Ruby ships with wrappers for the DBM, gdbm, and sdbm database libraries. These libraries are a family, of which the original member is DBM. The GNU Database Manager version is gdbm, and sdbm (Substitute DBM) is a public-domain version based on the earlier ndbm (New Database Manager, a successor to DBM). We'll focus on gdbm here, though the examples should work with any of the three *dbm libraries included with Ruby.

Problem

You want a simple contact manager, and you need to share the files with someone who may not have access to YAML.

Solution

Our hypothetical YAML crisis provides a chance to look at a gdbm-based solution. We'll aim for something that's as close as possible to the YAML version of the contact manager, and the best way to guarantee that closeness is to use a similar test suite.

The tests are shown in listing 9.8. Note that we're loading contacts_g, implying that the implementation of the two classes will be in contacts_g.rb.

Listing 9.8   The contact application tests

```
require 'test/unit'
require 'contacts_g'

Dir.mkdir("gdbm_contacts") unless File.exist?("gdbm_contacts")       ❶

class GDBMTest < Test::Unit::TestCase
  def setup
    @list = ContactList.new("gdbm_contacts")
    @contact = Contact.new("Joe Smith")
    @list << @contact                              ❷

    @contact.home["street1"] = "123 Main Street"       ❸
    @contact.home["city"] = "Somewhere"
    @contact.work["phone"] = "(000) 123-4567"
    @contact.extras["instrument"] = "Cello"
    @contact.email = "joe@somewhere.abc"
  end

  def test_retrieving_a_contact_from_list
    contact = @list["Joe Smith"]
    assert_equal("Joe Smith", contact.name)
  end

  def test_delete_a_contact_from_list
    assert(!@list.empty?)
    @list.delete("Joe Smith")
    assert(@list.empty?)
    assert(@list.contact_cache.empty?)
  end

  def test_home
    contact = @list["Joe Smith"]
    assert_equal("123 Main Street", contact.home["street1"])
  end

  def test_email
    contact = @list["Joe Smith"]
    assert_equal("joe@somewhere.abc", contact.email)
  end

  def test_non_existent_contact_is_nil
    assert_equal(nil, @list["Some Person"])
  end

  def teardown
    @list.delete("Joe Smith") if @list["Joe Smith"]
  end
end
```

The test suite for the gdbm implementation is similar to the one for the YAML implementation, but there are a few differences. One extra step here is creating the gdbm_contacts directory, so that the tests will be able to find it ❶. Also, some tests have been replaced to show you some of what you might want to do specifically for gdbm (though neither test suite is exhaustive). It's now necessary to add the contact to the list *before* setting any of the contact's properties ❷. The reason is the hash-to-database magic only works if the contact's components—home, work, extras—are gdbm file handles. And that will only happen when the Contact objects become part of a ContactList; it's the ContactList object that knows where the directory of gdbm files is.

Another tweak is that all keys are now strings, instead of symbols ❸. gdbm doesn't like symbols; it wants everything to be strings. Nonetheless, the goal of preserving the API in the gdbm reimplementation has been largely met, assuming we can get the tests to pass. On now to the implementation itself.

The way gdbm works is very different from the way YAML works. gdbm is definitely more of a real database, but it is simpler in terms of the kinds of data structures it can store. gdbm stores key/value pairs. The Ruby gdbm extension is programmed almost exactly like a hash.

Here's a simple example of using gdbm. First, run this code from a file—it will create a file called movies.db, so make sure you're not clobbering one!

```
require 'gdbm'

movies = GDBM.new("movies.db")
movies.update(
      { "Vertigo" => "Alfred Hitchcock",
       "In a Lonely Place" => "Nicholas Ray",
       "Johnny Guitar" => "Nicholas Ray",
       "Touch of Evil" => "Orson Welles",
       "Psycho"  => "Alfred Hitchcock",
       })

movies.close
```

Notice the use of the update method, which is familiar as a hash operation. Now, go into irb and do this:

```
>> require "gdbm"
=> true
>> movies = GDBM.new("movies.db")
=> #<GDBM:0xb7ef12cc>
>> movies.values.uniq
```

You'll get a list of all the directors in your database:

```
=> ["Orson Welles", "Nicholas Ray", "Alfred Hitchcock"]
```

The gdbm API is designed to be as hash-like as possible, with all the hash operations automatically writing to, or reading from, the database file.

The contact data we're storing isn't a simple hash, though. A contact has a name and an email address, which are just strings and could serve as hash keys, but the additional information, such as the home data, comes in the form of nested or embedded hashes.

One way to use gdbm in a situation where you need hashes within hashes is to serialize the inner hashes with YAML, and store them as strings. There's nothing terrible about doing that, but we've already looked at a YAML solution, so we'll do it a different way here. For our gdbm implementation of the contact list, the entire list will be represented by a *directory*, and each contact will have its own *subdirectory*. Inside that subdirectory, there will be individual gdbm files for each of the inner data structures: home, work, extras.

In the YAML implementation, a `ContactList` object was a kind of proxy to the actual array of `Contact` objects. In the gdbm implementation, `ContactList` objects will be proxies to directories. It's desirable to keep the API as transparent as possible. As API users, we don't want to have to know the details of how the files are being handled, so all of that can be encapsulated in the `ContactList` class.

The `Contact` objects can do their share of the lifting, too. A `ContactList` is in charge of a whole directory, and each contact has a subdirectory. It makes sense, then, for the `Contact` object to know the name of its directory.

Let's start this time with the `Contact` class. It's shown in listing 9.9.

Listing 9.9   The `Contact` class for the gdbm implementation of the contacts library

```
class Contact
  COMPONENTS = ["home", "extras", "work"]          ❶
  attr_accessor :name, *COMPONENTS                 ❷
  attr_reader :dirname          ❸

  def initialize(name)          ❹
    @name = name
    @dirname = @name.gsub(" ", "_")
  end

  def components        ❺
    COMPONENTS.map {|comp_name| self.send(comp_name) }
  end

  def open
    COMPONENTS.each do |component|
      self.send(component + "=", GDBM.new(component))        ❻
    end
  end

  def close
    components.each do |component|
      component.close unless component.closed?        ❼
    end
  end

  def email          ❽
    extras["email"]
  end

  def email=(e)
    extras["email"] = e
  end
end
```

One addition to the `Contact` class is the `COMPONENTS` constant ❶, which contains an array of strings corresponding to the nested containers in the `Contact` objects. The point of having this constant is to encapsulate these names in one place. That way, both the `Contact` and `ContactList` objects can find all of them easily, and the names will not have to be hard-coded in specific methods. Moreover, as you'll see when we look at the `ContactList` class, each component is actually going to be the name of a gdbm database: one each for `home`, `work`, and `extras`.

We want a read-write attribute for name, and one for each of the components ❷. Using the unary * operator on `COMPONENTS` has the effect of turning the array into a bare list, so it's as if we'd written this:

```
attr_accessor :name, :home, :work, :extras
```

We also want each `Contact` object to have a reader attribute in which it can store the name of its directory ❸, which will be a subdirectory of the master directory of the contact list to which the contact belongs.

The `initialize` method preserves the name (which is the actual name of the person whose contact information this is), and also stores the directory name ❹. The creation of the directory name involves replacing spaces in the name with underscores. You can adjust this if you prefer a different munging algorithm, as long as the result is a valid directory name (and preferably a reasonably cross-platform one).

The `components` method provides a translation from the component names to the actual components ❺. This, in turn, allows the `close` method to walk efficiently through all the components, performing a `close` operation on any that are not already closed.

Speaking of the `close` method, the `Contact` class provides both `open` and `close` methods. The `open` method creates a new gdbm object for each component ❻, assigning that new object to the relevant component attribute of the contact. If there's already a file with the appropriate name (for example, "extras"), gdbm will open it for reading and writing; otherwise, it will be created. (There are some further subtleties to the way gdbm handles read and write access, but we'll assume for the purposes of the contact list that it's private and only being accessed by one program at a time.)

The `close` method goes through the components corresponding to the filenames in which the data is stored, and performs the gdbm `close` operation on each one. This terminates the database connection to each file ❼.

Finally, we include special methods for handling the contact's email address ❽. The email address gets stored in, and retrieved from, the `extras["email"]` slot. The point of writing these methods is to enable us to set and retrieve the email address as if it were a simple attribute, even though storing it is a little bit involved. (A contact might have separate home and work email addresses, of course. But we'll keep it simple, as we did in the YAML implementation, and assume that each contact has only one email address.)

Now, let's look at `ContactList`. The specifics of implementing this class derive partly from the way gdbm works, and partly from the way directories work. We want to be able to get a contact from a contact list:

```
contact = @list["Joe Smith"]
```

The list object is going to need to go to the directory, look for a directory with the right name, and load all the gdbm files into a Contact object. Fair enough, but not very efficient. It might pay to keep a cache of Contact objects on hand, so the search doesn't have to be repeated if the same contact is requested twice.

With that in mind, look at listing 9.10, which shows the first segment of the ContactList class, including the initialize method, the [] method (which retrieves a Contact object by name), and a helper method called populate_contact. You can add this code to the top of the file containing the Contact class (or the bottom, though if you do that, it's best to follow the convention of keeping the two require lines at the top of the file).

Listing 9.10   The ContactList class for storing contact records

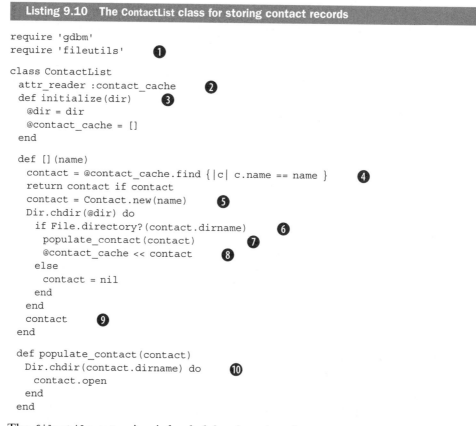

```ruby
require 'gdbm'
require 'fileutils'                    1

class ContactList
  attr_reader :contact_cache           2
  def initialize(dir)                  3
    @dir = dir
    @contact_cache = []
  end

  def [](name)
    contact = @contact_cache.find {|c| c.name == name }    4
    return contact if contact
    contact = Contact.new(name)        5
    Dir.chdir(@dir) do
      if File.directory?(contact.dirname)     6
        populate_contact(contact)             7
        @contact_cache << contact             8
      else
        contact = nil
      end
    end
    contact                            9
  end

  def populate_contact(contact)
    Dir.chdir(contact.dirname) do      10
      contact.open
    end
  end
end
```

The fileutils extension is loaded for the sake of one or two utility methods to be used later ❶.

Then, upon initialization ❸, the list stores its directory and creates an array that will serve to cache Contact objects. That array is available as a reader attribute ❷. When you try to retrieve a contact from the list, the list object first checks the cache ❹. If the contact is there, it returns it. If the contact isn't there, the real fun starts.

First, a new Contact object is created ❺. Then, the ContactList object switches to its own directory, where it looks for a subdirectory whose name is the same as the directory name reported by the Contact object—"Joe_Smith" for the contact "Joe Smith," for example ❻. If such a directory exists, the contact's components get initialized to a new gdbm database object, based on the component name ❼. The contact is now added to the list's contact cache ❽, so that the whole directory-based instantiation won't have to be repeated during this session. If, however, the directory corresponding to the requested component name does not exist, the contact variable is reset to nil. This indicates a request for a nonexistent contact. (Remember, you're just trying to fetch an existing contact, not create one.)

Finally, the value of the contact variable—which is going to be either nil or a gdbm object—is returned from the method ❾. If it's nil, you know that the contact you requested does not exist on this list. The populate_contact utility method navigates from the top directory of the list down to the specific subdirectory for this contact ❿. It then calls the open method on the contact—which, as you'll recall, calls GDBM.new on each of the contact's components, creating database handles on the relevant files.

Now let's look at adding an object to a list and removing one from the list. We're shooting for the same API as the YAML version:

```
@list << contact        # add a contact
@list.delete(contact)   # delete a contact
```

As listing 9.11 shows, these operations require attention to the filesystem and directory structure.

Listing 9.11   Adding and removing a contact

```
def <<(contact)
  Dir.chdir(@dir) do
    Dir.mkdir(contact.dirname) unless File.exists?(contact.dirname)     ❶
    populate_contact(contact)
  end
  @contact_cache << contact       ❷
end

def delete(name)
  contact = self[name]
  return false unless contact     ❸
  contact.close       ❹
  Dir.chdir(@dir) do
    FileUtils.rm_rf(contact.dirname)      ❺
  end
  contact_cache.delete_if {|c| c.name == name }     ❻
  true      ❼
end
```

To add a contact, we need to create a new directory, unless one exists ❶ (which is possible; there could already be a Contact object corresponding to this directory, even if it's not part of a contact list). We also need to go into the directory and populate the contact's components based on the gdbm files in the directory, creating them as necessary or just opening them for reading if they're already there. Finally, we add the contact to the list's contact cache ❷.

Removing a contact involves several steps. First, we only want to delete contacts we actually have, so the method returns `false` if the contact is unknown ❸. Second, we ask the contact to close itself, which means walking through the components and closing each gdbm connection in turn ❹. Then we use the `FileUtils.rm_rf` method to delete the contact's directory ❺, remove it from the cache if it's there ❻, and return `true` to indicate a successful deletion ❼.

Arguably, directory removal is a rather harsh step; it means that the information is really gone, not just hidden from the list. The reasoning, though, is that the list is really in charge of the contact, and that in practice we'll always access contacts through their lists. You can, of course, soften the code, if you want to devise a way to keep the contact but remove it from the list, or a way to copy contacts from one list to another.

We can now add, remove, and retrieve contacts from the list. We just need a few query methods: `directory_names` (the names of all the list's directories, which will be the munged versions of the names of the contacts), `empty?`, and `size`. Listing 9.12 shows the remaining code necessary to complete the `ContactList` class.

Listing 9.12   The remaining methods for the `ContactList` class

```
def directory_names
  Dir["#{@dir}/*"]
end

def size
  directory_names.size
end

def empty?
  directory_names.empty?
end

end
```

This class, along with the `Contact` class, now gives us all the functionality we need to make our tests pass.

```
$ ruby contacts_g_test.rb
Loaded suite contacts_g_test
Started
.....
Finished in 0.071413 seconds.

5 tests, 7 assertions, 0 failures, 0 errors
```

The key, again, is the directory structure, which we have to walk through explicitly, but which adds an extra level of nesting so that a `Contact` object can present us with what amounts to a collection of hashes.

Discussion

The gdbm version of the contact manager is a bit more sprawling, in terms of file space and directory structure, than the YAML version, and gdbm files, unlike YAML files, are not human-readable. But gdbm is a real database tool, not a different tool being recruited for database-like operations (such as a data-serialization tool, in the case of YAML). In practice, that means gdbm is optimized for database operations. Furthermore, having the entries spread out over many file directories means that you don't have to read them all in at the same time.

If you're just dealing with a few contacts or a small amount of data in whatever domain you're writing this code for, it's not going to make any noticeable difference whether you load in all the data at once or traverse a directory looking for it. If you've got a lot of data, you'll probably hit a point where splitting the data out into many gdbm files will speed things up. Of course, as with all performance questions, you have to try it out and measure for yourself. If you're using these tools for relatively small operations, you'll likely find any of them acceptable in terms of performance. That's part of their merit: they're easy to write and usually fast enough in operation.

One interesting programming issue arising in connection with the gdbm implementation of the contact manager is the issue of how much functionality should be embodied in the `Contact` objects, and how much should be delegated to the `ContactList` objects. Notice, for example, that a `Contact` object does not know how to populate itself, in the sense of opening connections to all of its gdbm files. The list handles that, through the `populate_contact` method. Would it be better to teach a contact how to populate itself, and then have the list call

```
contact.populate
```

instead of calling its own `populate_contact` method? You could certainly make a case for that; it puts the knowledge inside the object that's nearest to the operation. On the other hand, the contact list is really what we're modeling here. In a sense, the `Contact` class only exists as a convenient way to split out some of the list's functionality. If that's true, then how *much* functionality we split out is pretty much discretionary. And there's certainly no harm in experimenting with different ways of doing the same thing.

We'll turn next to the Ruby MySQL module, which takes us into the realm of relational databases.

9.3   *The MySQL driver*

We've now got enough usable code for manipulating contacts and contact lists to put it to some use. This will also allow us to delve into the world of relational databases and the available APIs for Ruby.

Overall, the story is that there are individual (database) drivers for MySQL, PostgreSQL, SQLite, and others. Any of these can be programmed individually. On top of these, you can also use the DBI (Database Interface) package, which provides an abstract API that can serve as a frontend to any of the DBD packages available.

We'll look at a use case for the "pure" MySQL driver here, and in section 9.4 we'll do something with DBI. Unlike the YAML and gdbm examples, these examples will not involve writing an API for a contact list but, rather, moving contact list data around: *to* a MySQL database first, and *from* a MySQL database second. It's not uncommon to use database tools in situations where you're moving data from one storage system to another. The nice thing about the facilities available in Ruby is that you can do quite a lot of this at a rather high level of abstraction.

Problem

You've got a YAML file of contact information, and you want to store it in a relational database.

Solution

Let's tackle this problem by using the MySQL driver. This driver is available as a gem or as a non-gem Ruby package. To install it as a gem, simply run the following command:

`gem install mysql`

To get started, take a look at listing 9.13, which shows several `Contact` objects in the YAML format.

Listing 9.13   An example of a YAML file for contact records

```
--- !ruby/object:ContactList
contacts:
- !ruby/object:Contact
  extras:
    :sport: bowling
    :car: Toyota
    :pets: armadillo

  home:
    :postal: "12345"
    :state: NJ
    :country: USA
    :street1: 123 Main
    :city: Somewhere
  name: David Black
  work: {}
  email: dblack@somewhere

- !ruby/object:Contact
  extras: {}

  home:
    :postal: "23456"
    :state: AB
    :country: USA
    :street1: 234 Main
    :city: Somewhere
  name: David Smith
  email: dsmith@somewhere
  work:
    :company: The Somewhere Consultants
    :street1: 234 Main
    :street2: Suite 33943
    :city: Somewhere
    :postal: "23456"
    :state: AB
    :country: USA

- !ruby/object:Contact
  extras:
    :instrument: violin
    :car: Honda
```

```
  :pets: cat
home:
  :postal: "00000"
```

contacts to a MySQL database is designing and creat-
the contact's email address as the primary key for the
ɜn key for all the other tables. Listing 9.14 contains
ting this database in MySQL. Running listing 9.14 as a
ɛrmissions, should create the database.

r creating the contacts database

```
IODB;
```

```
contact_email varchar(50),
foreign key(contact_email)
  references contacts(email)
  on delete cascade) ENGINE=INNODB;
```

```
drop table if exists work;
create table work (
  company varchar(100),
  street1 varchar(100),
  street2 varchar(100),
  city varchar(50),
  postal varchar(20),
  state varchar(20),
  country varchar(25),
  contact_email varchar(50),
  foreign key(contact_email)
    references contacts(email)
    on delete cascade) ENGINE=INNODB;

drop table if exists extras;
create table extras (
  label varchar(50),
  description varchar(150),
  contact_email varchar(50),
  foreign key(contact_email)
    references contacts(email)
    on delete cascade) ENGINE=INNODB;

grant all on contacts.* to 'contacter'@'localhost' \
  identified by 'secret'
```

The last command (grant) gives all the necessary privileges to the "contacter" user. You can, of course, make up your own username and password for that command. The main thing is to create a non-root user, since the username and password are going to appear in a plain-text program file. (Not that you'd be handing the file around anyway, but it's always better not to put very important passwords in plain text anywhere.)

The next step is to create the "glue" program that will take us from YAML to MySQL. This program is going to read the YAML file in, which will create a ContactList object containing several Contact objects, and write it out again, this time to the MySQL database. The input, however, isn't entirely congruent with the output; we have to do a little work to make it fit.

Contacts have home and work components, which map very easily from a hash (the structure by which they're represented inside the Contact object) to a database table. In fact, the keys of the home and work tables in the database schema are simply lifted from the key names in the home and work hashes.

The extras component is a little different. Here, keys are arbitrary, which means they cannot match up to database column names, since those names have to exist in advance. (It's possible to create columns on the fly using the MySQL API, but that's just asking for confusion and trouble.) Instead of storing each value in a column named for its key, the extras table has two storage columns: label and description. It also has a contact_email column, where the email address of the contact will be stored.

What this means is that while there will be one record in the home table and one in the work table for each contact, there will be one record in the extras table for every entry in the contact's extras hash. The key/value combination in the hash becomes the label/description combination in an extras record.

Most of the rest of the work of writing the program involves creating query strings and shipping them off to the database via the MySQL API. Each Contact object will trigger a three-part cycle of insertions:

- The query that creates the entry in the contacts table itself
- The loop that creates the entries in the home and work tables
- The loop that creates the entries in the extras table

First things first. Before any of this happens, we need to load in the necessary libraries, as well as our application code (contact_y.rb), and make connections on both the YAML side and the MySQL side:

```
require 'yaml'
require 'mysql'
require 'contact_y'

conn = Mysql.new("localhost", "contacter", "secret", "contacts")    ❶
list = YAML.load(File.read("contacts.yml"))    ❷
```

The assignment to conn gives us a new Mysql object—essentially an addressable handle on a database connection ❶. Note the arguments given to Mysql.new: host, username, password, and database name. The variable list ❷ will contain the ContactList represented in the YAML file; this contact list, in turn, contains and manages the specific contacts.

Now, let's take care of the first of the three major stages: creating the entry in the contacts table. Just for fun, here's how to do it using Ruby's % interpolation operator:

```
list.contacts.each do |contact|
  conn.query "INSERT INTO contacts (`name`, `email`)
    VALUES ('%s','%s')" % [contact.name, contact.email]
```

The %s format specifiers work as they do in the sprintf method family: they serve as placeholders for a string to be determined later. The two necessary strings are provided in an array after the main string, and between the main string and the array comes another %-sign—this is what triggers the interpolation operation.

Amidst all this handy string manipulation, notice what's actually happening here: a call to conn.query. We're using conn, the database connection handle, to send a SQL query to the database.

Next up: the home and work components. For each of these, the goal is to send a query that will insert the right values in the right fields. The fields into which we'll insert values are those that have the same names as the hash keys from the YAML structure ("postal", "state", etc.), plus the extra field contact_email—the primary key column in the home and work tables, which has no corresponding value in the YAML structure.

We first want to drill down from the contact to its components. Then we want to isolate each component's keys and create a query string that uses them as field names, together with the component's values as the database values. Here's the code that will do this:

```
%w{ home work }.each do |component|
  data = contact.send(component)    ❶
```

```
    items = data.keys                    ❷
    fields = (["contact_email"] + items).map {|field|
      "`#{field}`"
    }.join(",")        ❸
    values = [contact.email] + items.map {|field| data[field]}      ❹
    values.map! {|value| "'#{value}'"}     ❺
    values = values.join(",")         ❻
    conn.query("INSERT INTO #{component} (#{fields}) VALUES (#{values})")      ❼
  end
```

The data object is the entire component hash; we acquire it by sending the name of the component (home or work) to the Contact object ❶. Then we isolate the keys, which will be things like street1, street2, and phone, as items ❷. If we add the string "contact_email" to this list of items, we'll have all the necessary column names for the relevant database table. (There's no contact_email field in the YAML version, so we have to shoehorn it in to please the MySQL database schema.) These field names get inserted into backticks and are strung together with commas ❸. That will give us something like this for the fields variable:

```
`contact_email`, `street1`, `street2`, `city`, etc.
```

Those are the fields we'll be inserting values into. The values themselves come from a similar, but not identical, mapping of the actual value for contact.email, plus the actual values for the items (as retrieved from the data hash). Here, we put the array together first, because that's a somewhat longer operation, in this case ❹. Then the array gets mapped—map!ped, actually, because the values get changed in place—and then joined with commas to make a values string out of the array ❺, ❻. The result will be something like this:

```
'jsmith2@somewhere', '123 Main', '', 'Somewhere', etc.
```

Thus, the values string lines up nicely with the fields string, ready for insertion into the appropriate table ❼.

You may be wondering why it's necessary to march through all the keys and dig out all the values for each hash, when there's a values method that would do the same thing in one step. The reason is order—or, rather, lack thereof in a hash. Hashes are unordered, which means that the order in which their entries are returned is not guaranteed. While it's very likely that the keys, when returned separately via the keys method, will line up with the values as returned by the values method, it's a good idea nonetheless to go ahead and retrieve each value explicitly, so as not to depend on hash ordering in any guise.

The handling of extras comes next. It's actually a bit less involved than the handling of the home and work components, though it does potentially create more records:

```
    contact.extras.each do |label, description|
    conn.query("INSERT INTO extras (`contact_email`, `label`,
  `description`) VALUES ('#{contact.email}', '#{label}',
  '#{description}')")
    end
  end
```

Encapsulating component references

You'll recall that for the purpose of the gdbm contracts implementation, we neatened things up by setting a COMPONENTS constant inside the Contact class, so that it wasn't necessary to hard-code the names of the components wherever they were used. There are a couple of reasons it's probably not worth doing that here. First, the extras component has to be split out anyway. Second, the remaining components have to correspond exactly to table names in the database.

It is possible to query the database for its table names, and if you subtract "extras" and "contacts" from the list, you'll have (as it's currently engineered) the names of the other components. Still, while it's great to automate things as much as possible, you'll probably find that with more or less one-time conversion scripts, it's inevitable that certain things are going to have to be hard-coded, and in some cases will require individual treatment (like "extras").

Each entry in the extras hash gets an entry in the database, with its foreign key (contact_email) set to the current contact's email field. And that last end tells you that the big loop—the loop through all the contacts—is finished.

Discussion

The MySQL API may seem a bit raw to you, especially if you're used to a full-blown object-relational mapper (ORM) like ActiveRecord or Og. When you use the API directly, you write a lot of SQL yourself, and that may or may not be to your taste.

Keep in mind that having the programming interface available can make a big difference. It gives you all the power of Ruby in front of your SQL generation. You can, of course, grep through a YAML file and try to piece together queries yourself, but all you'll learn by doing that is how much easier it is when you have a programmatic layer, even if it's not an ORM.

If you do have an ActiveRecord-friendly database, you can of course use the higher-level commands available to you to handle the data more abstractly. It all depends on what your starting point and goal happen to be in a given project.

One thing that isn't covered in the preceding solution is error handling. Our script will simply die if something goes fatally wrong in a database operation, and that could leave the database in an inconsistent state. To prevent this, you can wrap each contact's set of queries up as a transaction.

To do this, you first need to turn off auto-commit mode:

```
...
conn = Mysql.new("localhost", "contacter", "secret", "contacts")
list = YAML.load(File.read("contacts.yml"))

conn.autocommit(false)
```

Now, you need to put each contact's worth of querying inside a begin/rescue/end block, where rescuing from a Mysql::Error will result in a rollback:

```
list.contacts.each do |contact|
  begin
    # rest of code, through the "extras" loop
```

```
  rescue Mysql::Error => e
    puts "Problem with contact #{contact.name}: #{e}"
    conn.rollback
    next
  end

  conn.commit
end
```

The commit only happens if no Mysql::Error gets raised along the way. Doing it this way will help you avoid getting the database into an inconsistent state (such as where a contact record is saved but the home record is not), and it will also avoid stopping the whole program just because of one malformed record.

So far, we've looked at sending insert queries to the database, which is important, but it's not the whole story. Our next problem will take us in the other direction: starting from a relational database and reading data out in order to store it in a different format. Moreover, we'll take this opportunity to turn the corner to DBI, the high-level Ruby database interface library.

9.4   *Using DBI*

DBI, Ruby's database interface library, ships separately, and it provides a high-level interface that allows you to come about as close as you can to programming different relational databases with the same programming tools. The goal is to abstract away the differences between various databases, and focus on what they have in common. At the same time (though we won't pursue it in detail here), DBI can also take advantage of features that one database has but others don't.

DBI rests on top of, and needs, one or more database driver (DBD) packages, such as the MySQL library we used in section 9.3. At time of writing, DBI supports 12 DBDs (plus a deprecated one). If you learn how to use DBI, it's almost one-stop-shopping for database APIs.

Problem

You need to read out some contact records from a relational database and save them to a gdbm database.

Solution

We're going to use the MySQL database from section 9.3, but this time we'll address the database with DBI. The goal is to migrate the data to the gdbm-style contacts database. That means we'll need to load contacts_g.rb, as well as DBI. Loading contacts_g.rb will in turn cause the gdbm driver to be loaded. We also need to create the output directory, if it doesn't exist already.

```
require 'dbi'
require 'contacts_g'
Dir.mkdir("migrated_contacts") unless File.exist?("migrated_contacts")
```

Now we need a ContactList object, which will serve as the receptacle for the data coming in from the MySQL database; the data will be massaged, of course, so as to fit the shape of Contact objects. (Make sure that the directory you use already exists, or add something to the script to create it.) We also need a database connection. And, finally, we need a list of all the tables in the database, *except* contacts and extras; those two tables require special handling.

```
list = ContactList.new("migrated_contacts")
conn = DBI.connect("DBI:Mysql:contacts", "contacter", "secret")
tables = conn.select_all("show tables").
          flatten - %w{ extras contacts }
```

The first argument to DBI.connect is the name of the database, contacts, qualified with DBI:Mysql to point DBI to the correct driver. Note that the separators here are single colons, not the double-colon operator that indicates nested constants in Ruby. The whole thing is just a string; none of the characters have significance until they're scanned and interpreted by DBI itself. The host will default to localhost.

To get the list of tables, we use select_all to return an array of rows. In this case, each row is a table name. Rows are returned as arrays inside arrays, and flattening the array takes out the nesting. Finally, we remove the names of the tables that require special treatment: extras and contacts.

The processing of the data from the database consists of a big loop, an iteration through all the rows of the contacts table. Inside the big loop is another loop, which handles all the tables in the tables array. Finally, the data from the extras table is read and transferred.

Listing 9.15 shows the big loop, and what happens inside it.

Listing 9.15   The loop through the contacts table

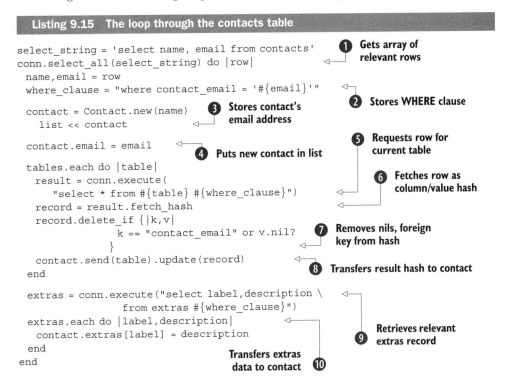

```
select_string = 'select name, email from contacts'     ① Gets array of
conn.select_all(select_string) do |row|                    relevant rows
  name,email = row
  where_clause = "where contact_email = '#{email}'"      ② Stores WHERE clause

  contact = Contact.new(name)          ③ Stores contact's
    list << contact                       email address

  contact.email = email                                  ⑤ Requests row for
                                     ④ Puts new contact in list    current table
  tables.each do |table|
    result = conn.execute(                               ⑥ Fetches row as
      "select * from #{table} #{where_clause}")             column/value hash
    record = result.fetch_hash
    record.delete_if {|k,v|
              k == "contact_email" or v.nil?             ⑦ Removes nils, foreign
              }                                             key from hash
    contact.send(table).update(record)
  end                                     ⑧ Transfers result hash to contact

  extras = conn.execute("select label,description \
              from extras #{where_clause}")
  extras.each do |label,description|
    contact.extras[label] = description
  end                                                    ⑨ Retrieves relevant
end                                                         extras record
         Transfers extras
         data to contact  ⑩
```

The table names will match the relevant components of the gdbm contact: specifically, home and work.

As with the previous script, where we went from YAML to MySQL, we're dealing with three major phases: creating the Contact objects, handling the miscellaneous tables, and handling the extras table. In preparation, we get hold of all the contact rows ❶, and store a WHERE clause that we're going to use repeatedly ❷, just to save having to type it out.

Creating and storing a new contact is easy ❸, thanks to the API we've already developed for the gdbm contacts database. After storing the contact, we set its email address, using the email= method, which transparently puts the email address into extras["email"] ❹.

Then we go through the list of tables. For each table (remembering that we've subtracted extras and contacts from the list), we execute a query returning the relevant row for this contact ❺. This request returns an object of class DBI::StatementHandle, which takes requests for actual delivery of the rows. The relevant request here is fetch_hash ❻, which returns the next row in the form of a hash of column names against values. (A certain amount of error-checking has been left to the reader, including making sure that there is only one row returned per table for each contact!) We then cleanse the hash of the irrelevant contact_email key, as well as any entries with nil values ❼ (which gdbm doesn't like; it only wants strings, and there's not much point storing empty strings for nils). The hash of columns and values is then transferred to the relevant component of the contact ❽. The hash update method is effective because the component is actually a gdbm object, and gdbm objects are programmed like hashes.

Next comes the extras special case. Here we get all the extras records belonging to this contact ❾, and make the appropriate assignments in the extras component ❿.

Discussion

DBI is a great tool for addressing a variety of database systems. Like the individual drivers, it keeps you fairly close to the SQL, and like the MySQL driver, DBI is not as abstracted or high-level as ActiveRecord or Og. But even if you're writing the statements mostly by hand, the ability to embed them inside Ruby logic and string handling is extremely valuable.

In this example, we see again the special casing of the extras table. Going from YAML to MySQL, the special casing involved the need to create a separate record for each key/value pair in the extras hash, using the column names label and description, because the keys for extras are arbitrary, and it was impossible to have a separate column name for each one. Going the other way, extracting the data *from* the MySQL database and putting it back into a Ruby hash structure (which is what gdbm objects essentially are), it's possible to shed the label/description wrapper and go back to having each label be a hash key and the corresponding description its value.

This kind of massaging of structure is fairly common when you migrate around the different data-storage facilities available in Ruby (and, of course, not just in Ruby).

The decisions you make about the shape of the containers are as important as any other feature of the storage process.

9.5 *Summary*

In this chapter, we've looked at a representative set of database and data-storage facilities in Ruby. We looked at YAML, the data-serialization format, as a kind of database tool, having the particular dual merit of allowing for direct storage of Ruby data structures and offering a human-readable, editable text representation of the data it's storing. From there we went to gdbm, one of the drivers in the DBM Berkeley database family. gdbm objects are tied invisibly to files and are programmed like Ruby hashes, making for another quick and easy data-storage tool.

In both YAML and gdbm, we developed library code for creating and managing a list of contacts. The rest of the chapter involved using this code in the service of trying out the relational database facilities available for Ruby. We undertook the task of migrating a YAML database of contact objects to a MySQL database, and then we migrated the same MySQL database back out, into gdbm contact-list format. Both of these projects were written "script-style" (with no classes, just procedural code), and both shed some light on the process of formulating and implementing data structures across different storage systems.

We haven't covered everything in the Ruby database realm, by any means, but you've seen enough to give you a toolset for writing your own scripts, and to give you your bearings as you explore some of the other available tools. You'll likely find that these techniques have some very practical uses—if not every single day, then at critical junctures in data-migration and -reorganization projects. In the next chapter, we'll take these ideas further and look at handling structured data files more in depth.

Structured documents *10*

This chapter covers

- Using XML to read configuration files
- Working with HTML
- Generating XML with Hpricot
- Reading RSS feeds

Almost any Ruby program you write will involve either loading data from an external source or exporting data produced in your program to an external source, which will be reloaded later or loaded by another program. You might use a dead-simple representation like YAML or a more complex one like Atom to store the data, but the basic principles will remain the same.

While you'll have the ability to choose the data format for your configuration files or external storage, you will often run into situations where you need to use data produced by someone else, often by programs written in other programming languages or even created manually by human beings. In these cases, you might need to be able to read in, and correctly interpret, broken data files. The most common example of this is reading HTML files from the internet, which are frequently impossible to parse without first repairing the data.

Thankfully, almost every structured format you might come across has an associated Ruby library that will make reading in data for use by your program, or writing out information you've collected, a trivial matter. Some of these libraries, like the Hpricot library that we will discuss later, also specialize in fixing broken input before giving you a simple API to parse and manipulate the data.

In this chapter, we'll look at XML, including specific forms like RSS, Atom, and XHTML. We'll also look at YAML, Ruby's built-in, simple serialization format, and CSV, which is commonly exported by programs like Microsoft Excel and Outlook.

10.1 XML in practice

The most common data-interchange format is XML. It is used to encode all sorts of information from documents produced in Microsoft Word to the votes of members of Congress made available online. Virtually all programming languages have extremely good support for XML, so it's virtually guaranteed that information exported by one program will be easily interpreted by any other. Vendors frequently use XML as a format for configuration files because they have to do little or no custom work to read or write them.

Because XML is such a common interchange format, there are a number of extremely common uses, like using XHTML for web pages and RSS or Atom for online feeds. We'll get to those cases later, but another extremely common use of XML is for storing configuration data for applications. Sooner or later, you will likely need to parse legacy or configuration data in the form of XML, and Ruby has a nice set of XML libraries to help you out.

For our first couple of examples, we'll look at parsing the configuration for a fictitious calculator program that performs similarly to the calculator built into Apple's Mac OS X or Microsoft Windows. Let's assume that the calculator supports two modes, standard and scientific, and that we'll store its starting position in our configuration file. We'll also store information about the decimal-point precision, as well as the number currently in memory, if any.

10.1.1 Using XML to read configuration files

One of the most common uses for XML in both development and consumer environments is storing configuration values. XML is a staple of Java and C# development, where many project presets are managed by XML files. XML files are an excellent way to integrate with an existing codebase or to use existing configuration data in a new Ruby (or other language) application.

Problem

You need to load and parse an XML configuration file for a new application.

Solution

For our calculator, we need to be able to read in the configuration details and instantiate a calculator object with the settings that were previously saved by the user. A sample configuration file for the calculator is shown in listing 10.1.

Listing 10.1 Our calculator's XML configuration file

```
<?xml version="1.0" encoding="ISO-8859-15"?>
<calculator>
  <startup mode="standard" precision="2" />
```

```
<memory type="float">16.24</memory>
<keyboard type="Macintosh">
  <numeric-keypad enter="=" clear="C" />
  <max-fkey>F16</max-fkey>
</keyboard>
</calculator>
```

This is a very simple configuration file, but it offers enough variance to explore the features of Ruby's built-in XML parser, REXML. Figure 10.1 shows the XML represented graphically as a tree of nodes.

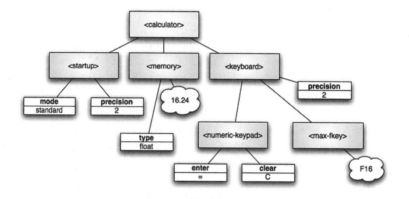

Figure 10.1   A graphical representation of the calculator XML document. Element nodes are represented by rounded rectangles, attributes by squared rectangles, and text nodes by bubbles.

There are a number of libraries that allow us to parse XML in Ruby. For this simple case, REXML, the XML parser that is built into Ruby, will do the trick. Check out listing 10.2 to see how natural the implementation is.

Listing 10.2   Getting our XML into Ruby with REXML

```ruby
require 'rexml/document'
include REXML

module Calculator
  class Config
    def initialize(memory, startup, keyboard)
      @memory = memory, @mode = mode, @keyboard = keyboard
    end
  end

  class Keyboard
    def initialize(type, numeric_keypad, max_fkey)
      @type = type, @numeric_keypad = numeric_keypad,
      @max_fkey = max_fkey
    end
  end

end
```

```
string = File.read("calculator.xml")
calculator = Document.new(string)
root = calculator.root
memory = root.elements["memory"]
memory = memory.text.send("to_#{memory.attributes['type'][0.1]}")
startup = {:mode => root.elements["startup"].attributes["mode"],
    :precision => root.elements["startup"].attributes["precision"]}

keyboard = root.elements["keyboard"]
keyboard_type = keyboard.attributes["type"]
numeric_keypad = keyboard.elements["numeric-keypad"].attributes
max_fkey = keyboard.elements["max-fkey"].text

keyboard = Calculator::Keyboard.new(keyboard_type,
    numeric_keypad, max_fkey)

config = Calculator::Config.new(memory, startup, keyboard)
```

In listing 10.2, we started by producing a hypothetical API for our calculator configuration object. Because, in this example, we are producing both the application and the XML configuration we'll read in, we are free to create an API for our application that closely mirrors the XML format. In this case, we used the simple XML reading methods of REXML to extract the information we needed from the configuration file and populate our configuration object. In a real-world scenario, this configuration object would presumably be passed into the application when it was instantiated.

For simplicity, we have left out any error handling, but you would probably want to handle errors caused by incorrectly formatted XML more gracefully than simply throwing an error and exiting the application, as this example would.

Discussion

Because this example is so simple, there are only a few things that need discussion. First off, the example uses a common Ruby trick to produce the correct value for the starting memory value. The XML format can only return strings, but we wanted to be able to specify that the value in memory was some other type. In our case, we wanted to allow integers or floats to be loaded in. Because Ruby allows conversion from string to numeric formats via to_f for floats and to_i for integers, we were able to provide a single character in the type attribute of memory, and then easily call the appropriate conversion function by using the send method.

REXML allows you to use XPath selectors and returns the appropriate node type based upon the selector. For instance, when getting the precision, we used the object's methods: root.elements["startup"].attributes["precision"]. We could have instead used an XPath attribute selector: root.elements["startup/@precision"]. Because the @ sign indicates that it's an attribute selector, the expression will return an attribute's value. In other cases, if we were to select elements, we could get elements back.

Another neat trick is that the attributes method on an element returns a Hash. As a result, if you structure your API to accept a Hash, you can simply pass in the result of the attributes method, as we did for numeric_keypad. This allows us to support an arbitrary (and even changing) set of options for the numeric keypad without having to change the way we parse the configuration file.

10.1.2 *Writing configuration data to disk*

Now that we've put together some code for reading in configuration data from an XML file, what happens if you want to save changes to the XML? Unless you expect your user to modify the document by hand, you need a way to output any changes back to the configuration file.

Problem

Now that you've read in the configuration file, you need to write an edited configuration file to disk.

Solution

For the purposes of this example, let's assume that we need to produce a function that will take a configuration object, as we defined it previously, and serialize it back into outputtable XML. Because we're doing more than just pulling in some data from a file, we'll get a bit more object oriented this time, and take the opportunity to write tests proving that our function works.

In addition to creating a mechanism for outputting our configuration object to XML, we'll pull our input conversion into `Calculator::Config`. We'll create `to_xml` and `from_xml` methods on the `Config` class. And to make things even more encapsulated, we'll create `to_xml` and `from_xml` methods on the `Keyboard` class, which will allow us to specify how we want keyboard specification objects to be saved and restored within the larger specification XML. See listing 10.3 for our implementation.

Listing 10.3 Reading and writing the configuration

```
require 'rexml/document'
include REXML

module Calculator
  class Config
    attr_accessor :memory, :startup, :keyboard
    def initialize(memory, startup, keyboard)
      @memory, @startup, @keyboard = memory, startup, keyboard
    end

    def self.from_xml(xml_file)                          ◁─┐ Loads Config
      string = File.read(xml_file)                          │ instance from XML
      calculator = Document.new(string)
      root = calculator.root
      memory_el = root.elements["memory"]
      memory =
➥ memory_el.text.send("to_#{memory_el.attributes['type'].slice(0,1)}")

      startup = {"mode" => root.elements["startup"].attributes["mode"],
      ➥ "precision" => root.elements["startup"].attributes["precision"].to_i}

      keyboard = Calculator::Keyboard.from_xml(root.elements["keyboard"])

      return new(memory, startup, keyboard)
    end

    def to_xml                   ◁─┐ Serializes Config
      doc = Document.new           │ instance to XML
```

```
      doc << XMLDecl.new(1.0, "ISO-8859-15")
      root = doc.add_element("calculator")
      root.add_element("startup", @startup)
      root.add_element("memory", "type" =>
      ➥ @memory.class.to_s.slice(0,1).downcase).add_text(@memory.to_s)
      root.add_element(keyboard.to_xml)
      doc
    end
  end

  class Keyboard
    attr_accessor :type, :numeric_keypad, :max_fkey
    def initialize(type, numeric_keypad, max_fkey)
      @type, @numeric_keypad, @max_fkey = type, numeric_keypad, max_fkey
    end
```

— Deserializes Keyboard instance from XML

```
    def self.from_xml(keyboard)
      keyboard_type = keyboard.attributes["type"]
      numeric_keypad = keyboard.elements["numeric-keypad"].attributes
      max_fkey = keyboard.elements["max-fkey"].text
      new(keyboard_type, numeric_keypad, max_fkey)
    end
```

```
    def to_xml
```
— Dumps Keyboard instance to XML
```
      el = Element.new("keyboard")
      el.add_attribute("type", @type)
      el.add_element("numeric-keypad", @numeric_keypad)
      el.add_element("max-fkey").add_text(@max_fkey)
      el
    end
  end

end
```

All of the code inside the new from_xml method should look very familiar, as it's basically cribbed out of our example in section 10.1.1. However, we moved the logic dealing with the Keyboard into a from_xml method on the Keyboard object, which allows us to pass in the root <keyboard> XML node, and have it return a Keyboard object, which we can use to instantiate our specification object.

Note that Keyboard.from_xml is a class method on the Keyboard class, just as Config.from_xml is a class method on the Config class. There's a slight incongruity between the two in that Config takes a filename, while Keyboard takes a DOM node. This is because of the way we expect to instantiate the objects: Configs will pull in an external file, while Keyboards will receive part of an existing DOM structure.

The to_xml function we wrote in the Config class is even simpler to understand than the original parsing function. First, we create a new XML Document. We then add an XML declaration (which should appear at the top of the XML files, if we're following good form), and then the root element (<calculator>). The add_element function has a nice property that makes the next step very simple. It takes an element name as its first parameter, and an optional Hash object for any attributes you wish to instantiate. Well, holy attributes, Batman! We already store the startup attribute of Config as a Hash, so we can simply pass it in. Elegant, huh?

We're not quite as lucky with memory, because we have to reverse the procedure we used in from_xml to store the number and its type. For type, we slice off the first character of the memory object's class, lowercase of course (s for String, i for Integer, and f for Float). For the value, which we store as text inside the <memory> node, we use to_s to stringify the value. The real trick, however, comes next, with our encapsulated Keyboard object.

As you recall from section 10.1.1, we decided to keep the Keyboard information in its own object, which would encapsulate information about a Keyboard. At the time, there was very little utility in this decision, but when we made our code more object oriented, we got to make further use of this encapsulation. Since our Config object has a Keyboard object in its keyboard attribute, we can simply call keyboard.to_xml to get the appropriate XML for the keyboard.

The Keyboard#to_xml function is also pretty simple. We start by creating a new wrapper element (<keyboard>), and adding the type attribute based upon the object's @type instance variable. You might have thought you could use the shortcuts we use with add_element to add the attributes when you create the elements, but unfortunately Element.new does not support that shortcut. We then use the shortcut syntaxes we used earlier to finish up the element, and we return it.

Discussion

The takeaway from all this XML creation is that writing somewhat elegant REXML code requires a good knowledge of the chaining and shortcut possibilities. Because add_element returns the element in question, for instance, we can immediately throw an add_text on top of it. We can also use existing hashes that we have created for our application for the attributes of any node—a trick we made extensive use of.

So far, we've been parsing and working with plain vanilla XML, but in the next section we're going to look at how to work with a domain-specific variety of XML: HTML.

10.2 *Parsing HTML and XHTML with Hpricot*

With the explosion of the web more than a decade ago, a tremendous amount of information has become available on the internet in HTML form. Unfortunately, that information is rarely, if ever, presented in fully valid, parsable form. Since we can't control the creation of the data we'll be reading in, it is important for us to have fast, dead-simple tools for taking broken markup and converting it into machine-readable content.

Fortunately, Hpricot, an XML parser written by Ruby luminary "why the lucky stiff" (http://github.com/why/hpricot/tree/master), provides us with just that. Its most performance-related features are written in C, so it's very fast, and it uses CSS3 selectors (plus a number of custom CSS extensions), so finding precisely the nodes you want, which is very important in massive, markup-heavy HTML pages, is much simpler than in REXML. Finally, it was born out of the philosophy of the popular jQuery JavaScript library, so you'll find that certain common tasks, like adding a class to a series of elements in a document, become extremely simple.

In this section, we will explore processing HTML documents that we create, as well as reading files in from the wild.

10.2.1 *Post-processing HTML output*

Suppose you use a Ruby web framework like Ruby on Rails, Merb, or Nitro, and you have a number of pages that produce tables. You want all of the tables to have zebra-striping (even numbered rows should be colored light blue) when your pages are rendered by the browser. You've already explored a few options, but none of them have met your needs.

You've tried using client-side JavaScript code, but some of your tables are quite large, and those pages can take minutes to load with this solution. You've considered manually ensuring that your tables are properly striped, but you have so many different mechanisms for creating tables that trying to manually ensure that the striping occurs has quickly become tedious. That said, it is not difficult for you to ensure that all tables that need to be striped have a specific class, such as `zebra`.

Problem

You need to process and transform HTML output from your web application.

Solution

We'll use Hpricot to post-process the rendered page and set an appropriate style on every other row. Then, we'll use a CSS stylesheet to pull in the style. We'll use Ruby on Rails for this example, but the general solution is framework-agnostic. As long as you have access to the rendered response, you can use the technique outlined here to post-process your HTML. See listing 10.4 for our implementation; the CSS is in listing 10.5.

Listing 10.4 A simple postprocessing filter

```
class ApplicationController < ActionController::Base

  after_filter :zebra

  def zebra
    doc = Hpricot(response.body)
    doc.search("table.zebra tbody
➥ tr:nth-child(even)").add_class("even")
    response.body = doc.to_s
  end

end
```

Listing 10.5 The associated CSS

```
.zebra .even {
  background-color: #ddf;
}
```

First off, note that we kept the example very simple, just to demonstrate the technique at hand. Later in this chapter, we will explore more features of Hpricot, which you will be able to use together with this technique to do more advanced postprocessing of HTML data.

With that said, let's look at the example. You can ignore the Rails-specific semantics. All that we're doing is saying that the postprocessing should occur for all pages in the application (by including it in `ApplicationController`), and specifying that we will do the postprocessing via an `after_filter`. The real action happens in the `zebra` method, and you're probably surprised at how short the code is.

The first line simply grabs the existing response body and parses it via Hpricot. Next, we find the rows we want to change. This might look a bit odd, but it's just a simple CSS3 selector. We find all tables with the class `zebra`, which is how we're going to specify that we want a table zebra-striped. Then, we'll jump down to the `<tbody>`, because we probably don't want to be striping our rows in the table head (if we have any).

Once we have the `tbody`, we get all the even-numbered rows, relative to their parent. We need to use `:nth-child` (rather than the `:even` selector supported by Hpricot) in case we have multiple tables on the page. If we simply used `:even`, if the first table ended on an odd row, the next table would have the striping skewed by one. Using `:nth-child` scopes the evenness to the table in question.

Once we've gotten the rows we need, we can use the `add_class` convenience method provided by Hpricot to add the `even` class to every matched row.

As we'll see later, Hpricot returns the `Elements` set that was matched by the original selector from `add_class`, so you can chain further modifications onto the end of it. Finally, we reset `response.body` to our modified document, and we're off to the races. Simple, huh?

Discussion

While we noted one important difference in behavior between the `:even` selector and `even`, there is another. The `:even` selector and `even` also index the rows in the tables differently. When you use the `:even` selector, the table is indexed as 0-based, which causes it to get the first, third, fifth rows, and so on. This differs from `even`, which indexes the table's rows starting with 1, fetching the second, fourth, sixth rows, and so on.

In the next section, we'll look at solving a nearly inevitable problem for developers working with HTML: fixing a broken HTML document.

10.2.2 Reading broken HTML

Broken HTML is a regular problem for developers who work with HTML for any period of time. Whether the cause is bad editors or web designers who fail to follow conventional web standards, there's a big, busted world of HTML to deal with. Fortunately, parsers have reached a point of reasonable intelligence and can fairly easily render broken HTML into something usable.

Let's say we have an application that reads in data from a series of blogs and aggregates the data for our readers. In most cases, the blogs provide a nice RSS feed, and we can happily use the feeds to get the data. Unfortunately, a few of them don't provide any kind of feed, and the HTML is extremely sloppy. On the bright side, they haven't updated their layout in at least a decade or two, and you can be pretty sure that the template they're using isn't going to change any time soon. An example of a typical post can be seen in listing 10.6.

Listing 10.6 A sample blog entry

```
<h3>Open Thread </h3>

<p class="byline"><i>by</i>
<a href="http://foo.com/">Mr. Foo</a>, Fri Aug 17, 2007
at 11:15:45 PM EST</p>

<div class="story_summary">
<p>Some Text Here</p>

<p>Lorem ipsum dolor sit amet, consectetur adipisicing
elit, sed do eiusmod tempor incididunt ut labore et
dolore magna aliqua. Ut enim ad minim veniam, quis
nostrud exercitation ullamco laboris nisi ut aliquip ex
ea commodo consequat. Duis aute irure dolor in
reprehenderit in voluptate velit esse cillum dolore
eu fugiat nulla pariatur. Excepteur sint occaecat
cupidatat non proident, sunt in culpa qui officia
deserunt mollit anim id est laborum.</p>

<p>
</div>

<p class="byline story_trail">
<br><a href="/story/2007/8/17/55555/5555">Permalink</a>
 :: 5 <a href="/story/2007/8/17/55555/5555#commenttop">Comments</a>

<br>Tags: <a href="http://www.myblog.com/tag/foo%20tag">
  foo tag
  </a>

  (<a href="http://www.myblog.com/tag">all tags</a>)

<br>
</p>
```

The post in listing 10.6 uses a typical blog engine and includes information about the person who wrote the article and when it was created, a permalink to the entry, and some tags, among other things. We want to get the information from the blog entry into an object we can use elsewhere in our application.

Problem

You need to parse and manipulate chunks of broken HTML.

Solution

Although it would be very common to store the information from the post in an `ActiveRecord` object, which is exposed by the Ruby on Rails framework and used on its own by other applications, we will use a run-of-the-mill class for this example. The code to accompany this chapter (available at the Manning website) includes an example of using `ActiveRecord` to scrape and store information that is very similar to the solution we'll use here.

First, you'll notice that there's a little bit of broken HTML in listing 10.6. While it's mostly acceptable, it's a far cry from perfectly valid XHTML (there's an open <p> tag on its own before the close of the <div> tag, and the <br> tags aren't self-closing).

Hpricot will attempt to fix these problems when it parses the HTML, so the output you'll eventually get will be, at the least, parsable. Listing 10.7 shows how to use Hpricot to implement this.

Listing 10.7   Getting the HTML into a `Post` object

```
require 'rubygems'
require 'hpricot'
require 'time'

module RubyInPractice
  class Post

    attr_accessor :title, :body, :by, :posted_on, :permalink, :tags
    def initialize(title, body, by, posted_on, permalink, tags)
      @title, @body, @by, @posted_on, @permalink, @tags = title, body,
      by, posted_on, permalink, tags
    end

    def self.from_blog_html(html, base_url)
      doc = Hpricot(html)                              ❶
      title = (doc/"h3").inner_text
      body = (doc/"div.story_summary").inner_html.gsub(/\n/, "").
        gsub(/<\/p><p>/, "<br/>").gsub(/<\/?p>/, "")
      by = (doc/"p.byline:first a").inner_text
      posted_on = Time.parse(doc/"p.byline:first
      :last").inner_text.gsub(/^\,\s*/, ""))           ❷
      permalink = base_url +
      (doc/search("a:contains(Permalink)").attr("href")
      tags = (doc/"p.story_trail a:gt(1)")[0..-2].map {|x|
      x.inner_html}.join(", ")
      new(title, body, by, posted_on, permalink, tags) ❸
    end

  end
end
```

The example in listing 10.7 is fairly rudimentary, but it allows us to take a look at a number of techniques you can use with Hpricot to get very specific pieces of information quickly and easily. But first, let's peruse the structure we're using here.

As in listing 10.3, where we read and wrote the configuration data, we have separated out the initialization of the class from the function that will pull the information from an external source.

This is an important technique, because it will allow us to extend this class later with additional parsers that can scan different types of blog entries. You might have `Post.from_wordpress_entry`, `Post.from_typo_entry`, and `Post.from_mephisto_entry` methods (and while all of those methods have RSS feeds, let's pretend we needed to do some screen-scraping for the sake of argument). Because we've left the initialization method so generic, we can easily plug into it after doing whatever complex parsing we need to do. That said, let's take a look at the actual code we use to get the various pieces of information out of the HTML fragment in listing 10.6 that we pulled from the web page.

The first thing we do, as in listing 10.4, is create an `Hpricot` object from the HTML ❶. To get the title, we simply grabbed the `inner_text` from the document's `<h3>` element. Marvel at the simplicity of the API before we move on ❷. The body of the article was in a `<div>` with the class of `story_summary`. All we need to do to get the contents of that element is to use elementary CSS knowledge: `div.story_ summary` represents a `<div>` with the class `story_summary`, so that's all we need here. We do some fancy `gsub`bing to normalize line spacing, and we're done.

Getting the byline is a bit trickier. Examining the HTML, we see that it's inside a link that's inside a `<p>` element with the class `byline`. Unfortunately, there are two `<p>` elements with that class on the page, but that poses no difficulty for the dexterity of Hpricot. Using the custom `:first` extension to the typical CSS3 syntax, we can grab just the first matched element. Putting it together, `p.byline:first a` matches the link we need, and, as before, `inner_text` will grab the text inside it.

We then move on to find the date and time the post was created, and we encounter another difficulty. The time is formatted well enough for our needs, but it's not surrounded by any tags. That, too, poses no problem for Hpricot. Examining the HTML, we see that the time is in the first `<p>` element with the `byline` class, and that it's the very last thing in the `<p>`. Because all of the text is grouped together, Hpricot considers it a single text node, so the selector `p.byline:first :last` matches it. The `:last` selector is another one of Hpricot's custom extensions, and the space in between the two parts of the selector indicate that Hpricot should find the last child of the first `p.byline`. Using `Time.parse`, which is included from the standard library when we did `require 'time'` wraps it all up.

Getting the permalink proves easy compared to the last two problems. Hpricot supports the CSS3 selector `:contains`, which returns all elements whose text contents match the text passed in to `:contains`. In this case, the link we want has the text "Permalink" helpfully embedded, so we get the element and use the handy `attr` method to get its `href` attribute. We then append the `href` to the `base_url` passed in, because we can see that the permalink provided in the HTML is a relative URL.

Then we get the tags attached to the article. Looking at the HTML, we can see that the tags are all enclosed inside links in a `<p>` element with the class `story_trail`. Looking closer, we see that we don't want to include the first, second, or last links. Using Hpricot's `:gt` selector, we can filter out the first two elements. Once we have those, we can use Ruby's `Array#[]` operator (since an Hpricot element collection is simply an extension of the base `Array` class) to remove the last link. We then create an array containing the `inner_text` of the links, and `join` them with a comma, producing a nice comma-separated list of tags.

Finally, we feed all this harvested data into a new object ❸.

Discussion

All in all, using Hpricot to scrape information from typical HTML sites is a piece of cake once you learn the supported selectors. But it's key that you do. Most of the power of Hpricot comes from being able to drill down into the dark corners of the document you're parsing without resorting to manually iterating through them. Since

Hpricot supports all of the same selectors as jQuery, you can get documentation on supported selectors by visiting docs.jquery.com/Selectors.

Now that we've learned a bit about Hpricot, let's take a brief detour to look at how we could rewrite our configuration example from section 10.1.2 using Hpricot.

10.3 *Writing configuration data: revisited*

A rare but valid use case for Hpricot is generating XML. It's not that Hpricot is *bad* at generating markup; it's just that that's not what it's built for. Fortunately, because we have tests for the class we wrote (included in the downloads for this book), we can simply reimplement our serialization methods and make sure they work.

Problem

You want to use Hpricot to generate the XML configuration file rather than adding another library to the requirements list.

Solution

We're going to show only the modified #to_xml methods from Config and Keyboard, which reflect the usage of Hpricot instead of REXML (which was shown in listing 10.2). Using the code in listings 10.8 and 10.9, all tests written for section 10.1.2 still pass.

Listing 10.8 Redone Config#to_xml

```
def to_xml
  doc = Hpricot.XML("<?xml version='1.0' encoding='ISO-8859-
➧    15'?><calculator/>")
  (doc/"calculator").append("<startup/>").
➧    search("startup").attr(@startup)
  (doc/"calculator").append("<memory>#{@memory.to_s}</memory>").
    search("memory").attr("type" => @memory.class.to_s.slice(0,1).downcase)
  (doc/"calculator").append(keyboard.to_xml)
  doc.to_s
end
```

Listing 10.9 Redone Keyboard#to_xml

```
def to_xml
  el = Hpricot.XML("<keyboard/>")
  (el/"keyboard").attr("type" => @type).
    append("<numeric-keypad/>").
    append("<max-fkey>#{@max_fkey}</max-fkey>").
    search("numeric-keypad").attr(@numeric_keypad)
  el.to_s
end
```

Using Hpricot for XML creation involves a lot of literal node creation. You create fragments of XML and stick them where they belong, and Hpricot takes care of creating XML nodes out of them. In listings 10.8 and 10.9, we also used a fair amount of chaining, taking advantage of the fact that Hpricot tends to return the original Elements array from operations performed on it.

Quickly looking through Config#to_xml (listing 10.8), you can see that we replaced our individual calls that created the XML document, its root node, and the

XML declaration with a single call to Hpricot.XML. We use Hpricot.XML rather than the typical Hpricot call when we want the parser to use strict XML semantics instead of HTML semantics. We then find the <calculator> node and append the empty <startup> node. Because the append method returns the original Elements array, we can then search for the new <startup> node and set its attributes in the same way we did in the REXML solution (listing 10.2). We use the same techniques until the end of the method, when we append the XML returned by Keyboard#to_xml.

Because Hpricot uses string-based manipulation, we put together the XML for the Keyboard in much the same way that we created the Config's XML in listing 10.7, but we return a String so that it can be appended to the <calculator> node in the Config object. Rerunning the tests gives us solid green, so we're good to go.

Discussion

The main thing to remember about using Hpricot to produce XML is that you'll be mostly producing XML fragments and using methods like append, inner_html=, and attr to set up your document. Once you get comfortable with this, it's extremely powerful.

Now that we've taken a look at HTML and generic XML, let's take a look at another form of rich markup: RSS.

10.4 Reading RSS feeds

Over the last few years, RSS has become a common way for content authors to keep readers updated about the material they are posting. Blog authors use RSS to keep their readers updated with their freshest content, booksellers use RSS to let people know about new books they are selling, and podcasters use a specialized form of RSS to point listeners to their latest episodes.

Because RSS content is so consistent, it's very easy to write web applications that take advantage of its aggregation capabilities. Feed readers galore have popped up, allowing users to enter their favorite feeds and giving them different ways to view the contents. We're going to take a look at how Ruby allows us to read through an RSS document, and we'll build a rudimentary feed reader to get information about our favorite feeds.

NOTE While we will not provide details in this book on how to integrate this solution with a web application framework such as Ruby on Rails, code samples along those lines are available in the downloadable materials for this book.

Problem

You want to build a simple feed reader that will allow your users to get the titles, URLs, brief descriptions, and publication dates for the articles in a feed. You want to be able to display the data on the command line by accepting command-line arguments, or on the web, as formatted HTML.

Solution

In this solution, we'll be using familiar tools, like Hpricot, and some not so familiar, like open-uri, to parse RSS. Listings 10.10 and 10.11 show our implementation of a simple RSS feed reader.

Listing 10.10   A simple RSS parser

```ruby
require 'rss'
require 'open-uri'
require 'rubygems'
require 'hpricot'

module RubyInPractice
  class RssParser

    attr_accessor :rss
    def initialize(file, options = {})
      f = open(file)
      s = f.read
      @rss = RSS::Parser.parse(s)
      @options = {:truncate => 500}.merge(options)
    end

    def titles
      @rss.items.map {|x| x.title}
    end

    def short_info
      @rss.items.map {|x| [x.title, Hpricot(x.description).
➥   inner_text[0..100] + "..."]}
    end

    def details
      @rss.items.map do |item|
        [ item.title,
          item.pubDate,
          item.link,
          Hpricot(item.description).

          ➥    inner_text[0..@options[:truncate]] + "..."
        ]
      end
    end

    def to_html
      @rss.items.map do |item|
        %{
        <h3><a href="#{item.link}">#{item.title}</a></h3>
        <h4>#{item.pubDate}</h4>
        <div class="body">#{item.description}</div>
        }
      end
    end

  end
end
```

Listing 10.11   A small command-line script for running the RSS parser

```ruby
#!/usr/bin/env ruby
require 'optparse'
require 'rss_parser.rb'
```

```
module RubyInPractice
  class RssRunner

    def self.parse_options
      @config = {}
      OptionParser.new do |opts|
        opts.banner = "Usage: rss_parser [options]"
        opts.separator ""
        opts.on "-f", "--file [FILE]",
➥ "the file or URL you wish to load in" do |file|
          @config[:file] = file
        end
        opts.on "-t", "--titles", "specify titles only" do |titles|
          @config[:titles] = true
        end
        opts.on "-s", "--short",
➥ "show a short version of the feed" do |short|
          @config[:short] = true
        end
        opts.on "-r", "--truncate [NUMBER]",
➥ "the number of characters to truncate the long
➥ version to (defaults to 500)" do |trunc|
          @config[:truncate] = trunc.to_i
        end
      end.parse!
    end

    def self.run
      parse_options
      file = @config.delete(:file)
      r = RubyInPractice::RssParser.new(file, @config)
      if !@config[:titles] && !@config[:short]
        r.details.each do |item|
          puts "\"#{item[0]}\" published at #{item[1]}"
          puts "Available at #{item[2]}"
          puts
          puts item[3]
          puts
          puts
        end
      elsif !@config[:titles]
        r.short_info.each do |item|
          puts "\"#{item[0]}\""
          puts item[1]
          puts
        end
      else
        puts r.titles.join("\n")
      end
    end

  end
end

RubyInPractice::RssRunner.run
```

There are two parts to the solution provided here. First up, we created a small class to read in an RSS feed and extract the useful information into some useful configurations (listing 10.10). Second, we created a command-line script written in Ruby that accepts a filename and spits out a human-readable version of the feed (listing 10.11), using the class we created in the previous listing. Before we take a look at the command-line script, let's take a look at the class that does the hard work.

At the very top, we initialize our class with a filename. Because we have required `open-uri`, we can provide either a local filename or an internet URL, which makes the code more versatile than it appears at first glance. We use `RSS::Parser.parse` to read the file into an RSS object, which will give us access to its contents. We also provide default options, which we will allow to be set using command-line switches later on.

We'll then create the methods that will aggregate the information from the feeds that we'll need later. Pretty much all you need to know here is that the RSS object exposes an `items` array, and that each `Item` has several pieces of information associated with it, including its title, a link to the URL, the publication date, and a description. The description will frequently have HTML data in it, so we'll strip that out using Hpricot if the data is being dumped to the terminal.

We also create a `to_html` method, which can be used by web frameworks to take the RSS feed and produce simple web-ready content. To see how it might be used, look at the `rss_controller.rb` file included with the downloadable files for this chapter. Note that we do not strip out the HTML content in the `to_html` method, because we are assuming it provides useful formatting instructions. You could use the techniques we covered in the previous sections to convert the description HTML into a more usable format.

In the command-line script (listing 10.11) we use simple techniques to make the class we just created produce useful content. It's not important that you fully understand how it works, but the basic principles should be obvious. We're using Ruby's built-in option parser to accept options to pass into our RSS parsing class. We accept a file parameter, which will be passed directly into our class (and, as a result, will support either a local file or a URL). We also support a choice of long, short, or titles-only display. Finally, we allow the user to specify how many characters to retain when we truncate the long version's descriptions.

Because we are using `optparse`, we automatically support -h (or --help), which will provide usage instructions based upon the information we specified. You can see for yourself by running `parse_it.rb`, which is provided with the downloadable materials for this chapter. Try entering the URL to the feed for your favorite blog. If you don't have one, check out the official Rails blog's feed at http://feeds.feedburner.com/RidingRails.

Returning briefly to the command-line script, you can see two main sections: `#parse_options` and `#run`. These names are not required, but they're conventional. At the end, you can see that we call `RubyInPractice::RssRunner.run`, which itself calls `parse_options`. The option parser will take apart the arguments you passed in to the function and set up the `@config` instance variable, which we use in `#run` to determine the filename and to pass configuration options to the RSS parser.

Discussion

We used `optparse` to handle our argument parsing in this section, mostly because it's built into Ruby's standard library, but there are a few libraries out there that handle the same functionality in a prettier shell. For example, the Trollop library (http://trollop.rubyforge.org/) offers a much nicer syntax at the cost of a bit of power. Here is a Trollop version of our arguments code from listing 10.11:

```
require 'trollop'

opts = Trollop::options do
  banner "Usage: rss_parser [options]"

  opt :file, "the file or URL you wish to load in"
  opt :titles, "specify titles only"
  opt :short, "show a short version of the feed"
  opt :truncate,"the number of characters to truncate
                 the long version to (defaults to 500)",
                :type => :int,
                :short => "r"
end
```

You'll notice you can't use a `proc` like we did in listing 10.11, so if you need to do any processing other than setting a value, perhaps this isn't the library for you. Other libraries include Optiflag (http://optiflag.rubyforge.org/), a very nice library with a rather powerful syntax, and Choice (http://choice.rubyforge.org/), a concise DSL for handling argument parsing. Any of these will work well; the choice largely hinges on the sort of syntax and the amount DSL-driven syntactic sugar you like to work with.

　　　Now that we've taken a look at reading feeds, let's turn our attention to generating our own feeds.

10.5　*Creating your own feed*

Now that you've learned how to read feeds from other sites, you might be thinking that you'd like to create your own feed. Unfortunately, there are a number of feed formats, and creating a program that exports only to RSS1, for instance, will leave some of your potential readers in the dark. Thankfully, a library called FeedTools will allow you to create a generic feed and then export it in multiple formats.

Problem

You want to create a feed for your website, but you only want to have to create a single feed and have it export feeds in the formats you want. Ideally, you would be able to decide at a later point exactly which feed formats you want to support, so the Ruby class should be flexible enough to support various formats.

Solution

We'll create a wrapper around FeedTools that will allow us to easily create a new feed and export it to whichever format we want. We'll only wrap a few commonly used functions for demonstration purposes, but it's trivial to extend this wrapper to provide additional functionality.

First, you'll need to install the `feedtools` gem:

```
gem install feedtools
```

Once you have FeedTools installed, the code in listing 10.12 will implement a feed generator.

Listing 10.12   Wrapping FeedTools

```ruby
require 'rubygems'
require 'feed_tools'

module RubyInPractice
  module Feeds

    class Feed
      attr_accessor :feed
      def initialize(options)
        @feed = FeedTools::Feed.new
        options.each do |option, value|
          @feed.send("#{option}=", value)
        end
      end
                                              Builds Atom feed
                                              based on object
      def to_atom
        @feed.build_xml("atom", 1.0)
      end
                                              Wraps FeedTools's RSS
                                              generation method
      def to_rss(version=2.0)
        @feed.build_xml("rss", version)
      end

      def add_entry(options)
        @feed << Item.new(options).item
      end

      def add_entries(*args)
        args.each do |entry|
          add_entry(entry)
        end
      end

      def set_author(name, email, href=nil)
        a = FeedTools::Author.new
        a.name = name
        a.email = email
        a.href = href if href
        @feed.author = a
      end

      def add_links(hash)
        hash.each do |href, title|
          l = FeedTools::Link.new
          l.href = href
          l.title = title
          @feed.links << l
```

```
        end
      end

    def method_missing(meth, *args)
      if meth.to_s =~ /=$/
        @feed.send(meth, *args)
      end
    end
  end

  class Item
    attr_accessor :item
    def initialize(options)
      @item = FeedTools::FeedItem.new
      options.each do |option, value|
        @item.send("#{option}=", value)
      end
    end

    def method_missing(meth, *args)
      if meth.to_s =~ /=$/
        item.send(meth, *args)
      end
    end
  end

  end
end
```

While FeedTools is quite cool, in that it provides a single API for multiple feeds, it suffers from extreme API complexity. Adding an author to a feed, for instance, requires creating a new `FeedTools::Author` object (trying to call `set_author` on a feed with a `String` will populate only the `name` field of the object). To simplify things a bit, we have created a new class called `RubyInPractice::Feeds::Feed`, which accepts a series of fields and instantiates the feed quickly and easily.

Because most of the fields on the `FeedTools::Feed` object are set by calling methods like `link=`, `id=`, and `copyright=`, we've instantiated our wrapper object with a `Hash` with corresponding values. For instance, to create a new `Feed` object with the feed's ID set to "http://www.manning.com", you would use this one-liner:

```
RubyInPractice::Feeds::Feed.new(:id => "http://www.manning.com")
```

Adding entries is a similarly complex process with FeedTools, so we have created a similar API for adding new entries. Once you have your wrapper object (let's call it feed), you would call add_entry:

```
feed.add_entry(:id          => "http://www.manning.com/foo",
          :title       => "NEW!",
          :abstract    => "Brand new feed entry",
          :description => "This is the first feed entry for our feed",
          :content     => "Some longer content would go here")
```

If you were creating an iTunes feed, there would be additional properties, like enclosure, `itunes_summary`, `itunes_image_link`—more than can be set using this method.

Keep in mind that Atom feeds require unique IDs; those IDs must be URLs, or you will not be able to generate an Atom feed.

Because setting up an author correctly using FeedTools can also be complex, we have added a `set_author` method that takes a `name`, `email`, and optional `href`, creates the required `FeedTools::Author` object, and associates the object with the wrapped feed. We do a very similar thing with the `add_links` method, which allows the creation of a `FeedTools::Link` object by simply passing in a hash of `href` => `title` pairs. You would do something like this:

```
feed.add_links("http://www.manning.com" => "Manning Publications")
```

To facilitate the creation of RSS and Atom feeds, we have also created two generation methods: `to_rss` and `to_atom`. Both methods simply delegate to the `build_xml` method of the underlying `FeedTools::Feed` object.

Discussion

Listing 10.13 shows an example of the feeds that will be generated using our wrapper script.

> **Listing 10.13   Creating a new feed**

```
f = RubyInPractice::Feeds::Feed.new(:id =>
    "http://rubyinpractice.manning.com", :title => "Ruby in Practice Feed",
    :description => "A sample feed for the Ruby in Practice chapter on Data
    parsing")
f.set_author "Yehuda Katz", "wycats@gmail.com"
f.add_entry(:title => "NEW!", :abstract => "This is a new feed",
    :summary => "This is a new feed for testing", :id =>
    "http://rubyinpractice.manning.com/new", :content => "There might
    normally be some long content here")
```

The API using our wrapped set is fairly simple, as you can see. Now, let's see what happens when we go to generate the feeds using our `to_atom` and `to_rss` methods. Listings 10.14 and 10.15 show markup generated by our code.

> **Listing 10.14   Generating RSS 2.0**

```
<?xml version="1.0" encoding="utf-8"?>
<rss xmlns:taxo="http://purl.org/rss/1.0/modules/taxonomy/" xmlns:rdf="http://
    www.w3.org/1999/02/22-rdf-syntax-ns#" xmlns:itunes="http://
    www.itunes.com/dtds/podcast-1.0.dtd" version="2.0" xmlns:media="http://
    search.yahoo.com/mrss" xmlns:dc="http://purl.org/dc/elements/1.1/"
    xmlns:content="http://purl.org/rss/1.0/modules/content/"
    xmlns:trackback="http://madskills.com/public/xml/rss/module/trackback/">
  <channel>
    <title>Ruby in Practice Feed</title>
    <link>http://rubyinpractice.manning.com/</link>
    <description>A sample feed for the Ruby in Practice chapter on
    Data parsing</description>
    <managingEditor>wycats@gmail.com</managingEditor>
    <ttl>60</ttl>
```

```
<generator>http://www.sporkmonger.com/projects/feedtools/</generator>
<item>
  <title>NEW!</title>
  <link>http://rubyinpractice.manning.com/new</link>
  <description>This is a new feed for testing</description>
  <content:encoded>
    <![CDATA[There might normally be some long content here]]>
  </content:encoded>
  <pubDate>Tue, 28 Aug 2007 13:37:55 -0000</pubDate>
  <guid isPermaLink="true">http://rubyinpractice.manning.com/new</guid>
</item>
</channel>
</rss>
```

Listing 10.15 Generating ATOM 1.0

```
<?xml version="1.0" encoding="utf-8"?>
<feed xml:lang="en-US" xmlns="http://www.w3.org/2005/Atom">
 <title type="html">Ruby in Practice Feed</title>
 <author>
  <name>Yehuda Katz</name>
  <email>wycats@gmail.com</email>
 </author>
 <link href="http://rubyinpractice.manning.com/" rel="alternate"/>
 <subtitle type="html">A sample feed for the Ruby in Practice chapter
➡ on Data parsing</subtitle>
 <updated>2007-08-28T13:38:09Z</updated>
 <generator>FeedTools/0.2.26 -
➡ http://www.sporkmonger.com/projects/feedtools/</generator>
 <id>http://rubyinpractice.manning.com</id>
 <entry xmlns="http://www.w3.org/2005/Atom">
  <title type="html">NEW!</title>
  <author>
   <name>n/a</name>
  </author>
  <link href="http://rubyinpractice.manning.com/new" rel="alternate"/>
  <content type="html">There might normally be some long content
➡ here</content>
  <summary type="html">This is a new feed for testing</summary>
  <updated>2007-08-28T13:37:55Z</updated>
  <id>http://rubyinpractice.manning.com/new</id>
 </entry>
</feed>
```

As you can see, we get back two very different feeds with all of the required feed-specific data, even though we were able to create them very simply. As we said previously, the wrapper API is far from complete, but the code should provide you with enough to get started adding more functionality for working with RSS. Unfortunately, the RDoc for FeedTools is not easily available online; however, it is installed with the gem. The easiest way to take a look at it would be to run `gem_server` and navigate to http://localhost:8808/doc_root/feedtools-0.2.29/rdoc/index.html.

Now let's take a look at YAML, another markup format that isn't based on XML at all.

10.6 *Using YAML for data storage*

We first looked at YAML in chapter 9. It is a lightweight alternative to XML, which, even in its more structured and parsable forms, requires quite a bit of code to get simple things done. At first glance, YAML can store and reload simple objects like hashes, arrays, integers, and strings, which will allow you to develop a serialization and load strategy for your configuration objects. For instance, Ruby on Rails uses YAML files to store information about the database it uses in different operating modes.

YAML is even more powerful, however, in that it is able to do quick-and-dirty serialization of your custom objects, as long as they're relatively simple. In this section, we'll take one final foray into the land of calculator configuration to see how we can use YAML to make the entire process of serializing a configuration object and reloading it later absolutely trivial.

Problem

You want to take an existing `Calculator::Config` object and store it to disk. When your application starts, you want to load in the file from disk and create a new `Calculator::Config` object for use.

Solution

In section 10.1, we looked at how to use XML as a configuration store. Now, we'll use Ruby's built-in YAML functionality to replace our previous XML plumbing. Listings 10.16 and 10.17 show our implementation.

Listing 10.16 Using YAML to solve the calculator config problem

```
require 'yaml'

module Calculator
  class Config
    attr_accessor :memory, :startup, :keyboard
    def initialize(memory, startup, keyboard)
      @memory, @startup, @keyboard = memory, startup, keyboard
    end

    def save_to(file)
      f = File.open(file, "w")
      f.puts(self.to_yaml)        ❶
    end

    def self.get_from(file)
      YAML.load(File.read(file))     ❷
    end
  end

  class Keyboard
    attr_accessor :type, :numeric_keypad, :max_fkey
    def initialize(type, numeric_keypad, max_fkey)
      @type, @numeric_keypad, @max_fkey = type, numeric_keypad, max_fkey
    end
  end

end
```

In listing 10.16, you can see that we kept the same API to the outside world but replaced the guts of our configuration parser with YAML. The API here is beautifully simple. To save our configuration to a file, we use the to_yaml method and write that data to the file ❶. Most of Ruby's core objects implement to_yaml in one form or another, so it should work for most values. We also load in the file and get a usable Ruby object in one fell swoop using the load method ❷. This process is simple and straightforward (much like the YAML format itself!). Our class should now behave the same as before, except that our configuration file will have to be in the YAML format.

Now that the guts are in place, we need to test and make sure it works. Listing 10.17 shows a short script that does that.

> **Listing 10.17 Using the YAML solution in an equivalent manner to our XML solution**

```
k = Calculator::Keyboard.new("Macintosh", {"enter" => "=",
➥ "clear" => "C"}, "F16")
c = Calculator::Config.new(16.24, {"mode" => "standard",
➥ "precision" => 2}, k)

c.save_to("config.yml")
Calculator::Config.get_from("config.yml")
```

Using Ruby's built-in YAML serialization, we are able to take a complex problem that we previously solved using XML serialization in section 10.1, and convert it to a one-liner.

Discussion

YAML serialization isn't the solution for every problem, because it can only serialize data structures, not objects that contain baked-in code (like procs and metaclass methods). However, for most configuration requirements, simple data structures are more than adequate. If you're getting much more clever than this, you're probably doing something wrong. Creating a separate Keyboard class to hold keyboard information was pushing it for us, but it was useful for the examples at hand.

For more complex examples, you can configure the YAML serialization. By defining the to_yaml_properties method to return an array of the properties you wish to serialize, you can cause YAML#dump to ignore properties that are not appropriate for serialization. You can also define yaml_dump and yaml_load methods on the object you are serializing to use a custom serialization strategy. You can get more information about customizing the default load and dump in the Pickaxe book (*Programming Ruby: The Pragmatic Programmers' Guide*, by Dave Thomas, with Chad Fowler and Andy Hunt).

10.7   *Summary*

Ruby's toolset for working with structured documents is excellent. Ruby can handle any major interchange format: XML, HTML, or YAML.

XML has bindings for almost any language, and Ruby's built-in REXML library is excellent for parsing XML. The Hpricot gem is even better, since it can handle the rich context of formats like HTML and can generate markup. Paired with the Feed-Tools gem, Hpricot can even handle RSS.

If YAML is your preference, Ruby's built-in YAML library is one of the best available. As such, YAML is used extensively in a lot of Ruby applications; it's preferred to XML not only for its superior bindings but also for its low visual noise and human readability.

In the next chapter, we're going to take a look at using authentication and authorization in Ruby and Rails applications.

11
Identity and authentication

Trust is the foundation of successful networked systems. If you are providing a personalized service over a network, you need to be able to trust that your users are who they say they are, and your users must trust you with their identity and their personal data. This chapter looks primarily at how you can trust your users—by implementing a robust authentication mechanism. How well you execute that authentication will influence how much trust your users will place in your application. Your approach to security has a big impact, whether you are ensuring that

233

users' passwords are safe, or you are offering an authentication option that involves a trusted third party.

In this chapter, we take a look at how to use Ruby and Rails to implement your own secure authentication schemes as well as integrate with established authentication mechanisms like Lightweight Directory Access Protocol (LDAP), Active Directory, and OpenID.

11.1 Securely storing a password

With few exceptions, your users' passwords should never be persisted in a way that would allow anyone access to them. For example, if a hacker were to get hold of your site's database, he shouldn't find a column filled with passwords as plain text. Hopefully, this is obvious, but enough sites on the web violate this rule that it is worth making sure your applications don't make this mistake.

Problem

You need to store a password for later authentication, and do it securely.

Solution

Securely hash the password using a salt, and store the resulting string. When it is time to authenticate a user, run the submitted password through the same one-way process and compare the result to what you stored.

> **Hashes with salt**
>
> A salt is the common term for a secondary input to a cryptographic function. It is typically used with a hash function, in order to make dictionary attacks on encrypted data difficult. A good summary of how this works can be found in Philippe Oechslin's article, "Password Cracking: Rainbow Tables Explained" (http://www.isc2.org/cgi-bin/content.cgi?page=738).

Listing 11.1 shows an example of an `ActiveRecord` class implementing this approach.

Listing 11.1 An `ActiveRecord` class implementing password hashing

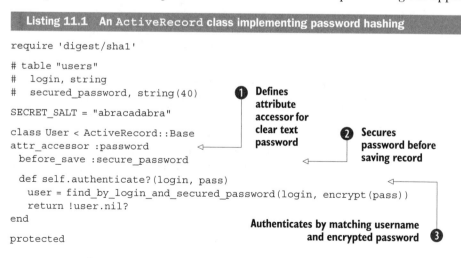

```
require 'digest/sha1'

# table "users"
#   login, string
#   secured_password, string(40)          ❶ Defines
                                              attribute
SECRET_SALT = "abracadabra"                   accessor for
                                              clear text      ❷ Secures
class User < ActiveRecord::Base               password          password before
attr_accessor :password          ◀───────┘                     saving record
  before_save :secure_password                    ◀──────┘

  def self.authenticate?(login, pass)                          ◀─────────┐
    user = find_by_login_and_secured_password(login, encrypt(pass))      │
    return !user.nil?                                                    │
end                                                                      │
                                    Authenticates by matching username   │
protected                              and encrypted password  ❸ ───────┘
```

```
def secure_password
  if password
    self.secured_password = self.class.encrypt(password)
  end
end

def self.encrypt(password)
  Digest::SHA1.hexdigest("--#{SECRET_SALT}--#{password}--")
end

end
```

In this example, the database table has a column named `secured_password`. This code supports setting the user's password, as well as authenticating a user. The password is assigned as clear text to the `password` attribute defined using `attr_accessor` ❶. The `before_save` callback encrypts the value of that attribute and stores it as the `secured_password` ❷, which gets persisted to the database. When it is time to authenticate a given username and password, the `authenticate` method searches for a matching username and password, using the one-way encrypted password value ❸.

Discussion

An implementation of the SHA1 algorithm is included in the Ruby standard library—it was written in C to make it perform as quickly as possible. The properties of this government-standard algorithm make it a great solution to the problem of storing passwords. Specifically, it is repeatable and nonreversible. It is important that it be *repeatable* so that the same password will always produce the same result, which can be compared to previous results. It is important that it be *nonreversible* so that if someone gains access to the encrypted string, it is computationally infeasible to discover the actual password.

The salt makes it more difficult to do a dictionary attack against your encrypted passwords—computing a list of the encrypted versions of common passwords and checking them against yours.

Although the SHA1 algorithm is in wide use, vulnerabilities have been discovered. The vulnerabilities are not believed to be serious, because to make use of them, an attacker would need much greater computational power than is typically available. Still, developers with healthy paranoia would do well to consider the more secure cousins of SHA1, known collectively as SHA2. The implementations of SHA2 that are included in Ruby's standard library are SHA256, SHA384, and SHA512. Here is some sample usage:

```
require 'digest/sha1'

puts Digest::SHA256.hexdigest("Please hash me.")
puts Digest::SHA384.hexdigest("Please hash me.")
puts Digest::SHA512.hexdigest("Please hash me.")
```

There is also an alternate approach to the solution that adds complexity but offers a more secure system overall. Instead of using a single salt, we will create a salt for each user and store it as an additional field. This dramatically increases the resources necessary for a dictionary attack. It also means that if two users choose the same password, the encrypted versions will still be different. If one of them had access to the encrypted passwords, it could not discover that it was using the same password as the other user. Listing 11.2 shows an implementation of this approach.

Listing 11.2 Per-user salt for password hashing

```ruby
require 'digest/sha1'
require 'openssl'                              ◁── Provides cryptographically
                                                   secure random numbers
# table "users"
#   login, string
#   secured_password, string(40)
#   salt, string(40)

class User < ActiveRecord::Base

  attr_accessor :password
  before_save :secure_password

  def self.authenticate?(login, pass)
    user = find_by_login(login)
    return false unless user
    return user.authenticate?(pass)             Authenticates
  end                                           against username and
                                          ◁──   encrypted password
  def authenticate?(pass)
    secured_password == self.class.encrypt(pass, salt)
  end

  protected

  def secure_password
    self.salt = generate_salt if new_record?
    self.secured_password = encrypt(password) if password
  end                                           Generates
                                                new salt from
  def generate_salt                       ◁──   random string
    Digest::SHA1.hexdigest(OpenSSL::Random.random_bytes(128))
  end

  def encrypt(password)
    Digest::SHA1.hexdigest("--#{salt}--#{password}--")
  end

end
```

In this version, a row must be retrieved from the database in order to validate a password. This is because the salt is stored alongside the login and secured password. At first glance, this seems like it might be insecure, and indeed, the separate location of the salt and secured password is an advantage of the original implementation. However, that advantage is outweighed by how much more difficult we are making life for an attacker by having a unique salt for each user.

To generate a different salt for each user, we need to pick a random value. Don't make the mistake of using the system time—if the attacker can guess when the account was created, it's easy for her to generate all the possible salt values and crack the password. And quite often, we'll store the account creation time directly in the users table. Using Ruby's rand method doesn't help either, because the random numbers it generates are not that random. They're based on the system clock, and even though they look secure, they can be cracked in a few seconds with today's hardware. Instead, we opted to use the OpenSSL library to generate a cryptographically secure random number to protect our salt from brute force attacks.

NOTE This use of multiple salts is the approach used by the restful_authentication Rails plugin, discussed in section 11.3.

If we go through great efforts to avoid persisting our users' passwords in plain text, it would be careless to write passwords to our log files. To avoid this in your Rails applications, add the following code to the controller that handles authentication, where password is the name of your password parameter:

```
class UsersController < ApplicationController
  filter_parameter_logging :password
  ...
end
```

This will replace the value of any parameter whose name contains "password" with the string [FILTERED].

Now that we've looked at a simple authentication scheme, let's take a look at authentication and identity with LDAP.

11.1.1 *Authenticating against LDAP*

LDAP is an open standard for interacting with hierarchical sets of people, groups, or resources. Popular open source LDAP servers include OpenLDAP and Fedora Directory Server (FDS). Commercial offerings include Sun's Java System Directory and Novell's eDirectory.

LDAP servers are well-suited to hold information about people and their security credentials. As a result, they are commonly used for authentication purposes. Let's take a look at how we can accomplish this with Ruby.

Problem

You need to authenticate users against an LDAP server.

Solution

We can use a Ruby LDAP library like the ruby-net-ldap gem to validate a username/password pair. Listing 11.3 shows an implementation of LDAP authentication with Ruby.

Listing 11.3 Authenticating with ruby-net-ldap

```
require 'net/ldap'

def valid_user?(username, password)
  ldap = initialize_ldap(username, password)
  ldap.bind
end

def initialize_ldap(username, password)
  Net::LDAP.new(:base => 'dc=example,dc=com',
```

```
                :host => 'your-ldap-server',
                :auth => {:username => "uid=#{username},cn=users",
                      :password => password,
                      :method => :simple})
end
```

The method `LDAP.bind` attempts to connect to the LDAP instance using the credentials we supply. It returns `true` if successful, and `false` if not.

Discussion

The primary alternative to the ruby-net-ldap gem used in listing 11.3 is ruby-ldap. While ruby-net-ldap is a pure Ruby LDAP client implementation, ruby-ldap is a wrapper around the OpenLDAP C library. As you might guess, this means that ruby-net-ldap is far more portable and easier to install, though ruby-ldap offers significantly better performance.

Ruby-ldap has an interesting library built on top of it called Ruby/ActiveLdap. ActiveLdap maps LDAP entries to objects in much the same way that ActiveRecord maps database rows to objects. Here is an example of defining a `User` class using ActiveLdap:

```
class User < ActiveLdap::Base
  ldap_mapping :dn_attribute => 'uid', :prefix => 'cn=users',
           :classes => ['top','account']
  belongs_to :groups, :class => 'Group', :many => 'memberUid',
          :foreign_key => 'uid'
end
```

ActiveLdap is likely overkill if your only use for LDAP is authentication. In that case, ruby-net-ldap is probably fast enough and your best bet. On the other hand, if your application is doing a lot with LDAP entries, like queries and read-write operations, ActiveLdap is definitely worth a look.

Leveraging a central corporate LDAP directory is a great strategy for applications being deployed internally. Your users will thank you for not making them create and remember yet another password!

11.2   *Authenticating against Active Directory*

Active Directory from Microsoft is used by many businesses for identity management. Integrating your authentication system with Active Directory is a great way to provide a good logon experience for internal applications and help the business keep identity and password management centralized.

Problem

You need to authenticate users against an existing Active Directory installation.

Solution

Fortunately, Active Directory is compatible with the LDAP spec, so we can use a Ruby LDAP library, like the ruby-net-ldap gem, to validate a username/password pair. See listing 11.4 for an example.

> **Listing 11.4   Authenticating against Active Directory using ruby-net-ldap**

```
equire 'net/ldap'

def valid_user?(username, password)
  ldap = initialize_ldap(username, password)
  ldap.bind
end

def initialize_ldap(username, password)
  Net::LDAP.new(:base => 'dc=example,dc=corp',
           :host => 'exampledomaincontroller',
           :auth => {:username => "#{username}@example.corp",
                :password => password,
                :method => :simple})
end
```

Ask your Active Directory administrator for the name of the domain controller—that's the LDAP host in the case of an Active Directory installation.

This example takes advantage of a convenience offered by Active Directory: you can send user@domain as the username for the purposes of binding, and Active Directory will handle it properly. Normally, LDAP instances expect a distinguished name (DN) in this spot.

Discussion

The approach in listing 11.4 is suitable for an application that should be available to any member of the Active Directory instance, but if you need more information about a user, you can call the search method, which returns a collection of LDAP entries, in place of the bind method, which simply confirms that the provided credentials are valid. This would be useful, for example, to validate that a user is not only who she says she is (via password), but also that she is a member of a particular group. The search method uses a filter based on the sAMAccountName attribute, which is the closest thing to a simple username attribute in Active Directory's schema.

Here's an example:

```
def valid_app_user?(username, password)
  ldap = initialize_ldap(username, password)
  entries = ldap.search :filter => "sAMAccountName=#{username}"
  return false unless entries && !entries.empty?
  return member_of_ad_group?("G-MyAppUsers", entries.first)
end

def member_of_ad_group?(group, ldap_entry)
  group_names = ldap_entry[:memberof] # returns a collection of fully-
                            # qualified Active Directory groups
  group_names.any?{|name| name.include? 'CN=#{group},' }
end
```

The array of groups returned by the :memberof attribute of an Active Directory LDAP entry contains the distinguished name of the groups. Something like this:

```
CN=G-MyAppUsers,OU=Groups Security,OU=Example,DC=example,DC=corp
```

In the `member_of_ad_group?` method, we're looking for a match in the first part, the common name (CN).

If you want a solution specific to Active Directory, ruby-activedirectory takes all the features and idiosyncrasies of Active Directory into account. It provides classes for `Users`, `Groups`, and `Computers`. The `ActiveDirectory::User` authenticate method will validate a particular user's password. Using it is straightforward:

```
require 'activedirectory'

def valid_user?(username, password)
  user = ActiveDirectory::User.find('jdoe')
  user.authenticate(password)
end
```

This library depends on ruby-ldap being installed, which can be a little tricky, as it wraps the OpenLDAP C library. If you can get over that hurdle, ruby-activedirectory is quite useful in working with an Active Directory installation.

11.3   *Adding authentication to your Rails application*

Most nontrivial Rails applications offer a personalized experience to each user of the site. The most common solution to personalization needs is letting users sign up for an account and authenticating them when they visit the site. While implementing a username/password authentication system eventually leads to various decisions and custom code, adding a basic implementation isn't particularly difficult.

Problem

You need to add authentication to a Rails application...quickly!

Solution

The easiest and most well-trodden route to getting user authentication in a Rails application is by using the restful_authentication plugin to generate the necessary code. First, you'll need to install the plugin:

```
script/plugin install restful_authentication
```

You'll see some text scroll by, and if it's successful, you should see the plugin's README and you'll have a vendor/plugins/restful_authentication folder in your Rails application.

> **TIP**   You may have to provide the source for the plugin (the plugin's source repository). In this case, you'll need to add `--source=http://svn.techno-weenie.net/projects/plugins/restful_authentication/` to the script/plugin call.

The next step is generating the code. We need a `User` model, a `UsersController`, and a migration, along with tests and a couple of useful library classes. The plugin rolls all of these into one convenient generator:

```
script/generate authenticated User
```

To get access to all of the helpers and other code, we need to mix the `Authenticated-System` module into `ApplicationController` instead of `UsersController`, where the plugin will place it, so that it is available to all of our controllers. We need to remove the include AuthenticationSystem line from users_controller.rb:

```
class UsersController < ApplicationController
  # Be sure to include AuthenticationSystem in
  # Application Controller instead
  include AuthenticatedSystem
  ...
end
```

We also need to move the AuthenticatedSystem module to ApplicationController in application.rb:

```
class ApplicationController < ActionController::Base
  include AuthenticatedSystem
  ...
end
```

The restful_authentication plugin enforces its authentication through before_filters. To restrict a controller, we can add before_filter :login_required to its class body, like this:

```
class TodosController < ApplicationController
  before_filter :login_required
  ...
end
```

Next, we'll need to set up the database tables for users and their sessions. This just involves running the database migration generated by the plugin.

```
rake db:migrate
```

That's all the setup we need. If you start your application using script/server, you can create the first account by pointing your web browser to http://0.0.0.0:3000/users/new.

TIP   Rick Olson is a member of the Ruby on Rails core team and is known online as "technoweenie." You can find some incredibly useful plugins (including this one) and learn a lot by browsing his repository at http://github.com/technoweenie/plugins/.

Discussion

It is easy to assume that authentication on the web is simple because thousands of web-sites have implemented it. The truth is that the possible variations and nuances are manifold. Can any visitor sign up and create an account, or are accounts created only by users with administrative privileges? Does a user log in with her username, or does she log in with an email address? Perhaps either is possible? What sort of confirmation or activation step is necessary? The purpose of the restful_authentication plugin is not to support all these scenarios, but rather to put into place the most common mechanisms for username/password authentication and give you a solid base to build upon.

Our favorite thing about the restful_authentication plugin is the quality of the tests (or specs) it adds to a project. Both the generated model and the controller are accompanied by tests that together sport 100 percent code coverage. When you're ready to start customizing your application's authentication logic, start with the tests—either adding tests to drive new features, or modifying tests to drive changes to the generated code.

TIP   The generator will generate tests and test helpers for you by default, but you can tell the plugin to give you specs for RSpec instead by giving it the --rspec option or by simply adding a spec/ directory to your Rails application.

The restful_authentication plugin also provides very useful helper methods you can use in your own tests. Inside of your lib directory, you'll notice that the generation process has added authenticated_test_helper.rb. It defines a module that is mixed into the two test classes generated (test/unit/user_test.rb and test/functional/users_controller_test.rb in the previous example). Let's look at how to use a few of these helper methods.

The login_as method takes a symbol (:quentin in the following example) that is used to look up a user from the YAML fixtures:

```
def test_index_ok_for_logged_in_user
  login_as :quentin
  get :index
  assert_response :ok
end
```

It then sets that user as the logged-in user by setting session[:user] to the ID of the specified user. This helper lets you interact with controllers in your tests as if a user were logged in to your application. You can also interact as an anonymous user; when the login_as method is passed nil, it clears any existing value of session[:user], thereby simulating an anonymous user:

```
def test_index_not_available_to_anonymous_user
  login_as nil
  get :index
  assert_response 401
end
```

The power of Ruby's block syntax is evident in the assert_difference method. In the following example, the count method of User is called twice. In between, the content of the block is executed—a POST to the create action, in this case:

```
def test_create_increments_user_count
  assert_difference 'User.count', 1 do
    post :create, :user => {:login => 'foo', :password => 'test'}
  end
end
```

The return values of the two calls are compared to verify that the difference is equal to the value of the second argument to assert_difference: 1 in our example.

Conversely, assert_no_difference works just like assert_difference but instead ensures that the return value of the specified method is the same before and after the block executes:

```
def test_create_with_invalid_login_does_not_change_user_count
  assert_no_difference User, :count do
    post :create, :user => {:login => nil, :password => 'test'}
  end
end
```

If you're thinking, "Wow! Some of these test helpers are really handy," you would be right. It is a good idea to mix this module into the `Test::Unit::TestCase` class defined in test/test_helper.rb. You can then remove it from the generated tests and use it in any of your tests for the rest of your application.

The restful_authentication plugin consists entirely of code generators, so there's really no need to keep it installed once you're happy with the code you've generated. You can either delete the directory or remove it like this:

```
script/plugin remove restful_authentication
```

The code you generated with it will still be present and working, but you won't be transferring an extra directory with every deployment for no reason.

Let's take a look at putting authentication into action by creating semi-private per-user feeds.

11.4 *Semi-private, personalized feeds*

RSS and Atom feeds are a great way for users to keep a connection to your site. In the case of a data-driven site, the information in a feed is likely unique or at least personalized for each user. Unfortunately, many feed readers don't support username/password authentication, or don't do so securely.

Problem

You need to offer feeds that are personalized and semi-private but that still work with typical feed readers.

Solution

We'll create and associate a secret token with each user that can be used to authenticate for feeds only. Listing 11.5 shows a sample ActiveRecord migration that adds a column to hold our secret token. In the subsequent listings, we'll modify the User class to populate the token for new users, and demonstrate how to integrate it with a controller.

Listing 11.5   An ActiveRecord migration to add our token column

```
require 'digest/sha1'
require 'openssl'

class AddUserToken < ActiveRecord::Migration

  class User < ActiveRecord::Base      ❶
  end

  def self.up
    add_column :users, :token, :string, :limit => 40      ❷
    User.find(:all).each do |user|
      user.token = Digest::SHA1.hexdigest(
  ➥     OpenSSL::Random.random_bytes(128))      ❸
```

```
    user.save
  end
end

def self.down
  remove_column :users, :token
end
end
```

We want to work with a clean version of the User class, so that any future changes to the application code won't risk breaking this migration ❶. After adding the column ❷, the migration populates it with a random token ❸. We'll make use of that in the listings that follow.

Next, our User model should automatically create a token when a new user is added. As such, we'll need to add a before_create call to generate the token before the User is created. Listing 11.6 shows our implementation.

Listing 11.6   A User model that generates tokens upon creation

```
require 'digest/sha1'
require 'openssl'

class User < ActiveRecord::Base
  before_create :generate_token
  ...
  def generate_token
    self.token = Digest::SHA1.hexdigest(OpenSSL::Random.random_bytes(128))
  end
end
```

We are creating a random 40-character token, and using SHA1 is a convenient way to do that. We will then add these tokens to the personalized feed URLs that our application exposes, and use them to associate the incoming requests for feeds with the right user's data. If our application's actions require a login by default (via a filter in ApplicationController called login_required), a CommentsController that implements this concept might look like the one in listing 11.7.

Listing 11.7   A comments controller implementing our token authentication

```
class CommentsController < ApplicationController
  skip_before_filter :login_required, :only => [:index]
  prepend_before_filter :login_or_feed_token_required, :only => [:index]

  def index
    @comments = current_user.comments
    respond_to do |format|
      format.html
      format.rss  { render_rss_feed_for @comments }
      format.atom { render_atom_feed_for @comments }
    end
  end

  ...

end
```

Here, for the `index` action only, the controller will bypass the default `login_required` filter, but add a filter that calls the `login_or_feed_token_required` method. This method allows the request to proceed if either the user is logged in or the request is for an RSS or Atom feed and the request `params` hash contains the correct secret token.

The following code should be added to our `ApplicationController`:

```
def login_or_feed_token_required
  if params.has_key?(:token) &&
➥ (request.format.atom? || request.format.rss?)
    return true if @user = User.find_by_token(params[:token])
  end
  login_required
end
```

We attempt to authenticate using the token if appropriate, and otherwise fall back to the `login_required` method.

Discussion

The solution relies on providing an alternate means of authentication (a secret token) to each user. This alternate authentication provides only limited rights: read-only access to XML feeds. In the event that the secret is leaked, this approach limits exposure. Contrast that with having a user's password compromised because your application forced him to embed it in a feed URL used from a web-based feed reader.

Since we want to support users in keeping their data secure, it is a good idea to provide a mechanism that allows users to replace their secret tokens on demand. You can provide this with a Rails controller action like this one:

```
class UsersController < ApplicationController
  ...
  def refresh_token
    @user.generate_token
    @user.save!
  end
  ...
end
```

It is important that users realize that changing their tokens will break any externally stored URLs.

You might consider using the same token, or a separate one, as an authentication mechanism for your application's API. If your API provides both read and write operations, this would obviously increase risk. Still, your users would probably prefer embedding a randomly generated 40-character string in a script than in their passwords.

When you detect that you are handling an RSS or ATOM request, you can be fairly confident that an RSS reader or a script is the requestor. In these situations, you can more efficiently handle the request by turning off the session for that request, like this:

```
class CommentsController < ApplicationController
  ...
  session :off, :only => :index,
          :if => Proc.new { |req| is_feed_request?(req) }
  ...
  def self.is_feed_request?(request)
```

```
    request.format.atom? || request.format.rss?
  end
end
```

Note that `is_feed_request` is defined as a class method of the controller. For the method to resolve in the `session :off` statement, it must be a class method.

If the data in the feeds is not sensitive, keep it simple and skip authentication for feeds altogether. You could also consider making the feed content a shallow, nonsensitive indicator of the content with links back into the site, where the user would have to authenticate normally. Another approach you may want to consider is simple, time-tested HTTP Basic Authentication.

11.5   *HTTP Basic Authentication*

Sometimes you need some very simple authentication capabilities. HTTP Basic Authentication is a well-known standard supported by practically every web browser and web automation library. It offers a simple way to secure an API or application meant to be consumed by simple scripts.

Problem

You need to access the username and password sent via HTTP Basic Authentication in a simple Ruby CGI application.

Solution

Listing 11.8 shows how we can extend CGI to allow access to HTTP Basic data.

Listing 11.8   Authenticating with HTTP Basic using CGI

```
class CGI
  def basic_auth_data
    user, pass = '', ''
    header_keys = ['HTTP_AUTHORIZATION', 'X-HTTP_AUTHORIZATION',
                'X_HTTP_AUTHORIZATION',
                'REDIRECT_X_HTTP_AUTHORIZATION']
    header_key = header_keys.find{ |key| env_table.has_key?(key) }
    authdata = env_table[header_key].to_s.split if header_key
    if authdata && authdata[0] == 'Basic'
      return Base64.decode64(authdata[1]).split(':')[0..1]
    end
  end
end

# Here's an example usage:
cgi = CGI.new
username, password = cgi.basic_auth_data
```

In this example, we open up the `CGI` class and add `CGI.basic_auth_data`, a method that can extract the relevant HTTP headers according to the HTTP spec. Note how two of Ruby's language features (open classes and multiple return values) allow us to create nicer usage syntax than we could in less flexible languages.

Discussion

As you can tell from the code in listing 11.8, the username and password is Base64-encoded. This makes the user's credentials extremely easy for an attacker sniffing

HTTP traffic to access. Ensuring that HTTP traffic occurs over HTTPS is one way to make this technique more secure.

While a programmatic web client can be written to always send authorization headers, most graphical web browsers prompt for basic authentication upon receiving a response with a 401 status code and a WWW-Authenticate header. While testing using a browser, you may not see any authorization headers until you challenge the browser, like this:

```
cgi.out("status" => "AUTH_REQUIRED",
  "WWW-Authenticate" => 'Basic realm="My Application"') { "And you are…?" }
```

Since most developers use Rails for web development these days, people have ported HTTP Basic Authentication to the framework. Rails 2.0 provides this functionality in `ActionController::Base`, specifically the `authenticate_or_request_with_http_basic` method.

NOTE With the release of Rails 2.3, Rails now supports digest authentication in addition to basic authentication.

11.6 *Integrating OpenID into your application*

OpenID is an open standard for decentralized single sign-on. It seeks to address the problem that every internet user is familiar with—too many usernames and passwords.

If a site supports OpenID, a user can simply enter her OpenID (janedoe. myopenid.net, for example) and get redirected to her OpenID provider's website, where she agrees to allow the originating site to authenticate before being redirected back to the originating site with a token that proves the user is the owner of the ID.

Of course, this explanation is a slight simplification of the OpenID protocol. We recommend you familiarize yourself with the details of the interactions. A great resource is the documentation embedded in the ruby-openid gem source code. Check out lib/openid/consumer.rb in particular.

Problem

You need to support single sign-on via OpenID.

Solution

We're only going to use OpenID in our application, so we can use the `ruby-openid` gem to abstract the details of the inter-server communication and initiate and complete the process in controller actions. Listing 11.9 shows a simple controller that handles logging in with OpenID.

Listing 11.9 A simple OpenID login controller

```
require 'openid'

class LoginController < ApplicationController
  def index
    #show the OpenID login form
  end

  def begin
    openid_url = params[:openid_url]
```

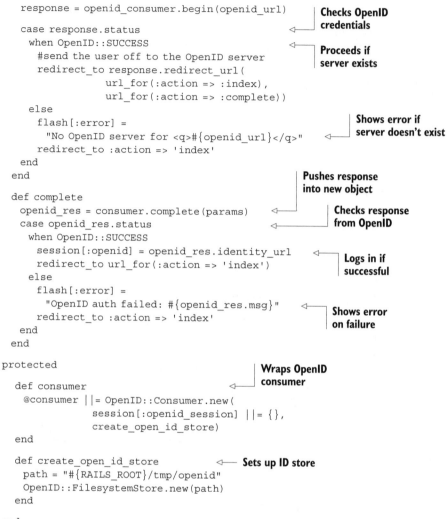

```
    response = openid_consumer.begin(openid_url)          Checks OpenID
                                                          credentials
    case response.status
      when OpenID::SUCCESS
        #send the user off to the OpenID server           Proceeds if
        redirect_to response.redirect_url(                server exists
                  url_for(:action => :index),
                  url_for(:action => :complete))
      else
        flash[:error] =                                   Shows error if
          "No OpenID server for <q>#{openid_url}</q>"     server doesn't exist
        redirect_to :action => 'index'
      end
  end

  def complete                                            Pushes response
                                                          into new object
    openid_res = consumer.complete(params)                Checks response
    case openid_res.status                                from OpenID
      when OpenID::SUCCESS
        session[:openid] = openid_res.identity_url         Logs in if
        redirect_to url_for(:action => 'index')            successful
      else
        flash[:error] =
          "OpenID auth failed: #{openid_res.msg}"          Shows error
        redirect_to :action => 'index'                     on failure
    end
  end

  protected                                               Wraps OpenID
                                                          consumer
    def consumer
      @consumer ||= OpenID::Consumer.new(
                session[:openid_session] ||= {},
                create_open_id_store)
    end

    def create_open_id_store          Sets up ID store
      path = "#{RAILS_ROOT}/tmp/openid"
      OpenID::FilesystemStore.new(path)
    end

end
```

We'll need a login form, of course, so the view for the index action of the controller would look like this:

```
<% form_tag url_for(:action => 'begin') do %>
  <%= text_field_tag 'openid_url' %>
  <%= submit_tag 'Login' %>
<% end %>
```

Submitting this form results in a request that is handled by our `begin` action, which starts the OpenID transaction. Taken all together, this code will allow you to check the session for an `:openid` key and use that to determine whether the user is authenticated.

For a simple, readable way to check whether a user has authenticated, we could define a helper method like so:

```
class ApplicationController < ActionController::Base
  ...
  def authenticated?
    session.has_key? :openid
  end
  ...
end
```

You could also have a `User` model backed by a database table if you need to store per-user preferences or attributes. You could access it based on the user's OpenID, like this:

```
class ApplicationController < ActionController::Base
  ...
  def current_user
    User.find_by_open_id_url(session[:openid])
  end
  ...
end
```

Discussion

As one would expect, there are a number of OpenID plugins, the most prominent of which is open_id_authentication from the Rails core team. There are two major differences between these plugins and the previous example code. First, the plugins attempt to encapsulate most of the logic within modules in the plugin, naturally. Second, the plugins all default to using a database store instead of a filesystem store. For an application that is load-balanced across multiple servers, the filesystem store is inadequate.

A common idiom is to allow users to choose between a username/password login scheme or OpenID. Integrating open_id_authentication with restful_authentication to achieve this effect is not very difficult. First, we'll need to add a field to our user model and a field to the forms to edit them. Listings 11.10 and 11.11 show a migration and edited view to allow for this logic.

Listing 11.10 A database migration to create the OpenID tables

```
class AddOpenIdAuthenticationTables < ActiveRecord::Migration
  def self.up
    create_table :open_id_authentication_associations,
            :force => true do |t|
      t.integer :issued, :lifetime
      t.string :handle, :assoc_type
      t.binary :server_url, :secret
    end

    create_table :open_id_authentication_nonces, :force => true do |t|
      t.integer :timestamp, :null => false
      t.string :server_url, :null => true
      t.string :salt, :null => false
    end

    add_column :users, :identity_url, :string
  end

  def self.down
```

```
      drop_table :open_id_authentication_associations
      drop_table :open_id_authentication_nonces
      remove_column :users, :identity_url
    end
  end
```

Listing 11.11   Edited view to support OpenID authentication

```
<% form_tag session_path do -%>

<p><label for="email">Login</label><br/>
<%= text_field_tag 'login' %></p>

<p><label for="password">Password</label><br/>
<%= password_field_tag %></p>

<p><label for="identity_url">Identity URL:</label><br />
<%= text_field_tag :openid_url %></p>

<p class="submit"><%= submit_tag 'Log in' %></p>
<% end -%>
```

Next, we'll need to edit (or basically replace) our controller to allow for OpenID authentication and non-OpenID authentication. This requires us to add some conditional logic as shown in listing 11.12.

Listing 11.12   A new `SessionsController` that supports OpenID

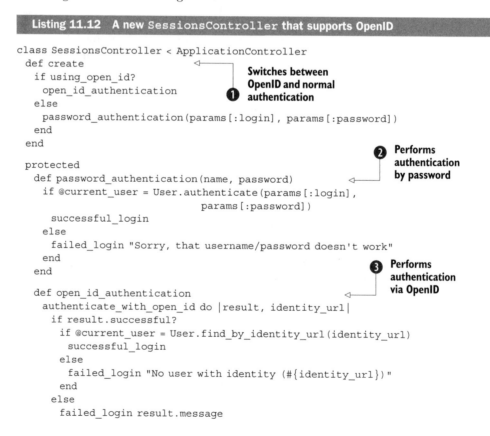

```
class SessionsController < ApplicationController
  def create
    if using_open_id?                         ◄——  ❶ Switches between
      open_id_authentication                         OpenID and normal
    else                                             authentication
      password_authentication(params[:login], params[:password])
    end
  end

  protected                                                  ❷ Performs
    def password_authentication(name, password)      ◄——       authentication
      if @current_user = User.authenticate(params[:login],     by password
                               params[:password])
        successful_login
      else
        failed_login "Sorry, that username/password doesn't work"
      end
    end                                                      ❸ Performs
                                                                authentication
    def open_id_authentication                       ◄——         via OpenID
      authenticate_with_open_id do |result, identity_url|
        if result.successful?
          if @current_user = User.find_by_identity_url(identity_url)
            successful_login
          else
            failed_login "No user with identity (#{identity_url})"
          end
        else
          failed_login result.message
```

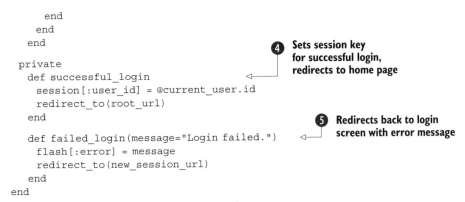

```
        end
      end
    end
  private
    def successful_login
      session[:user_id] = @current_user.id
      redirect_to(root_url)
    end

    def failed_login(message="Login failed.")
      flash[:error] = message
      redirect_to(new_session_url)
    end
  end
end
```

❹ Sets session key for successful login, redirects to home page

❺ Redirects back to login screen with error message

In this new controller (listing 11.12), we first need to replace our earlier create method with one that can differentiate between standard authentication and OpenID ❶. In this implementation, we use the plugin's convenience method using_open_id? (which, in turn, checks for the presence of a value for params[:identity_url]).

Next, we need to create two methods for handling the types of authentication: password_authentication ❷ and open_id_authentication ❸. The password_authentication method is basically the previous create method, except renamed and using calls to our successful_login and failed_login methods. The open_id_authentication method consists of the logic that we previously wrote in listing 11.9, except now it's abstracted away into a plugin and condensed down to a single method.

Finally, we create two methods that are called when logins succeed ❹ (or fail ❺), regardless of authentication type.

Now we need to add a route to config/routes.rb that the OpenID plugin can use to handle communication with the OpenID server:

```
map.open_id_complete 'session', :controller => 'sessions',
                     :action => 'create',
                     :requirements => { :method => :get }
```

Now our users should be able to log in with either a username/password pair or their favorite OpenID provider.

OpenID is rapidly gaining support in the industry. Companies that provide an OpenID account to all their customers include AOL, Yahoo!, WordPress, SixApart, Orange, and France Telecom. Although it is primarily targeted for the public web, applications for the enterprise are quite interesting. A company could run a public OpenID server for just its employees, thereby vouching for the identity of anyone with an OpenID provided by the company. Also, because OpenID libraries are available for practically every web development platform, it has become an option for single-sign on in a heterogeneous environment. You might easily layer an OpenID server atop your Active Directory or proprietary authentication system. If you're interested in this, there are several open source OpenID servers, including some written in Ruby cataloged on the OpenID website (http://wiki.openid.net/Libraries).

11.7   *Summary*

Teenagers today are fond of vintage T-shirts, or simply those that appear to be vintage. This style has been dubbed "authenticitude" by marketing wonks—the attitude of authenticity. For Rubyists, though, we think "authenticitude" should be the attitude of treating authentication seriously, and letting your users know that you do.

Whether your application lives in a corporate environment or on the public web, whether your users are open standards junkies, newbies, or mindless client applications, we hope this chapter has what you need to implement a great authentication system. Take it seriously. Know your users and let them know that their data and identities are safe with you.

If you want to wear a faux-vintage T-shirt while you're coding it, that's your business.

Searching and indexing 12

This chapter covers

- Searching databases
- Indexing content using Ferret and Solr
- Searching with other technologies
- The scraping technique

Throughout this book, and throughout your entire programming life, you've been used to dealing with data, because it forms the input and output for all computer programs. So far, we have mostly looked at transforming data from one state to another, but in this chapter we're going to investigate Ruby's abilities to let you *search through* data.

Unfortunately, as a language that has reached maturity only in the last few years, Ruby is not blessed with hundreds of search-related libraries. This is not necessarily a bad thing, as search technologies progress quickly, and most of the available Ruby search solutions are up to date and ready to use in production immediately.

In this chapter, we'll look at Ruby-specific techniques for searching and indexing data, and we'll examine some solutions to common search-related problems.

We're going to look at standalone libraries and techniques available to Ruby developers, and we'll walk through the process of indexing content using two

Apache Lucene-based libraries, Ferret and Solr, as well as a performance-driven Ruby-only library called FTSearch. We'll also look at integrating search features with other technologies, and at searching the web, searching databases, and adding indexing and search features to Ruby on Rails applications.

First, we'll define searching and indexing, as well as other related terminology.

NOTE   We will only cover search libraries that are under active development and that have been updated in the last year. There are several older libraries that you may hear about, but we feel it's important to focus on up-to-date, well-supported tools, so that the level of documentation and support you would expect is still present.

12.1 *The principles of searching*

Searching refers to the process of taking a collection of data, processing it so that it can be scanned quickly, then enabling a program or a user to find small elements of data within the larger set. Google provides the most ubiquitous form of search technology in our lives today. If you want to find a web page that contains a certain word, or set of words, you go to http://www.google.com, type in your query, and receive your results almost instantaneously.

The amount of data Google can search across is somewhere in the range of billions of pages, which take up thousands of gigabytes of space. Google, therefore, certainly can't scan every page, byte by byte, looking for results to your query. It could take days (or longer!) to get your search results that way, although it would still, technically, be a "search engine."

The process that allows Google to produce search results in under a second is *indexing*, and the performance benefits of indexing are so significant that every search library or tool must provide indexing services of one form or another.

Indexing technologies can be extremely advanced, but at their most basic, they work in the same way as an index in a book. For example, if you turn to the index of this book and search for a particular term, you know roughly where in the index to look, because the index is in alphabetical order. Furthermore, once you find your desired term, you're provided with a set of page numbers to refer to. This contrasts significantly with having to read through every page of the book to find something. Computers use similar techniques. A search engine's indexer makes a note of words and phrases on a page, and links those terms (using, for performance and efficiency, a unique numeric ID that references each distinct term) to the page it is indexing. When a search is run, the query engine can quickly look up the IDs of pages that match the terms provided by a user's search query.

12.2 *Standalone and high-performance searching*

In this section, we're going to look at generic, standalone searching and indexing scenarios with the simplest problem we can provide: indexing, and then querying, a corpus of documents. This contrasts with the latter half of this chapter, where we will look at how to use and integrate search techniques in busier situations, such as on the web or within a database-driven web application.

12.2.1 Standalone indexing and search with Ferret

Ferret is a Ruby implementation of Apache Lucene, an open source search and indexing library written in Java. Lucene is incredibly popular in the open source world, and a significant amount of software, and many libraries, use it for implementing large and small search systems. Lucene is an indexing and search library, and so does not include any features relating to obtaining or specially parsing content. These features are provided by other libraries, or by the software using Lucene. As a Ruby implementation of Lucene, Ferret shares the same characteristics.

Ferret will not crawl the web for you, download emails, or index different types of content in unique ways. Instead, you have to use Ferret from your Ruby programs in a generic way. Like Lucene, Ferret can deal with different data formats, and as long as you can extract the textual content of the data you wish to index, Ferret can handle it. Ferret works with the concepts of *documents* and *fields*, where documents represent individual groups of content to be indexed (such as a single web page, an email message, or the lyrics of a song) and fields are more detailed elements of data with documents (such as dates, author information, and other metadata).

In this section, we're going to look at using Ferret to index and search through documents we provide.

Problem

You wish to be able to index, and then search via query, an arbitrary set of documents (that may or may not contain multiple fields of metadata, such as titles, descriptions, and author information) quickly and efficiently. You do not care if the index is usable only from Ruby.

Solution

We'll look at three solutions to the problem. The first, in listing 12.1, implements a basic text-only indexing and searching system. The second, in listing 12.2, looks at indexing and searching through content that contains metadata and multiple fields. The third solution, in listing 12.3, looks at storing an index to disk and then loading it from another program (which allows the index to persist).

Each solution assumes that you have installed the ferret gem. This is very simple to do on a system running Ruby and RubyGems; use `gem install ferret`.

Listing 12.1 Basic document search

```
require 'rubygems'
require 'ferret'

index = Ferret::Index::Index.new        ①

index << "This is a test document to test Ferret."
index << "Here is another test document."          ②
index << "And now, for something totally different!"
```

```
query = "test"

index.search_each(query) do |id, score|
  puts "Found #{query} in document #{id} (scoring #{score})"
end
```
❸

Listing 12.2   Multifield document search

```
require 'rubygems'
require 'ferret'

# Begin to build a set of fields for content to use
fields = Ferret::Index::FieldInfos.new(:store => :yes, :index => :yes)
```
❹
```
# Give a boost to titles, as their content is likely to confidently
# reflect the document
fields.add_field(:title, :boost => 10)

# No boost for general content
fields.add_field(:text)
```
❺
```
# Give a big boost to author information in terms of searches

fields.add_field(:author, :boost => 20)

# Build a local index object
index = Ferret::Index::Index.new(:field_infos => fields)
```
❻
```
# Add some example documents to the index
index << {  :title  => "My Test Document",
            :text   => "This is a test to demonstrate Ferret",
            :author => "Fred Bloggs" }

index << {  :title  => "Irrelevant Title",
            :text   => "Another test document",
            :author => "Anon" }
```
❼
```
index << {  :title  => "Third Document",
            :text   => "This document contains nothing of interest",
            :author => "Fred Bloggs" }

# Perform a query
puts "What do you want to search for?"
query = gets.chomp
search_results = index.search(query).hits

# Sort the search results by score descending and show the results
search_results.sort_by{ |h| h.score }.reverse.each do |hit|
  print "Found '#{index[hit.doc][:title]}' by "
  puts "'#{index[hit.doc][:author]}' (score: #{hit.score})"
end
```

Listing 12.3   Separate indexer and query client programs

```
# Indexer (file: indexer.rb)
require 'rubygems'
require 'ferret'

fields = Ferret::Index::FieldInfos.new(:store => :yes, :index => :yes)
fields.add_field(:title, :boost => 10)
fields.add_field(:text)
```

```
fields.add_field(:author, :boost => 20)

# Create an index on the filesystem (stored in /tmp/our_index)
index = Ferret::Index::Index.new(:path => '/tmp/our_index',
                          :field_infos => fields)

# Add some example documents to the index
index << {  :title => "My Test Document",
            :text  => "This is a test to demonstrate Ferret",
            :author => "Fred Bloggs" }

index << {  :title => "Irrelevant Title",
            :text  => "Another test document",
            :author => "Anon" }

# Query client (file: query_client.rb)
require 'rubygems'
require 'ferret'

index = Ferret::Index::Index.new(:path => '/tmp/our_index')

# Perform a query
puts "What do you want to search for?"
query = gets.chomp
search_results = index.search(query).hits

# Sort the search results by score descending and show the results
search_results.sort_by{ |h| h.score }.reverse.each do |hit|
  print "Found '#{index[hit.doc][:title]}' by "
  puts "'#{index[hit.doc][:author]}' (score: #{hit.score})"
end
```

These three solutions are very similar, but they show different approaches and levels of complexity. All of them use a Ferret index, with the first two solutions storing the index in memory for immediate use only, and the final solution storing the index to and loading it from the disk.

In listing 12.1, we can see how simple it is to create an index by creating a new object from the Ferret::Index::Index class ❶.

Next, we supply the index with multiple documents to be indexed ❷. We used strings, but we could have used almost any form of data in Ruby that can translate to a string (such as an array or a hash).

Whether we use an in-memory or on-disk index, "pushing" documents to the index causes them to be indexed immediately. Finally, we query the index using the search_each method, which performs a search and iterates over each result, passing in the document ID of the matching document, along with a quality score, each time ❸.

We did not give our documents ID numbers, but Ferret did this for us in the order that we supplied the documents. For example, the first solution performs a query of "test", which nets the following results:

```
Found test in document 0 (scoring 0.70710676908493)
Found test in document 1 (scoring 0.5)
```

Because the word "test" wasn't mentioned in the third document (the document that has an ID of 2, due to 0-indexing), it's not returned as a result.

Listing 12.2 shows how the previous solution can be extended with an option to include information about a set of fields that exist on the supplied documents. We define these fields first into a group using class `Ferret::Index::FieldInfos`, then pass that composite object through to the index as an option.

Defining fields to be indexed and managed separately by Ferret is easy. First, we create the `FieldInfos` object that will hold all of the information ❹.

This constructor takes many different options, but the important ones are `:store` and `:index`. These options act as the default choices for all the fields we define from here on out. The `:store` option lets us choose whether the index will store the *actual content* of a field (or whether the content should be compressed and/or processed and then discarded entirely) and `:index` specifies whether a field should be indexed at all. In our case, we want the default to be yes for both.

Next, we define three fields: a "title" field, a "text" or content field, and an author field ❺. Adding the fields is as easy as calling `add_field` on the `FieldInfos` object. Then we specify the field name, along with any options. In this case, the default options of `:store => :yes` and `:index => :yes` are used on all of the fields, but on two of the fields we provide a "boost."

Boosting is useful when you have columns that contain data that's more important than data in other columns. In this case, for example, we give document titles more importance in the rankings than the main content (in the `text` field). We then give the author name even more importance than the title, so that if one document contains "Fred" in the title, and another was written by someone named "Fred," the latter document would probably score more highly.

Once the fields are defined in the `FieldInfo` set, we define the index much like in our first example, but we also pass through the field data ❻.

Then, to add documents with defined fields, we use hashes ❼. Because the fields are delimited in these sample documents, Ferret knows how to handle them in relation to the fields defined in the index.

If we run this example and provide it with a test query, we can see how the boosts affect the results:

```
What do you want to search for?
> document
Found 'Third Document' by 'Fred Bloggs' (score: 1.97577941417694)
Found 'My Test Document' by 'Fred Bloggs' (score: 0.922030389308929)
Found 'Irrelevant Title' by 'Anon' (score: 0.065859317779541)
```

Notice that even though each document contains the word "document," the document that ranks highest is the one with the word in both the title and the content, whereas the second result lacks the word in the content, and the third document, with an extremely low score, merely contains it in the `text` field.

Listing 12.3 demonstrates how to store and retrieve an index from disk. Ferret makes it extremely simple; it is only necessary to specify the pathname within the construction of the index object ❽.

If the directory specified using the :path parameter doesn't exist, it'll be created, as it is in the first example of this third solution. In the second example, the index is loaded in much a similar fashion **❾**.

Because the index should already exist, and the field information is predefined, we don't need to construct and pass through the field information to Ferret, as it's already part of the index's structure. The rest of the third solution then uses the same querying code as used earlier.

Discussion

While the queries we performed in the solutions were simple, single-word queries, Ferret has support for complex queries, as you'd expect from a search tool. You can search for phrases, perform Boolean operations ("fred OR martha" or "foo AND bar"), and use wildcards (such as "fre*").

You can learn more about the query syntax supported by Lucene at http://lucene.apache. org/java/docs/queryparsersyntax.html.

You can also learn more about how to use Ferret by looking at the official tutorial at http://ferret.davebalmain.com/api/files/TUTORIAL.html.

Next, we're going to look at a true Apache Lucene instance, installed and made available remotely by another Apache product: Solr.

12.2.2 *Integrating with the Solr search engine*

In the previous section, we looked at using Ferret, a Ruby implementation of Apache Lucene, to index and search data. As we discovered, Ferret and Lucene are indexing and searching libraries, and the ability to parse the data to be indexed, as well as to interpret the results of searches, rests with the client application.

In this section, we're going to look at Lucene from a different angle, using the Solr search server. Solr, another Apache project, is an open source search server that uses Lucene. Whereas Lucene is only a searching and indexing library, Solr provides higher-level features such as XML and JSON HTTP-based APIs, replication, caching, and a web-based administration interface. If Lucene is the guts of a searching and indexing system, Solr provides the friendly face necessary to use it at a higher level.

Whether you choose to use Ferret or Solr depends on your preferences and the fit between your requirements and the pros and cons of each technology. Even though both provide Lucene-based functionality, their interfaces are so radically different that careful consideration is required. Solr wins out if you need features like replication and the ability to rapidly scale or to easily access indexes over a network, or if you want to provide the same index to multiple applications, including non-Ruby applications. Ferret wins out if you want a simple, single-machine, Ruby-only solution, because it can be installed in one step using RubyGems, whereas Solr requires you to install several pieces of software just to get started.

The solution covered in this section expects that you have Apache Solr installed and running correctly. The installation of Solr is beyond the scope of this chapter, but the official home page is at http://lucene.apache.org/solr/, and information about its dependencies, such as Java 1.5 (or higher), and how to download Solr, is available in the main tutorial provided on the site.

Problem

You wish to use a Solr installation to index and query a set of documents, whether the Solr server is local or remote. This will give you the ability to perform searches over HTTP and to use Solr's features to gain access to a more robust, scalable, cross-application search solution.

Solution

In our solution in listing 12.4, we assume Solr is installed and running, and that access to the admin interface is possible at http://localhost:8983/solr/admin/. If the server is running on a different machine or port, replace `localhost` references in the code with the relevant hostname, IP address, and/or port.

Listing 12.4   The `MySolr` class

```ruby
require 'net/http'
require 'uri'
require 'open-uri'

# Very basic client library for Solr
class MySolr
  def initialize(server)
    @server = server
  end

  def << (doc)
    # Put together the XML for Solr in a basic fashion
    xml = %q{<add><doc>}
    doc.each do |key, value|
      xml << %Q{<field name="#{key}">#{value}</field>}
    end
    xml << %q{</doc></add>}

    # Send the request
    make_xml_request xml
  end

  # Commit any new documents to the index
  def commit
    make_xml_request %q{<commit waitFlush="false"
                  waitSearcher="false" />}
  end

  # Delete an item from the index
  def delete(id)
    make_xml_request %Q{<delete fromCommitted="true">
                  <id>#{id}</id></delete>}
  end

  # Perform a query / search on the Solr server
  def query(q)
    params = %Q{?q=#{q}&wt=ruby}                          ❶
    uri = @server + "select/" + params
    eval(open(uri).read)['response'] rescue nil           ❷
```

```
end

private

# Makes an HTTP POST request to Solr and sends the data we supply
def make_xml_request(body)
  uri = URI.parse(@server + "update")
  res = Net::HTTP.new(uri.host, uri.port).start do |http|
    http.post(uri.path, body, { 'Content-Type' => 'text/xml' })
  end
  raise "Error - #{res.class}" unless res.class == Net::HTTPOK
end
end
```

A class is specially provided here, as current libraries available are focused on integration with Ruby on Rails, rather than for use directly from Ruby. As such, this basic library demonstrates how Solr works at a deeper level by making the HTTP requests directly. Once you become familiar with Solr, you may choose to take a different approach, or to use one of the Rails/ActiveRecord-based solutions.

The MySolr class (listing 12.4) is used by the remainder of this solution, so you'll need to `include` it at the top of the code in listings 12.5 through 12.7 or `require` it in. These three code examples give demonstrations of some of the most basic functions provided by both Solr and the MySolr interface class.

Listing 12.5 Adding and indexing documents

```
# Create an index object using the MySolr class
index = MySolr.new("http://localhost:8983/solr/")

# Add documents to the index
index << { :id   => 1,
        :name => "My Test Document",
        :text => "This is a test to demonstrate Solr" }

index << { :id   => 2,
        :name => "Irrelevant Title",
        :text => "Another test document" }

# Commit the documents to the index
index.commit
```

Listing 12.6 Querying the index

```
results = index.query('title')

# Print the results
puts "#{results['numFound']} result(s) found!"
puts
results['docs'].each do |result|
  puts "Document ID: #{result['id']}"
  puts "     Title: #{result['name']}\n\n"
end
```

Running listing 12.6 after the indexing routine in listing 12.5 should produce a result like the following:

```
1 result(s) found!
```

```
Document ID: 2
     Title: Irrelevant Title
```

Listing 12.7   Deleting items from the index

```
index.delete(1)
index.delete(2)
index.commit
```

As a search engine system with a network-accessible API, most of the code that makes up the `MySolr` library is concerned with making HTTP connections and moving XML data around. This contrasts with our earlier experiments with Ferret, which work in a very natural, Ruby-coded way. Solr, on the other hand, accepts XML instructions over HTTP, although its internal operation is somewhat similar to that of Ferret.

The `MySolr` class is not to be considered a particularly reliable Solr client library, although it works well for our demonstration of how to integrate with Solr at the HTTP level. One major flaw with the library is that it doesn't construct XML documents in a reliable way. (The intricacies of building XML documents is long-winded and beyond the scope of this chapter.)

This solution depends on a Solr server being installed and running when `MySolr` is used. It also expects you to be using the "example" Solr server that's built by default when you install Solr. This example server includes a schema with predefined field types that we use in the solution (namely, id, name, and text). If you wanted to build your own schema from scratch, you would need to cater for this in the documents you index from Ruby, and ensure that they only present the legitimate fields to Solr; otherwise an error will result.

From the client's point of view, using `MySolr` is similar to using the Ferret library. In listing 12.5, we create an index and push documents onto it. Querying is quite different, as you can see in listing 12.6. Solr accepts queries over HTTP to a URL like so:

```
http://hostname:port/solr/select?q=query
```

If you have Solr running, you can use such a URL and see the results come back in XML format. For our purposes, we add an extra option that makes Solr return the results in a Ruby-friendly format, by using a URL like this:

```
http://hostname:port/solr/select?q=query&wt=ruby
```

This technique is apparent in the query method of `MySolr` (listing 12.4) when we put the URL together ❶. Solr will return a string that can be evaled by Ruby:

```
{'responseHeader'=>{'status'=>0,'QTime'=>0,'params'=>{'q'=>'title',
  'wt'=>'ruby'}},'response'=>{'numFound'=>1,'start'=>0,'docs'=>
  [{'name'=>'Irrelevant Title','id'=>'2','sku'=>'2','popularity'=>0,
  'timestamp'=>'2007-07-12T03:56:49.618Z'}]}}
```

We evaluate this and return the relevant section from the query method (❷ in listing 12.4). This eval line downloads the results (using open-uri's convenient technique), evaluates the Ruby-friendly text response, then returns only the response section, because the `responseHeader` section only contains information about the request and how long it took to complete.

The information that gets returned to the main client is then a hash that looks like this:

```
{'numFound'=>1,'start'=>0,'docs'=>[{'name'=>'Irrelevant Title','id'=>
➥ '2','sku'=>'2','popularity'=>0,'timestamp'=>'2007-07-12T03:56:49.618Z'}]}
```

With this information, it's rudimentary to walk through the information and present the results.

Deleting items indexed by Solr is achieved, again, by a simple HTTP call. The code in listing 12.7 demonstrates how this feature of MySolr is used, and the code in the library illustrates the API call at a more direct level.

Discussion

In this section we have interfaced with Solr, a system that provides a network-accessible API using HTTP to a search indexer and query engine. Ruby is particularly well equipped to deal with engaging with remote APIs, and Solr is a great example of where using a system built upon a non-Ruby technology can still have a good fit with Ruby code.

Our solution focused primarily on the mundane indexing and querying, but behind the scenes were many API calls produced by MySolr and delivered using HTTP.

You can learn more about Solr's HTTP API calls and how to index data and configure Solr at the Solr Wiki at http://wiki.apache.org/solr/FrontPage.

Later in this chapter, we will look briefly at how to use Solr from a Ruby on Rails application, where the acts_as_solr plugin takes care of all of the intricacies of XML and HTTP.

12.2.3 *Ultrafast indexing and searching with FTSearch*

The previous two sections have looked at Apache Lucene-based searching and indexing tools. In this section, we're going to look at a more grassroots, specialized, and high-performance library called FTSearch.

FTSearch is a performance-focused search library written primarily in Ruby (with a little C, for performance) by Mauricio Fernandez. FTSearch began its life when Fernandez wanted to create a tool that could search Ruby's documentation faster than the existing `ri` tool. He decided to start by writing a basic suffix-array-based full-text search engine, and his first pure Ruby implementation—achieved in merely 300 lines—was already many times faster than `ri`'s existing search.

With further work, and the addition of a little C code, FTSearch became so fast that Fernandez began to test FTSearch on the source code for Linux rather than on the trivial amount of Ruby documentation available. At the end of 2006, Fernandez's benchmarks showed that FTSearch was outperforming Ferret (and therefore the Lucene approach in general) by between 3 and 30 times.

These characteristics, coupled with FTSearch's current lack of many features Ferret and Solr provide, mean FTSearch is ideally equipped for situations where you have a massive set of text files (such as source code) and all you need to do is index and perform queries on their raw contents very rapidly.

Problem

You want to index, and then search via query, an arbitrary set of documents or files extremely quickly, without using an Apache Lucene derivative. Raw indexing and query performance are the overriding considerations, as opposed to features.

Solution

We will use an indexer (listing 12.8), which will define the fields, iterate through the files, and index them. We'll then use a query script (listing 12.9) to query the index we created.

Listing 12.8   Using FTSearch to build an indexer

```
# Add ./lib and ./ext/ftsearch to the path search for "require"s
$:.unshift *%w{lib ext/ftsearch}

# Load the necessary parts of the FTSearch library
require 'ftsearch/fragment_writer'
require 'ftsearch/analysis/simple_identifier_analyzer'
require 'ext/ftsearch/ftsearchrt'

# Define a set of fields for the index to use, as with our Ferret example
field_infos = FTSearch::FieldInfos.new
field_infos.add_field(:name => :uri,     :analyzer =>
            FTSearch::Analysis::SimpleIdentifierAnalyzer.new)
field_infos.add_field(:name => :content, :analyzer =>
            FTSearch::Analysis::WhiteSpaceAnalyzer.new)

# Create an index that uses the fields defined above
index = FTSearch::FragmentWriter.new(:path => "testindex",
                        :field_infos => field_infos)

# Get a list of files to index
files_to_index = Dir["data/**/*.*"]

# Go over each file and add it to the index
files_to_index.each do |file|
  puts "Adding to index: #{file}"
  index.add_document(:uri => file, :content => File.read(file))
end

# Write index to disk from memory
index.finish!
```

❶

Listing 12.9   Querying the index

```
# Add ./lib and ./ext/ftsearch to the path search for "require"s
$:.unshift *%w{lib ext/ftsearch}

# Load the necessary parts of the FTSearch library
require 'ftsearch/suffix_array_reader'
require 'ftsearch/fulltext_reader'
require 'ftsearch/document_map_reader'
require 'ftsearchrt'
```

```
# Set up readers for each stage of the searching and ranking process
fulltext_reader     = FTSearch::FulltextReader.new(:path =>
                                    "testindex/fulltext")
suffix_array_reader = FTSearch::SuffixArrayReader.new(fulltext_reader,
                          nil, :path => "testindex/suffixes")
doc_map_reader      = FTSearch::DocumentMapReader.new(:path =>
                                    "testindex/docmap")

# Get a query from the user
puts "What do you want to search for?"
query = gets.chomp

# Get the raw "hits" for the query in the index
hits = suffix_array_reader.find_all(query)          ❷
puts "#{hits.size} found"

offsets = suffix_array_reader.lazyhits_to_offsets(hits)     ❸
puts "#{offsets.size} documents found"

# Sort the documents based on weights of fields
# This gives the first field "uri" more weight than the content
sorted = doc_map_reader.rank_offsets(offsets, [1000000, 10000])    ❹

# Print the sorted results
puts "Results:"

sorted.each do |doc_id, score|
  puts "Document ID: #{doc_id}"
  puts "    Score: #{score}"                                        ❺
  puts "  Filename: #{doc_map_reader.document_id_to_uri(doc_id)}\n\n"
end
```

Before we look at how the FTSearch library is used, it's necessary to cover its installation process. As a prerelease library, FTSearch requires a manual installation. The library, in its current state, can be installed using the Darcs package manager (darcs.net/), like so:

```
darcs get http://eigenclass.org/repos/ftsearch/head/
```

Or, if you don't want to download and install Darcs, you can mirror or manually download all of the files directly from eigenclass.org/repos/ftsearch/head/.

Once you have all of the files, the README file explains how to compile the C portion of the library. On most systems, this is as easy as running this command:

```
cd ext/ftsearch && ruby extconf.rb && make
```

The FTSearch solution is split into an indexer and a program that performs queries upon the index. The indexer (listing 12.8) looks very similar to the Ferret indexer. Fields are defined, again using a FieldInfos class ❶. Notice that we specify different analyzers to be used on the two fields. The content is indexed with each word being parsed once it is broken up by whitespace. But filenames are divided up by other separators, and the SimpleIdentifierAnalyzer looks for groups of alphanumeric characters, whether or not separated by whitespace. This will allow the query client to search for words within filenames.

The rest of the indexer retrieves a list of files from the data subdirectory and provides them to the index object to be indexed. Finally, the `finish!` method is called on the index to write the data to disk.

The querying program (listing 12.9) looks a little more complex. Due to FTSearch's young age, it's necessary to do more work than you need to do with Ferret. We have to require quite a few library files (which, in future, will hopefully be replaced with a single `require "ftsearch"`!) and create instances of readers for the different types of files in the index. Usually these functions would be abstracted away within a library, and it's anticipated that this will happen with FTSearch in the future.

Once the reader objects are prepared and the user has supplied a query, the first step is to get a list of all of the "raw hits" for the query ❷. With the list of raw hits in the bag, it's time to refer them to the documents ❸, and then sort our results by the scores with `rank_offsets` ❹. The second argument to `rank_offsets` is an array with weights for each field used in the index. Whereas with Ferret the `boost` values could be provided up front and stored in the index, with FTSearch it is currently necessary to provide these figures at the time of search. Therefore, we're giving words within the filename a "boost" of 1,000,000, and words within the files themselves a boost of only 10,000.

Displaying the sorted results is easy, as `rank_offsets` returns an array containing document IDs and scores ❺.

Discussion

If the source code to the Linux 0.01 kernel (http://www.kernel.org/pub/linux/kernel/Historic/linux-0.01.tar.gz) is extracted into the "data" directory, the code in listing 12.9 is run, and a query of "Linus" is supplied, the results should look like this:

```
2 found
2 documents found
Results:
Document ID: 68
    Score: 2
  Filename: data/linux/kernel/vsprintf.c

Document ID: 28
    Score: 1
  Filename: data/linux/include/string.h
```

If you want to run your own tests, make sure you provide a large corpus, such as the large collection of source code found in the Linux kernel. FTSearch's techniques are better suited to indexing and searching large sets of data, not small sets, so it makes sense to test it out properly!

The FTSearch installation comes with a README file and several excellent examples, all of which are more in-depth than the simple solution demonstrated here. By reading through the examples, the full power of FTSearch becomes apparent. A FTSearch vs. Ferret benchmarking tool is also included, so you can see FTSearch's significant speed advantages for yourself.

12.2.4 *Indexing and searching Rails data with Ferret and Solr*

When approaching search with Rails, you might be asking, "Why use Ferret or Solr or Sphinx from Rails? Can't I search with a database and ActiveRecord?"

Rails and ActiveRecord provide an abstraction between classes, objects, and data stored in a database. Rails supports a number of different database systems, such as MySQL, PostgreSQL, Microsoft SQL Server, and Oracle. Unfortunately all of these database systems work in different ways.

Some of the database engines Rails supports include advanced full-text search features and others do not. Furthermore, different data and table types within each engine can have different search characteristics. This has meant that Rails and ActiveRecord have not been able to provide a generic, easy way to perform full-text searches on tables within Rails applications, instead leaving users to perform sloppy, non-portable SQL hacks like this (for MySQL):

```
results = Post.find(:all, :conditions => "title LIKE '%search phrase%'")
```

The downside to the preceding code line is that it forces the database to go through every row in the posts table to find an entry with a title containing the necessary word or phrase. As we discussed in section 12.1, this is considered to be a search, but without any indexing process it's extremely inefficient and slow, particularly on larger datasets.

To get around the performance problems, it's possible to use the Lucene-inspired Ferret library that we looked at in section 12.2.1 to index data that's in our database, and then query the index when we want to perform searches, rather than querying the database directly. Once Ferret returns the correct document IDs, we can use standard ActiveRecord methods to extract the data from the live database.

Problem

You want to index, then search via query, data stored in a single Rails model using a Ferret- or Solr-based index.

Solution

We are going to focus on a Ferret-based solution, and then we'll take a quick look at how to change the solution to work using Solr. As the interfaces of the two plugins are so similar, a full, second solution for Solr is not necessary.

Note that this solution relies on having Ferret installed (as explained in section 12.2.1). You will also need the acts_as_ferret Rails plugin, which can be installed simply:

```
gem install acts_as_ferret
```

Once acts_as_ferret is installed, add the following line to the end of your config/environment.rb file, and the remainder of the solution will work:

```
require 'acts_as_ferret'
```

Once acts_as_ferret is installed and included in our Rails application, using Ferret's features on our models becomes extremely trivial. To get started, open your model file (app/models/post.rb or whichever model you please), and edit it so it looks similar to listing 12.10. Note the call to `acts_as_ferret`; this tells the plugin that this model is searchable.

> **Listing 12.10   A simple search-enabled class using acts_as_ferret**

```
class Post < ActiveRecord::Base
  has_many :comments
  belongs_to :user

  acts_as_ferret :fields => {
              :title   => { :boost => 10 },
              :content => { }
            }
end
```

❶

Querying the index is very simple and offers helpers that will work from models, controllers, and views:

```
Post.find_by_contents("test").each do |post|
  result_title = post.title
  result_score = post.ferret_score
end
```

The `acts_as_ferret` line throws a whole set of gears into action that take care of indexing and tracking the `title` and `content` fields/attributes on our `Post` objects. But a more powerful style to follow is the style shown in listing 12.10 ❶. This style is more complex, but it allows us to specify options for each field, much as we did in section 12.2.1. Similar to our example in listing 12.2, we apply a `boost` to a particular field. This means that words contained within the `title` of a post are considered more important than those in the `content`. Because titles are usually more concise and targeted than the content of blog posts, this is a good use of the `boost` technique.

You can also specify whether or not Ferret should store the data it's indexing by using the `:store` option, much as we did in listing 12.2 (by default, storing is off):

```
acts_as_ferret :fields => {
            :title   => { :boost => 10, :store => :yes },
            :content => { }
          }
```

Now let's add posts to be indexed to our database (you can do this using the script/console tool to make it easier):

```
Post.create(:title => "Test Post", :content => "A test document!")
Post.create(:title => "Another Post", :content => "More test stuff!")
Post.create(:title => "Third Post", :content => "End of testing")
```

The acts_as_ferret plugin takes care of the indexing automatically, so we can immediately start making queries using the `find_by_contents` method that `acts_as_ferret` adds to models it's supporting:

```
Post.find_by_contents("test").each do |post|
  puts "#{post.title} - #{post.ferret_score}"
end
```

With our example data, we get these results:

```
Test Post - 1.0
Another Post - 0.025548005476594
```

Naturally, more complex examples are possible, as you get the full range of Boolean, wildcard, and other searches that Ferret supports:

```
Post.find_by_contents("te*").each { |p| puts p.title }
```

It's also possible to query the index without returning each matching object. This could be useful if you just wanted to count the number of results, do pagination, or get access to the metadata:

```
Post.find_id_by_contents("test*")
```

The preceding search results in an array like the following:

```
[3, [{:score=>1.0, :model=>"Post", :id=>"1", :data=>{}},
    {:score=>0.0157371964305639, :model=>"Post", :id=>"2", :data=>{}},
    {:score=>0.0157371964305639, :model=>"Post", :id=>"3", :data=>{}}]]
```

The `find_by_contents` method also supports the `:limit` and `:offset` features that will be familiar from other finders:

```
Post.find_by_contents("*", :limit => 1, :offset => 1)
```

This search will return not the first result, but the second result, and it can also be useful for pagination.

You can learn a lot more about how acts_as_ferret works from the official wiki at http://projects.jkraemer.net/acts_as_ferret/wiki.

Discussion

Now that we've covered acts_as_ferret sufficiently, let's look at using the same code with Solr, a Lucene-based search server. The acts_as_solr plugin provides a very similar interface to acts_as_ferret, and its API documentation is available at http://api.railsfreaks. com/projects/acts_as_solr/.

The acts_as_solr plugin is installed in the same way as most Rails plugins, using the script/plugin tool (which requires Subversion to be installed):

```
ruby script/plugin install
⇨  svn://svn.railsfreaks.com/projects/acts_as_solr/trunk
```

The plugin can use a remote Solr install (as we did in section 12.2.2—you should even be able to use the same example install that we used previously) but it also comes with its own version of Solr, which makes things easier. To run it, type this:

```
cd vendor/plugins/acts_as_solr/solr/
java -jar start.jar
```

Solr will then be running permanently, and you can continue developing on another shell or terminal.

Before we change any code in the Rails application, the configuration file in db/solr.yml must be updated to use the correct address and port number for the currently running version of Solr. Update this for both production and development environments before continuing, or the acts_as_solr plugin might break in one or the other environment. The address of the Solr server will have been printed on the screen when you ran the Solr server.

Changing the Post model from that in the Ferret example to using acts_as_solr, results in the following:

```
class Post < ActiveRecord::Base
  has_many :comments
  belongs_to :user

  acts_as_solr :fields => [{:title => {:boost => 10}}, :content]
end
```

The syntax is a little different for specifying the boost (and any other options you might choose to use), but the technique is almost the same as for acts_as_ferret. For example, querying is very similar:

```
Post.find_by_solr("test")
```

Or, if you'd like to get a full set of results:

```
Post.find_by_solr("test").records.each { |p| puts p.title }
```

Both of these solutions (Ferret and Solr) are great in themselves, but they can sometimes suffer from corrupted indexes, complex deployments, or performance problems. The Sphinx full-text search engine, covered in the next section, isn't perfect, but it does solve some of these problems and offers a compelling alternative to Lucene-based solutions.

12.2.5 *Searching in Rails with Ultrasphinx*

Ferret and the other search options we discuss in this chapter are tested and proven to work well in most situations, but some environments call for more-performant and better-scaling solutions. Sphinx, a search daemon written by Andrew Aksyonoff, is a high-performance full-text search engine that works with MySQL and PostgreSQL. In this section, we'll look at using Sphinx in your Rails applications using a plugin.

Before getting started, you'll need to install the Sphinx search engine, available from http://www.sphinxsearch.com/. Once you get it installed, we can look at how to use it with Ruby.

Problem

You need to do high-performance indexing and searching in our Rails application.

Solution

The Ultrasphinx plugin by Evan Weaver is by far the best Sphinx interface for Ruby. It supports all the basic features of Sphinx (plus a few extras like spell-checking), and wraps all this in an incredibly simple API that works with ActiveRecord.

NOTE   If the Ultrasphinx syntax doesn't work for you, try Thinking Sphinx. It offers nearly the same functionality with a different syntax. You can get it at http://github.com/freelancing-god/thinking-sphinx

To get the Ultrasphinx plugin working, you'll first need to install it. Ultrasphinx requires the Chronic gem, so you'll have to install it too:

```
sudo gem install chronic
script/plugin install -x
➡ svn://rubyforge.org/var/svn/fauna/ultrasphinx/trunk
```

After you get that installed, copy the default.base file from the plugin's examples directory to your config/ultrasphinx directory. Now we can add the Ultrasphinx calls to the models we want to index. Listing 12.11 shows a basic indexed model.

Listing 12.11   A model that's indexed with Ultrasphinx

```
class Article < ActiveRecord::Base
  is_indexed :fields => ['title', 'content', 'byline']
end
```

Note that we specify the fields to index along with the call to is_indexed. Only the fields we indicate here will be indexed.

Finally, we need to let Ultrasphinx set up the Sphinx daemon and build the index. Ultrasphinx encourages you *not* to edit the configuration files by hand, because they include a lot of Ultrasphinx- and Rails-specific options that need to stay the way they are for the plugin to work. To get everything set up, run the following Rake tasks:

```
rake ultrasphinx:configure
rake ultrasphinx:index
rake ultrasphinx:daemon:start
```

The Sphinx daemon should now be configured, the models indexed, and the daemon started.

TIP   You can also run rake ultrasphinx:bootstrap to do the same thing as the Rake commands.

Listing 12.12 shows how to execute a search.

Listing 12.12   Executing a full-text search with Ultrasphinx

```
@search = Ultrasphinx::Search.new(:query => 'excellent food')
@search.run
@results = @search.results
```

After the search in listing 12.12 is run, the @results variable will have an enumerable collection of ActiveRecord objects returned for "excellent food", and you can use them as you would anything else that includes Enumerable (e.g., #each, #[], and so on).

When it comes times to rotate your Sphinx index, you can do so by running the following Rake task:

```
rake ultrasphinx:index
```

This will rotate the index leaving the daemon in its current state (started or stopped).

Discussion

We've just covered the basic case here, but there are a lot of useful options available in Ultrasphinx that go beyond a simple use case.

One great feature of the Ultrasphinx plugin is its built-in support for the de facto standard pagination plugin: will_paginate from Mislav Marohni? and P.J. Hyett. To get paginated results from your searches, you'll first want to install will_paginate:

```
script/plugin install git://github.com/mislav/will_paginate.git
```

Then, in your controller, feed a page parameter to the initializer for `Ultrasphinx::Search`. In this case, we'll use `params[:p]` as the value:

```
@search = Ultrasphinx::Search.new(:query => @query, :page => params[:p])
```

Then, in your views, you'll need to use the `will_paginate` view helper.

```
<%= will_paginate(@search) %>
```

You can then operate on your search results like other collections you previously paginated using will_paginate.

If you'd like to have your results highlighted to show matches in the fields, you can tell Ultrasphinx to highlight matched sections by calling `excerpt` instead of `run`:

```
@results = @search.excerpt
```

After this, the model instances in `@results` will be frozen and have their contents changed to the excerpted and highlighted results.

If you'd like to weight the results of your search, you can provide a hash with the field-to-weight ratios in them. For example, if we wanted the title and byline of an article to have more weight in the results than the body, we'd do something like this:

```
@search = Ultrasphinx::Search.new(:query => @query, :weights =>
➥ { [CA]'title' => 2.0, 'byline' => 2.0})
```

Now the search results will be ordered by the weight of the matches on the indexed fields.

You can also provide a number of options for indexing. If you want to cut down on indexing overhead, you can switch to delta indexing, which lets you provide a constraint on what values will be indexed. For example, if we wanted to only index records that had been changed in the last day, we could do something like the following in our .base file in config/ultrasphinx/:

```
delta = <%= 1.day + 30.minutes %>
```

To tell Ultrasphinx that models should use the delta index, you'll need to change the call to `is_indexed` slightly to add `:delta => true`:

```
is_indexed :fields => ['title', 'body'], :delta => true
```

The only catch to this is that it builds a separate index. This means you'll need to rotate it using a different Ultrasphinx Rake task (`rake ultrasphinx:index:delta`) and you'll need to merge the changes into the main index inside the delta period (for example, if your delta is one day, you'll need to do it daily). If you keep this in mind, a delta index is an excellent way to keep your indexing overhead to a minimum.

You can also assign arbitrary conditions to indexing. For example, if you only want to index videos that have not been marked as "deleted," you could do something like the following:

```
class Video < ActiveRecord::Base
  is_indexed :fields => ['title', 'desc'], :conditions => "deleted = 0"
end
```

From now on, Sphinx will only index records whose `deleted` attribute is `false` (or, in SQL, 0). This is useful for situations where content may be hidden or otherwise masked from users and, as such, should not show up in searching.

Next, we're going to change gears significantly. We'll move away from the dry, technical world of directly interfacing with indexing and querying routines and rely on more-automated indexing solutions.

12.3 Integrating search with other technologies

So far, we've focused on indexing and querying various collections of local data, but now we're going to look at how we can use and integrate searching and indexing techniques with other technologies, such as the web and database-driven applications.

12.3.1 Web search using a basic API (Yahoo!)

In the eyes of many, search means Google. We know that there's a lot more to search than that, but it's impossible to escape the fact that, to many people, "search" relates to the ability to search the web. This isn't a bad assumption to make, because the web, coupled with search engines like Google and Yahoo!, provides a relatively device- and format-agnostic way to search large sets of data. In the rest of this chapter, we're going to look at how you can perform your own web searches with Ruby on both Google and Yahoo! using two different techniques, a search API and "scraping."

In this solution, we'll query Yahoo! and process the results it returns in a basic XML format, although a similar approach can be used for many systems that provide basic APIs where the query can be specified on a URL and the results are returned in a structured format (such as searches made with Amazon.com's developer APIs).

Problem

You want to perform web searches using search engines, such as Yahoo!, that return structured data.

Solution

We'll use the Yahoo! Web Search API to search for the five top results for "ruby"; our implementation is in listing 12.13.

> **Listing 12.13 Searching for "ruby" using Yahoo!'s API**

```
require 'open-uri'
require 'rexml/document'

# Specify some parameters for the search
```

```
results = 5
query  = 'ruby'
appid  = 'YahooDemo'

# Construct the URL using our parameters and retrieve the XML data
url = "http://api.search.yahoo.com/WebSearchService/V1/webSearch"
url += "?query=#{query}&appid=#{appid}&results=#{results}"
xml = open(url).read

# Print search results extracted from XML
REXML::Document.new(xml).elements.each('ResultSet/Result') do |result|
  puts result.text('Title') + " => " + result.text('Url')
end
```

❶

❷

Yahoo! provides access to its Web Search API via simple URLs. The first half of our program is concerned entirely with loading up the libraries we need to use (code omitted below) and building up one of these URLs **❶**.

The basic parameters required by Yahoo! are the number of results to return (in this case, 5), an application ID (YahooDemo), and a query (in this case, ruby). There are about ten other parameters that access advanced features, like removing adult sites, choosing sites from certain countries, and so forth. They are covered in detail at http://developer.yahoo.com/search/web/V1/webSearch.html.

The application ID in our example is YahooDemo, which Yahoo! provides for test purposes only. It should work for a few queries, but if you want to use the Yahoo! Web Search API seriously, you'll need to apply to Yahoo! for your own application ID and agree to their terms and conditions. You can learn more about this, and the rest of Yahoo!'s APIs at http://developer.yahoo.com/search/.

After the URL has been put together, we use open-uri's useful open method to download the XML:

```
xml = open(url).read
```

The resulting XML is too long and complex to print in this book, but its format becomes apparent from the code we use to parse it **❷**. This code uses Ruby's standard XML process library, REXML, to iterate over each Result element of the XML from Yahoo!, and then to print out the contents of the inner Title and Url elements in each case:

```
Ruby Programming Language => http://www.ruby-lang.org/en
Ruby (programming language) - Wikipedia, the free encyclopedia =>
http://en.wikipedia.org/wiki/Ruby_programming_language
Ruby Central => http://www.rubycentral.com/
Ruby Annotation => http://www.w3.org/TR/ruby/
Ruby Programming Language => http://ruby-lang.org/
```

Discussion

The Yahoo! Web Search API represents, to us as programmers, an excellent web search API because the results are returned in a programmer-friendly XML format. This format has been defined by Yahoo! and will remain consistent and documented (at Yahoo!'s developer site).

The results of running this program—a Yahoo! web search using the query "ruby"—will look something like this:

```
Ruby Programming Language => http://www.ruby-lang.org/en
Ruby (programming language) - Wikipedia, the free encyclopedia =>
http://en.wikipedia.org/wiki/Ruby_programming_language
Ruby Central => http://www.rubycentral.com/
Ruby Annotation => http://www.w3.org/TR/ruby/
Ruby Programming Language => http://ruby-lang.org/
```

Next, we're going to move on to a rougher approach to searching—a Google "screen scraping" approach.

12.3.2 Web search using a scraping technique (Google)

Let's face it, Google is the granddaddy of search, so it's natural to want to be able to use its results in a programmatic fashion. Or how about other sites, like the Internet Movie Database (http://www.imdb.com) or a typical e-commerce site? Unfortunately, we need to resort to the dark magic of scraping.

Problem

You want to perform web searches and extract data from search engines or other websites that don't present their results in a structured way. This forces you to use a scraping technique.

Solution

Until the end of 2006, Google provided access to a SOAP-based search API, but this has been withdrawn from use for all except existing users. As this system is now deprecated and closed to the public, we cannot go into its operation. Google replaced the SOAP-based API with an AJAX-based one to be used directly on web pages, but this API is not of significant use to us.

It should be noted that scraping search results in an automated fashion is against Google's terms of service, although it is generally allowed for nonautomated, personal use. We expect you to use any code provided in this section in good faith and in compliance with Google's terms of service (or those of any other site you choose to scrape).

To start, you need to install the scRUBYt! library. scRUBYt! (http://scrubyt.org/) is a Ruby library, developed by Peter Szinek, that makes it easy to automate and process data on the web. It is available as a gem and can be installed as follows:

```
gem install scrubyt
```

On some platforms, you may also need to install an extra gem (only do this if there is an error when running this solution):

```
gem install ParseTreeReloaded
```

Now, let's get down to scraping. Listing 12.14 shows how to fetch a Google results page and scrape the results from it.

Listing 12.14   Scraping Google for results for "ruby"

```
require 'rubygems'
require 'scrubyt'

query = "ruby"

results = Scrubyt::Extractor.define do
  fetch 'http://www.google.com/'            ❶
  fill_textfield 'q', query                 ❷
  submit

  result('/html/body/div/div/div', { :generalize => true }) do
    link_title '/a[1]'
    link_url '/a/@href'                                          ❸
  end
end

puts results.to_xml        ❹
```

The conciseness of the main part of our code emphasizes how easy scRUBYt! makes processing data on the web.

The steps involved should be clear. As scRUBYt! features its own domain-specific language (DSL), we define an extractor through the `Scrubyt::Extractor` class, and then the fun can begin.

The first step of the extraction process is to fetch the http://www.google.com homepage ❶. That done, we can fill out the search form with our desired query and submit the form. In this case, it's easy to see by looking at the source code that the Google search form uses a text field with a name of q to accept the user's query, so we use `fill_textfield` to do this job for us, and submit the form ❷.

Once the form is submitted, a results page will be returned, and we need to define a pattern to match against each result. scRUBYt! is powerful enough to allow us to specify example results, obtained by hand, and then work out the XPath rules to scrape that data from a page. In this case, to ensure that the example works, I have specified the XPath rules explicitly ❸.

The result block gives us access to each result (found with an XPath query of /html/body/div/div/div) and allows us to define which elements of the result we want to extract. In this case, we're extracting the title and URL of the links, although you could extract the result descriptions too, with an extra rule. These methods are simple patterns and could use any name, other than `link_title` and `link_url`. scRUBYt!'s DSL is clever enough to work out that these are the names we're giving to the respective elements, and it will use these names in the resulting XML. For example, this code is as valid and would result in XML output using slightly different element names:

```
result_title '/a[1]'
result_url '/a/@href'
```

The resulting XML that comes from the final `puts` line ❹ can then be processed using any XML library, such as REXML or SimpleXML.

The results returned by this program, after a whole collection of raw debugging information, should look something like this:

```
<root>
  <result>
    <link_title>Ruby Programming Language</link_title>
    <link_url>http://www.ruby-lang.org/</link_url>
  </result>
  <result>
    <link_title>Ruby Home Page - What's Ruby</link_title>
    <link_url>http://www.ruby-lang.org/en/20020101.html</link_url>
  </result>
  <result>
    <link_title>
        Ruby (programming language) - Wikipedia, the free encyclopedia
    </link_title>
    <link_url>
      http://en.wikipedia.org/wiki/Ruby_programming_language
    </link_url>
  </result>
  <result>
    <link_title>Ruby - Wikipedia, the free encyclopedia</link_title>
    <link_url>http://en.wikipedia.org/wiki/Ruby</link_url>
  </result>

  [.. extra results removed to preserve space ..]

</root>
```

Discussion

As Google doesn't supply a programmer-friendly API, we had to resort to scraping Google's data from the regular HTML pages. As explained earlier, automating this process on a mass scale is against Google's terms and conditions, so tread with caution. That said, you will be able to use this same technique with other websites and search engines, and the scraping library, scRUBYt!, comes with many examples of using the library to scrape sites like IMDB, Yahoo! Finance, Amazon.com, and so on.

12.4 Summary

This chapter has covered a tight niche, in terms of Ruby. As we've seen, only a handful of search libraries and techniques have been developed in Ruby so far, but all of them are reasonably powerful and ready to be used in production scenarios.

We first looked at the general principles of searching and indexing, and then looked at some high-performance, standalone solutions in the guises of Ferret, a Ruby Apache Lucene port, Solr, an HTTP-based search server and interface to Lucene, and FTSearch, a high-performance suffix-array-based indexer and search library. We then discussed how to search in your Rails applications using solutions like acts_as_ferret, acts_as_solr, and Ultrasphinx—plugins that bridge the gap between Rails applications and search libraries.

Finally, this chapter has shown you how to get your bearings with the search technologies available to you in Ruby. It's also shown you some further technologies and libraries you can explore and look out for in the future.

In the next chapter, we're going to move on to document processing and report generation.

13
Document processing and reporting

This chapter covers

- Reading and writing CSV data
- Generating daily reports
- Producing a comparison report
- Generating customized printable reports

Though we'd all love to be video game programmers or lead developers for the Next Big Web 2.0 multimedia experience, most programmers have less glamorous problems to solve. This inevitably includes processing documents exported from sources, ranging from legacy systems to industry-standard SQL databases. Of course, collecting the data and translating it into a useable form is only half the challenge. Aggregated data then needs to be manipulated, analyzed, and formatted in ways that clearly communicate what that data represents. The field of reporting ranges from quick sales reports for a small business to massive statistical analyses for the enterprise.

There are numerous canned solutions for processing one form of document and translating it to another, or for running standard reports against data. For many uses, these applications are the way to go. However, these solutions aren't golden hammers. When developing custom software, it's often desirable to get exactly the kinds of results you're looking for, instead of using prebuilt solutions that may or may not be what you need. For this kind of problem, Ruby shines.

In this chapter, we'll be looking at several solutions to common reporting problems. We'll cover processing and formatting libraries such as FasterCSV, and we'll look at the lightweight reporting system, Ruport. Through these solutions, you'll be able to see how rolling your own solutions isn't as scary as it sounds. By providing a solid but malleable foundation to work from, Ruport provides a way to quickly build your own customized reporting applications.

We'll start with simple CSV processing to show off FasterCSV's feature set, then show how to use Ruport's code generator to trivially script a database-backed report that automatically emails its results when run. We'll then show how you can use Ruby's text-processing capabilities to compare a CSV file to a nonstandard data format. After covering the ins and outs of data manipulation, we'll dive into printable documents, showing how you can leverage Ruport and PDF::Writer to generate attractive customized PDF reports. Finally, we'll talk about how to optimize for performance when dealing with large datasets in Ruport.

13.1 *Processing CSV data*

One of the most common tasks in document processing is handling CSV data. Used as a generic text format for tabular data from any range of sources, the CSV format is simple and fairly easy to process. However, Ruby's standard library for handling CSVs is a bit awkward, and also very slow. Luckily, James Edward Gray II's FasterCSV library has become the de facto standard for CSV processing in Ruby. We'll take a look at a simple example to show the library in action, and then we'll go over some of the key features that you might find useful.

To install FasterCSV, simply install the gem:

```
gem install fastercsv
```

Since FasterCSV is pure Ruby, it should work without modification on all platforms.

Problem

You need to read and write CSV data efficiently in Ruby via FasterCSV.

Solution

We're going to implement a simple currency conversion tool to show FasterCSV in action. The CSV data we will use for this example is quite simple:

```
Currency,Code,USD/1 Unit,Units/1 USD
Andorran Franc,ADF,0.1339,7.4659
Andorran Peseta,ADP,0.005372,186.167
Utd. Arab Emir. Dirham,AED,0.2723,3.6741
Afghanistan Afghani,AFA,0.01998,50.25
Albanian Lek,ALL,0.01136,91.678
Armenian Dram,AMD,0.002895,345.41
NL Antillian Guilder,ANG,0.5682,1.8
```

The small utility shown in listing 13.1 performs conversions to and from any of the currencies listed in the CSV file, using USD as the base currency for interchange.

Listing 13.1   Currency converter

```ruby
require "rubygems"
require "fastercsv"

class CurrencyConverter

  def self.load_data(file,currency="USD")
    @to_us = { "USD" => 1 }
    @from_us = { "USD" => 1 }

    FasterCSV.foreach(file, :headers => true,
                      :converters => :numeric) do |r|
      @from_us[r["Code"]] = r["Units/1 USD"]
      @to_us[r["Code"]]   = r["USD/1 Unit"]
    end
  end

  def self.convert(amount,options={})
    from = options[:from] || "USD"
    to   = options[:to] || "USD"

    amount * @to_us[from] * @from_us[to]
  end

  def self.high_low_report
    high, low = @from_us.partition { |code,ratio| ratio < 1 }
    write_file high, "high.csv"
    write_file low, "low.csv"
  end

  private

  def self.write_file(data,filename)
    FasterCSV.open(filename,"w") do |csv|
      csv << ["Code","USD/1 Unit"]
      data.each { |record| csv << record }
    end
  end

end
```

As you can see, nothing about the implementation is particularly surprising. Two lookup tables are generated for rates when `CurrencyConverter.load_data()` is called. It is then possible to make arbitrary currency conversions. For example, you could convert 100 USD to Andorran francs:

```ruby
CurrencyConverter.convert 100, :to => "ADF"
```

You can go in reverse as well (back to USD):

```ruby
CurrencyConverter.convert 12240.0, :from => "ADF"
```

The implementation also allows for non-U.S. to non-U.S. conversion:

```ruby
CurrencyConverter.convert 100, :from => "ADF", :to => "AMD"
```

In addition to this conversion feature, you can see that this little utility also offers a simple reporting facility. It will determine which currencies are higher and which are lower in value than the USD and generate two CSV files, high.csv and low.csv. Providing that you have loaded a CSV file with the exchange ratios, generating this report is easy:

```
CurrencyConverter.high_low_report
```

We end up with two output files:

```
high.csv:
```

```
Code,USD/1 Unit
XPT,0.0007819
OMR,0.386
GRD,0.7345
ITL,0.7345
DEM,0.7345
```

```
low.csv:
```

```
Code,USD/1 Unit
XCD,2.725
SAR,3.7509
RUB,25.6764
NOK,5.8243
NIO,18.743
```

As you can see, FasterCSV makes the task of CSV processing nearly trivial. Of course, it's worth discussing in a little more detail how the library works, as well as the advantages it offers over Ruby's built-in CSV standard library.

Discussion

As the name implies, FasterCSV is much faster than Ruby's standard CSV processor. In most cases, it is about 800 percent faster. Plus, it has more advantages than speed alone. If we look back at the currency conversion code, the CSV processing seems to take a back seat, letting us focus on the actual problem we're trying to solve. It seems this way because there are a lot of nice things that FasterCSV is handling for us.

If you work with Ruby's standard CSV processor, there is no direct support for CSV headers. This means that instead of saying r["Code"], you'd be saying r[2] in our example, or rolling your own mapping of names to indices. Whenever you give any of FasterCSV's reading methods the option :headers => true, it will try to use the first line of a CSV file as the headers, and will automatically allow you to refer to cells by column name in addition to their ordinal position.

Because CSV files might have nonunique column names, FasterCSV supports minimum ordinal indices. The following simple Interactive Ruby (IRB) session shows how a row with two a columns can still be nicely handled using this feature:

```
>> a = FasterCSV.read("simple.csv", :headers => true)
>> a[0].to_a
=> [["a", "1"], ["b", "2"], ["c", "3"], ["a", "4"]]
>> a[0]["a"]
=> "1"
>> a[0]["a",1]
=> "4"
```

Rubyists often enjoy using symbols for keys rather than strings. FasterCSV allows arbitrary conversions of data and has a built-in converter, which makes this trivial:

```
>> a = FasterCSV.read("simple.csv", :headers => true,
?>                        :header_converters => :symbol)
>> a[0].to_a
=> [[:a, "1"], [:b, "2"], [:c, "3"], [:a, "4"]]
>> a[0][:a]
=> "1"
>> a[0][:a,1]
=> "4"
```

In addition to header conversions, FasterCSV allows you to do conversions on your entire dataset, which we'll now take a look at. One thing you'll notice from our calculations is that we never explicitly converted the ratio fields to Float objects. However, it's pretty clear why we didn't have to, if you look at the main loading code in listing 13.1:

```
FasterCSV.foreach(file, :headers => true, :converters => :numeric) do |r|
  #...
end
```

The :converters => :numeric code tells FasterCSV to use a built-in formatter to inspect the fields and convert numeric values to their proper Ruby objects (Fixnum, Float, etc.). This comes in handy, as it prevents us from having to do explicit to_f calls for each field that needs to be converted. Other built-in converters are available, such as :date, :datetime, :integer, and :float.

It is also quite easy to build your own converters, if needed. The process is essentially as simple as passing Proc objects that accept a field as an argument and do any necessary manipulations. You might have noticed in listing 13.1 that FasterCSV.open() looks a whole lot like File.open(). Listing 13.2 shows this method in use again.

Listing 13.2   File output for currency converter

```
FasterCSV.open(filename,"w") do |csv|
  csv << ["Code","USD/1 Unit"]
  data.each { |record| csv << record }
end
```

The primary difference is that instead of a File object, a FasterCSV object is yielded. This object will automatically convert arrays into CSV rows, doing any necessary escaping.

If we had wanted to output to a string instead of a File object, you can use FasterCSV.generate. Our original code could be rewritten as follows:

```
csv_string = FasterCSV.generate do |csv|
  csv << ["Code","USD/1 Unit"]
  data.each { |record| csv << record }
end
```

This especially comes in handy when generating CSV files in the context of web applications, where you may wish to build files on the fly for download without ever storing them server-side.

For the most part, the fact that FasterCSV acts a lot like a Ruby I/O object makes life a lot easier, since it is very rare to be working with CSV data without the need for I/O operations. We have only scratched the surface here, of course.

Most programmers will encounter CSV processing jobs from time to time. Though we didn't cover all the edge cases, most jobs will involve some of the basic techniques shown here. You can consult the FasterCSV documentation on its website (http://fastercsv.rubyforge.org/) or in the gem package for more information on special cases.

Of course, CSV processing is only part of the picture. We'll now take a look at Ruby Reports, which is a comprehensive reporting foundation that makes use of FasterCSV and other popular Ruby libraries to make building custom reporting applications a whole lot easier.

13.2 *Generating and emailing daily reports*

A common task in reporting is generating scheduled reports. These take on several flavors, but they usually share the same core process: query a database for records that match a given date or time period, process the report, then send it somewhere for use or archival. Here we'll look at how to solve this type of problem for a basic sales report in Ruport.

Ruport is a gem, so installation is straightforward. We'll want to grab the latest versions of ruport, ruport-util, and acts_as_reportable, so the easiest way to do this is to grab the ruport/murdoch meta-gem, which can be installed as follows:

```
sudo gem install murdoch
```

Problem

You need to produce simple custom reports based on raw SQL queries, and automatically email their results, all using Ruport.

Solution

We'll use Ruport's code generator, called rope, to script away the boilerplate code and cut down on hand configuration. The rope tool is part of the `ruport-util` package, which is officially maintained by the Ruby Reports developers.

The following commands create a basic code skeleton and then create templates for our report and its controller:

```
$ rope store_reports
$ cd store_reports
$ rake build report=daily_sales
$ rake build controller=sales
```

Our report will run against a MySQL database and email it automatically upon generation. The configuration in listing 13.3 is the minimum necessary to allow us to do so.

Listing 13.3   Rope Configuration (config/environment.rb)

```
require "ruport"

# Uncomment and modify the lines below if you want to use query.rb
#
```

```
Ruport::Query.add_source :default, :user => "root",
                         :dsn => "dbi:mysql:storefront"

Ruport::Mailer.add_mailer :default, :host => "mail.adelphia.net",
                          :address => "gregory.t.brown@gmail.com"
```

We set up our main report to execute a simple query, and we tell the report to render with the Sales controller. The code in listing 13.4 generates text and PDF output for the report, and emails both upon execution.

Listing 13.4 Sales Report (lib/reports/daily_sales.rb)

```
require "lib/init"
require "lib/controllers"

class DailySales < Ruport::Report

  renders_with Sales

  def renderable_data(format)

    query %q{ select product,quantity,customer_name from sales
           where sale_date = ? order by quantity }, :params => [today]
  end

  def today
    Date.today.strftime('%Y-%m-%d')
  end

end

DailySales.generate do |report|
  report.save_as("sales_report.pdf")
  report.send_to("gregory.t.brown@gmail.com") do |m|
    m.subject = "Sales Report for #{report.today}"
    m.text    = report.to_text
    m.attach "sales_report.pdf"
  end
end
```

Our controller for this report is fairly simple, as you can see in listing 13.5. It simply calculates the total number of items sold in a day and the number of customers. The formatters display this information, as well as the table that is returned from the SQL query.

Listing 13.5 Sales Report Controller (lib/controllers/sales.rb)

```
require "lib/init"

class Sales < Ruport::Renderer
  stage :report_table

  module Helpers

    def today
      Date.today.strftime("%m/%d/%y")
    end

    def total_sales
      data.sum("quantity")
    end
```

```
  def total_customers
    data.column("customer_name").uniq.length
  end

end

formatter :text do
  build :report_table do
    output << "Sales Report for #{today}\n\n"
    render_table(data)
    output << "\n\nTotal Sales: #{total_sales}  " <<
            "Total Customers: #{total_customers}"
  end

end

formatter :pdf do
  build :report_table do

    title = "Sales Report for #{today}\n"

    render_table(data,:formatter => pdf_writer,
                 :table_format => { :title => title })

    pad(10) do
      add_text "Total Sales: #{total_sales}  " <<
            "Total Customers: #{total_customers}",
            :justification => :center
    end

  end
end

end
```

The report is invoked by running the following command:

```
$ rake run report=daily_sales
```

You can see the text output next, which is sent as the body of the email:

```
Sales Report for 07/17/07

+-------------------------------------------+
|   product     | quantity | customer_name  |
+-------------------------------------------+
| Tollbooth     |      1 | Joe Rasta       |
| Tomato        |      1 | Al Green        |
| Vacuum Cleaner |     3 | Joe Loop        |
| Vacuum Cleaner |     5 | Al Green        |
+-------------------------------------------+

Total Sales: 10  Total Customers: 3
```

The PDF output (shown in figure 13.1) is sent as an email attachment.

By using rope, you're automatically given a common structure for your application that is ideal for this sort of problem. At this point, the only task remaining is to hook up scheduling software (such as cron)—but we'll leave that part up to you.

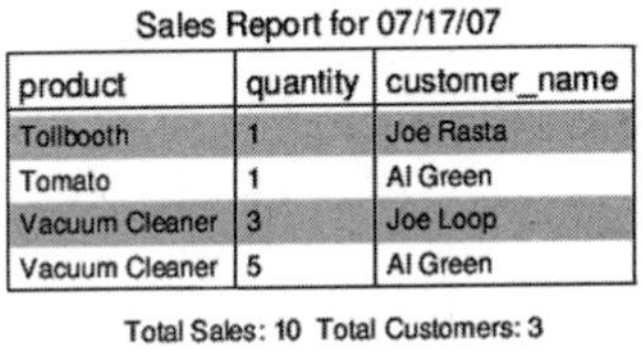

Sales Report for 07/17/07

product	quantity	customer_name
Tollbooth	1	Joe Rasta
Tomato	1	Al Green
Vacuum Cleaner	3	Joe Loop
Vacuum Cleaner	5	Al Green

Total Sales: 10 Total Customers: 3

Figure 13.1 Ruport's PDF output

Discussion

Now let's look at the parts of this application in more detail. When you run the rope command, you're actually generating a simple skeleton for Ruport applications. The files generated are listed on the screen when the command is run:

```
$ rope store_reports

creating directories..
  store_reports/test
  store_reports/config
  store_reports/output
  store_reports/data
  store_reports/data/models
  store_reports/lib
  store_reports/lib/reports
  store_reports/lib/controllers
  store_reports/templates
  store_reports/sql
  store_reports/log
  store_reports/util
creating files..
  store_reports/lib/reports.rb
  store_reports/lib/helpers.rb
  store_reports/lib/controllers.rb
  store_reports/lib/init.rb
  store_reports/config/environment.rb
  store_reports/util/build
  store_reports/util/sql_exec
  store_reports/Rakefile
  store_reports/README
```

In our report, we needed to configure our database and mailer information, which was done in config/environment.rb (listing 13.3). For both of these, we showed the most basic form of configuration. If you need to authenticate your SMTP session, the following configuration can be used to connect to an SMTP mail server that requires authentication:

```
Ruport::Mailer.add_mailer :default, :host => "mail.adelphia.net",
                    :address => "test@test.com",
                    :user => "joe", :password => "secret",
                    :auth_type => :login
```

As you can see, it's simply a matter of providing a username and password and specifying that the mail server uses login authentication. You can also use the following configuration to specify a database username and password and a remote location of your database.

```
Ruport::Query.add_source :default, :user => "joe",
                    :password => "secret",
                    :host => "192.168.1.101",
                    :dsn => "dbi:mysql:storefront"
```

If you are working with a database other than MySQL, you can set the :dsn accordingly. For example, if you're working with ODBC it would look like this:

```
:dsn => "dbi:odbc:storefront"
```

You can consult the RubyDBI documentation (or our information about DBI in chapter 9) to find out what DSN to use for your data source.

You can see that for both the Mailer and Query configurations in listing 13.3, we've called our configurations :default. This is because Ruport will use these sources if others are not specified, but it can handle multiple sources. For example, you could easily define a test database:

```
Ruport::Query.add_source :test, :user => "root"
                      :dsn => "dbi:mysql:storefront_test"
```

In our report, we could rewrite our query to use this test database, as follows:

```
query %q{ select product,quantity,customer_name from sales
        where sale_date = ? order by quantity }, :params => [today],
                               :source => :test
```

Mailer works in a similar fashion and can be configured through the Report#use_mailer() method if needed.

We'll now take a look at Report objects and how they tie in with the rest of Ruport.

The main purpose of Ruport's Report class is to keep report definitions from looking like a shell script. It's entirely possible to live without it, and when working within other frameworks, it is even advisable to do so. For standalone reports with reasonably basic needs, Report provides a handy base class that simplifies common Ruport tasks.

If we look back at our report definition (listing 13.4), you'll see it is more or less split into two parts. The first part simply ties a query's result set to the controller and provides a helper method for formatting dates:

```
class DailySales < Ruport::Report

  renders_with Sales

  def renderable_data(format)

    query %q{ select product,quantity,customer_name from sales
            where sale_date = ? order by quantity }, :params => [today]

  end

  def today
    Date.today.strftime('%Y-%m-%d')
  end

end
```

The renderable_data method will pass its return value as the :data option to the controller specified by renders_with() when you generate your report.

The second part of our definition is our output generation code, which sends an email of PDF and text output when it is run:

```
DailySales.generate do |report|
  report.save_as("sales_report.pdf")
  report.send_to("gregory.t.brown@gmail.com") do |m|
    m.subject = "Sales Report for #{report.today}"
    m.text    = report.to_text
    m.attach "sales_report.pdf"
  end
end
```

One thing you might notice is that when you save files to disk, Ruport ensures that the proper formatter is called. This means that this code

```
report.save_as("sales_report.pdf")
```

is equivalent to this code:

```
File.open("sales_report.pdf","wb") { |f| f << report.to_pdf }
```

This should work with arbitrary format definitions, so that `save_as("foo.some-thing")` will be equivalent to this line:

```
File.open("foo.something","w") { |f| f << report.to_something }
```

By structuring your reports this way, you gain the ability to swap out data sources very easily. It can be useful to work with CSV dumps to design a report, and later hook it up to the actual database. As long as the data is represented in the same way, Ruport doesn't care where it's coming from.

This means that if you had a CSV dump of your sales table, you could rewrite just the renderable_data method and not touch anything else:

```
class DailySales < Ruport::Report

  renders_with Sales

  def renderable_data(format)
    Table("products.csv")
  end

end
```

With that in mind, we'll look at how to avoid raw SQL by using ActiveRecord instead. The change is surprisingly simple. We can get our model hooked up via a simple rake task:

```
$ rake build model=sale
```

We won't need to change anything for this report, but you can see that the model definition in data/models/sale.rb is quite basic:

```
class Sale < ActiveRecord::Base

  acts_as_reportable

end
```

This allows us to use a method called `report_table` to get a `Ruport::Data::Table` back from an ActiveRecord find. Listing 13.6 shows our new ActiveRecord-backed report definition. The `Report.generate` code and renderer needn't be changed at all.

> **Listing 13.6   Sales Report, modified for AR (lib/reports/daily_sales.rb)**

```
require "lib/init"
require "lib/controllers"
require "data/models"

class DailySales < Ruport::Report
```

```
renders_with Sales

def renderable_data(format)

  Sale.report_table(:all,
    :only => ["product","quantity","customer_name","sale_date"],
    :conditions => ["sale_date = ?", today],
    :order => "quantity")
end

def today
  Date.today.strftime('%Y-%m-%d')
end

end
```

You'll also notice that our controllers don't look any different from when we used them in the context of rope (in listing 13.5). They're just the same as you'd use anywhere else. The only particularly interesting bit about these controllers is that they make use of a helper module to encapsulate tasks common to the formatters:

```
module Helpers

  def today
    Date.today.strftime("%m/%d/%y")
  end

  def total_sales
    data.sum("quantity")
  end

  def total_customers
    data.column("customer_name").uniq.length
  end

end
```

This module allows us to call these methods in our formatters and fit them into our format as needed. There is nothing tricky going on here—the Helpers module is mixed into the formatters at render time.

You've seen here how rope provides a way to partition your code so it can easily be reused without having to write a ton of boilerplate code. The common task of writing a quick report that's capable of being run by a scheduler and delivered via email to the people that need it should be easy, and rope tries to make sure that it is. We'll now take a look at how to use Ruport with data that isn't coming from a convenient source, such as a database or CSV file.

13.3 Comparing text reports to well-formed data

Although it is desirable to report against well-formed data, it's not always an option. Most systems we deal with from day to day make use of relational databases, or at least offer standardized export formats, but this isn't true for our legacy systems. Luckily, Ruby is an excellent text-processing language, so it can handle most obscure data formats with ease.

Problem

You need to produce a comparison report that analyzes a flat file and compares it to a
CSV data source. Your data looks like the files in listings 13.7 and 13.8.

Listing 13.7   Transaction report, legacy data file

```
                            Transaction Report
                          1/1'6 Through 11/16'6
11/16'6                                                      Page 1
ETS Checking


     Date     Num     Description               Category
     ---------------------------------------------------------------------

          BALANCE 12/31'5


     1/2'6    38-487   misc adj                  Misc
     1/3'6    38-490   John Parlian                Sales
     1/3'6    38-491   Tolland                   Sales
     1/3'6    38-492   New Alliance...           Misc
     1/4'6    38-494   James Farall...           Misc
     1/4'6    38-495   Returned Check              Misc
     1/4'6    38-496   Craig Winter...            Dinners
     1/4'6    38-497   York                      Dinners
     1/4'6    38-498   York                      Misc
     1/4'6    38-499   York                      Sales
     1/4'6    38-500   York                      Sales
     1/4'6    38-501   Wooster                    Sales
     1/5'6    38-502   Tolland                    Sales
     1/5'6    38-503   Bankcard Ser...            Dinners
```

Listing 13.8   Transaction report, CSV database dump

```
Date,Num,Description,Category
1/2/2006,38487,misc adj,Misc
1/2/2006,38489,John Parlian,Salary
1/3/2006,38490,John Parlian,Sales
1/3/2006,38491,Tolland,Sales
1/3/2006,38492,New Alliance...,Msc
1/4/2006,38493,James Farell...,Salary
1/4/2006,38494,James Farall...,Misc
1/4/2006,38495,Returned Check,Misc
1/4/2006,38497,York,Misc
1/4/2006,38498,York,Misc
1/4/2006,38499,York,Sales
1/4/2006,38500,York,Sales
1/4/2006,38501,Wooster,Sales
1/5/2006,38502,Tolland,Sales
```

Solution

The report in listing 13.9 is quite simple, but useful. At work, we use this to catch syn-
chronization issues with a two-way bridge between a legacy system and a standard SQL
server. It parses both files to create Table objects, which can then be compared to see

which records are missing from each, and which records are different, based on their record numbers.

```
require "rubygems"
require "ruport"
require "ruport/util"

module Analysis

  module_function

  def process_text_file(filename)
    Table(%w[Date Num Description Category]) do |t|
      File.foreach(filename) do |r|
        next unless r =~ /\A\d+\/\d+'\d+\s{4}\d/
        row = r.split(/\s\s+/)
        row[0].sub!(/'\d+/) { |m| "/#{m[1..-1].to_i + 2000}" }
        row[1].delete!("-")
        row[-1].chomp!
        t << row
      end
    end
  end

  def missing_data(options = {})
    from,compare,by = options.values_at(:from,:compared_to,:by)
    keys = compare.column(by) - from.column(by)
    compare.sub_table { |r| keys.include?(r[by]) }
  end

  def unmatched_data(options = {})
    grouping = Grouping(options[:old] + options[:new], :by => options[:by])
    Table(options[:old].column_names + ["file"]) do |t|
      grouping.each do |n,g|
        if g.length == 2 && g[0] != g[1]
          t << g[0].to_hash.merge("file" => "old", "Num" => n)
          t << g[1].to_hash.merge("file" => "new", "Num" => n)
          t << []
        end
      end
    end
  end

end

table_from_txt = Analysis.process_text_file("checking.txt")
table_from_csv = Table("checking.csv")
```

The final report generation is fairly simple:

```
puts "The following data was missing from the Text file\n"
puts Analysis.missing_data( :from => table_from_txt,
                 :compared_to => table_from_csv,
                 :by => "Num")

puts "\nThe following data was missing from the CSV file\n"
```

```
puts Analysis.missing_data( :from => table_from_csv,
                            :compared_to => table_from_txt,
                            :by => "Num" )

puts "\nThe following data did not match in the two files\n"
puts Analysis.unmatched_data( :old => table_from_txt,
                              :new => table_from_csv,
                              :by => "Num" )
```

This outputs a nicely formatted text report that shows what data is out of sync between the two files:

```
The following data was missing from the Text file
+----------------------------------------------------+
| Date    | Num   | Description    | Category |
+----------------------------------------------------+
| 1/2/2006 | 38489 | John Parlian   | Salary   |
| 1/4/2006 | 38493 | James Farell... | Salary   |
+----------------------------------------------------+

The following data was missing from the CSV file
+----------------------------------------------------+
| Date    | Num   | Description    | Category |
+----------------------------------------------------+
| 1/4/2006 | 38496 | Craig Winter... | Dinners  |
| 1/5/2006 | 38503 | Bankcard Ser... | Dinners  |
+----------------------------------------------------+

The following data did not match in the two files
+------------------------------------------------------------+
| Date    | Num   | Description    | Category | file |
+------------------------------------------------------------+
| 1/3/2006 | 38492 | New Alliance... | Misc     | old  |
| 1/3/2006 | 38492 | New Alliance... | Msc      | new  |
|         |       |                |          |      |
| 1/4/2006 | 38497 | York           | Dinners  | old  |
| 1/4/2006 | 38497 | York           | Misc     | new  |
|         |       |                |          |      |
+------------------------------------------------------------+
```

Though the solution for this is basically straightforward, we're playing with some of the most powerful features in Ruby and Ruport. We'll take some time to go through some of the more interesting parts in depth, so that you can use these tricks in your own reports.

Discussion

The first task we must deal with, before doing any comparisons or formatting, is parsing the text file input. Our process_text_file() method handles this, building up a table of data as it iterates through the lines of the text file. An individual record in our text file looks like this:

```
1/2'6   38-487   misc adj                      Misc
```

To keep things simple, we tell our processor to skip any rows that don't have this basic format:

```
next unless r =~ /\A\d+\/\d+'\d+\s{4}\d/
```

The actual check is fairly simple. In English, you can read this as: Starting at the beginning of the line, match one or more digits followed by a / character, followed by one or more digits, followed by a ' character, followed by four spaces, followed by a digit.

This means that the pattern is really only matching the following part of the preceding record:

```
1/2'6    3
```

As there are only three types of data present in our file—header data, empty lines, and records—this check turns out to be sufficient. Only records will match this pattern. By jumping to the next line if this check fails, we can immediately skip processing headers and blank lines.

If we've matched a record, we then process it to make it into well-formed data for comparison. Let's look at it line by line.

Split by at least two spaces:

```
row = r.split(/\s{2,}/)
row #=> ["1/2'6","38-487","misc adj","Misc\n"]
```

Convert the year into a four-digit year:

```
row[0].sub!(/'\d+/) { |m| "/#{m[1..-1].to_i + 2000}" }
row[0] $=> "1/2/2006"
```

Remove the dashes from the `Num` column:

```
row[1].delete("-")
row[1] #=> "38487"
```

Remove the newline from the `Category` column:

```
row[-1].chomp!
row[-1] #=> "Misc"
```

This provides us with a nicely formed record, looking something like this:

```
row #=> ["1/2/2006","38487","misc adj","Misc"]
```

Notice that each field is now in a comparable format to the records in our CSV data. We append the record to the table we're building up, and the final result of the `process_text_file()` method a `Table` object with all the processed records aggregated. Because the CSV is well formed, there is no need to manipulate the data, and it is loaded via a simple call:

```
table_from_csv = Table("checking.csv")
```

With both files processed, we can begin our comparison report.

Figuring out what data is in one file but not the other is simple, because all records have a unique primary key in their `Num` field. Our `missing_data()` method definition follows:

```
def missing_data(options = {})
  from,compare,by = options.values_at(:from, :compared_to, :by)
  keys = compare.column(by) - from.column(by)
  compare.sub_table { |r| keys.include?(r[by]) }
end
```

We invoke this method twice: once to show what is missing from the text file, and once more to show what is missing from the CSV file.

In either case, this performs a simple set difference on the values in the Num field to find out which keys are present in one file but not in the other:

```
keys = compare.column(by) - from.column(by)
```

In our "missing from text file" report, this results in keys being set to the two values that are not present in the text file's Num field, which are:

```
["38949","38503"]
```

We then create a subtable from the CSV data, including only those records that are missing from the text file:

```
compare.sub_table { |r| keys.include?(r[by]) }
```

The result is our familiar text table output, looking like this:

```
+-----------------------------------------------+
| Date    | Num   | Description    | Category |
+-----------------------------------------------+
| 1/2/2006 | 38489 | John Parlian   | Salary   |
| 1/4/2006 | 38493 | James Farell... | Salary   |
+-----------------------------------------------+
```

The same process is repeated to find the records that exist in the text file but not in the CSV file. As you can see, it is fairly trivial to do this kind of filtering, so long as you have a unique key to work with.

The more interesting part of this report is seeing which records exist in both files but do not match. We use a Grouping object in unmatched_data() to simplify things. The very first line joins the two tables together and then groups them:

```
grouping = Grouping(options[:old] + options[:new], :by => options[:by])
```

The real purpose of this grouping is to collect the data in groups by their Num fields. This leaves us with two possible group lengths, either 1 or 2. The length 1 groups are ones that exist in only one file, and the length 2 groups are ones that exist in both files. As we're building up the table for our report, we immediately reject the data that isn't in pairs, and then compare the first record to the second record to see if they are equal. If they aren't, we add them to our report:

```
Table(options[:old].column_names + ["file"]) do |t|
  grouping.each do |n,g|
    if g.length == 2 && g[0] != g[1]
      t << g[0].to_hash.merge("file" => "old", "Num" => n)
      t << g[1].to_hash.merge("file" => "new", "Num" => n)
      t << []
    end
  end
end
```

In the preceding code, we are yielded the group name and actual group object for each iteration. Our group name represents the Num value for the records, and our group object contains our tuple of records, with the old values preceding the new values. We simply append these values to the table we are building up, adding an empty row as a spacer for each group. The resulting table looks familiar:

```
+-----------------------------------------------------------+
| Date     | Num   | Description     | Category | file |
+-----------------------------------------------------------+
| 1/3/2006 | 38492 | New Alliance... | Misc     | old  |
| 1/3/2006 | 38492 | New Alliance... | Msc      | new  |
|          |       |                 |          |      |
| 1/4/2006 | 38497 | York            | Dinners  | old  |
| 1/4/2006 | 38497 | York            | Misc     | new  |
|          |       |                 |          |      |
+-----------------------------------------------------------+
```

This allows us to inspect the data very easily and see the rows with unmatched values.

That finishes off all the interesting implementation details of the actual report. However, it's worth making a comment about the structure of our report definition, as it deviates a little from the norm.

Our solution finds itself very near the crossroads between a quick one-off script and a more structured application. Ruby's object-oriented model is very pleasant to work with, but to a minimalist, it might seem a little excessive for a problem like this. For this reason, we use a modular design.

By using `module_function`, we can create modules that encapsulate functions that can be called directly on the module itself, rather than needing to be mixed into another object. This means we don't need to define a class to hold our functions; the module alone will do.

This provides a namespace for our code to live in, which means that we can reuse bits of this code in other scripts without worrying about a method name like `process_text_file` clashing with other definitions. This sort of structure is ideal for scripts that are around this size and complexity. It makes the code still easy to test, which is something you throw away with one-off scripts, and it still prevents you from having to manage state, which is inevitable if you use an object-oriented solution.

It's very common to reuse bits and pieces of reporting code, so structuring your scripts in this way may make it easier for you to do so without having to think much about design.

As you can see, it is quite easy to quickly parse a nonstandard text format and then compare it to other data using Ruby's regular expressions and Ruport's table-manipulation capabilities. Though this report was somewhat basic, the general approach is useful for more complex applications as well.

We've covered a lot of useful material so far, but you can't exactly call the reports we've been generating beautiful. We'll now take a look at how Ruport handles printable document output, which provides some better eye candy than we've been offering so far.

13.4 *Creating customized documents for printing*

Generating customized printable reports is something most programmers will need to do from time to time. Though Ruport handles the most common cases without any modification, you'll often need to extend its PDF formatter to get the results you need. We'll walk through a common PDF formatter extension to show how to begin customizing your reports.

Problem

You need to produce sharable documents from data groupings, and you want to generate custom PDF documents.

Solution

The controller and formatter in listing 13.10 takes a CSV file and does a simple grouping operation on the data. The result is then displayed on a landscaped page, with a header and information panel in addition to the table of grouped data.

Listing 13.10   Purchase Notes PDF renderer and formatter

```
require "rubygems"
require "ruport"

class PurchaseNotes < Ruport::Controller

  prepare :report
  stage :header, :info_panel, :table

  formatter :pdf do
    def prepare_report
      options.paper_orientation = :landscape
    end

    build :header do
      draw_text "FooBar Enterprises", :font_size => 36, :left => 50
      hr
    end

    build :info_panel do
      info = "Daily Record for FooBar Enterprises," <<
          " prepared by #{options.preparer}\n\n" <<
          "Please process the following orders for shipping.\n" <<
          "If there are any questions, email the Sales Department"

      rounded_text_box(info) do |o|
        o.radius = 3
        o.width = 300
        o.height = 80
        o.heading = "Purchase Log for #{Date.today.strftime('%m/%d/%y')}"
        o.font_size = 12

        o.x = 450
        o.y = 580
      end
    end

    build :table do
      move_cursor -50
      render_grouping data, :style => :separated,
        :table_format => { :width => 700 },
        :formatter => pdf_writer
    end

  end

end
```

The following code shows how this controller is used:

```
t = Table("products.csv")
puts PurchaseNotes.render_pdf(:data => Grouping(t, :by => "Name"),
                 :preparer => "Sam Jackson")
```

Our input CSV is fairly simple:

```
Name,Recipient Name,Recipient Location,Order Number,Quantity,Unit Price,Total
Accordian,Joe Gainsville,"43 Orange Street
Smockton,VT 01010",10123,3,10.25,30.75
Toy Piano,Mark Union,"100 Telpha Lane
Silverberg, MD 02020",10124,1,200.00,200.00
Kite,Al Hooligan,"50 Staley Road
Sandspring, MI 03030",10125,2,50.00,100.00
Toy Piano,Joe Gainsville,"43 Orange Street
Smockton,VT 01010",10126,2,200.00,400.00
Kite,Ralph Eggert,"109 Salt Rock Road,
Trist, CA 04040",10127,1,50.00,50.00
Kite,Allen Spitz,"300 Telian Court
Apartment 3A
East Bay, FL 05050",10128,5,50.00,250.00
```

After grouping and applying the formatting we've specified, we get nice PDF output, as shown in figure 13.2.

| Purchase Log for 07/23/2007 |
| Daily Record for FooBar Enterprises, prepared by Sam Jackson |
| Please process the following orders for shipping. |
| If there are any questions, email the Sales Department |

FooBar Enterprises

Name	Recipient Name	Recipient Location	Order Number	Quantity	Unit Price	Total
Accordian	Joe Gainsville	43 Orange Street Smockton,VT 01010	10123	3	10.25	30.75
Toy Piano	Mark Union	100 Telpha Lane Silverberg, MD 02020	10124	1	200.00	200.00
	Joe Gainsville	43 Orange Street Smockton,VT 01010	10126	2	200.00	400.00
Kite	Al Hooligan	50 Staley Road Sandspring, MI 03030	10125	2	50.00	100.00
	Ralph Eggert	109 Salt Rock Road, Trist, CA 04040	10127	1	50.00	50.00
	Allen Spitz	300 Telian Court Apartment 3A East Bay, FL 05050	10128	5	50.00	250.00

Figure 13.2   The PDF output from our Purchase Notes renderer and formatter

Although it definitely involves rolling up your sleeves, you can see that it isn't terribly difficult to get really fine-grained control over document rendering.

Discussion

Most customized formatting jobs in Ruport begin with defining a controller. This class is responsible for describing the process that should be carried out by formatters, and it serves as the interface to rendering data in whatever formats you wish to support. For this particular application, our definition is quite simple:

```
class PurchaseNotes < Ruport::Controller

  prepare :report
  stage :header, :info_panel, :table

  # ...

end
```

With the preceding definitions, when told to render a specific format, the following hooks will be called on the formatter, in order:

```
* prepare_report
* build_header
* build_info_panel
* build_table
```

Any hooks that are not implemented are simply ignored. This allows the formatters to retain some degree of independence from the renderers. This independence is actually necessary, because the controllers do not need to know about the formatters at all when they are defined. Take a look at our formatter definition:

```
formatter :pdf do
  # ...
end
```

This shortcut interface is simply syntactic, and it is functionally equivalent to this code:

```
class PDF < Ruport::Formatter::PDF

  renders :pdf, :for => PurchaseNotes

  # ...

end
```

It is this callback that allows us to render our results as follows:

```
puts PurchaseNotes.render_pdf(:data => Grouping(t, :by => "Name"),
                :preparer => "Sam Jackson")
```

This turns out to be a handy feature. As there is no need to follow a specific convention, format names are simply labels. So for example, if we had used this code,

```
renders :landscaped_pdf, :for => PurchaseNotes
```

our call would look like this:

```
puts PurchaseNotes.render_landscaped_pdf(
  :data => Grouping(t, :by => "Name"),
  :preparer => "Sam Jackson"
)
```

Now that we've gone through the basic structure of a formatting extension, we can walk through each of the stages of the report and take a look at what's going on. The first thing to notice is that we are working on a subclass of Ruport::Formatter::PDF, which allows us to gain access to a number of helper methods to do customized PDF output. Because this particular report has many columns, we want a landscaped report. We can set an option for this in our prepare_report hook:

```
def prepare_report
  options.paper_orientation = :landscape
end
```

It is important to set this option before calling any methods that would draw on the PDF object. Once you begin drawing, you cannot change the paper orientation. For this reason, our prepare hook is the best place to put this instruction to ensure it is called before anything else.

Once we've established the paper orientation, we can begin drawing our report. Starting with the header, we need our company name in large font, followed by a horizontal rule:

```
build :header do
  draw_text "FooBar Enterprises", :font_size => 36, :left => 50
  hr
end
```

We're doing a bit of measured text here, describing a specific distance from the left margin in pixels. We could have also specified this in terms of ruler measurements, so long as we converted the values before passing them. This would require us to make use of a PDF::Writer helper. For example, if we wanted to place our text two inches from the left margin, we could do something like this:

```
draw_text "FooBar Enterprises", :font_size => 36,
                    :left => pdf_writer.in2pts(2)
```

Of course, you don't always need to be so specific about where text is placed on the screen. If you want Ruport's PDF formatter to handle flow control for you, the add_text() method works fine.

In our report, we overlay a rounded text box with additional information. This text box has dynamic elements to it, but they're mostly trivial. Let's look at this stage so we can talk about what's going on with it.

```
build :info_panel do
  info = "Daily Record for FooBar Enterprises," <<
       " prepared by #{options.preparer}\n\n" <<
       "Please process the following orders for shipping.\n" <<
       "If there are any questions, email the Sales Department"

  rounded_text_box(info) do |o|
    o.radius = 3
    o.width = 300
    o.height = 80
    o.heading = "Purchase Log for #{Date.today.strftime('%m/%d/%Y')}"
    o.font_size = 12

    o.x = 450
    o.y = 580
  end
end
```

The `rounded_text_box` method is fairly straightforward. We provide the body text info as an argument, and set the formatting details and our text box header via the block. All of these fields (with exception of `heading`) are required to create a rounded text box, so be sure to include them. If you have to draw several similar boxes, you can, of course, create a helper method that simplifies things.

The more interesting part of this code is that we make use of formatting options, allowing us to pass in extra data at rendering time to populate the dynamic parts of our report. If you look back at the code that actually renders the report, you'll see we pass an option as `:preparer => "Sam Jackson"`. In the preceding code, this is represented by `options.preparer`. Ruport's formatting-option system is very simple, and this is one of three ways to use it.

Another way you can invoke this is to use the block form of rendering to access the `options` object directly:

```
PurchaseNotes.render_pdf do |r|
  r.data = Grouping(t, :by => "Name"),
  r.options.preparer = "Sam Jackson"
end
```

The `options` object is shared by the controller and whatever formatter it invokes, so you can actually make use of it in both the formatter and controller as needed. They can also be accessed like an indifferent hash, such as `options["preparer"]`, which can come in handy for highly dynamic reports.

If you want to be sure an error is raised when this option is not set, you can use `required_option()` in your renderer definition. This will make it so that an invocation like the following will raise a `RequiredOptionNotSet` error:

```
PurchaseNotes.render_pdf(:data => Grouping(t, :by => "name"))
```

Whether or not you choose to use this feature is entirely up to you, and will probably depend on your needs.

That essentially covers things you can do with options processing in Ruport, so let's take a look at how data is handled by the formatting system.

The data object we're passing in is a `Ruport::Data::Grouping`, and because this already has a built-in formatter that will work for our needs, we don't need to reinvent the wheel. We can make use of a simple rendering helper to call that formatter. The only caveats are that we need to pass our `PDF::Writer` object into it to make sure that the grouping renders on our object instead of creating a new PDF file, and that we need to manually position it on our document. The following code does exactly that:

```
build :table do
  move_cursor -50
  render_grouping data, :style => :separated,
    :table_format => { :width => 700 },
    :formatter => pdf_writer
end
```

The `move_cursor` call lets us move our drawing cursor down the page 50 pixels, leaving sufficient room between the start of the table and the end of the header content.

When we call `render_grouping`, we simply pass it our data object, and tell it to use the separated grouping style. We also set some `PDF::Writer` objects via `:table_format`. Any attributes you specify via this method are used to set accessors on the underlying `PDF::SimpleTable` object, which means that you have full control over the table generation. For more details on this, check the Ruport API documentation for `Ruport::Formatter::PDF` and possibly the `PDF::Writer` documentation.

We've walked through a nontrivial PDF report that hits some of the common elements you will need: custom headers, text boxes, and tabular output. Though it can get to be a little low-level, you can more or less accomplish anything you might need with `PDF::Writer` and a little help from Ruport. There are copious PDF examples for Ruport distributed with the source, but you may be able to get by with what you've seen here for the most common cases.

One thing worth mentioning is that `PDF::Writer` has notable performance issues. With this in mind, we'll now talk a little about doing performance optimizations while working with Ruport.

13.5 *Reporting against large datasets*

It's no secret that Ruby is a slow language. Combine this with the common task of generating reports based on anywhere from ten thousand to ten million records, and it seems as if you're asking for trouble. However, in many cases, it is still possible to squeeze out enough performance to make it worthwhile to stick to Ruby.

Problem

You need to report against a very large dataset without eating up all the resources available to your server.

Solution

For this solution, we'll build a row-based processor to generate text, HTML, and PDF reports. Although Ruport is most comfortable with processing and formatting tables, it isn't impossible to work with rows. In fact, Ruport has a built-in row-rendering system that can be easily customized. For this example, we have trivial data, but it spans over 20,000 lines. Here is a small sample of what it looks like:

```
date,chart,amount
2/20/2007,453175.2S,$325.00
2/20/2007,453175.2S,$300.00
2/20/2007,453175.2S,$250.00
11/17/2006,233089,$58.00
11/17/2006,233089,$58.00
11/17/2006,233089, $-
11/17/2006,233089,$58.00
11/17/2006,233089,$58.00
1/22/2007,233089,$84.00
1/22/2007,233089,$84.00
1/22/2007,233089,$84.00
```

The code in listing 13.11 uses Ruport, `PDF::Writer`, and FasterCSV to process this data and do the necessary format conversions.

Listing 13.11   Custom row rendering report

```ruby
require "rubygems"
require "ruport"
require "pdf/writer"
require "fastercsv"

class MyPDF < Ruport::Formatter::PDF

  renders :pdf, :for => Ruport::Controller::Row

  def build_row

    pdf_writer.start_new_page if cursor < 50

    pad(5) do
      ypos = cursor
      draw_text data[0], :y => ypos
      draw_text data[1], :y => ypos, :left => 150
      draw_text data[2], :y => ypos, :left => 250
    end

    horizontal_rule
  end

end

pdf = PDF::Writer.new
renderer = Ruport::Renderer::Row
widths = [10,12,10]

File.open("out.txt", "w") do |text|
  File.open("out.html", "w") do |html|
    html << "<table>"
    FasterCSV.foreach("big.csv") do |r|
      next unless r[2] =~ /\d|(amount)/

      html << renderer.render(:html, :data => r)

      text << renderer.render(:text, :data => r,
        :max_col_width => widths, :ignore_table_width => true)

      renderer.render(:pdf, :data => r, :formatter => pdf)
    end
    html << "</table>"
  end
end

pdf.save_as("out.pdf")
```

If you noticed, it seems like we've unraveled the system a bit, creating our own custom PDF renderer, using ordinal values instead of column-based access, and even resorting to using some of the methods of Ruport's dependencies directly. The reasons for this can be summed up in two words: speed and memory.

On our machines, this takes about one minute to run. Better than 75 percent of that time is spent generating the PDF, which is over 500 pages long. Since this is all done in pure Ruby, speed usually comes at the cost of elegance.

We'll now take a closer look at the different techniques used and get a feel for how to attack similar problems when you encounter them.

Discussion

When dealing with smaller datasets, it's often convenient to think and work in terms of tables rather than rows. This becomes less and less feasible the larger your dataset gets. This is a problem where with every new row, your cost increases in both time and space. By cutting the tables out of the equation, we can process, manipulate, and format each row as we receive it, then let garbage collection pick up the discarded ones as needed.

That's why in the code, you'll notice that we only need to store one row at a time, instead of having the whole result set in memory:

```
FasterCSV.foreach("big.csv") do |r|
  next unless r[2] =~ /\d|(amount)/

  text << renderer.render(:text, :data => r,
    :max_col_width => widths, :ignore_table_width => true)

  html << renderer.render(:html, :data => r)

  renderer.render(:pdf, :data => r, :formatter => pdf)
end
```

The drawbacks of row-based processing are that it makes for uglier code. If we weren't trying to be conservative about resources, the preceding code could be written like this:

```
table = Table("big.csv")
table.reduce { |r| r.amount =~ /\d/ }

text << table.to_text
html << table.to_html
pdf  << table.to_pdf
```

Nothing here is particularly efficient, and it falls down and dies under high data volumes. You can see in the latter case that column names are automatically detected, but that in our row processor, we need to check for them explicitly:

```
next unless r[2] =~ /\d|(amount)/
```

Though it's ugly, this lets us filter a specific column without applying the filter to the header row. In cases where simple pattern matching like this won't work, you may need to take a different approach. Because our data isn't being rendered as a table, but rather as a series of rows, we need to roll up our sleeves a bit here. Ruport provides a base-row renderer for HTML, text, and CSV, but not PDF. It also requires a little tweaking to make use of the text formatter.

For HTML, you'll notice that we don't need to provide any special directives:

```
html << renderer.render(:html, :data => r)
```

HTML turns out to be an excellent format for streaming, because we don't need to worry about column widths, page breaks, or anything like that for the basic cases. We really just need to generate something like this for each row:

```
<tr><td>1/22/2007</td><td>233089</td><td>$84.00</td></tr>
```

This is exactly what the preceding line of code does, with some whitespace consider-ations for easier hand-editing. It is implemented very efficiently, and if we were only rendering HTML in this report, it would take less than five seconds to generate the HTML from our CSV.

You'll notice that the text formatting isn't nearly as straightforward. We need to make use of fixed column widths and turn off table-width detection:

```
text << renderer.render(:text, :data => r,
     :max_col_width => widths, :ignore_table_width => true)
```

The problem with doing row-based text output is that in order to format the rows properly, we need to set fixed widths for the columns. For example, if we did not spec-ify column widths, we'd likely end up with something like this:

```
| a | this is a long field |
| bc | this is short |
| d | this is another long field |
```

By specifying fixed widths, we can get better looking output, more like this:

```
| a  | this is a long field       |
| bc | this is short              |
| d  | this is another long field |
```

In the preceding code, `:ignore_table_width => true` simply tells Ruport not to try to truncate the table to fit the console, making it suitable for output to file.

As another minor performance note, the text-generation code might have read a little more clearly if we embedded the widths directly:

```
text << renderer.render(:text, :data => r,
     :max_col_width => [10,12,10], :ignore_table_width => true)
```

However, the problem here is that Ruby would create a new array each time a new record was rendered, and since these values do not change from row to row, we can speed things up a little by defining these values before entering the loop.

Ruport is capable of generating very nice tables using `PDF::SimpleTable`. This tool is notoriously slow and becomes painful to work with when you have a relatively small number of pages. The reason for this is similar to why tabular output of text is tricky: every cell needs to be inspected in order to figure out the right column widths, and for PDFs, tables also need to properly span pages, reprinting the column names when needed.

Our approach here is to create a very simple, fixed-width PDF output that properly spans pages and is easy to read. The following chunk of code does exactly that:

```
class MyPDF < Ruport::Formatter::PDF

  renders :pdf, :for => Ruport::Controller::Row

 def build_row

  pdf_writer.start_new_page if cursor < 50

  pad(5) do
```

```
    ypos = cursor
    draw_text "Date: #{data[0]}",    :y => ypos
    draw_text "Chart: #{data[1]}",   :y => ypos, :left => 150
    draw_text "Amount: #{data[2]}",  :y => ypos, :left => 250
  end

  horizontal_rule
 end

end
```

This formatter produces the simple output seen in figure 13.3

You may have more complex needs for your reports, and you can certainly tweak the formatter a whole lot more before it becomes too costly. You'll notice that we manually check to see whether we need to advance the page before rendering a new row. This prevents records from spanning multiple pages and provides us with a buffer zone between the end of the page and our last record on the page.

Also remember that PDF is not a format that can easily be streamed, and even if it were possible, the PDF::Writer API does not provide a way to do it. This is why you'll notice that we need to instantiate the PDF::Writer object outside of the main processing loop:

```
pdf = PDF::Writer.new
```

We then pass this to our row renderer so that it uses this object instead of creating a new PDF::Writer object with a single row each time:

```
renderer.render(:pdf, :data => r, :formatter => pdf)
```

Finally, we can save the full PDF once it has been generated:

```
pdf.save_as("out.pdf")
```

In practice, we've found that this approach scales fairly well, so long as you stick to primitive drawing methods, text rendering, and manual page advancement. It's when you need to either inspect the entire data source before producing a report, or when you need to do complex checks to determine whether or not your data will fit properly on a page or in a column that things slow down greatly.

date	chart	amount
2/16/2007	170831	$210.00
2/16/2007	170831	$270.00
12/29/2006	450316	$330.00
12/29/2006	450316	$330.00
12/2/2006	439626S	$58.00
12/2/2006	439626S	$58.00
12/18/2006	288087S	$150.00
12/18/2006	288087S	$150.00

Figure 13.3 Row-based PDF output

The general patterns shown here should help when you need to squeeze a little more speed out of a report or conserve some memory. The CSV file in this example can be replaced with any streaming data source, including result sets from databases or other sources, such as files processed with `StringScanner`.

The key things to remember here apply to most applications, but they're worth repeating:

- Avoid loading full data structures in memory if they can be streamed
- Use lightweight data structures if possible
- Avoid repeatedly creating new objects with the same values in loops
- Use fixed column widths if possible in formatted output
- Disable as much auto-detection as possible, and tune for your specific problem
- Use lower-level tools when necessary to avoid overhead

If you're generating batch reports at night, or have processes that can run for a few minutes without causing problems, it's entirely feasible to use Ruby to process large datasets. If you're not in that boat, you'll need to consider ways to parallelize your task, or think about writing C extensions. However, for a lot of common cases, this general approach should do the trick.

13.6   *Summary*

The five recipes in this chapter should give you a solid base in building reporting applications with Ruby and Ruport, and you should be able to adapt the examples to solve your actual problems. Ruport is ultimately more about helping you define your reporting process and helping with the low-level bits than it is about solving any particular reporting problems. The general approach here will be sufficient to get you well on your way with your work.

appendix A:
Installing Ruby

Installing Ruby is a fairly trivial affair, but there are a few things worth paying attention to. You will want to use gems extensively, and not all installations include Ruby-Gems by default. You may also want to use gems that take advantage of C extensions (for example, MySQL drivers and the Mongrel web server), which require that you have the proper development libraries and tools. In this appendix, we provide you with the simplest steps for installing a fully functional and up-to-date version of Ruby 1.8 on Windows, Mac OS X, and Linux.

Once Ruby is running, look at the A.4 section, where we provide useful tips for improving IRB (the Interactive Ruby Interpreter) and accessing documentation for all gems installed on your machine.

A.1 Installing on Windows

If you're using Windows, you have three options. You can get the latest version of Ruby directly from the ruby-lang.org web site, with downloads for either Ruby 1.8 or 1.9. When you download the Ruby interpreter, it includes command-line tools like RDoc, IRB, and RI, but does not include RubyGems or many of the other libraries you need to get started.

In our experience, hunting down and installing libraries like RubyGems, FCGI, or OpenSSL is not fun, and we've got better things to do. A better alternative is to use the one-click Ruby installer, available from http://rubyinstaller.rubyforge.org. It includes many of the common libraries you need to get started, libraries for accessing various Windows APIs, a good programmer's text editor (Scite), and a PDF copy of the first edition of *Programming Ruby*.

If you're interested in building Rails applications, consider Instant Rails, available from http://instantrails.rubyforge.org. Instant Rails includes all the same libraries as the One-Click Ruby Installer, and adds recent versions of Rails, Mongrel, MySQL, and Apache. It's the quickest way to install a working environment for developing and deploying web applications.

Before you get started, we recommend upgrading to the latest version of Ruby-Gems, which offers important performance and usability improvements:

```
$ gem update -system
```

Now you're all set and ready to go.

A.2   Installing on Mac OS X

Mac OS X 10.5 (Leopard) comes with Ruby 1.8.6 preinstalled and also includes Rails, Mongrel, Capistrano, and a few other gems.

It works well, but before you get started, we recommend upgrading to the latest version of RubyGems, which offers important performance and usability improvements:

```
$ sudo gem update --system
```

The different release schedules mean that Leopard does not include the most recent versions of Rails and Mongrel, but this is not a problem, since those are safe to upgrade using sudo gem update.

Mac OS X 10.4 (Tiger) includes Ruby 1.8.2, but many of the libraries you will want to use no longer support 1.8.2. For example, Rails requires 1.8.4 or later. The easiest way to upgrade to a more recent version of Ruby is using the Ruby One-Click installer for OS X available from http://rubyosx.rubyforge.org.

Alternatively, you can install Ruby using either MacPorts or Fink. For example, to install Ruby with RubyGems using MacPorts, run this command:

```
$ sudo port install ruby rb-rubygems
```

Ruby support on Mac OS X is excellent, but in spite of that we did run into a couple of gotchas. Occasionally, gems that use C extensions will fail to recognize libraries installed outside the main directories (for example, libraries installed using MacPorts). These are easy to fix by passing specific compile/build options to gem install, like this:

```
$ sudo gem install oniguruma -- --with-opt-lib=/opt/local/lib
```

MySQL adds another twist. By default, C extensions are built as universal binaries, but MySQL ships with per-architecture binaries. You can force Ruby to build extensions for a particular architecture by setting the ARCHFLAGS environment variable. To install MySQL on the Intel architecture:

```
$ sudo -s
$ export ARCHFLAGS="-arch i386"
$ gem install mysql -- --with-mysql-dir=/usr/local/mysql
```

For PowerPC, replace -arch i386 with -arch ppc.

A.3   Installing on Linux

You can compile from source on any Linux distribution, but most of them offer a binary package also. For example, installing Ruby on Red Hat Fedora couldn't be easier. Just go into the terminal and use the package manager:

```
$ sudo yum install ruby ruby-devel rubygems gcc
```

The ruby package provides the generic command-line utilities, while ruby-devel provides header files, and gcc the compiler, both of which are necessary for installing gems that use C extensions, such as Mongrel and MySQL.

Most likely, this will install an older version of RubyGems. We recommend upgrading to the latest version, which offers important performance and usability improvements:

```
$ sudo gem update --system
```

Installing Linux on Ubuntu/Debian takes a bit more effort. For starters, the ruby package will install the Ruby interpreter but none of the command-line tools (RDoc, IRB, etc.). Use the meta-package ruby-full to install all the relevant command-line tools.

To build gems that use C extensions, you'll need both ruby1.8-dev and, if you don't already have them, the various build tools like GCC and Make, provided by the build-essentials package:

```
$ sudo apt-get install ruby-full ruby1.8-dev libopenssl-ruby
$ sudo apt-get build-essential
```

If you install the Debian rubygems package, you may find that it only supports installing Ruby gems using apt-get. Only a fraction of Ruby gems are available through the Debian package manager. We recommend you install a fully functional version of RubyGems by downloading it from the RubyForge project:

```
$ curl -OL http://rubyforge.org/frs/download.php/38646/rubygems-1.2.0.tgz
$ tar xzf rubygems-1.2.0.tgz
$ cd rubygems-1.2.0
$ sudo ruby setup.rb
$ sudo ln -s /usr/bin/gem1.8 /usr/bin/gem
```

Remember that certain gems use C extensions, which in turn require header files to compile. For example, to install the Ruby MySQL gem, it is not enough to have MySQL installed on your machine; you must also install the MySQL developer package:

```
$ sudo apt-get install libmysqlclient15-dev
$ sudo gem install mysql
```

A.4 More tips

Now that you have Ruby installed, it's time to customize your environment to use Ruby gems and IRB effectively. We're going to cover three simple setups that we find indispensable in every environment. They'll make it easier to run Ruby scripts, enhance the IRB, and let you access documentation for the various gems you install.

A.4.1 Requiring RubyGems with RUBYOPT

One thing we find annoying about Ruby is that it still treats RubyGems as an optional extension that you have to install separately. And since it's optional, you also have to require 'rubygems' in any program that uses gems.

You can get around this by setting the RUBYOPT environment variable to the value rubygems. On Windows, you can set this environment variable using the Control Panel—the One-Click Ruby Installer will automatically do that for you.

On Mac OS X, Linux, and other flavors of UNIX, you can add this line to your .profile:

```
export RUBYOPT=rubygems
```

A.4.2   *Improving IRB with Wirble*

If, like us, you work from the command line and use IRB or the Rails console, which itself uses IRB, we highly recommend installing Wirble. Wirble adds tab-completion, history, a built-in `ri` command, and colorized output.

NOTE   *UtilityBelt*   If you're really into extending irb, a library named Utility Belt adds more extensions to irb than we could cover in this whole book. Grab it from http://github.com/gilesbowkett/utility-belt.

Once you install Wirble (`gem install wirble`), create a file called .irbrc in your home directory and add the following lines to it:

```
require 'rubygems'
require 'wirble'
# start wirble (with color)
Wirble.init
Wirble.colorize
```

Don't add the last line if you don't like colors in your console, or if you are running from the Windows command line, which doesn't support ANSI colors.

Once you have Wirble installed, you can use tab-completion on Ruby classes, modules, and methods. For example, begin by typing `Obj` and press the Tab key once to expand it to `Object`. Continue by typing a period (`.`) and press the Tab key again to reveal all the methods on the `Object` class.

Not sure what a class or method does? You can get help from within IRB by running the `ri` method with a class, module, or method name, like this:

```
>> ri "MatchData"
>> ri "Object.dup"
>> ri "open"
```

You can also use the up and down arrow keys to go back in history.

A.4.3   *Accessing Ruby's documentation*

As intuitive as Ruby is, you won't get far without knowing the APIs, and that means looking up the documentation. Ruby comes with two tools that let you access documentation using the command line or your web browser.

You can use the command-line tool `ri` to request information about any class, module, or method from both the core library and any installed gem, like this:

```
$ ri Enumerable
$ ri lambda
$ ri String.to_i
```

You can use the gem server to access documentation for all installed gems from your web browser. This method makes it much easier to navigate through the documentation. In addition to class and method documentation, many gems also include a README file containing valuable information about the gem and its usage, alongside links to the official web site.

Start by running the gem server from the command line:

```
$ gem server
```

Then point your browser to http://localhost:8808. You now have documentation for all of your gems at your fingertips.

appendix B:
JRuby

JRuby is an implementation of the Ruby language that runs on the Java Virtual Machine (JVM). The main benefits of using JRuby are the ability to mix Ruby and Java code, the performance benefits gained from running on the JVM, and the ability to deploy web applications to Java servers like Tomcat and J2EE. This appendix provides an overview that will help you get started exploring the many facets of JRuby.

B.1   Installing and using JRuby

The steps required to install JRuby are the same on all operating systems. First, make sure you have Java installed and that the `java` command is accessible from the path. Next, download the most recent version of JRuby available from dist.codehaus.org/jruby, expand the archive to a directory of your choice, and set the path to point to the `bin` directory that contains the various JRuby executables (`jruby`, `jirb`, etc.). Verify that JRuby is installed correctly by running `jruby --version` from the command line.

For example, on Linux you could download and install JRuby 1.1.2 like this:

```
$ curl -OL http://dist.codehaus.org/jruby/jruby-bin-1.1.2.tar.gz
$ tar -xz < jruby-bin-1.1.2.tar.gz
$ mv jruby-1.1.2 /opt/jruby
$ echo "export PATH=\$PATH:/opt/jruby/bin" >> .profile
```

To run Ruby programs using JRuby, use the `jruby` command:

```
$ jruby myprog.rb
```

You can also use `jirb`, the JRuby Interactive Interpreter, the same way you would use `irb` (see appendix A for instructions on how to install Wirble).

JRuby includes a recent version of RubyGems, and you can start installing and managing gems using the `gem` command. Make sure to read the next section to avoid conflicts between the Ruby and JRuby gem repositories.

If you need specific JVM settings, you can pass them along to JRuby using command-line options with the prefix -J, or by setting the environment variable JAVA_OPTS. For example,

```
$ export JAVA_OPTS=-client
$ jruby -J-Xmx512m myapp.rb
```

Next, we'll look at how to use JRuby and Ruby side by side on the same machine.

B.2 JRuby and Ruby side by side

Ruby and JRuby maintain separate gem repositories, and any gem you install for one will not be available for the other. While most gems are identical across platforms, gems that use C extensions install different code depending on the target platform. On Windows machines (mswin32), they will use JRs, and on most other platforms, they will compile shared libraries during installation. Gems that use C extensions will not install on JRuby. Fortunately, many popular gems, such as Mongrel and Hpricot, were ported over to JRuby and install using Java libraries instead of C extensions.

RubyGems handles this for you by installing the right gem for the target platform, so gem install mongrel will work the same way for all Ruby platforms and for JRuby. There are a few cases where you will be using different gems, such as mysql for Ruby but jdbc-mysql for JRuby.

Many gems install command-line scripts; for example, Rake provides rake while RSpec uses spec. Installing the gem on both platforms will result in two command-line scripts in two different locations, both available from the path. This may be a source of confusion at first, but it is easy to work around using the -S command-line argument, as the following example illustrates:

```
$ ruby -S spec specs/*
$ jruby -S gem install rspec
$ jruby -S spec spec/*
```

This is also the suggested way to install gems when using Ruby and JRuby side by side. If Ruby's gem command shows up first on the path, you can run it directly to install gems in the Ruby repository and use jruby -S gem to install gems in the JRuby repository, or vice versa.

When working on Rails applications, many of the scripts you will be using (e.g., script/server, script/plugin) are used from the current directory, not the path. In this case, you cannot use the -S option nor do you need to. Simply run the script with the right interpreter, like this:

```
$ ruby script/server
$ jruby script/server
```

If you're writing Ruby code that behaves differently on each platform, you can detect when it runs in JRuby by looking at the value of the RUBY_PLATFORM constant. This constant holds a string that depends on the target platform (e.g., i386-mswin32 or universal-darwin9.0). Since Java code behaves the same way on all operating systems, JRuby always sets this constant to java. You can still determine the underlying operating system by requiring rbconfig and checking the value of Config::CONFIG['host_os'].

Next, let's see how we can use JRuby to build Ruby applications that use Java libraries and tightly integrate with Java code.

B.3   *Mixing Ruby and Java*

As you can imagine, JRuby is all about easy Java and Ruby integration. You can access any Java class or interface available in the class path through the Java module. Here's an example:

```
>> foo = Java.java.lang.String.new('foo')
=> #<Java::JavaLang::String:0xe704bd @java_object=foo>

>> bar = Java.java.util.HashMap.new
=> #<Java::JavaUtil::HashMap:0xcd022c @java_object={}>
```

Calling Java methods is just as easy:

```
>> foo.toString
=> "foo"
>> foo.to_string
=> "foo"
>> foo.to_s
=> "foo"
```

As you can see from this example, you can call methods using either Java or Ruby naming conventions (either toString or to_string). Since these are also Ruby objects, you can call their Ruby methods as well, in this case to_s.

The conversion works both ways. Here's an example of passing Ruby objects to Java:

```
>> array = Java.java.util.ArrayList.new([1, "foo", Object.new])
=> #<Java::JavaUtil::ArrayList:0xc7c7bc @java_object=[1, foo,
     #<Object:0xa0a9a>]>

>> array.to_s
=> "[1, foo, #<Object:0xa0a9a>]"
```

Primitive types like strings and integers automatically convert to the right Java types. Since Ruby objects are also Java objects, you can define Ruby classes that extend Java classes. Java interfaces are exposed as modules, so to implement an interface, you simply include it:

```
class MyIterator
  include Java.java.util.Iterator
  def hasNext
    false
  end
end
```

If you need to cast arrays, use the to_java method, as this example illustrates:

```
>> ['foo', 'bar'].to_java
=> #<#<Class:01x96f94>:0x7a00b @java_object=[Ljava.lang.Object;@9c5304>

>> ['foo', 'bar'].to_java(Java.java.lang.String)
=> #<#<Class:01xf3941>:0x8fc43e @java_object=[Ljava.lang.String;@9cce04>
```

As with Java, you can use import to save yourself typing the full package name:

```
>> import Java.java.util.Hashtable
=> Java::JavaUtil::Hashtable
>> Hashtable.new
=> #<Java::JavaUtil::Hashtable:0x3584f9 @java_object={}>
```

To access Java libraries, add them to the class path using the `-J-cp` command-line argument, by setting the `CLASSPATH` environment variable, or simply by requiring them:

```
>> require '/usr/share/ant/lib/ant.jar'
>> Java.org.apache.tools.ant.Project
=> Java::OrgApacheToolsAnt::Project
```

The Java system properties are always available from `ENV_JAVA`:

```
>> ENV_JAVA['java.runtime.version']
=> "1.5.0_13"
```

You've now seen how to use Java code from Ruby. Next we'll show you how to mix Ruby code into Java applications using the scripting support provided by Java 6.

B.4 Scripting with Ruby

With JRuby you can also run Ruby scripts and use Ruby libraries inside your Java applications. You will need Java 6, which adds scripting support, the JRuby libraries in the class path, and `javax.script.EngineManager` to create a `ScriptEngine` that can evaluate Ruby code.

This simple example shows how you can load a Ruby file and call one of its methods:

```
ScriptEngine jruby = new ScriptEngineManager().getEngineByName("jruby");
jruby.eval(new FileReader("myscript.rb"));
String hello = (String) jruby.eval("hello_world");
System.out.println("Ruby says " + hello);
```

The last JRuby feature we're going to cover is the ability to package Ruby applications as WAR files and deploy them directly into your Java web server.

B.5 Deploying web applications

You can use JRuby to deploy Rails applications to Java web servers like Tomcat or JBoss. Start by installing the Warbler gem (`jruby -S gem install warbler`) and head over to the root of your Rails project to package it as a WAR file:

```
$ jruby -S warble war
```

Warbler creates a WAR file that places the core of your Rails application in the WEB-INF directory, including Rails itself, any plugins you use, and any gem dependencies. Public files go in the root of the WAR file, and you can use additional Java libraries that are copied over from the lib directory to WEB-INF/lib. The result is a self-contained, ready-to-run application.

If you need to customize the WAR file to your specific needs, start by creating a new configuration using the `warble config` command, and edit the config/warble.rb file before running `warble war` again.

appendix C:
Deploying web apps

In chapter 8, we looked at tools to deploy Ruby (both web and off-the-web) applications. Here, we'll look at specifics and the architecture for deploying web applications. There is certainly no shortage of options. So which deployment method is right for you?

We'll start by briefly reviewing the available options, then narrow it down to one particular architecture that works best across the board, from local use during development to deploying for production on a server farm. We'll show you how to deploy for this architecture using Apache 2 and Nginx as frontend web servers and Thin and Mongrel as backend application servers.

C.1 An overview of deployment options

The original model for deploying applications behind web servers was CGI. When using CGI, the web server starts a new process to handle each incoming request. That may be good enough for simple and oft-used scripts, but if you're using a web framework or opening database connections, the cost of setting these up for each request will quickly bring your server to its knees. Since most web applications fall into the latter category, we'll turn our attention to better-performing options.

To work around the limitations of CGI, modern web servers start the application once and keep that process alive, dispatching incoming requests as they come along. One approach that emerged early on consists of the web server and application running in separate processes, using protocols like FastCGI or SCGI to connect the two. A fair number of web servers support FastCGI, SCGI, or both, either natively or through add-ons, and on the Ruby side you'll find both the ruby-fcgi and scgi gems. In spite of their availability, we do not recommend either option. As it stands, FastCGI and SCGI fell behind and are harder to set up and administer, and they offer lackluster performance compared to the alternatives.

The second approach involves a web server that can run Ruby code in the same process. Most web servers support this model through modules, plugins, or components, although with limited availability—the choice of language dictates the choice of web servers able to run the code, and few servers are able to run Ruby code in the same process. As we'll see in a minute, this is not necessarily a problem.

Apache uses modules for running applications in the same process, the most popular being mod_php. You won't hear much about mod_ruby because its development stagnated, in no small part due to its inability to deal with Rails applications. Java web servers use components that are packaged and deployed as WAR files. These must be written in Java and use the Servlet API, but they fortunately do support Rails applications, using JRuby to run Ruby applications on the JVM, and Warble to package Rails applications as WAR files (as discussed in appendix B).

There are three web servers designed specifically for running Ruby applications. WEBrick is a pure-Ruby implementation bundled as part of the core Ruby library. When you're running Rails in development mode, you'll notice that it uses WEBrick by default. WEBrick's best feature is being available everywhere Ruby is, but don't expect much in terms of performance or scalability.

Mongrel is a lightweight web server that incorporates a native library—C code on most platforms, and Java code when running on JRuby—to handle the CPU-intensive portion of HTTP processing, offering simple setup and configuration with real-world performance. Thin is another lightweight web server that uses the Mongrel HTTP processing library in combination with Event Machine, a high-performance I/O network library, offering better throughput and scalability.

Mongrel and Thin are both viable options, and while Thin has the edge on performance and scalability, Mongrel has been around for longer and has better tooling support and more extensive documentation.

It was difficult for us to choose one server to cover. Fortunately, they're similar enough in principles and basic usage, so we decided to base our examples on Thin, and to highlight the differences in sidebars.

Although Thin and Mongrel are excellent choices for handling the dynamic portion of an application, and they support a variety of frameworks (Rails, Merb, Camping, to name but a few), they do not offer the same capabilities you would expect from a full-fledged web server. Neither one is a web server we would expose directly to the internet. Rather, we're going to delegate that task to a more capable frontend web server, and configure it to reverse proxy into our Thin/Mongrel application servers. We'll explain the basics of this architecture next.

C.2   *Reverse proxying*

Proxy servers are commonly used as outbound gateways; they handle traffic emanating from clients on the local network, directed at servers on the internet. Reverse proxy servers act as gateways for inbound traffic, responding to requests coming from clients on the internet and dispatching them to applications deployed on the local network.

Reverse proxies are compelling for several reasons. To clients, they look like a single web server and provide a central location for handling encryption, access control, logging, virtual hosting, URL rewriting, static-content caching, throttling, load balancing, and everything else a web server is tasked with. That leaves the backend web servers to deal exclusively with the business logic, simplifying management and configuration when you have many different applications deployed throughout the network. The two communicate with each other using the HTTP protocol.

One obvious benefit of a reverse proxy architecture is the ease of scaling, from a single instance used during development all the way to a large-scale server farm. You can start small, deploying the frontend web server and a handful of application servers on the same machine. Since the intensive portions of the workload are handled by these application servers, scaling is a matter of adding more machines and distributing the application servers across them. A single frontend web server can handle massive traffic before it reaches its scalability limits. Beyond that, you can start looking at load-balancing proxy servers like Varnish, Pound, or PenBalance, or even go down the route of dedicated hardware appliances.

Another benefit is the variety of options available and the ability to mix and match them to create a best-of-breed configuration. Standardizing on the HTTP protocol allows you to pick from any number of frontend web servers and load balancers, and just as easily mix in different backend web applications, from the simplest ones all the way to mainframes. Because we're exercising management and control through the frontend web server, we don't have to standardize on a single provider for our web applications, and can easily mix languages and platforms, running Ruby side by side with PHP, Python, J2EE, and .Net.

The last benefit is application isolation. Since all backend applications run independent of each other—the shared-nothing architecture—we can add new applications without impacting existing ones. For example, we can roll out a new Rails 2.0 application and run it alongside an older Rails 1.1 application, without having to migrate the older but fully functional code, just because we're using the newer framework for future development.

The ability to scale with ease, mix and match best-of-breed solutions, and roll out new applications alongside legacy ones makes reverse proxy our favorite deployment model. So let's look at actual deployment. We'll start by showing you how to set up Thin and Mongrel for the application servers, and then proceed to cover Apache and Nginx for the frontend web servers.

C.3   *Setting up Thin*

True to its name, Thin is a light web server that's incredibly easy to set up (visit http://code.macournoyer.com/thin/ for more information). We're going to start from an existing Rails application and work our way to having an operating system service that manages multiple application instances.

If you don't already have Thin, now is the time to install it by running gem install thin. We'll be conservative and start out by testing a single instance of the application. From the root directory of your Rails application, issue the following command:

```
$ thin start -e production --stats /stats
```

After you start Thin, you should see some output about a server starting up and serving on port 3000. Thin is quick enough that you'll want to use it in development

> ### Performance benefits of a frontend web server
>
> A well-tuned frontend web server does more than just shield your web applications from the internet and provide a central point for management and control. Here are five ways in which it can speed up your web applications:
>
> - It can serve static content directly, freeing your application to deal with dynamic content.
> - It can compress responses before sending them to the client, cutting down bandwidth and improving response time.
> - It can buffer responses on behalf of slow clients. Slow clients keep the application busy, waiting to transmit the full response; buffering frees the application to cater to the next incoming request.
> - Acting as a proxy server, it adds another layer of caching between client and server. Make sure to mark responses that are publicly cacheable by using the right `Cache-Control` directive.
> - By keeping connections open without tying up processing threads, it can take advantage of HTTP keep-alives and scale to a larger number of concurrent connections.

instead of WEBrick, and it knows that, so it defaults to run in development mode. Here we're dealing with deployment, so we need to force Thin to run in production mode just to make sure we got the configuration right. It's easier to check for issues now than later on, when we run Thin as a background service.

Next, point your web browser to http://localhost:3000. We added the `--stats` option, so you can also navigate to http://localhost:3000/stats and investigate HTTP requests and responses. A common issue with reverse proxy configuration is forgetting to forward an essential request header, and the `--stats` option helps you spot these problems.

Once you have verified that everything works as expected, it's time to create a configuration file. Now let's generate a simple configuration that will run three instances of Thin that listen on ports 8000 through 8002:

```
$ thin config -s 3 -a 127.0.0.1 -p 8000 -e production -C myapp.yml
```

In this configuration, the frontend web server and Thin all run on the same machine, and since we don't want to expose Thin to clients directly, we told it to only accept requests using the loopback address 127.0.0.1. If you're running Thin on a separate machine from the frontend web server, use an IP address that is directly accessible to the frontend web server. The default (0.0.0.0) will work if you don't care which IP address receives incoming requests.

We now have a configuration file called myapp.yml. Let's see what it looks like:

```
---
pid: tmp/pids/thin.pid
log: log/thin.log
timeout: 30
port: 8000
max_conns: 1024
```

```
chdir: /var/www/myapp
environment: production
max_persistent_conns: 512
daemonize: true
address: 127.0.0.1
servers: 3
```

If we wanted to add more servers, we could change the port, or IP assignment, or any other configuration option; we could run the command with different options; or we could edit this YAML file in a text editor.

Later, we're going to run Thin as a service. We're going to have one Thin service per machine, and that service may run any number of applications, so each configuration file must point to the root directory of the application it runs. If you move the application to a different location, make sure to change the value of the chdir configuration property.

Next, let's start Thin using this configuration:

```
$ thin start -C myapp.yml
```

To check that it's running, point your browser to each of the ports, http://localhost:8000 through 8002, or use the lsof command:

```
$ lsof -i tcp@127.0.0.1 -P
COMMAND PID   USER  FD   TYPE    DEVICE   SIZE/OFF NODE NAME
ruby    3321  assaf 3u   IPv4  0x4e74270      0t0  TCP localhost:8000 (LISTEN)
ruby    3324  assaf 3u   IPv4  0xaf1e66c      0t0  TCP localhost:8001 (LISTEN)
ruby    3327  assaf 3u   IPv4  0xb0a0e64      0t0  TCP localhost:8002 (LISTEN)
```

How you get Thin to run as a service depends on the operating system you're using. On Linux, you can do that with a single command:

```
$ sudo thin install
```

This command creates a new directory for storing the configuration files (/etc/thin) and adds a script in /etc/init.d to control the Thin service. When you start the Thin service, it enumerates all the configurations it finds in the /etc/thin directory and starts a server based on each. If you have more than one application, make sure they all use different port ranges. If you run the same configuration on multiple machines, you could keep the configuration file in the application and link to it from the /etc/thin directory, like this:

```
$ sudo ln -s myapp.yml /etc/thin/myapp.yml
```

Finally, we're going to set up the service to start and stop automatically, and then get it started. On Red Hat/CentOS, use these commands:

```
$ sudo /sbin/chkconfig --level 345 thin on
$ thin start --all /etc/thin          .
```

On Debian/Ubuntu, use these commands:

```
$ sudo /usr/sbin/update-rc.d thin defaults
$ thin start --all /etc/thin
```

Now that we've got Thin up and running, let's configure the frontend web server using either Apache or Nginx.

Setting up Mongrel

Mongrel and Thin are similar enough that we can follow the same workflow and just highlight where they differ (visit http://mongrel.rubyforge.org for more information about Mongrel). To run a cluster (several instances) of Mongrel, you'll want to install the mongrel and mongrel_cluster gems with this command:

```
$ gem install mongrel mongrel_cluster
```

We'll first start a single instance in production mode:

```
$ mongrel_rails start -e production
```

To create a configuration that runs three instances on ports 8000 through 8002, use this command:

```
$ mongrel_rails cluster::configure -e production \
-N 3 -p 8000 -a 127.0.0.1 -c $PWD
```

You need to point Mongrel to the root of your Rails application explicitly, which we did here using the -c $PWD argument. This command will create a new configuration in config/mongrel_cluster.yml.

When run as a service, Mongrel picks up all the configuration files it finds in the /etc/mongrel_cluster directory, so either move your configuration file there, or create a symbolic link, like this:

```
$ sudo mkdir /etc/mongrel_cluster
$ sudo ln -s config/mongrel_cluster.yml /etc/mongrel_cluster/myapp.yml
```

To start and stop the service from the command line, use these commands:

```
$ mongrel_cluster_ctl start
$ mongrel_cluster_ctl stop
```

To deploy Mongrel as a service on Linux, find the resources/mongrel_cluster file in the Mongrel gem directory, and copy it over to the /etc/init.d diretory using gem contents mongrel_cluster. Make it an executable with chmod +x, and configure it to start and stop at the appropriate run levels. On Red Hat/CentOS, use this command:

```
/sbin/chkconfig --level 345 mongrel_cluster on
```

On Debian/Ubuntu, use this command:

```
sudo /usr/sbin/update-rc.d mongrel_cluster defaults
```

On Windows, start with this command:

```
gem install mongrel_service
```

Then install a service by running the following command, which takes the same command-line arguments or configuration file:

```
mongrel_rails service::install
```

C.4   Setting up Apache load balancing

With Thin up and running, we can turn our attention to the frontend web server. To set up Apache for reverse proxy and load balancing, you need Apache 2.1 or later, loaded with mod_proxy, mod_headers, and mod_proxy_balancer. These modules are included and activated in the default Apache configuration.

We're going to create a new configuration file for our application, myapp.conf, and place it in the Apache configuration directory. We'll start by defining the proxy balancer to point at the three Thin instances:

```
<Proxy balancer://myapp>
  BalancerMember http://127.0.0.1:8000
  BalancerMember http://127.0.0.1:8001
  BalancerMember http://127.0.0.1:8002
</Proxy>
```

Put this at the head of the configuration file. If you add more instances (ports), move Thin to a different server (IP address), or if you need to fine-tune how the workload is distributed (assigning a different load factor to each instance), this will be the place to make these changes.

Next, and still using the same configuration files, we're going to create a virtual host that handles incoming requests using the proxy load-balancer:

```
<VirtualHost *:80>
  ServerName example.com
  ServerAlias www.example.com
  DocumentRoot /var/www/myapp/public

  # Redirect all non-static requests to application,
  # serve all static content directly.
  RewriteEngine On
  RewriteCond %{DOCUMENT_ROOT}/%{REQUEST_FILENAME} !-f
  RewriteRule ^/(.*)$ balancer://myapp%{REQUEST_URI} [P,QSA,L]
</VirtualHost>
```

Our application serves dynamic content, but also includes static content like images, CSS stylesheets, JavaScript, and so forth. Apache can handle these efficiently and without burdening the backend server, so we tell Apache to serve any file it finds in the document root directory, and to dispatch all other requests to the backend server. Rails puts all the static content under the public directory, so point DocumentRoot there. Never point it to the root directory of the Rails application unless you want people to download your application's source code and configuration files.

The reverse proxy forwards requests to the backend application using HTTP, so when configuring a virtual host to handle HTTPS requests, the proxy must inform Rails that the original request came over HTTPS by setting the forwarded protocol name. You can do that by adding this line to the virtual host configuration:

```
RequestHeader set X_FORWARDED_PROTO 'https'
```

Now we're ready to restart Apache (sudo apachectl -k restart), open the browser to http://localhost, and watch the application in action.

Before we finish off, here's another trick to add to your arsenal. Apache includes a Load Balancer Manager that you can use to monitor the state of your workers and change various load-balancing settings without restarting Apache. The following configuration will enable local access to the Load Balancer Manager on port 8088:

```
Listen 8088
<VirtualHost *:8088>
  <Location />
    SetHandler balancer-manager
    Deny from all
    Allow from localhost
  </Location>
</VirtualHost>
```

Setting up Nginx

Nginx is an up-and-coming web server. It isn't as popular as Apache and unfortunately isn't as well documented, but it offers better performance and scalability. At its core, Nginx has a smaller memory and CPU footprint and uses nonblocking I/O libraries, so it can scale to larger workloads and maintain a higher number of concurrent connections. We recommend giving Nginx a try, and we'll show you how to configure it as we did for Apache (you can read more about it at http://nginx.net).

We're going to create a new configuration file for our application, myapp.conf, and place it in the Nginx configuration directory. Some setups of Nginx will include all the configuration files placed in a certain directory (typically /etc/nginx/enabled), but if not, make sure to include it from within the `http` section of the main configuration file.

We'll start by defining the upstream web server that points to our three Thin instances:

```
upstream myapp {
  server 127.0.0.1:8000;
  server 127.0.0.1:8001;
  server 127.0.0.1:8002;
}
```

Next, and still using the same configuration files, we're going to define a virtual host that handles incoming requests by dispatching them to the upstream server:

```
server {
  listen      80;
  server_name  example.com;
  gzip on;
  proxy_buffering on;

  location / {
    proxy_set_header  X-Real-IP  $remote_addr;
    proxy_set_header  X-Forwarded-For $proxy_add_x_forwarded_for;
    proxy_set_header Host $http_host;

    root /var/www/myapp/public;
    if (!-f $request_filename) {
      proxy_pass http://myapp;
      break;
    }
  }
}
```

> **Setting up Nginx** *(continued)*
>
> When dealing with HTTPS requests, add the following line to the list of forwarded headers:
>
> ```
> proxy_set_header X-Forwarded-Proto 'https';
> ```
>
> If you're running Nginx and Thin on the same machine, you can take advantage of Unix sockets by configuring the upstream server to use them:
>
> ```
> upstream  backend {
>     server   unix:/tmp/thin.0.sock;
>     server   unix:/tmp/thin.1.sock;
>     server . unix:/tmp/thin.2.sock;
> }
> ```
>
> You will also need to configure Thin to use sockets instead of IP ports:
>
> ```
> $ sudo thin config -s 3 -S /tmp/thin.sock -e production -C /etc/
>     thin/myapp.yaml
> ```

C.5   *Summary*

In this appendix, we covered options for deploying Ruby-based web applications, focusing specifically on the reverse-proxy architecture. The benefits of this architecture are the ability to scale from a single-server deployment to a cluster of application servers, and the ease of mixing different web applications and languages. We showed you how to set up a cluster using two different lightweight Ruby servers, Thin and Mongrel. We also showed you how to set up a sturdy frontend server using either the popular Apache or the blazing fast Nginx.

index

MORE TITLES FROM MANNING

The Well-Grounded Rubyist
by David A. Black

   ISBN: 1-933988-65-7
   525 pages
   $44.99
   March 2009

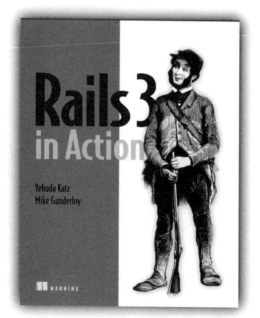

Rails 3 in Action
by Yehuda Katz and Mike Gunderloy

   ISBN: 1-935182-27-7
   400 pages
   $44.99
   August 2009

For ordering information go to www.manning.com

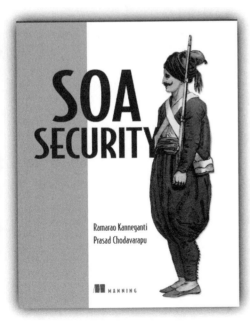

MORE TITLES FROM MANNING

Becoming Agile
...in an imperfect world
by Greg Smith and Ahmed Sidky

   ISBN: 1-933988-25-8
   400 pages
   $44.99
   April 2009

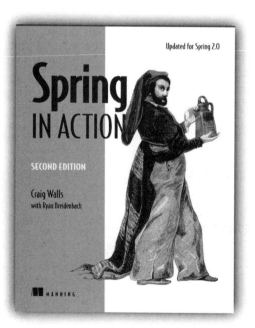

Spring in Action
Second edition
by Craig Walls with Ryan Breidenbach

   ISBN: 1-933988-13-4
   768 pages
   $49.99
   August 2007

For ordering information go to www.manning.com